RECENT DEVELOPMENTS IN
THE FOUNDATIONS OF UTILITY AND RISK THEORY

RECENT DEVELOPMENTS IN THE FOUNDATIONS OF UTILITY AND RISK THEORY

Edited by

L. DABONI
Institute of Finance Mathematics, University of Trieste, Italy

A. MONTESANO
Faculty of Political Science, University of Milan, Italy

and

M. LINES
Faculty of Business and Economics, University of Venice, Italy

D. REIDEL PUBLISHING COMPANY

A MEMBER OF THE KLUWER ACADEMIC PUBLISHERS GROUP

DORDRECHT / BOSTON / LANCASTER / TOKYO

Library of Congress Cataloging in Publication Data

Recent developments in the foundations of utility and risk theory.

(Theory and decision library; v. 47)
Papers delivered at the Second International Conference on Foundations of Utility and Risk Theory, Venice, June 1984.
Includes index.
1. Utility theory–Congresses. 2. Risk–Congresses. I. Daboni, Luciano. II. Montesano, Aldo. III. Lines, M. (Marji) IV. International Conference on Foundations of Utility and Risk Theory (2nd ; 1984 : Venice, Italy) V. Series.
HB201.R35 1986   330.15'7   86–594
ISBN 90–277–2201–3

Published by D. Reidel Publishing Company,
P.O. Box 17, 3300 AA Dordrecht, Holland.

Sold and distributed in the U.S.A. and Canada
by Kluwer Academic Publishers,
190 Old Derby Street, Hingham, MA 02043, U.S.A.

In all other countries, sold and distributed
by Kluwer Academic Publishers Group,
P.O. Box 322, 3300 AH Dordrecht, Holland.

CONTENTS

PREFACE

The Second International Conference on Foundations of Utility and Risk Theory was held in Venice, June 1984. This volume presents some of the papers delivered at FUR-84. (The First International Conference, FUR-82, was held in Oslo and some of the papers presented on that occasion were published by Reidel in the volume <u>Foundations of Utility and Risk Theory with Applications</u>, edited by Bernt P. Stigum and Fred Wenstøp). The theory of choice under uncertainty involves a vast range of controversial issues in many fields like economics, philosophy, psychology, mathematics and statistics. The idea of discussing these problems in international conferences has been successful: two conferences have been held and others will follow. The climate of the debate has changed in the meantime, partly as a result of these conferences. It is no more only a question of attacking or defending the neo-Bernoullian assumptions, but also of proposing wider generalizations and including new elements in the analysis of the decision process.

For instance Amartya Sen - comparing the two current notions of rationality, internal consistency and self-interest pursuit - introduces the concept of reasoning and considers the irrationality which may result from the failure of a positive correspondence between reasoning and choice or from a limited capacity of reasoning. Rationality is also considered with respect to the controversial axiom of strong independence. John C. Harsanyi introduces the concept of practical certainty, i.e. the instrumental decision of accepting some empirical statements as true based on the judgement that the loss which the agent may incur in using the policy determined by that acceptance is smaller than the gain obtained by simplifying the decision problem. Donald Davidson expands on Ramsey's original problem of discovering probabilities and values, considering also the meaning of sentences whose interpretation is not predetermined. Thus decision theory is combined with interpretation in an analysis which adheres to Jeffrey's theory. Max Black argues against the tendency to view any departure from the standard model of expected utility maximization as a manifestation of inconsistency and shows some sensible reasons for what might look like a perverse choice, Robert Sugden points out that regret theory concerns the decisions of people in difficult situations, when they do not have a complete master plan for choosing the best action, and he laments the fact that the lack of such a plan is considered irrational.

While the papers we have mentioned above discuss the rationale behind decision making, those that follow are concerned with people's value, i.e. with utility. Maurice Allais determines an invariant cardinal utility function which agrees with empirical data of his 1952 and 1975 tests. This function is loglinear on a large domain and is the same for all agents up to only one parameter. Georges Bernard shows that it is necessary to abandon the independence axiom in order to establish a general utility function, non-linear in probabilities, of uncertain prospects. Three approaches are considered, the last of which, proposed by the author, is examined mainly with regard to the principle of dominance. Allan Gibbard outlines the conditions under which decision matrices (introduced by Savage) yield the instrumental expected utility, which is a general kind of expected utility. Luciano Daboni and Guido A. Rossi in their papers use de Finetti's original approach in order to determine a utility function for uncertain situations. Hector A. Munera proposes a generalized means model of which the expected utility model and the linearized moments model are particular cases. Munera also uses the concept of mean introduced by de Finetti and Kolmogoroff. After recapitulating his measure of the intensity of preference which considers the choice situation among sequences of elementary alternatives, Antonio Camacho shows how these cardinal utilities could be used for determining social choice in special cases. Ole Hagen analyzes some inplications - among them utility dominance - of the expected utility theory which survive in competing theories. Robin Pope considers Savage's explanation of his error in answering Allais's test and goes on to indicate a timing inconsistency in von Neumann-Morgenstern's set of axioms. Giorgio Leonardi, E. Fabio Arcangeli and Aura Reggiani give a new axiomatic reconstruction of random utility models (already considered by Luce and Mc Fadden) and use the resulting theory in order to analyze observations of aggregate choice with respect to the standard ordinal utility and revealed preference theories. Peter Wakker specifies the properties of the preference relations necessary and sufficient to guarantee the existence of continuous concave functions of utility.

The connection between information and utility is considered in two papers. Morris H. DeGroot, following a Bayesian approach, analyzes the measure of information with respect to the probability distribution and the utility function of a decision maker. He introduces the notion of expected information and of retrospective information presenting their properties and role. Anio O. Arigoni treats the evaluation of the informational utility of linguistic variables in descriptions of facts for which statistical and semantic features are considered jointly.

The attitude of decision makers towards risk is the focus of the following papers. Kenneth R. MacCrimmon and Donald A. Wehrung have undertaken a large-scale study to assess the risk propensity of practicing decision makers. The results have the important characteristic of being obtained by considering many different situations and attitutes. Lola L. Lopes gives four propositions about how people process risks and explains the gap between behavioural phenomena and neo-Bernoullian theory using explanations provided by the subjects. Aldo Montesano introduces a measure of risk aversion which does not require the existence of the neo-Bernoullian utility function but only the existence of a certainty equivalent for every action. Gerald L. Nordquist considers the problem of how to measure risk aversion in the case of a utility function dependent on the state of nature.

The last part of the volume discusses some problems of economic activity deriving from uncertainty. Karl Aiginger examines the conditions that make firms produce more (or less) under uncertainty than they would under certainty. János Ács evaluates the application of risk management in strategic planning.

ACKNOWLEDGEMENTS

The University of Venice, Ca' Foscari hosted the Second International Conference on the Foundations of Utility and Risk Theory. The Program Committee consisted of Werner Leinfellner, Ole Hagen and Aldo Montesano. Marji

Lines served as Conference Secretariat. Many thanks to Lucia Dal Mistro and Roberta Nordio for their help in the preparation of this volume.

Financial support for the conference was given by the following organizations:

Consiglio Nazionale delle Ricerche (National Council of Research).

Regione Veneto (Regional Administration of Veneto).

Comune di Venezia (municipality of Venice).

Provincia di Venezia (Provincial Administration of Venice).

Banca Nazionale del Lavoro.

Assicurazioni Generali.

Istituto Nazionale delle Assicurazioni

and the University of Nebraska.

We also wish to thank all of the participants at the conference for contributing to the remarkable atmosphere of friendly critique and finally, for making these FUR conferences a recurrent source of reference in the field of utility and risk theory.

Venice, October 30, 1985
Luciano Daboni
Aldo Montesano
Marji Lines.

PART I

RATIONALITY AND UNCERTAINTY IN DECISION THEORY

Amartya Sen

RATIONALITY AND UNCERTAINTY

1. Consistency and Interest

There are, it can be argued, two dominant approaches to rational choice extensively used in decision theory and economics:
(1) Internal consistency: Rational choice is seen, in this approach, simply in terms of internal consistency of choice.
(2) Self-interest pursuit: The rationality of choice is identified here with the unfailing pursuit of self-interest.
        The two approaches both have fairly straightforward interpretations in choices with certainty. The internal consistency approach has been much used in the theory of "revealed preference", with various "axioms" of revealed preference serving as conditions of internal consistency of choice (see Samuelson, 1947).[1] In much of modern economic theory, "rational choice" is seen as no more - and no less - than consistent choice, and a choice function is taken as "rationalizable" if and only if it is consistent enough to have a binary representation (or, in a more exacting interpretation, representation by an ordering).
        The self-interest approach is crucial to the derivation of certain results in traditional and modern economic theory, e.g., the Pareto optimality of competitive equilibria.[2]
        The traditional theory of utility provides a seemingly firm basis for the rationality of pursuing one's utility - defined either in terms of Benthamite hedonism of pleasure calculus, or in terms of various formulation of desire-fulfilment. In fact, ambiguities in the concepts of "utility" and "preference" have played quite a substantial part in intermediating between self-interest and choice, giving the appearance of tying rational choice firmly to the pursuit of self-interest.[3]
        The self-interest approach is some times confounded with the internal consistency view, through defining

3

L. Daboni et al. (eds.), Recent Developments in the Foundations of Utility and Risk Theory, 3–25.
© *1986 by D. Reidel Publishing Company.*

interest or utility as the binary relation of "revealed preference" (i.e., the binary relation that can represent the choice function if it satisfies certain conditions of internal consistency).

But, obviously, that definitional trick does not establish a correspondence of choice with any independently defined notion of self-interest. There is a world of difference between the claim that a person is trying to pursue his or her self-interest through choice, and the announcement that whatever the person can be seen as maximizing (if such a binary relation does exist[4]) will be _called_ that person's utility (or interest). The internal consistency approach and the self-interest approach are fundamentally different.

I would like to argue that neither approach adequately captures the content of rationality. Consider the internal consistency approach first. Take a choice function C(.), assumed to be "rationalizable" (i.e., "binary") and let R be the binary relation representing it[5]. Construct the binary relation R* from R by "reversing" every strict preference, and let C*(.) be the choice function generated by (and "rationalizable" with respect to) R*. If a person with unchanged nonchoice characteristics (i.e., the same feelings, values, tastes, etc.) were to end up choosing in exactly the "opposite" way in each case, i.e., according to C*(.) rather than C(.), it would be hard to claim that his or her choices have remained just as "rational". But the "opposite" choices are exactly as consistent!

Rationality has to include some correspondence of choice with _other_ characteristics, and it cannot be fully captured by any notion of _internal_ consistency - however exacting it may be. In this sense, the internal consistency approach is too permissive (though it may _also_ bo too restrictive in other ways, if the consistency conditions turn out to be unduly exacting). A person need not be involved in any lapse of reasoning or rationality if he or she decides to pursue some goals other than self-interest.[6] People in real life may or may not be entirely self-seeking, but it would be absurd to claim that anyone who does not pursue what he or she recognizes to be his or her own interest _must be_ just irrational!

It is arguable that what goes wrong with these two standard approaches to rationality is their failure to pay adequate and explicit attention to the role of reasoning in distinguishing the rational from the irrational. Reasoning may demand more than consistency.[7] (Also, it need not be seen as requiring - though this is a more debatable point - that consistency must take a binary form.[8]) There is also no convincing ground for insisting that a person's reasoning must be employed only in the pursuit of his or her self-interest. The internal consistency approach can bring in reasoning only indirectly - only to the extent (and in the form) that is allowed by the nature of the consistency conditions imposed. The self-interest approach refuses to admit reasoned choice in pursuit of any goals other than self-interest. Both approaches sell reasoning very short indeed, in characterising rationality.

The view is often expressed that the notion of rationality is quite "unproblematic" when the object of attention is choice under certainty, and that the difficulties arise from trying to "extend" the notion of rationality - obvious in the case of certainty - to cases involving uncertainty. I shall argue that this view is hard to defend, and the enormous difficulties of getting a grip on the notion of rationality under <u>uncertainty</u> include a great many problems that also arise in characterising rationality in choices <u>without</u> uncertainty.

2.   Reasoning and Correspondence

Rationality must deal with the correspondence of actual choice with the use of reason. There are two distinct types of failures of rationality. A person can fail to do what he would decide to do if he were to reason and reflect on what is to be done. The failure may arise from one of several causes, e.g.,

(i)   the person has acted "without thinking",
(ii)   the person has reasoned lazily about what to do and has not used his faculties properly,
(iii) the person has reasoned carefully and decided to do x, but has ended up doing y for, say, the weakness of will (what the Greeks called "akrasia").

All these cases have one point in common, to wit, the person would reject his own choice on careful reflection - there is, in this sense, a failure of positive correspondence between the person's reasoning and his choice. I shall call this "correspondence irrationality".[9]

In contrast with "correspondence irrationality", a person may fail to be rational because of the limited nature of the reasoning of which he is capable. A person may have reflected as carefully as he can on a choice, but not seen something significant that a sharper reasoning would have revealed. I shall call this "reflection irrationality". In the case of "correspondence irrationality", the person fails to do the right thing as he himself sees it (or would have seen it if he had carefully reflected on the matter), whereas with "reflection irrationality" the person fails to see that the objective he wishes to pursue would have been better served by some other choice (on the basis of the information he has).

To illustrate, take the case of Buridan's ass, which died of starvation dithering between two haystacks both of which looked alluring. Was the ass irrational? We can't, of course, know whether it was or not without knowing more about the story. Perhaps it was an extremely noble and do-gooding ass, commiting suicide to leave the haystacks for other asses, and pretending to dither to avoid embarassing the other asses? If so, Buridan's ass may have been far from irrational (even though members of the "self-interest" school of rationality would not see this).

Let us assume, however, that the ass did indeed wish to live and was not intending to bequeath the haystacks to other asses. Why didn't it choose one of the haystack, then? Did it fail to see that touching neither haystack and dying of starvation was the worst of the three alternatives, no matter how it ranked the haystacks? If it saw this and was still paralysed (say, by greed), or - alternatively - would have seen it if it had reflected carefully but did not so reflect (say, because of nervousness), then this is a case of "correspondence irrationality". Another possibility is that the ass would not have been able to figure this out at all (i.e., to see that even if it could not decide which of the two haystacks was the larger, it was still sensible to choose either of them rather than neither).[10] If this was the case, then this exemplifies "revealed irrationality". Perhaps the ass had read too much "revealed preference" theory, and felt unable to choose x when y was available without being sure that x was superior to (or even at least as good as) y, and - relevantly for the "weak axiom" - without being sure that it would never choose y in the presence of x.

Both these issues of rationality are deeply problematic in the sense that it is not easy to find simple criteria that will diagnose rationality or irrationality of either type in a decisive way. "Correspondence rationality" involves the use of counterfactuals (what the person would have decided on careful relection). While social science is hard to do without counterfactuals,[11] the no-nonsense operationalist dreads the excursion into "what would have happened if...". Similarly, it is not easy to be sure how much reasoning to demand in diagnosing "reflection irrationality". For example, is a choice "reflection irrational" if the person chose wrongly because he was unable to figure out (relevantly for his choice of action) a hard mathematical puzzle the solution of which was "contained" - analytically - in the problem itself. Where do we draw the line?

I should make it absolutely clear that I do not regard it at all embarrassing to the approach I am presenting here that decidability is a problem for both "correspondence irrationality" and "reflection irrationality". Quite the contrary. My claims include: that the notion of rationality involves inherent ambiguities; that the decidability problems of correspondence rationality and reflection rationality merely make these ambiguities clear; that many of the sources of ambiguities are present with or without uncertainty; that the standard approaches to rationality avoid these ambiguities (insofar as they do avoid them) by misspecifying the problem of rationality. I would also argue that to try to jettison all the ambiguities of rationality and to aim at a sure-fire test that will work in every case would tend to take us away from the reasons that make rationality an important concept. The partial undecidabilities of rationality are, in fact, part and parcel of my thesis.

Decidability problems do not make a concept useless. The identification of many unambiguous cases may well be both easy and useful. Ideed, the belief - often implicit - that a satisfactory criterion must be a "complete" one has done, it can be argued, a good deal of harm in the social sciences by forcing us to choose between groundless defeatism and arbitrary completion.

I have tried to argue the case for systematically accomodating "incompleteness" in such contexts as interpersonal comparison of utilities, measurement of inequality, making real income comparisons, quantifying poverty, and measuring capital.[12] A similar approach may be useful in dealing with rationality. There will be clear cases of "correspondence irrationality", where the person himself accepts unambiguously that he would have chosen differently had he bothered to think at all on the matter. There are clear cases also when "correspondence irrationality" is caused by the "weakness of will" despite the person having made a reasoned decision to do something else.

Similarly, though there may be doubts about how much reasoning to incorporate in the standards of "reflection irrationality", some cases are clear enough. It is known that people learn techniques of decision making with practice. Indeed, one major objective of decision theory has been to improve people's ability to reason about decisions.[13] There may be great difficulties on drawing an exact line, but it may be easy enough to agree that some cases involve obvious reasoning failures of an uncomplicated kind, and which can very easily be avoided with just a little training.

3.   Uncertainty and Reasoning

Having outlined an approach to the problem of assessing rationality of choice, I should make a few remarks on the contrasts with other approaches. The differences with the approaches of "internal consistency" and "self-interest" in their pure forms must be obvious enough. But some approaches are more complex.

John Harsanyi presents his "rational-choice models of social behaviour" by noting that his theory "is a normative (prescriptive) theory" and that "formally and explicity it deals with the question of how each player should act in order to promote his own interests most effectively". One obvious difference between our approach and Harsanyi's lies in his apparent concentration on the person promoting "his own interest" (rather than any other goals that he may have). But this may not be a major problem here, since much of Harsanyi's analysis can be reinterpreted in terms of pursuit of general goals - subject to certain formal restrictions - rather than only the particular goal of self-interest maximization.

A second difference, which is more fundamental, arises from Harsanyi's firmly prescriptive motivation, and this relates ultimately to seeing decision-theoretic recommendations as consistency conditions that any person must obey to make sense of his practice. In contrast, "correspondence rationality" is not prescriptive, and "reflection rationality" is only conditionally prescriptive.

To illustrate the contrast - at the risk of being a little ad hominem - both Allais' own response to the choice in the paradox that bears his name and Savage's well-know first-blush response (in the same lines as Allais') are simply "irrational" in Harsanyi's framework since they violated the condition of "strong independence" which is seen as a "prescriptive requirement of rationality". In contrast, in our framework of "correspondence rationality", Allais' choices were not "correspondence irrational"; he did defend his choice by reasoned reflection and has continued to do so.[14] On the other hand, Savage's choices were clearly "correspondence irrational", and he did in fact reject his first-blush choices after reasoned reflection about the implications of his choices.

Regarding "reflection irrationality", there is more of a problem of decidability. But if anyone does claim that Allais' reasoning regarding these choices are "erroneous", he has to show why the apparent justification is not "really" acceptable. The issue of reflection rationality in this case may well be an important one to pursue, but that is a very different exercise from simply insisting on strong independence as a consistency condition. I shall take up that question for a closer examination in the next section.

The "internal consistency" approach has been used powerfully, in analysing decision making under uncertainty, in many rational decision models.[15] Some - like the von Neumann-Morgenstern utility model - have been successful both in raising important questions about rational behaviour under uncertainty and also - as Harsanyi notes - in "explaining or predicting real-life human behaviour" (1978, p. 16).[16] The latter question - that of explanation or prediction of actual behaviour -

involves   a   somewhat   different   issue   from   that   of
rationality - a distinction that is especially important
in   the   context   of   interpreting   various   "obviously
irrational" psychological responses found in experimental
research by MacCrimmon, Kahneman, Slovik, Tversky and
others.[17]

As far as rationality is concerned, the difficulties
with the internal consistency approach in the case of
decision under uncertainty are not radically different
from those in the case of certainty. A person can be
internally consistent and still be doing the opposite of
the things he should obviously do to pursue his own
goals. As was discussed earlier - no test of internal
consistency, however stringent, can deal with this
problem. Also, on reasoned reflection a person might
revise his choices substantially, even though the
first-blush responses had satisfied all the conditions of
internal consistency. It should be clear that whether
or not these consistency conditions are necessary for
rationality, they can scarcely be _sufficient_ for it.

The issue of _necessity_ raises problems similar to
those faced in the context of choice under certainty, but
with greater force. "Why binary choice?" has now to be
supplemented by such question as "Why strong
independence?" These are certainly matters for reasoning
for and _against_. This, in turn, leads to possible
applications of the concepts of "correspondence
rationality" (involving "self-policing") and "reflection
rationality" (involving a host of issues from decision
theoretic training to "agreeing to disagree").

4.   Independence and Rationality

The rationality axiom for choice under uncertainty that has
caused the most controversy is almost certainly the
condition of strong independence. One of several versions
of this condition demands that a lottery L^1 will be preferred to a lottery L^2 if and only if, for any lottery L^3,
the combined lottery $(pL^1, (1-p)L^3)$ will be preferred to the
combined lottery $(pL^2, (1-p)L^3)$ for all probability numbers
p. Mixing each lottery with a third one - in the same
proportion in the two cases - does not change the ranking.
It was this axiom that was clearly violated by Allais'
famous counterexample, and it has been the subject of

several other interesting counterexamples as well.

The strong independence axiom is indeed crucial to the expected utility approach. Given this axiom, the linear form of evaluation is pretty much unavoidable in choosing between lotteries, since the other axioms needed (including conditions of complete ordering and a mild condition of continuity) are not particularly exacting.[18] The battle of expected utility has been largely fought on the field of independence.

While strong independence has appeared to some to be self-evidently a necessary condition of rationality - indeed of internal consistency - it certainly does need a detailed defence. Violating it is not obviously silly in the way in which the behaviour of Buridan's ass clearly is. If an "error" is being made, it is a less immediate one, and more must be said on this than to assert that strong independence is self-evidently essential for reasoned choice.

One approach, among others, in defence of expected utility (including strong independence) that has persuasive features is Peter Hammond's (1982) derivation of expected utility from what he calls - taking a little liberty - "consequentialism". In Hammond's character-isation "consequentialism" requires that acts be chosen exclusively on the basis of choosing from the "feasible set of contingent consequences" - and these reflect "prizes" with the over-all uncertainties specified. The requirement builds in a bit of separability, and then adding a little continuity, Hammond gets home to expected utility on the basis of "probability consequentialism", with the uncertainty specified in terms of probabilities. The operative choices here are confined to "consequence lotteries" and the choice of acts follows from that.

Hammond's argument is interesting and important, but it is not adequate (nor is it claimed to be so) for establishing exclusive reasonableness of expected utility. Part of the difficulty arises from limitations of consequentialist reasoning that have received much attention in recent years in moral philosophy (see Williams, 1973, 1982; Nagel, 1980; Parfit, 1984). But the property defined by Hammond is, in some important respects, even more demanding than traditional consequentialism. The main "consequentialist" approach in moral philosophy has been based on the utilitarian view,

which   has   involved   restricting   attention   to   the
"utilities" of the persons in question in the consequent
states of affairs.[19]   In Hammond's formulation, these
mental attitudes do not figure at all, and true to the
tradition of von Neumann-Morgenstern type "expected
utility", "utilities" are determined <u>by the choices</u> over
lotteries rather than the other way round. This has, of
course, been a bone of contention between Allais and his
followers on one side who have preferred to   start with a
psychological cardinal utility that influences choice
over   the   lotteries.[20]   The   issue   is of   decisive
importance since   the   consideration of counterfactual
("could have been") outcomes can influence the contingent
choice over lotteries through affecting the person's
happiness and other psychological features.

     This is, of course, the door that opens to old
arguments on such subjects as the relevance of "regret"
(even the cogency of the old minimax regret and new
theories like those of Bell, 1982; and Loomes and Sugden,
1982), and a variety of other considerations that the
"expected utility" theorist tends to see as red herrings.
There is some scope for genuine confusion about two
distinct issues related to such matters as "regret". The
question of rationality of "regretting" has to be
distinguished from the question of the rationality of
taking note of regret if it were to occur. Even if it is
the case that it is irrational for me to regret something
that cannot be changed, if nevertheless I am willynilly
doomed to regretting the thing in question,[21] then I
must take note of that <u>fact</u> of regretting[22].

     Aside   from   psychological   sensitivity   to
"counterfactual outcomes", there are other considerations
that question the entire   consequentialist perspective,
e.g., the   relevance of   agency (<u>who</u>   took <u>what</u> decision). Information on this is lost in the "consequence
lotteries", which does not distinguish between the path
through a "decision node" as opposed to a "chance node" so
long as the "consequences" are the same. There is a more
information-preserving way of characterising "consequential
reasoning" that will permit such considerations to be
included in "consequential reasoning" (see Sen, 1982b,
1983), but for that we must go beyond "consequence
lotteries".

     I   would argue that the condition of strong
independence is deeply questionable from either of these

two   perspectives: (1)   "counterfactual   outcome
sensitivity", and (2) "agency sensitivity". To this we can
add a third, viz., (3) "information sensitivity". The
information that   a person gathers about prizes and
uncertainty does, of course, get reflected in the
specifications of "consequence lotteries", but also the
valuation that a person attaches to the consequence may
well depend on things about which a person learns more by
considering what lotteries he is, in fact, facing. There
is an odd asymmetry in the traditional "expected utility"
story whereby the observer (such as the decision analyst)
learns about the chooser's preferences by observing his
decisions, but the chooser does not use the nature of the
lotteries that he faces to learn about the nature of the
world, which may affect his valuation of consequences and
thus his choices.   To be sure, there is no formal
restriction on such learning, but once such learning is
systematically admitted, some of the axioms of expected
utility   (including   "strong   independence")   becomes
difficult to sustain. As lotteries are combined with
others, the determination of the person's valuation of the
states and acts can sensibly change, even within a broadly
consequentialist framework.

     Some of the "counterexamples" to expected utility
and its axioms (including "strong independence") that have
been offered in the literature (e.g., Allais', 1953;
Machina's, 1981; Tversky's, 1975) can be seen in the light
of these three considerations, in particular the first two
("counterfactual outcome sensitivity" and "agency
sensitivity").[23]

     I suggest three other "counterexamples" below.

Case I: The No-letter Response

     You come home after the day's work and check your
mail. You may possibly have won a prize in the national
draw (you think with probability p), in which case you
would find a letter waiting for you. If no letter, you
would choose to do something useful like painting the
garbage can, which needs doing some time. In another case,
there is the possibility (you think with probability p) of
your finding a court summons for a motoring incident - the
policeman was vague and the last day for summoning you
will pass tonight. If you find no letter, you would like
to open a bottle of champagne and enjoy yourself, rather
than painting the garbage can. The significance of the

no-letter situation depends on what could have been, but
hasn't (cash prize in one case, court summons in the
other).

So your preferences are the following:

[p, win cash, no summons;   [p, win cash, no summons;
 1-p, no win, no summons, preferred 1-p, no win, no summons,
 paint garbage can]   to   drink champagne]

and

[p, no cash win,   [p, no cash win,
   summons received;   summons received;
 1-p, no win, no summons, preferred 1-p, no win, no summons,
 drink champagne]   to   paint garbage can]

The same case of "no letter" - implying "no win, no
summons" - is read differently depending on whether the
alternative expectation was for a cash win, or for
getting a summons (depending on the nature of the lottery
with which the decision regarding drinking champagne and
painting garbage can is combined).
     You have violated strong independence all right, and
you must prepare to face the "expected utility" lot.[24]
But if you don't change your mind on further reflection
(showing no sign of "correspondence irrationality"), you
will not get the big stick of "reflection irrationality"
from me.

Case 2: The Doctor's Dilemma

     Dr. Chang faces the problem that he is in a remote
rural area, facing two critically ill persons, and with
just one unit of the medicine that can possibly help cure
each. If administered to Hao, there is - Dr. Chang
believes - a 90 per cent chance of cure for Hao. If given
to Lin, there is, Dr. Chang believes, an even higher
chance of cure - he thinks around 95 per cent. If the
medicine is divided between the two, neither will be
cured. Faced with the need for an unequivocal choice
between the two ("please say who"), Dr. Chang would decide
to give the medicine to Lin. But when he is given the
option of a 50-50 chance mechanism (either directly or
indirectly through the choices of the other doctors), he
opts for that lottery over either of the two certain

strategies. That is, he chooses trivial lottery L^1 = (0, Hao; 1, Lin) over trivial lottery L^2 = (1, Hao; 0, Lin) but chooses (.5, Hao; .5, Lin) over (0, Hao; 1, Lin), which is equivalent to (.5, L^1; .5, L^2) being chosen over (.5, L^1; .5, L^1).

The violation of strong independence and expected utility may be due to a sense of fairness in the treatment of Hao and Lin (not ignoring Hao just because he has a somewhat lower probability of cure, though it is very high anyway).[25] But it may also be due to Dr. Chang's dislike of having to make the choice himself between Hao and Lin, "condemning" - as it were - one of them to death. Dr. Chang may, in fact, even prefer that the lottery be won by Lin, who has a somewhat higher probability of cure, but nevertheless prefer to have the genuine lottery over simply giving the medicine to Lin, ignoring Hao's claims altogether. The agency of the actual choice - whether Dr. Chang has to name one of two to be saved (and the other left to die) - may make a difference to him. Whether Dr. Chang is morally right to prefer the lottery is, of course, a debatable issue (there are arguments on both sides), but certainty it is very hard to claim that Dr. Chang is being straightforwardly irrational in being "agency sensitive".

Case 3: Deportation Information

Ayesha - an immigrant to the United Kingdom - is wondering whether to become a civil rights lawyer or a commercial lawyer in her choice of career. Given that simple choice, she would be inclined towards the latter, i.e., commercial law practice. But she learns that since there were some minor technical irregularities in her immigration papers (and since she comes from what is politely called the "new" Commonwealth countries, as opposed to white ones), she has about a 50 per cent chance of being simply deported from the U.K. rather than doing either kind of practice there. She decides that if these are the prospects and if - in the event - she is not deported, then she will prefer after all to be a civil rights lawyer. However, everything in the real world (except in her mind) will be exactly the same if she is not deported as it would have been if that issue had not been raised at all. Is she being irrational in violating strong idependence?

Ayesha's choices can be given reasoned support in

line with "counterfactual outcome sensitivity", rather
like in the case of "the No-letter Response". She could
also believe that she has some "responsibility" now to
concentrate on civil rights issues having become involved
in one herself, at the receiving end. But I don't want to
pursue either of these lines here. (I assume that Ayesha
is psychologically unaffected and also does not accept any
special moral responsibility by virtue of facing the
prospects of her own deportation.) But the very fact of
her facing the probability of deportation herself may give
her more <u>knowledge</u> of the issue of immigration and of
the problems faced by fellow immigrants. The world is no
different, but her understanding of it is not unaffected
by the uncertainty she herself faces regarding
deportation. Her contingent preference reflects her greater
understanding of the realities of the U.K. immigration
policy and of the nature of the civil rights problem,
if she faces the prospect of deportation herself.

    If the nature of the uncertainties faced affects a
person's knowledge and if this affects the person's
<u>valuation</u> of the outcomes (without changing the
"outcomes", as they are defined in this literature), then
the axiomatic requirements of expected utility models may
well be seriously compromised.

5.   Concluding Remarks

Some of the main points of this paper can be briefly put
together.
    (1) The two standard approaches to "rational
choice", viz., "internal consistency" and "self-interest
pursuit", are both deeply defective.
    (2) The view that the problem of rationality is
"unproblamatic" for choice under certainty, with
difficulties arising only with uncertainty, is mistaken.
Many serious difficulties are present whether or not
uncertainty is faced by the chooser.
    (3) The problem of rational choice can be split
into two different types of problems, which are
respectively called here "correspondence rationality" and
"reflection rationality".
    (4) "Correspondence irrationality" is a matter of
failure of correspondence between the person's reasoned
reflection and his actual choices. The failure can arise

from various causes, e.g., (i) acting "without thinking", (ii) lazy reflection, and (iii) "weakness of will".

(5) "Reflection irrationality" is a matter of failure of careful reflection. Despite reflecting carefully, connections may be missed and relevant considerations ignored because of intellectual limitations, possibly due to lack of training on decision problems.

(6) Both "correspondence rationality" and "reflection rationality" have serious decidability problems. This is no embarrassment to the approach to rationality suggested in this paper. The notion of rationality involves inherent ambiguities, and the decidability problems of "correspondence rationality" and "reflection rationality" relate to these basic ambiguities. Sensible criteria for checking a property cannot lead to complete and clearcut answers when the property itself includes ambiguities. There is a strong case for systematically admitting incompleteness in rationality judgments, separating out clear cases of irrationality (of either type) from others.

(7) The approach of "expected utility" raises interesting issues of "reflection rationality". The axioms used (including "strong independence") and the demands of "probability consequentialism" both help to bring out the main contentious issues in the "expected utility" approach. While the approach has much appeal, there are serious arguments against it as well. The problem of "reflection rationality" has genuine ambiguities in dealing with violations of strong independence and probability consequentialism.

(8) Three different arguments for violating strong independence were identified and distinguished, viz., (1) "counter-factual outcome sensitivity", (2) "agency sensitivity", and (3) "information sensitivity". These arguments can be used to explain reasoned violations of the axioms of expected utility in some of the counterexamples that have been presented in the literature.

(9) Three counterxamples to the reasonableness of strong independence were presented, called respectively, (1) "The No-Letter Response", (2) "The Doctor's Dilemma", and (3) "Deportation Information". The first illustrates "counterfactual outcome sensitivity" and the second "agency sensitivity"; whereas the third can be seen as

exemplifying either "counterfactual outcome sensitivity" or "information sensitivity".

(10) Finally, rational choice is a matter of the correspondence of choice to the person's reasoning and of the quality of that reasoning. While both questions are hard to deal with, they have to be explicitly faced. To try to avoid these questions either by externally imposing specific objectives and substantive rules (e.g., self-interest maximization), or by imposing conditions of internal consistency (e.g., binariness, strong independence), amounts to losing important dimensions of the problem of rationality of choice. No set of internal consistency conditions - however stringent - can be <u>sufficient</u> for the rationality of choice. Nor - it appears - can the usual consistency conditions be seen as <u>necessary</u>. Rationality deserves a less mechanical approach.

All Souls College
Oxford

NOTES

1. See also Arrow (1959), Richter (1971), Sen (1971), Herzberger (1973).
2. See Arrow (1951b), Debreu (1959), Arrow and Hahn (1971). These results require <u>actual</u> behaviour to be self-interest maximizing, and this involves the further assumption that actual behaviour is also "rational" (seen as self-interest maximization).
3. See Sen (1972) for a critique; also Sen (1982a).
4. See Arrow (1959), Sen (1971), Herzberger (1973).
5. See Richter (1971), Sen (1971), Suzumura (1976).
6. See Nagel (1969), Sen (1972, 1977a), Hirschman (1977, 1982), Margolis (1982), Akerlof (1983), Schelling (1984), and Schick (1984).
7. In an illuminating review article, Mark Machina (1981) remarks: "It is not irrational, for example, to hate asparagus". It certainly isn't (though what rotten luck!). However, it would be difficult to take as rational the person who hates asparagus but continues eating it nevertheless, without being able to provide any convincing reason for choosing what he hates (e.g.,

seeking some particular vitamins present in asparagus, or facing a threat of being murdered by an asparagus-maniac gang if he does not eat "the good vegetable"). As formulated here, the issue of rationality of choice is connected with the correspondence of choice with reasoning and the quality of that reasoning. In the context of certainty, Machina sees rationality as "transitivity" of the person's preference.

8. The reasonableness of choices being "binary" has been differently assessed in Arrow (1951a), Sen (1970a, 1977a), Schwartz (1972), Fishburn (1973), Herzberger (1973), Plott (1973), Kanger (1976), Campbell (1975), Suzumura (1983), Sugden (1985).

9. I have discussed the motivational issues underlying "correspondence rationality" in Sen (1984b).

10. An alternative reading - perhaps even the most frequent reading - of the problem of Buridan's ass makes it indifferent between the two haystacks (rather than being unable to decide which one was preferable). In this case the ass should have even less problem in choosing either haystack (with a guarantee of maximization no matter which of the two haystacks it chose).

11. See Elster (1978).

12. In various papers, reproduced in two selections, Sen (1982a, 1984a).

13. See Raiffa (1968) and Keeney and Raiffa (1976). See also Harsanyi (1977).

14. See also Allais and Hagen (1979) and Stigum and Wenstøp (1983).

15. For an illuminating review, see Fishburn (1981).

16. See also Arrow (1970).

17. See MacCrimmon (1968) and Kahneman, Slovik and Tversky (1983). For a challenging defence of the rationality of some of the alleged irrationalities of observed psychology, see Cohen (1983). See also Jeffrey (1965), Levi (1974, 1982), Arrow (1982, 1983), Gärdenfors and Sahlin (1982), Machina (1983), McClennen (1983), among many other contributions.

18. The independence condition is strictly necessary for global linearity (i.e., fixed utilities), but can be dispensed with for more permissive "expected utility analysis" with "local utilities" (locally linear coefficients for weighting the probabilities); see Machina (1982).

19. I have tried to argue that even with consequentialism, this concentration on "utility consequences" <u>only</u> is a further severe limitation of the utilitarian approach; see Sen (1979).

20. For an illuminating analysis of the distinction between the "actual psychological reality" of a person's feeling about the choices (e.g., Allais'), and the "psychological values" assigned by the expected utility procedure, see Machina (1981).

21. Only an upper-class Englishman properly brought up by a strict nanny can believe that if a person decides that some psychological attitude is not sensible, then it certainty can be prevented from occuring. See also Schelling (1984).

22. One must also distinguish between regretting a <u>mistaken</u> decision and regretting a decision that turns out to be <u>wrong</u> (though not mistaken on the basis of the information available at the time of deciding). The latter may well be, in some sense, "silly", but if one knows that one will not be able to avoid that silliness, it is surely unreasonable to take no note of that psychological fact.

23. See also MacCrimmon (1968), Drèze (1974), Allais and Hagen (1979), Stigum and Wenstøp (1983).

24. An alternative way of dealing with the case is to allow your "disappointment" (at not getting the cash prize) or "relief" (not "getting" the summons) enter the description of the states of affairs or outcomes, but this goes against the approach of "expected utility" and also makes "strong independence" a rather vacuous restriction. A third possibility is to assume that the person does not <u>know</u> what the alternative outcomes might be (i.e., does not know whether a cash prize is expected, or a summons may be coming). However, to combine this ignorance with rational decision making over lotteries, we would have to assume that the person forgets what the nature of the lotteries (and the prices) are, <u>after</u> taking his decisions. Independence cannot be easily rescued by any of these "cunning" tricks.

25. Cf. Diamond (1967), Sen (1970a), Broome (1984), for a somewhat different case with symmetric individual positions.

REFERENCES

Akerlof, G.: 1983, "Loyalty Filters", _American Economic Review_ 73.

Allais, M.: 1953, "Le Comportement de l'Homme Rational devant le Risque: Critique des Postulates et Axiomes de l'Ecole Amèricaine", _Econometrica_ 21.

Allais, M., and O. Hagen (eds.): 1979, _Expected Utility Hypotheses and the Allais Paradox: Contemporary Discussion of Decisions under Uncertainty with Allais' Rejoinder_, D. Reidel, Dordrecht.

Arrow, K.J.: 1951a, _Social Choice and Individual Values_, 2nd edition (1963) Wiley, New York.

Arrow, K.J.: 1951b, "An Extension of the Basic Theorems of Welfare Economics", in J. Neymann, ed., _Proceedings of the 2nd Berkeley Symposium of Mathematical Statistics_, University of California Press, Berkeley.

Arrow, K.J.: 1959, "Rational Choice Functions and Orderings", _Economica_ 26.

Arrow, K.J.: 1970, _Essays in the Theory of Risk-Bearing_, North-Holland, Amsterdam.

Arrow, K.J.: 1982, "Risk Perception in Psychology and Economics", _Economic Inquiry_ 20.

Arrow, K.J.: 1983, "Behaviour under Uncertainty and Its Implications for Policy", in Stigum and Wenstøp (eds.), 1983.

Arrow, K.J., and F.H. Hahn: 1971, _General Competitive Analysis_, Holden-day, San Francisco, republished (1979) North-Holland, Amsterdam.

Bell, D.E.: 1982, "Regret in Decision Making under Uncertainty", _Operations Research_ 30.

Borch, K., and J. Mossin: 1968, _Risk and Uncertainty_, Macmillan, London.

Broome, J.: 1984, "Uncertainty and Fairness", _Economic Journal_ 94.

Campbell, D.E.: 1976, "Democratic Preference Functions", _Journal of Economic Theory_ 12.

Chipman, J.S., L. Hurwicz, M.K. Richter, and H.F. Sonneschein (eds.): _Preference, Utility and Demand_, Harcourt, New York.

Cohen, J.: 1982, "Are People Programmed to Commit Fallacies? Further Thoughts about Interpretation of Experimental Data on Probability Judgment", _Journal of the Theory of Social Behaviour_.

Davidson, D., P. Suppes, and S. Siegel: 1957, _Decision_

Making: An Experimental Approach, Stanford University Press, Stanford.

Debreu, G.: 1959, *A Theory of Value*, Wiley, New York.

Diamond, P: 1967, "Cardinal Welfare, Individualistic Ethics, and Interpersonal Comparisons of Utility: A Comment", *Journal of Political Economy*, 75.

Drèze, J.H.: 1974, "Axiomatic Theories of Choice, Cardinal Utility and Subjective Probability: A Review", in J.H. Drèze (ed.), *Allocation under Uncertainty: Equilibrium and Optimality*, Macmillan, London.

Edwards, W., and A. Tversky (eds.): 1967, *Decision Making* *Penguin Books*, Harmondsworth.

Elster, J.: 1978, *Logic and Society*, Wiley, New York.

Fishburn, P.C.: 1973, *The Theory o f Social Choice*, Princeton University Press, Princeton.

Fishburn, P.C.: 1981, "Subjective Expected Utility: A Review of Normative Theories", *Theory and Decision*, 13.

Gärdenfors, P., and N.E. Sahlin: 1982, "Unreliable Probabilities, Risk Taking and Decision Making", *Synthese* 53.

Hammond, P.J.: 1976, "Changing Tastes and Coherent Dynamic Choice", *Review of Economic Studies* 43.

Hammond, P.J.: 1982, "Consequentialism and Rationality in Dynamic Choice under Uncertainty", Technical Report 387, Institute for Mathematical Studies in the Social Sciences, Stanford University.

Harsanyi, J.C.: 1966, "A General Theory of Rational Behaviour in Game Situations", *Econometrica* 34.

Harsanyi, J.C.: 1977, *Rational Behaviour and Bargaining Equilibrium in Games and Social Situations*, Cambridge University Press, Cambridge.

Herzberger, H.G.: 1973, "Ordinal Preference and Rational Choice", *Econometrica* 41.

Hirschman, A.O.: 1977, *The Passions and the Interest*, Princeton University Press, Princeton.

Hirschman, A.O.: 1982, *Shifting Involvements*, Princeton University Press, Princeton.

Jeffrey, R.C.: 1965, *The Logic of Decision*, McGraw-Hill, New York, 2nd edition (1983), University of Chicago Press, Chicago.

Kahneman, D., and A. Tversky: 1979, "Prospect Theory: An Analysis of Decision under Risk", *Econometrica* 47.

Kahneman, D., P. Slovik, and A. Tversky: 1983, *Judgment under Uncertainty: Heuristics and Biases*, Cambridge University Press, Cambridge.

Kanger, S: 1976, "Choice Based on Preference", mimeographed, Uppsala University.

Keeney, R.L., and H. Raiffa: 1976, Decisions with Multiple Objectives: Preferences and Value Tradeoffs, Wiley, New York.

Levi, I.: 1974, "On Indeterminate Probabilities", Journal of Philosophy 71.

Levi, I.: 1982, "Ignorance, Probability and Rational Choice", Synthese 53.

Loomes, G., and R. Sudgen: 1982, "Regret Theory: An Alternative Theory of Rational Choice under Uncertainty", Economic Journal 92.

Luce, R.D., and H. Raiffa: 1957, Games and Decisions, Wiley, New York.

MacCrimmon, K.R.: 1968, "Descriptive and Normative Implications of Decision Theory Postulates", in K. Borch and J. Mossin, 1968.

Machina, M.: 1981, 'Rational' Decision Making vs. 'Rational' Decision Modelling?", Journal of Mathematical Psychology 24.

Machina, M.:1982, " 'Expected Utility' Analysis without the Independence Axiom", Econometrica 50.

Machina, M.: 1983, "Generalized Expected Utility Analysis and the Nature of Observed Violations of the Independence Axiom", in B. Stigum and F. Wenstøp (eds.) 1983.

McClennen, E.F.: 1983 , "Sure-Thing Doubts", in B.Stigum and F. Wenstøp (eds.), 1983.

Margolis, H.: 1982, Selfishness, Altruism and Rationality, Cambridge University Press, Cambridge.

Nagel, T.: 1970, The Possibility of Altruism, Clarendon Press, Oxford.

Nagel, T.: 1980, "The Limits of Objectivity", in S. McMurrin (ed.), Tanner Lectures on Human Values, Cambridge University Press, Cambridge.

Parfit, D.: 1984, Reasons and Persons, Cladendon Press, Oxford.

Plott, C.: 1973, "Path Independence, Rationality and Social Choice", Econometrica 41.

Raiffa, H.: 1968, Decision Analysis, Addison-Wesley, Reading, Mass.

Ramsey, F.P.: 1931, "Truth and Probability", in F.P. Ramsey, The Foundations of Mathematics and other Logical Essays, Kegan Paul, London.

Richter, M.K.: 1971, "Rational Choice", in Chipman,

Hurwicz, Richter and Sonneschein (eds.), 1971.

Savage, L.J.: 1954, The Foundations of Statistics, Wiley, New York.

Samuelson, P.: 1947, The Foundations of Economic Analysis, Harvard University Press, Cambridge, Mass.

Schelling, T.C.: 1984, "Self-Command in Practice, in Policy, and in a Theory of Rational Choice", American Economic Review 74, Papers and Proceedings.

Schick, F.: 1984, Having Reasons: An Essay on Rationality and Sociality, Princeton University Press, Princeton.

Schwartz, T: 1972, "Rationality and the Myth of the Maximum", Nous 7.

Sen, A.K.: 1970a, Collective Choice and Social Welfare, San Francisco, Holden-Day, republished by North-Holland (1979), Amsterdam.

Sen, A.K.: 1970b, "Interpersonal Aggregation and Partial Comparability", Econometrica, 38; 1972 "A Correction", Econometrica

Sen, A.K.: 1971, "Choice Functions and Revealed Preference", Review of Economic Studies 38.

Sen, A.K.: 1972, "Behaviour and the Concept of Preference", Economica 40.

Sen, A.K.: 1977a, "Social Choice Theory: A Re-examination", Econometrica 45.

Sen, A.K.: 1977b, "Rational Fools: A Critique of the Behavioural Foundations of Economic Theory", Philosophy and Public Affairs 6.

Sen, A.K.: 1979, "Utilitarianism and Welfarism", Journal of Philosophy 76.

Sen, A.K.: 1982a, Choice, Welfare and Measurement, Blackwell, Óxford, and Harvard University Press, Cambridge, Mass.

Sen, A.K.: 1982b, "Rights and Agency", Philosophy and Public Affairs 11.

Sen, A.K.: 1983, "Evaluator Relativity and Consequential Evaluation", Philosophy and Public Affairs 12.

Sen, A.K.: 1984a, Resources, Values and Development, Blackwell, Oxford: Blackwell and Harvard University Press, Cambridge, Mass.

Sen, A.K.: 1984b, "Rationality, Interest and Identity", written for a festschrift for A.O. Hirschman.

Simon, H.A.: 1957, Models of Man, Wiley, New York.

Sugden, R: 1985, "Why Be Consistent? A Critical Analysis of Consistency Requirements in Choice Theory", Economica 52.

Suzumura, K.: 1976, "Rational Choice and Revealed Preference", Review of Economic Studies 43.

Suzumura, K.: 1983, Rational Choice, Collective Decisions and Social Welfare, Cambridge University Press, Cambridge.

Stigum, B.P., and F. Wenstøp (eds.): 1983, Foundations of Utility and Risk Theory with Applications, Reidel, Dordrecht.

Tversky, A.: 1975, "A Critique of Expected Utility Theory: Descriptive and Normative Considerations", Erkenntnis 9.

Tversky, A., and D. Kahneman: 1974, "Judgment under Uncertainty: Heuristics and Biases", Science 185.

von Neumann, J., and O. Morgenstern: 1947, Theory of Games and Economic Behaviour, Princeton University Press, Princeton.

William, B.: 1973, "A Critique of Utilitarianism", in J. Smart and B. Williams, Utilitarianism: For and Against, Cambridge University Press, Cambridge.

Williams, B.: 1982, Moral Luck, Cambridge University Press, Cambridge.

John C. Harsanyi

PRACTICAL CERTAINTY AND THE ACCEPTANCE
OF EMPIRICAL STATEMENTS

1. Introduction

Both scientists and ordinary people accept the truth of some empirical statements, ranging from reports on directly observed, or personally remembered, or reliably reported, individual facts to general scientific hypotheses and to entire scientific theories--even though they do not have, and cannot possibly have, conclusive evidence for their truth.[1] What is the rational justification, if there is any, for an acceptance of such truth claims? To answer this question, I am going to propose a Bayesian theory of acceptance, which, however, unlike the theories of such distinguished authors as Hempel (1962), Levi (1967, 1980), and several others, and unlike the theory which I myself suggested on an earlier occasion (Harsanyi, 1983, p. 342), makes no use of special cognitive utilities (or epistemic utilities).

Informally speaking, my theory will be based on the assumption that the acceptance of an empirical statement is an instrumental decision. An ideally rational person will accept a statement, not on the expectation of deriving direct utility (cognitive utility) from doing so, but rather on the expectation that acceptance of this statement will simplify his or her decision problems in practical life and/or in science, without significantly distorting the actual decision he or she will reach--in spite of the fact that he or she cannot be absolutely sure that this statement is in fact true.[2] If we do not have enough evidence to assign probability 1 to a given statement, then its acceptance as a true statement can never be intrinsically justified, though it may be justified instrumentally as a policy simplifying our decision-making process.

Yet, before any further discussion of this problem, I will have to discuss two related topics. One is the importance of informal decisions. The other is the use of

27

L. Daboni et al. (eds.), Recent Developments in the Foundations of Utility and Risk Theory, 27–41.
© *1986 by D. Reidel Publishing Company.*

<u>imprecise</u>   (numerically   not   uniquely   determined)
subjective probabilities in Bayesian decision theory.

2. Formal and Informal Decisions

Many of our practical and theoretical decisions are based
on explicit and unambiguous criteria. These I will call
<u>formal</u> decision. Other decisions we are making are based on
rather vague criteria, or may not be based on any explicit
criteria at all. These I will call <u>informal</u> decision. We
often say that decisions of this latter type are based on
<u>personal judgment</u>.

  For   example, we have clear arithmetic criteria to
decide which particular shop is selling a given commodity
at the lowest price. Likewise, we have clear logical
criteria to determine whether a proposed mathematical
proof is a valid proof or not. On the other hand, we have
no clear criteria to decide what numerical probability to
assign to a particular horse coming in first in a given
horse race. We all know that informal decisions, i.e.,
personal judgments, play essential roles in science, in
business, in politics, and also in everyday life (cf.
Polanyi, 1967).

  In my opinion, it is one of the great virtues of
Bayesian theory that it clearly recognizes the important
roles played <u>both</u> by formal and by informal decisions in
human decision making. If a Bayesian decision maker wants
to find the best policy in a given situation, he first has
to choose a specific <u>model</u> for analyzing this situation.
Then he has to choose his <u>prior probabilities</u> and his von
Neumann-Morgenstern <u>utility function</u>. All these choices
are largely matters of personal judgment.[3] But once these
choices have been made, finding the expected-utility
maximizing policy is a matter of computation and, therefore,
represents a formal decision.

  I will argue below that, even though conventional
Bayesian theory already assigns an important role to
informal decisions, their actual importance is even
greater than conventional Bayesian theory suggests.

3. Imprecise Subjective Probabilities

Most Bayesian authors admit that many of our subjective

probabilities are rather vague and do not possess
well-defined unique numerical values (cf. Savage, 1954, p.
59). Yet, most of them prefer to base their formal theory
on the idealizing assumption that the decision maker under
consideration does entertain precise numerical
probabilities--or at least that he would do so if he were
an ideally rational person. But several authors, including
Schick (1958, pp. 63-77), Good (1962), and Levi (1980, pp.
192-204), have introduced numerically indeterminate
subjective probabilities even into their formal theories.
For instance, they admit the possibility that the decision
maker may allocate his subjective probability for a given
event merely to some interval, say, by placing it between
1/4 and 1/3, without assigning to it any definite numerical
value within this interval, etc.

I want to propose an intermediate approach. Suppose
we have a Bayesian decision problem with a well-defined
von Neumann-Morgenstern utility function U, and with a
finite number of alternative policies $\pi_1,\ldots,\pi_n$. Let F
be the set of all possible subjective probability
distributions f over the states of nature. Clearly, F
will contain infinitely many such probability
distributions f. Let F_i (i=1,...,n) be the set of all
probability distributions f that would make a given policy
π_i the expected-utility maximizing policy. Obviously,
the n sets $F_1,\ldots, F_n$ will all be convex and compact
sets. Moreover, apart from some degenerate cases, any
nonempty set F_i will contain infinitely many different
probability distributions f.

Now, the model I am proposing is this. In order to
choose a specific policy π_i, a Bayesian decision maker
will always have to decide which particular set F_i his
subjective probability distribution f belongs to. But in
order to choose this policy π_i, he need not undertake the
additional intellectual effort of choosing a specific
distribution f within this set F_i as being his actual
subjective probability distribution. Once he knows that
his subjective probability distribution belongs to F_i, he
can be sure that his optimal policy is π_i.

For example, suppose I am offered a choice between
two bets free of charge. One bet is that I will get $100 if
President Reagan is re-elected and will get nothing if
he is not. The other bet is that I will get $100 if he is
not re-elected and will get nothing if he is. Then,
assuming that the utility I would derive from $100 does

not depend on the results of the next presidential election, I will have to choose between the two bets by trying to decide whether Reagan's re-election or his failure to win re-election is the more probable outcome, (Of course, if I regard both possible outcomes as equally likely, then I can rationally choose either bet.)

No doubt, I may very much dislike to commit myself to either probability judgment. But by choosing one of the two bets I will in fact commit myself to assigning my subjective probability p for Reagan's re-election either to the closed interval [0.5, 1.0] or to the closed interval [0.0, 0.5]. That is to say, my choice between the two bets will commit me to a personal judgment as to the relative weight I want to assign to the reasons there are for expecting Reagan to be re-elected as against the relative weight I want to assign to the reasons there are for expecting him not to be re-elected.

On the other hand, once I have decided to assign p to (say) the interval [0.5, 1], I will obtain no practical benefit from trying to decide whether p=0.60 or < 0.60 or > 0.60. Thus, if it took me any mental effort at all to decide this latter question, it would be rational for me to leave this question undecided--unless I have some other reasons (e.g., sheer theoretical interest) for making a more precise probability judgment.

In fact, if I decide that p must be very close to 1/2, even though it might be either a little greater or a little smaller than 1/2, it may be rational for me to choose between the two suggested bets at random, without trying to determine wheter p > 1/2 or p < 1/2. For I may very well make the personal judgment that p is so close to 1/2 that my expected utility loss in case I choose the "wrong" bet will be smaller than (or at most equal to) the disutility cost of the mental effort required to determine whether I should set p > 1/2 or p < 1/2.

4. The Criteria For Practical Certainty

My theory of acceptance will be based on the concept of practical certainty. The conclusion we have reached in Sections 2 and 3 will provide useful guidance in discussing this latter concept. I will say that a person regards a statement as strictly certain if he assigns a subjective probability of 1 to it. In contrast, informally speaking,

I will say that he regards a statement as <u>pratically certain</u>
if he treats this statement <u>as if</u> he assigned probability 1
to it, even though in actual fact he assigns only a <u>lower</u>
probability to it.

More formally, let Prob (s) denote the decision
maker's true <u>unconditional</u> subjective probability for any
statement s. Let Prob (s| s*) denote his <u>conditional</u>
subjective probability for the same statement s on the
assumption that a given statement s* is true.

Now suppose this person wants to choose an optimal
policy for a given practical decision problem D. Let π be
the policy that would maximize his expected utility in
terms of his <u>true</u> subjective probabilities Prob (s). I
will call π his <u>true</u> optimal policy.[4] On the other
hand, let π' be the policy that would maximize his
expected utility if he replaced his <u>true</u> subjective
probabilities Prob (s) by his <u>conditional</u> subjective
probabilities Prob (s| s*). Of course, it may happen that
π' = π. But if in fact π' ≠ π, then I will call π' his
<u>second best</u> policy. Finally, I define assigning "direct"
<u>practical certainty</u> to a given statement s* within a
specific decision problem D as a decision to base one's
analysis of D on the <u>conditional</u> probabilities Prob (s|
s*) rather than on one's <u>true</u> subjective probabilities
Prob (s). Moreover, I will say that, by assigning <u>direct</u>
practical certainty to a given statement s* in this sense,
one also assigns <u>indirect</u> practical certainty to any
statement s^0 that is a <u>logical consequence</u> of s*. Note
that by relying on the conditional probabilities Prob (s|
s*), one automatically treats s* itself <u>as if</u> it had
probability 1 because, obviously, Prob (s*| s*) = 1 even
if Prob (s*) < 1.

Why would anybody want to assign practical certainty
to any statement s* in accordance with this definition?
Because by doing so he can often greatly <u>simplify</u> his
analysis of the relevant decision problem D.

In particular, suppose that the decision maker knows
that <u>one</u> and <u>only one</u> of several alternative hypotheses
$h_1, \ldots, h_n$ is true, but does not know which one it is.
Yet, if he could assume that it was <u>practically certain</u>
that the true hypothesis was one of the hypotheses
$h_1, \ldots, h_k$ with k < n, then he could restrict his
analysis to a <u>smaller number</u> of possibilities, and could
disregard the possibility that one of the <u>other</u>
hypotheses $h_{k+1}, \ldots, h_n$ represented the truth. This

would obviously simplify his analysis.

Of course, from a Bayesian point of view, an attempt to simplify one's analysis of a given decision problem D by treating a statement s* as practically certain can be justified only under some rather stringent conditions. The conditions I am going to propose will not be conditions for the various <u>individual</u> statements to which the decision maker wants to assign practical certainly, but will rather be conditions for a <u>composite</u> statement, representing the <u>conjunction</u> of all individual statements to which practical certainty is to be assigned.[5] Therefore, in what follows, s* will always denote this composite statement. Of course, under my definitions, if the decision maker assigns <u>direct</u> practical certainty to this composite statement s*, he will automatically assign <u>indirect</u> practical certainty to every component statement included in s*, because any such component statement will be a logical consequence of s*. The conditions we need are as follows.

1. We must require that this composite statement s* should be logically <u>consistent</u> (which entails that all the component statements included in s* must be <u>mutually</u> consistent).This requirement is needed both because the very concept of rationality implies that an ideally rational person will not entertain inconsistent assumptions; and also because the conditional probabilities Prob (s| s*) are not well defined if s* is an inconsistent statement.

2. We must also require that, given the decision maker's utility function (payoff function) and given his true subjective probabilities Prob (s), if he treats statement s* as practically certain he should not end up with an <u>unacceptable policy</u>. More specifically, treating s* as practically certain will be clearly justified if this will have <u>no effect</u> on his policy choice because $\pi' = \pi$. But it will be justified even if $\pi' \neq \pi$, as long as the expected utility loss α he may incur by using the <u>second best</u> policy π' instead of using the <u>true</u> optimal policy π will be offset, or more than offset, by the expected utility gain β he hopes to derive by simplifying his analysis of the relevant decision problem D.

Yet, how can the decision maker actually decide

whether this last condition is satisfied or not? Of course, he could decide this question by full analysis of <u>both</u> models, both the simpler model based on the conditional probabilities Prob (s| s*), and the more complicated model based on his true subjective probabilities Prob (s). By analysis of both models, he could find both of the two policies π and π', could compute their expected utilities in terms of his true probabilities Prob (s), and could compute the quantity β as the <u>difference</u> between these two expected utilities. He could also assess the utility costs of analyzing each of the two models, and then could compute the quantity α as the <u>difference</u> between these two utility costs.

Yet, this approach would be obviously self-defeating because it would amount to <u>giving up</u> in advance all the benefits he could possibly obtain by restricting his analysis to the simpler model.

Therefore, I conclude that the only sensible approach for him will be to make a <u>personal judgment</u>, before undertaking detailed analysis of either model, as to whether the expected utility gain β he will obtain by simplifying his analysis can be reasonably taken to be large enough to <u>compensate</u> him for the expected utility loss α he may incur by ending up with a second best policy π' rather than with a true optimal policy π.

Indeed, he may even decide the issue by making the somewhat <u>simpler</u> personal judgment as to whether this expected utility loss α would be small enough to be <u>acceptable</u> to him.[6]

Of course, if the decision maker does opt for using his conditional probabilities Prob (s| s*) rather than his true subjective probabilities Prob (s), he will be often well advised to estimate the former probabilities <u>directly</u>, rather than to compute them from the latter probabilities, because such direct estimation will often be a simpler procedure.

Note that under the proposed theory it will be normally unnecessary for us to decide which statements we want to regard as <u>strictly</u> certain, and which statements merely as <u>practically</u> certain. For we will treat both classes of statements in the same way, <u>as if</u> they had probability <u>1</u> of being true. This seems to be an important advantage of the proposed theory because it is often very hard for us to decide whether we really are, and are justified in being, <u>strictly certain</u> about specific matters. Moreover, it will not be necessary for us to decide what our true unconditional probabilities Prob (s) are for various statements s, because we will use only our conditional probabilities Prob (s|s*) in our actual analysis.

5. Persistent Practical Certainty

In Section 4 we have considered the criteria that will make it rational for a person to treat a given composite statement s* as practically certain with respect to <u>one</u> specific practical decision problem D. But any person can further simplify his decision-making procedure by choosing to assign practical certainty to a suitable composite statement s* in a <u>persistent</u> manner, with respect to <u>all</u> practical decision problems he will encounter--until he decides at some later time to make a <u>direct check</u> as to whether s* still satisfies the criteria for practical certainty with respect to his current decision problems.

No doubt, by assigning <u>persistent</u> practical certainty to a given statement s* in this sense, and, therefore, by not checking individually for each decision problem whether s* actually satisfies the criteria of practical certainty with respect to this decision problem, the decision maker will increase the risk of treating s* as practically certain in some cases where this is not really justified and, as a result, of ending up with nonoptimal policies on such occasions.

Thus, before assigning <u>persistent</u> practical certainty to a given statement, the decision maker will have to make a <u>personal judgment</u> as to whether the expected simplification in his decision-making procedure will compensate him for the expected losses from occasional nonoptimal policies--or as to whether these expected losses will be small enough to be <u>acceptable</u> to him.

If a person has decided to assign <u>persistent</u> practical certainty to a given composite statement s*, he may later come to <u>re-examine</u> this decision for two main reasons.

<u>Case 1</u>. One possible reason is that he is now facing a decision problem D in which the <u>penalty</u> (i.e., the expected utility loss) he would incur by acting on the assumption that statement s* (or some component statement s^0 of this composite statement s*) was <u>true</u> when in

fact it was <u>untrue</u> would be unusually high. This will be a perfectly valid reason even if he has <u>no</u> new evidence that would reduce the credibility of s* or of any of its component statements.

For example, in various minor matters I may have acted for many years on the assumption that the house next door is legally owned by the man who lives in it and may have taken it as practically certain that this was the case, even though I had only rather inconclusive evidence for it. This may have been a reasonable policy on my part because it really mattered very little to me whether he was the legal owner or not. But suppose I am now seriously considering the possibility of buying the house from him. This will obviously mean that I cannot any longer take it for practically certain that he is the legal owner (or at least that I cannot do so without much better evidence) because if I paid him for the house on the assumption that he was the legal owner even though in fact he was not, I might lose a lot of money.

<u>Case 2</u>. The other possible reason is that the decision maker has obtained <u>new evidence</u> that casts serious doubt on statement s* (presumably by impairing the credibility of one or more component statements included in this composite statement s*).

In <u>Case 1</u> the decision maker must proceed as follows. Let s** be the shorter composite statement he will obtain if he removes from the composite statement s* those component statements that seem to be responsible for the high-penalty problem. The decision maker will have to make a <u>personal judgment</u> as to whether the optimal policies he obtained in his current decision problems by use of the conditional subjective probabilities Prob (s| s**), based on the shorter composite statement s**, would yield him <u>significantly higher</u> expected utilities than the optimal policies he obtained by use of the conditional subjective probabilities Prob (s| s*), based on the longer composite statement s*, would yield him. (The expected utilities associated with <u>both</u> sets of policies, of course, would have to be evaluated in terms of the probabilities Prob (s| s**), which <u>do not prejudge</u> the question of whether or not to assign practical certainty to those component statements or statement s* that might be responsible for the high-penalty problem.)

If the decision maker decides that the new policies can be reasonably assumed to yield significantly higher expected utilities than the old policies would have yielded to him, then he must <u>give up</u> treating the longer composite statement s* as practically certain, and must assign practical certainty only to the shorter composite statement s**. But if he feels that the new policies would <u>not</u> yield significantly higher expected utilities than the old policies would yield, then he can <u>go on</u> assigning practical certainty to s*.

In <u>Case 2</u> the decision maker must proceed as follows. Let s** be the shorter composite statement he will obtain if he removes from the composite statement s* all component statements whose credibility has been impaired by the newly obtained evidence; and let e denote this new evidence itself. The decision maker will have to make a <u>personal judgment</u> as to whether the optimal policies he obtained in his current decision problems by use of the conditional subjective probabilities Prob (s| s**e), based on the shorter composite statement s* and on the new evidence e, would yield him <u>significantly higher</u> expected utilities than the optimal policies he obtained by use of the conditional subjective probabilities Prob (s| s*), based on the longer composite statement s*, would yield him. (Of course, the expected utilities associated with <u>both</u> sets of policies would have to be evaluated in terms of the probabilities Prob (s| s**e).)

If the decision maker decides that the new policies would in fact yield him higher expected utilities, then be must <u>give up</u> treating s* as a practically certain statement, and must assign practical certainty only to the shorter composite statement s**.[7] But if he feels that the new policies would <u>not</u> yield significantly higher expected utilities, then he can <u>go on</u> assigning practical certainty to s*.

6. A Bayesian Model of Scientific Activity

Up until now I have only discussed the role that practically certain statements play in <u>practical</u> decision making. Now I propose to consider their role in <u>scientific</u> decision making. Yet, science is in many ways an activity quite different from practical decision making. Therefore, before actually discussing the use of practically certain statements in science, I will first propose a <u>general Bayesian model of scientific activity</u>. In this model expected-utility maximization will play no formal role. Rather, the central role the latter usually plays in Bayesian models will be taken over by subjective probability judgments as to which particular theory has the best chance of being the correct theory among all alternative theories in any given scientific field.

Probably most people will agree that ideally the task of science is to come up with true theories that provide truthful explanations for the empirical facts. Yet, we can never be quite sure whether any given scientific theory is in fact completely true in all its specific details or not. Therefore, more realistically, we may say that the task of science is to identify, among all alternative theories existing in a given field, that particular theory that can be reasonably judged to have the highest probability of being true and of providing a correct explanation for the facts. A further task of science is to propose new theories whose probability of being true and of providing correct explanation is higher than that of any existing alternative theory.[8]

7. Practical Certainty in Science

On the basis of the proposed model of scientific activity, I now introduce the following definitions. Let s* again be the conjunction of all statements that a given scientist wants to treat as practically certain in one specific scientific decision problem, i.e., in evaluating alternative theories in one specific, narrowly defined, field of science. I will say that he assigns "direct" practical certainty to this composite statement s* in the relevant field of science if he decides to judge the probability of every scientific theory t in this field in terms of the conditional subjective probabilities Prob (t| s*) on the assumption that this statement s* is true, rather than in terms of his true unconditional subjective probabilities Prob (t) for these theories--in order to simplify his job of assessing the probabilities of all these theories. Again, I will say that by assigning direct practical certainty to this composite statement s*, he will automatically assign indirect practical certainty to each component statement included in s* and, more generally, to all logical consequences of s*.

Under what conditions will a scientist be justified

in assigning practical certainty to some statement s^* in this sense? According to the proposed model of science, he will be justified in doing so if this will not significantly impair his ability to identify the theory that has the <u>highest probability</u> of being the correct theory, among all alternative theories in this field.

More formally, let $t = t^0$ be the theory with the highest <u>unconditional</u> probability Prob (t). I will call t^0 the <u>true</u> optimal theory. Let $t = t^{00}$ be the theory with the highest <u>conditional</u> probability Prob $(t \mid s^*)$. Of course, it may happen that $t^{00} = t^0$. But in case $t^{00} \neq t^0$, than I will call t^{00} the <u>second-best</u> theory.

The scientist in question will be clearly justified in treating statement s^* as practically certain if he expects that $t^{00} = t^0$. But I would like to argue that he will be justified in doing so even if $t^{00} \neq t^0$, as long as he can reasonably expect that the second-best theory t^{00} he will choose will be a theory <u>almost as good</u> as the true optimal theory would be--in the sense that his true subjective probabilities Prob (t^{00}) and Prob (t^0) for t^{00} and for t^0 will <u>not be very far apart</u>. More exactly, we may require that he should have good reasons to expect that the <u>ratio</u> of these two probabilities would be very close to unity.

8. Persistent Practical Certainty in Science

A scientist can further simplify his job making the decision to assign practical certainty to a given composite statement s^* in a <u>persistent</u> manner, i.e., not only in <u>one</u> specific field of science but rather in <u>all</u> fields of science--until at some later time he has specific reasons to <u>re-examine</u> this decision. He will be justified in doing so if he expects that s^* will satisfy the criteria for practical certainty (as stated in Section 7) in <u>all</u> fields of science.

On the other hand, his basic reason for re-examining this decision at a later time will be that he has obtained <u>new evidence</u> that casts serious doubt on statement s^* or on some component statement included in s^*. (This reason corresponds to Case 2 of Section 5. The analog of Case 1 of Section 5 is less likely to arise in science.)

9. Conclusion: Acceptance of Empirical Statements

Let s* be the conjunction of all empirical statements that
a given person wants to accept as true. I propose that we
should interpret his acceptance of s*, and of every
component statement included in s*, as a decision to
assign <u>persistent</u> practical certainty to s* <u>both</u> in
his practical decisions <u>and</u> in his scientific activities
(if any).

Indeed, at a more fundamental level, we may interpret
acceptance of s* also as a decision to recommend it also to
all <u>other</u> members of society to assign persistent
practical certainty to this statement s*, both in their
practical and their scientific decisions, on the ground
that s* satisfies the criteria for practical certainty,
both in practical life and in science, from <u>their</u> points
of view as well.

Thus, our theory interprets the acceptance of an
empirical statement as an <u>instrumental</u> action. It is not
meant to satisfy our psychological needs by yielding us
<u>directly</u> any cognitive utilities. Rather, it is meant to
<u>simplify</u> our decision making process, both in practical
life and in science, yet do this without significantly
affecting the <u>quality</u> of the decisions we are likely to
reach.[9]

School of Business Administration
University of California
Berkeley

NOTES

1. I want to thank the National Science Foundation for
supporting this research through grant SES82-18938 to
the Center for Research in Management, University of
California, Berkeley. I want to thank also Professor
Isaac Levi of Columbia University, and Professor Teddy
Seidenfeld of Washington University, St. Louis, for
discussing topics related to those of this paper in
extensive and very helpful correspondence. But let me
add that they are not responsible in any way for the
views I will state, and may very well disagree with

most of them.

2. In what follows, for convenience in similar contexts I will omit the female pronouns.

3. Though, as I have argued elsewhere (Harsanyi, 1983, pp. 350-355), in some cases we can choose our prior probabilities on the basis of well-defined formal criteria.

4. I will make the simplifying assumption that this optimal policy π is unique (and so is the policy π' to be defined below). But my analysis can be easily extended to the general case.

5. In case the decision maker wants to assign practical certainty to _infinitely many_ individual statements, I will assume that he uses a rich enough propositional logic as to allow him to use infinite conjunctions, or to use set-theoretical formulae doing the same job.

6. If he chooses to rely on this simpler personal judgment, instead of undertaking an actual _comparison_ between his estimates of α and of β, he would act in the spirit of Simon's theory of _limited rationality_ (cf. e.g., Simon, 1979).

7. Or he may assign practical certainty to _both_ s** and e, i.e., he may assign practical certainty to their conjunction (s** and e). In the text I have spoken only about assigning practical certainty to s** itself, because the evidence e may contain statements asserting that the decision maker assigns positive subjective probabilities _less_ than 1 to some factual claims, rather than assigning practical certainty to them (cf. Jeffrey, 1968).

8. Lack of space prevents me here from discussing my model of scientific activity in any greater detail. See Footnote 9.

9. The interested reader is referred to a longer version of this paper, titled "Acceptance of empirical statements: a Bayesian theory without cognitive utilities", appeared in _Theory and Decision_ 18, 1.

REFERENCES

Bogdan, R.J. _et al._ (eds.): 1973, _Logic, Language, and Probability_, D. Reidel, Dordrecht, Holland.

Good, I. J.: 1962, "Subjective Probability as a Measure of a Nommeasurable Set," in E. Nagel _et al._ (eds.), _Logic,_

Methodology, and Philosophy of Science, Stanford University Press, Stanford, CA., pp. 319-329.

Harman, G.: 1965, "The Inference to the Best Explanation," _Philosophical Review_ 74, 88-95.

Harsanyi, J.C.: 1983,"Bayesian Decision Theory, Subjective and Objective Probabilities and Acceptance of Empirical Hypotheses," _Synthese_ 57, 341-345.

Hempel, C.G.: 1962, "Deductive-Nomological versus Statistical Explanation, " _Minnesota Studies in the Philosophy of Science_ 3, 98-169.

Hilpinen, R.: 1968, "Rules of Acceptance and Inductive Logic," _Acta Philosophica Fennica_ 22, 1-134.

Jeffrey, R.C.: 1965, _The Logic of Decision_, McGraw-Hill, New York, N.Y.

Jeffrey, R.C.: 1968, "Probable Knowledge," in I. Lakatos (ed.), _The Problem of Inductive Logic_, North Holland, Amsterdam.

Kyburg, H.E. Jr.: 1961, _Probability and the Logic of Rational Belief_, Wesleyan University Press Middleton, CT.

Levi, I.: 1967, _Gambling with Truth_, A. Knopf, New York, N.Y.

Levi, I.: 1980, _The Enterprise of Knowledge_, M.I.T. Press, Cambridge, MA.

Polanyi, M.: 1967, _The Tacit Dimension_, Routledge & K. Paul, London.

Savage, L.J.: 1954, _The Foundations of Statistics_, New York, N.Y.

Schick, F.: 1958, _Explication and Inductive Logic_, Doctoral Dissertation, Columbia University, New York, 1958. (Quoted in Levi, 1980, p. 447, note 12).

Simon, H.A.: 1979, "Rational Decision Making in Business Organizations," _American Economic Review_ 69, 493-513.

Swain, M. (ed): 1970, _Induction, Acceptance, and Rational Belief_, D. Reidel, Dordrecht, Holland.

Donald Davidson

A NEW BASIS FOR DECISION THEORY

In testing a theory of decision making under uncertainty it is usually assumed that subjects understand the words used by the experimenter to describe
the alternatives being offered. Or, perhaps more
accurately, the experimenter assumes he knows how the
subject understands the experimenter's words. Given the
complexity of wagers, the obscurity of the connection
that is supposed to exist between states of nature and
outcomes, and the many other ways misunderstandings can
occur, the assumption of perfect communication between
subject and experimenter is often not satisfied. Even if
it were, the assumption is unsatisfactory from a
theoretical point of view. For the interpretation of
another's language is a problem very similar to the
problem of discovering his subjective probabilities and
utilities: belief, desire and meaning are all attitudes
towards propositions. And the two problems are closely
interlocked, as will become clear.

The present approach is <u>foundational</u> in the
following sense: unlike standard versions of Bayesian
decision theory, this approach does not assume as given
the identity of the objects, states, events, or wagers
among which the subject makes his choices. In a fairly
clear way, it is just a matter of giving Frank Ramsey's
attitude to decision theory broader application[1]. Where
Ramsey treated quantified utilities and probabilities as
constructs derived from an observed pattern of ordinal
preferences among gambles, the theory to be described
treats not only quantified utilities and probabilities as
constructs but also the meanings of the sentences that
describe the objects of preference. Thus the problem of
identifying and individuating propositional contents is
conceived as an integral aspect of the overall project of
interpreting the thoughts and actions of an agent.

In this paper I suggest the form of a theory that
shows how in principle it may be possible not only to

43

L. Daboni et al. (eds.), Recent Developments in the Foundations of Utility and Risk Theory, 43–56.
© 1986 by D. Reidel Publishing Company.

determine an agent's utilities and subjective probabilities but also to identify the propositions to which the utilities and probabilities are assigned. The approach makes use of Richard Jeffrey's version of decision theory,[2] but where Jeffrey attaches probabilities and utilities to propositions assumed to be identified in advance, I propose to attach probabilities and utilities to the sentences of the subject's language. In application, the theory is designed to discover what the subject's sentences mean, thus fixing the contents of the subject's beliefs and desires. Of course there is no reason why the sentences involved should not also belong to the experimenter's language; the point is that identity of meaning is not taken for granted.

In most experimental tests of theories of decision making under uncertainty, subjects make a number of pairwise choices between options; the pattern of responses is then seen to be compatible or not with the theory. The responses are counted as responses to propositions, or, more precisely, to <u>interpreted sentences</u>. In the present approach, the experimental situation may be imagined as identical, but the same responses are recorded simply as responses to sentences, sentences the meanings of which are not known in advance to the experimenter. Thus the data with which the theory deals are responses to <u>uninterpreted sentences</u>. The central empirical concept is that of a weak preference that one (uninterpreted) sentence rather than another be true. There should be no complaint that this is an obscure or untestable concept, at least by comparison with the central empirical concept of other versions of decision theory, since the method of testing is identical in the two cases, but the present approach reads much less into the observed responses.

In spite of these remarks about testing and experiment, my interest in this paper is entirely theoretical. For reasons about to be adumbrated, I am profoundly sceptical about the possibility of significant experimental tests of theories of rationality.[3] This does not mean that such theories, or the considerations that lie behind them, have no empirical application. On the contrary, I think of such theories as attempts to illuminate an essential aspect of the concepts of belief, desire, intention and meaning. One criterion a theory of these concepts must meet is this: it must show how it is possible for one person (the 'experimenter') to come to understand another (the 'subject'). So the theory must begin with data that take as little as possible for granted, and it must be shown that the constraints imposed on the data by the theory are adequate to lead to understanding. The possibility of empirical application is therefore crucial. But since I think of the present enterprise as aiming not at experiment but at an idealized description of the patterns of behavior that make it possible for people to fathom one another's thoughts and meanings, I shall stop speaking of experimenters and their subjects and speak instead of agents, actors, people, and their human interpreters.

It is common to make a strong distinction between Bayesian theories as normative and as decriptive. As a picture of how the perfectly rational agent should act, such theories are sometimes allowed to be essentially correct, though perhaps oversimplified (through failure to consider the cost of information or computation, for example). As descriptive theories, however, they are considered to be at best limited in application and absurdly idealized. Many experiments seem to bear out this view.

I doubt that there is an interesting way of understanding the purported distinction. Until a detailed empirical interpretation is given to a theory, it is impossible to tell whether or not an agent satisfies its norms; indeed, without a clear interpretation it is hard to say what content the theory, whether normative or descriptive, has. Nor does it make sense to say that in a normative application one is not interested in the truth of the theory, since the question whether someone's acts, or preferences and beliefs, are in accord with the theory is just the question whether or not the theory is true of him. On the other hand (and more important) is the fact that the concepts of thought, choice, and intentional action are so laden with normative considerations that theories that employ these concepts cannot be tested for empirical validity without the use of normative standards. Decision theory deals with intentional choices, and supplies a rationale for such choices. But the general idea that intentional actions can be rationalized is no invention of decision theorists; it is part of the everyday concept of intentional action. For an intentional action is an action done with some intention, and this requires that there be a value the agent hopes to realize, and a belief that by acting as he does he has some chance of realizing the value. So, for example, if a composer adds a contrabassoon to the orchestration of his new symphony with the intention of strengthening and giving color to the bass, he must have set some positive value on strengthening and giving color to the bass, and must believe that by adding a contrabassoon to the orchestra he has a chance of achieving his aesthetic end. Thus the description of the intention with which he acted explains why he acted as he did, and at the same time rationalizes the action, that is, reveals a framework within which the action was reasonable from the point of view of the agent. Analogously, to give the propositional content of a belief or a desire is to describe that attitude as one which under appropriate circumstances is apt to cause, and so rationalize, a range of intentional actions.

The fact that a theory of decision contains a normative element cannot, then, be thought to rule out its use as a descriptive theory, since simply to denominate an action or choice as intentional is already to declare that it satisfies at least minimal norms of rationality. Familiar theories of decision do, of course, idealize the normative element by giving it holistic scope; but even in positing a consistent pattern in the totality of preferences and choices of an agent, decision theories depart from common sense only in degree and precision. Thus (to mention the simplest sort of case) we hesitate to attribute outright violations of transitivity of preference to an agent, and search instead for an explanation that rationalizes the apparent violation, perhaps by redescribing the choices or the alternatives from the agent's point of view.

It is clearly an error to suppose that the basic normative element in intentional choice is a dispensable ingredient supplied by the wit and reason of the agent, for as a matter of definition what is intentional meets minimal standards of rationality. To put matters this way shifts part of the burden of introducing rudimentary rationality into the description of an action from the agent to the interpreter. For unless an interpreter can discover a rational pattern in the behavior of an agent, he cannot describe or explain that behavior as intentional action.

The norms that must be employed whenever an action,

choice, preference, or intention is described or explained are thus those of a would-be interpreter as well as those of the person he wants to understand. To find someone else intelligible in the way that intentional actions are intelligible is to recognize one's own ground level norms realized in the behavior of the other.

The unavoidable mingling of the normative and descriptive in any theory of choice applies equally to the interpretation of speech. The possibility of understanding speech depends upon the interpreter's presumption that the pattern of attitudes a speaker has to his sentences (whether or not uttered) is largely, and in the most basic matters, consistent and correct. Thus if there is some sentential operator in the speaker's language that when applied to a sentence always converts assent to dissent and vice versa, the interpreter's best guess is that the operator should be taken to be negation. Is this 'principle' of interpretation descriptive or normative? It is normative in this respect: it imposes a small part of the interpreter's logic on the speaker, for it interprets him as inferring that a sentence is to be held to be false if it is the negation of a sentence held to be true. But it is descriptive in that no alternative strategy is available for deciding what the speaker means by that connective. (Of course these remarks directly concern only the speaker's private attitudes of assent and dissent to his sentences, and are related to his <u>utterances</u> in very complicated ways. Nevertheless a speaker who wishes to be understood must somehow convey his real attitudes to his most basic sentences, if only by allowing his hearers to believe he belongs to a certain linguistic community).

To interpret an utterance of a speaker is to assign truth conditions to the sentence uttered; roughly speaking, one assigns one of one's own propositions to his utterance. Since propositions are identified by their logical properties, inductive and deductive, their role in determining evaluations and actions, and their relations to the world, the interpreter can do no better in general than to interpret an utterance of a speaker by keying it to a proposition of his own such that if he (the interpreter) believed the proposition true it would play approximately the same role in his reasoning, actions, and feelings as it would play in the economy of the speaker were <u>he</u> to believe his utterance true. Naturally, many allowances for differences may become justified as understanding increases. But the principle remains: differences, like agreements, can only be understood against a very large shared background of beliefs and values. If this fact escapes our notice, it is because agreement is largely uninteresting in itself, and is more apt to focus on the obvious or the trite than on the recherchè.

So far, interpretation has been argued to demand sameness, or approximate sameness, in the patterns of belief of interpreter and interpreted and, with appropriate relaxation of standards, the same has been said of evidential relations, inductive methods, and other norms of consistency. All this entails, of course, that successful interpretation will result in agreement on the truth of many propositions. Thus it would make no sense to interpret some range of sentences as being about grouse while at the same time interpreting a large number of other accepted sentences as saying such things as that grouse have four legs, have fur, burrow in the ground, and are light green.

Obvious truth is involved more directly. For the best evidence that a sentence should be understood as true if and only if a grouse is present is that the speaker is caused to hold the sentence true by the clear proximity of grouse and caused to hold the sentence false by the apparent absence of grouse. Degrees of belief tuned to the appearances and other evidence would clearly make for a more subtle and convincing case.

The ineluctable normative element in interpretation has, then, two forms. First, there are the norms of pattern: the norms of deduction, induction, reasoning about how to act, and even how to feel given other attitudes and beliefs. These are the norms of consistency and coherence. Second there are the norms of correspondence, which are concerned with the truth or correctness of particular beliefs and values. This second kind of norm counsels the interpreter to interpret agents he would understand as having, in important respects, beliefs that are mostly true and needs and values the interpreter shares or can imagine himself sharing if he had the history of the agent and were in comparable circumstances.

It should be emphasized that these maxims of interpretation are not mere pieces of useful or friendly advice: rather they are intended to externalize and formulate (no doubt very crudely) essential aspects of the common concepts of thought, affect, reasoning and action. What could not be arrived at by these methods is not thought, talk, or action.

The problem of interpreting language at the same time as discovering the subjective probabilities and cardinal values of an agent is like Ramsey's original problem of sorting out the last two of these parameters given ordinal choices or preferences; it is like it, but harder, since it involves nothing less than identifying the propositional objects of the attitudes. The problem is similar also in that the theoretical concepts -- belief, preference, and now meaning -- are interdependent in the sense that none of them can be determined without determining the others. Ramsey realized that since choice is a function of both degree of belief and relative strength of desire, there could be no way to quantify one element first as a step to quantifing the other. He therefore outlined a series of steps an experimenter could in theory follow which would allow the two factors to be disentangled. To follow these steps is to appreciate the fact that the constraints imposed by the theory on the pattern of ordinal preferences suffices to yield appropriate measures of utility and subjective probability. Thus by outlining steps that lead to the separate measurements Ramsey in effect provided an informal proof of the adequacy of his axioms to their purpose.

I shall follow, though more sketchily (even) than Ramsey, the same method. The theory, as applied to a particular agent at a time, provides an interpretation of all his utterances, actual and potential; it does this in the form of a Tarski-style theory of truth which gives the conditions of truth for utterances of sentences.[4] The theory imposes the usual conditions on subjective probabilities, applied to the sentences of the agent, and also standard conditions on preferences, again applied to sentences. Thus the theory deals uniformly with the sentences of an agent, and aims to give the relative strength of the agent's desires that sentences be true, the degree of his belief that sentences are true, and the meaning of the sentences.

The basic empirical primitive is the agent's (weak) preference that one sentence rather than another be true; as remarked above, one may therefore think of the data as

being of the same sort as the data usually gathered in an
experimental test of any Bayesian theory of decision, with
the proviso that the interpretation of the sentences among
which the agent chooses is not assumed known in advance to
the experimenter or interpreter.

The   uniformity   and   simplicity of   the empirical
ontology of the system,   comprising as it does just
utterances and sentences, is essential to achieving the
aim of combining decision theory with interpretation. The
cost, however, is that gambles or wagers, which usually
provide the glue that relates beliefs and preferences,
are not available at the ground level. Here, as in much of
the rest of this paper, I   follow Jeffrey, whose theory
deals with propositions only, and therefore also cannot
directly incorporate gambles. Here then is the analogue of
Jeffrey's desirability axiom, applied to sentences rather
than propositions:

(D)   If prob(s and t)=0 and prob(s or t)$\neq$0, then

$$\text{des}(s \text{ or } t) = \frac{\text{prob}(s)\text{des}(s)+\text{prob}(t)\text{des}(t)}{\text{prob}(s)+\text{prob}(t)}$$

(I write 'prob(s)' for the subjective probability of
s and 'des(s)' for the desirability or utility of s.)
By relating preference and belief, this axiom does the
sort of work usually done by gambles; the relation is,
however, different. Events are identified with sentences
which on interpretation turn out to say the event occurs
('The next card is a club'). Actions and outcomes are also
represented by sentences ('The agent bets one dollar',
'The   agent wins five dollars'). Gambles do not enter
directly, but the element of risk is present, since to
choose that a sentence be true is usually to take a risk
on what will concomitantly be true. (It is assumed that
one cannot choose a logically false sentence). So we see
that if the agent chooses to make true rather than false
the sentence 'The agent bets one dollar', he is taking a
chance on the outcome, which may, for example, be thought
to depend on whether or not the next card is a club. Then
the desirability of the (truth of) the sentence 'The agent
bets one dollar' will be the desirability of the various
circumstances in which this sentence is true weighted in
the usual way by the probabilities of those circumstances.

Suppose the agent believes he will win five dollars if the next card is a club and will win nothing if the next card is not a club; he will then have a special interest in whether the truth of 'The agent bets one dollar' will be paired with the truth or falsity of 'The next card is a club'. Let these two sentences be abbreviated by 's' and 't', where not $\underline{s}$ is $\bar{\underline{s}}$ and not $\underline{t}$ is $\bar{\underline{t}}$. Then

$$des(\underline{s}) = \frac{prob(\underline{s} \text{ and } \underline{t})des(\underline{s} \text{ and } \underline{t})+prob(\underline{s} \text{ and } \bar{\underline{t}})des(\underline{s} \text{ and } \bar{\underline{t}})}{prob(\underline{s})}$$

This is, of course, something like Ramsey's gambles. It differs, however, in that there is no assumption that the 'states of nature' that may be thought to determine outcomes are, in Ramsey's term, 'morally neutral', that is, have no effect on the desirabilities of the outcomes. Nor is there the assumption that the probabilities of outcomes depend on nothing but the probabilities of the 'states of nature' (the agent may believe he has a chance of winning five dollars even if the next card is not a club, and a chance he will not win five dollars even if the next card is a club).

The 'desirability axiom' (D) can be used to show how probabilities depend on desirabilities in Jeffrey's system. Take the special case where $\underline{t} = \bar{\underline{s}}$. Then we have

$$des(\underline{s} \text{ or } \bar{\underline{s}})=des(\underline{s})prob(\underline{s})+des(\bar{\underline{s}})prob(\bar{\underline{s}}) \qquad (1)$$

Since $prob(\underline{s})+prob(\bar{\underline{s}})=1$, we can solve for $prob(\underline{s})$:

$$prob(\underline{s}) = \frac{des(\underline{s} \text{ or } \bar{\underline{s}})-des(\bar{\underline{s}})}{des(\underline{s})-des(\bar{\underline{s}})} \qquad (2)$$

In words, the probability of a proposition depends on the desirability of that proposition and of its negation. Further, it is easy to see that if a sentence $\underline{s}$ is more desirable than an arbitrary logical truth (such as 't or $\bar{\underline{t}}$'), then its negation ($\bar{\underline{s}}$) cannot also be more desirable than a logical truth. Suppose that (with Jeffrey) we assign the number 0 to any logical truth. (This is intuitively reasonable since an agent is indifferent to the truth of a tautology.) Then (2) can be rewritten:

$$\text{prob } (\underline{s})= \cfrac{1}{1 - \cfrac{\text{des}(\underline{s})}{\text{des}(\bar{\underline{s}})}} \tag{3}$$

It is at once apparent that des($\underline{s}$) and des($\bar{\underline{s}}$) cannot both be more, or both be less, desirable than 0, the desirability of any logical truth, if prob($\underline{s}$) is to fall in the interval from 1 to 0. If (once again following Jeffrey) we call an option good if it is preferred to a logical truth and bad if a logical truth is preferred to it, then (3) shows that it is impossible for an option (sentence) and its negation both to be good or both to be bad.

Taking 'not($\underline{s}$ and $\bar{\underline{s}}$)' as our sample logical truth, we can state this principle purely in terms of preferences:

If des($\underline{s}$)>des[not($\underline{s}$ and $\bar{\underline{s}}$)] then   (4)
    des[not($\underline{s}$ and $\bar{\underline{s}}$)]≥des($\bar{\underline{s}}$), and
if des[not($\underline{s}$ and $\bar{\underline{s}}$)]>des($\underline{s}$) then
    des($\bar{\underline{s}}$)≥des(not[$\underline{s}$ and $\bar{\underline{s}}$])

Since both negation and conjunction can be defined in terms of the Sheffer stroke '|' ('not both'), (4) can be rewritten:

If des($\underline{s}$)>des{($\underline{t}|\underline{u}$)|[($\underline{t}|\underline{u}$)|($\underline{t}|\underline{u}$)]} then   (5)
    des{($\underline{t}|\underline{u}$)|[($\underline{t}|\underline{u}$)|($\underline{t}|\underline{u}$)]}≥des($\underline{s}|\underline{s}$), and
if des{($\underline{t}|\underline{u}$)|[($\underline{t}|\underline{u}$)|($\underline{t}|\underline{u}$)]}>des($\underline{s}$) then
    des($\underline{s}|\underline{s}$)≥des{($\underline{t}|\underline{u}$)|[($\underline{t}|\underline{u}$)|($\underline{t}|\underline{u}$)]}

The interest of (5) for present purposes is this. If we assume that '|' is some arbitrary truth-functional operator that forms sentences out of pairs of sentences, then the following holds: if (5) is true for all sentences $\underline{s}$, $\underline{t}$, and $\underline{u}$, and for some $\underline{s}$ and $\underline{t}$, des($\underline{s}|\underline{s}$)≠des($\underline{t}|\underline{t}$), then '|' must be the Sheffer stroke (it must have the logical properties of 'not both'); no other interpretation is possible.[5] Thus data involving only preferences among sentences the meaning of which are unknown to the interpreter has led (given the constraints of the theory) to the identification of one sentential connective. Since all logically equivalent sentences are equal in desirability, it is now possible to interpret all the other truth-functional sentential connectives, since all are definable in terms of the Sheffer stroke. For example, if it is found that for all sentences s

$$\text{des}(\underline{s}|\underline{s})=\text{des}(\sim\underline{s})$$

we can conclude that the tilde is the sign for negation.

It is now possible to measure the desirability and subjective probability of all sentences, for the application of formulas like (2) and (3) requires the identification of only the truth-functional sentential connectives. Thus it is clear from (3) that if two sentences are equal in desirability (and are preferred to a logical truth) and their negations are also equal in desirability, the sentences must have the same probability. By the same token, if two sentences are equal in desirability (and are preferred to a logical truth), but the negation of one is preferred to the negation of the other, then the probability of the first is less than that of the second. This, along with appropriate existence axioms, is enough to establish a probability scale. Then it is easy to determine the relative desirabilities of all sentences.[6]

In Jeffrey's theory neither desirabilities nor probabilities are measured on scales quite as unique as in Ramsey's (or any other standard) theory. But the differences do not matter to the prediction or explanation of choice behavior, nor do they matter to the interpretation of language by the method under discussion.

At this point the probabilities and desirabilities of all sentences have in theory been determined. But no complete sentence has yet been interpreted, though the truth-functional sentential connectives have been identified, and so sentences logically true or false by virtue of sentential logic can be recognized. It remains to sketch the methods that could lead to a complete interpretation of all sentences, that is, to the construction of a theory of truth for the agent's language. The approach is one I have discussed in a number of articles, and is inspired by the work of W. V. Quine on radical translation.[7]

For an agent to have a certain subjective probability

for a sentence is for him to hold that sentence true, or
false, or for him to have some determinate degree of
belief in its truth. Since the agent attaches a meaning to
the sentence, his degree of confidence in the truth of the
sentence is also his degree of faith in the truth the
sentence expresses. Beliefs, as manifested in attitudes to
sentences, are the clue to meaning. We have already
observed that logically equivalent sentences are equal in
desirability. This in itself is no direct help in getting
at the meaning of logically equivalent sentences, though
it does help, as we have seen, in interpreting the
truth-functional sentential connectives. Patterns of
sentences held true or false will also lead to the
detection of the existential and universal quantifiers,
and thus to the structures that account for entailments
and logical truths in quantificational logic. To discover
the structures that account for entailments and logical
truths in quantificational logic is to uncover logical
form in general, that is, to learn how sentences are made
up of predicates, singular terms, quantifiers, variables,
and the like. The symbol for identity should be easy to
locate, given its role in promoting entailments based on
substitution; someone who holds sentences of the forms
'a=b' and 'Fa' true will also hold a sentence of the
form 'Fb' true, whatever the predicate 'F' means (unless it is intentional -- one of the problems I am here
overlooking).

Further steps in interpretation will require some
elaboration of the empirical basis of the theory; it will
be necessary to attend, not just to the agent's
preferences among sentences, but also to the events and
objects in the world that cause his preferences (and hence
also his beliefs). Thus it will be the observable
circumstances under which an agent is caused to assign high
or low probabilities to sentences like 'It is raining',
'That's a horse', or 'My foot is sore' that yield the most
obvious evidence for the interpretation of these sentences
and the predicates in them. The interpreter, on noticing
that the agent regularly assigns a high or low degree of
belief to the sentence 'The coffee is ready' when the
coffee is, or isn't, ready will (however tentatively
pending related results) try for a theory of truth that
says than an utterance by the agent of the sentence 'The
coffee is ready' is true if and only if the coffee is
ready.

   Pretty obviously, the interpretation of common predicates depends heavily on indexical elements in speech, such as demonstratives and tense, since it is these that allow predicates and singular terms to be connected to objects and events in the world. To accomodate indexical elements, theories of truth of the sort first proposed by Tarski must be modified; the nature of these modifications has been discussed elsewhere.[8]

   The interpretation of predicates less directly keyed to untutored observation will depend in large measure on conditional probabilities, which show what the agent counts as evidence for the application of his more theoretical predicates. Such evidence may also be expected to help account for errors in the application of observational predicates under less than ideal conditions.

   The approach to decision theory sketched here has many applications. It is easy to imagine how in general to add a dynamic dimension to the theory: the theory can be made to predict changes in the distribution of desirabilities and probabilities given new information, and hence also in the actions the agent will perform under various circumstances. Desirabilities will enter more directly than I have indicated in the interpretation of evaluative words and sentences. The development of these further applications I leave to other occasions.

Department of Philosophy
University of California
Berkeley

NOTES

1. See Ramsey (1931).
2. See Jeffrey (1983).
3. See Essay 12 in Davidson (1980).
4. See Tarski (1956). The application of Tarski's general approach to natural language is discussed in Davidson (1984).
5. I am indebted to Stig Kanger for showing me why an earlier attempt at a solution to this problem would not work. He also added some needed refinements to the present proposal.

6. For details see Jeffrey (1983).
7. See Chapter 2 of Quine (1960) and Essays 9--12 in Davidson (1984).
8. See Essays 2 and 4 in Davidson (1984).

REFERENCES

Davidson, D.: 1980, <u>Essays on Actions and Events</u>, Clarendon Press, Oxford.

Davidson, D.: 1984, <u>Inquiries into Truth and Interpretation</u>, Clarendon Press, Oxford.

Jeffrey, R.: 1983, <u>The Logic of Decision</u>, 2nd edition, University of Chicago Press, Chicago and London.

Quine, W. V.: 1960, <u>Word and Object</u>, The Technology Press and John Wiley, New York.

Ramsey, F.P.: 1931, "Truth and Probability" in <u>Foundations</u> of Mathematics, Routledge and Kegan Paul, London.

Tarski, A.: 1956, "The Concept of Truth in Formalized Languages" in <u>Logic, Semantics, Metamathematics</u>, Oxford University Press, Oxford.

Max Black

SOME QUESTIONS ABOUT BAYESIAN DECISION THEORY

Bayesian Decision Theory (BDT) is usually presented
nowadays in the form of (1) an uninterpreted axiom system
(plausibly regarded as a mathematical 'model', representation or blueprint) containing undefined constants (parameters), together with (2) a less formal 'interpretation' of
those parameters, expressed for the most part in non-techni-
cal layman's language. If the interpreted axioms are then
regarded as empirical assertions, the resulting BDT is a
fragment of a scientific theory of free human action.

I assume familiarity with such careful formulations of a
BDT as are to be found, for instance, in John C. Harsanyi's
writings (for example, see Harsanyi, 1977). In what follows
I shall mainly consider choices made 'with certainty', by a
single person, say 'Eligo'.

Although current BDTs, resulting from nearly four
decades of intensive study by mathematicians, economists,
psychologists and philosophers, have been sufficiently
impressive to be acclaimed as "among the jewels of intellectual accomplishment in our time" (see Simon, 1978) I believe
that the fundamental concepts employed in applying contemporary BDTs deserve the further critical scrutiny that the
following, necessarily brief, reflections may perhaps promote.

Descriptive or Normative?

The pioneers of BDT have characteristically regarded themselves as scientists, seeking mathematical models to represent in idealised and simplified fashion the actual behaviour of rational decision-makers. But since choices and
decisions (I shall not distinguish between them in this
paper) are prime instances of free actions by persons who
might have chosen otherwise had they wished, a 'science' of
human choice will necessarily have normative implications.
Thus the familiar admonition of Bayesian theorists to 'maximise expected utility' is part of what might be called a

57

L. Daboni et al. (eds.), Recent Developments in the Foundations of Utility and Risk Theory, 57–66.
© *1986 by D. Reidel Publishing Company.*

Bayesian code (BC) addressed to those who wish to behave
rationally when making decisions.

My chief question will be how far the Bayesian code
deserves to be respected. More specifically: I wish to
consider whether anybody who fails to conform to the BC in
some respects deserves to be reprimanded for 'inconsistency'
or 'defective rationality'.

A Simple Illustration

Let us suppose that Eligo, having won a prize in a booksel-
ler's promotion lottery, arrives in the store to choose one
of a given set of books. I imagine him to compare them two
at a time ('pairwise'), rejecting each time the one he less
prefers. For simplicity I assume for the present: (1) that
no 'ties' arise, i.e., cases in which Eligo has no relative
preference for either of the two books compared ('indifference'); and (2) no cases of indecision in which Eligo is
unable to make a pairwise rejection. The BC admonishes him
to take as his prize the ultimate survivor in this selective
procedure.

In this kind of case, BDT postulates that the binary
relation of 'preference' (call it 'P') shall be transitive
[i.e., that if Eligo accepts xPy ('I prefer x to y') and yPz
he is always committed to accepting xPz, not zPx). If
Eligo's behaviour violates this condition, so-called
'cycles' will result, such as xPy and yPz and zPx (a 'triadic cycle'). The emergence of such cycles (or those containing more than three terms -- having larger diameters as
it were) is held to convict Eligo of 'inconsistency' or
'irrationality'.

Qualms About the Transitivity of Preference

Most advocates of BDT consider the requirement of transitivity (and hence the absence of preference cycles) as self-
evident. But is it really so? If 'I prefer B1 to B2' were
to mean something like 'I would be happier to get B1 rather
than B2', transitivity of the preference relation might well
seem as obvious as the transitivity of, say, the relation of
'being more expensive than'. But contemporary Bayesians,
committed to a behaviouristic methodology, distrust any 'subjective' expressions of present inclination or anticipated

satisfaction. Accordingly, they interpret 'I prefer B1 to B2' to mean: 'If I were now offered a choice between B1 and B2 alone, I would take the first'. Let us call this preferential pairwise choice (PPC).

It is not obvious that Eligo's PPCs, thus construed, will in fact be transitive. For he is being viewed as making counterfactual predictions whose behaviouristic verifications would be actual choices between just two books, in situations differing from his actual situation. And even if those many counterfactual predictions were indeed all true, there is nothing in the nature of preference, thus defined, that guarantees transitivity and the consequent emergence of a unique linear ordering.

Eligo might not notice the cycles possibly lurking in the pairwise choice procedure I have postulated. If he thinks that he would reject b in favour of a (aPb) and a in favour c (cPa), he will be discarding both b and a and so will have no occasion to compare b and c. Yet if such a comparison would have yielded bPc, Eligo would have been faced with a triadic cycle. (Such unnoticed cycles might well arise in long chains of pairwise choices.)

In general, it is easily seen that the identity of a survivor of a cyclic set of pairwise choices will depend upon the order in which the pairwise comparisons are made. Thus Eligo might, in our example, be committed to cPa by one calculation and to aPc by another. To safeguard himself against this kind of possibility, Eligo ought theoretically to repeat the entire chain of hypothetical pairwise choices, examining all the pairs of available books in all possible sequences. Even if that yielded no cycles, there would always remain the disturbing possibility that the linear order he obtains might only be part of a large cycle including books not actually at his disposal.

Thus unless the preference relation is transitive a priori, a very conscientious user of BDT in the envisaged situation would have to discover whether his PPCs did in fact yield a unique linear ordering. This would require him to consider PPCs not only between the books actually available to him, but also between them and other books that might have been offered. For one added book might produce a 'cycle' that included all the books actually available and thus render the Bayesian injunction to maximise utility impossible to apply. This fantastically elaborate procedure must be viewed as a reductio ad absurdum of any methodology that requires it.

Questioning the Transitivity Requirement

Let us take another look at the alleged transitivity of
preference. When 'completeness' (xPy or yPx for all x and
y) holds for the relation of strong preference between three
alternatives, a, b and c, it can seem self-evident that aPb
and bPc together necessarily imply aPc.

For if not, and completeness holds for the pair a and c,
we could derive cPa, which, taken with bPc would yield bPa,
conflicting with the assumption that aPb. Still more obvious
at first sight seems to be the inconsistency of supposing
that Eligo might be led to assert aPa (as following from aPb
and bPa).

There is no a priori reason, however, why a given binary
relation should in general fail to produce cyclicity. An
instructive example can be drawn from the so-called pecking
behaviour of domestic or wild birds. We are told that when
a number of hens are kept in the same enclosure they arrange
themselves in a unique linear order, at whose head is an
unpecked pecker, while at its foot there is a wretched bird
that is, as it were, a pecked unpecker, pecked by all the
others. But if corresponding observations are made on a
group of three birds belonging to different species, say a
hen, a pheasant and a duck, circularity may result, with hen
pecking pheasant, pheasant pecking duck and duck pecking
hen (for further examples, see Gardner, 1974).

The following is a more directly relevant example. Suppose we have three football teams, say Leeds, Manchester and
Newcastle, in which each can be expected to beat the next,
on account of, say, decisively superior attack, defense or
stamina, respectively. Their strengths might then be represented in the following diagram (with higher marks indicating higher strengths):

	attack	defense	stamina
L(eeds)	3	2	1
M(anchester)	1	3	2
N(ewcastle)	2	1	3

I will now assume that the two-point superiority of L over M
in attack is sufficiently decisive to outweigh the lesser

inferiority of the former to the latter in the categories of
defense and stamina; and similarly for the other two cases.

Given such a possible situation, it would not be absurd
or self-contradictory to claim that L is overall a stronger
team than M; likewise, M over N and N over L. (The paradox-
ical flavour of such assertions results from the tug of the
comparative form of the expression 'stronger team than'.)

If one were now offered bets on the outcomes of all the
three possible matches between the teams in question, it
would be quite rational to bet on L against M, M against N,
and N against L. For no 'Dutch Book' could be made against
such a triplet of bets.

It might be objected that the imagined situation arises
only because football teams play against one opponent at a
time, while choices in general may and should be considered
in groups of three or some higher number. What would a
rational bettor do, it may be asked, if he had similarly
cyclical information about three racehorses in pairwise contests and was then considering a race in which all three
were running together for the first time? Well, of course,
one horse would win, if dead heats were excluded. But the
rational response would surely be to have, on the evidence
available, as yet no definitive preference. (Here again the
breakdown of transitivity is of decisive importance for
rational choice.)

It is instructive in this connection to examine Amartya
Sen's interesting attempt to show that transitivity is already guaranteed by the assumed asymmetry of the preference
relation (the inadmissibility of xPy and yPx).

In his inaugural address (1973) Amartya Sen assumes the
correctness of the so-called 'Weak Axiom of Revealed Preference', to the effect that if somebody "chooses x when y is
available, then he will not choose y in a situation in which
x is obtainable." Sen's derivation of the transitivity
axiom (here slightly modified to convert his argument into a
direct rather than an indirect one) runs as follows: Suppose that the chooser prefers x to y when offered a choice
between just these two options by themselves. Now let him
be offered a choice between the same x and y, in the presence of a new option, z, to which y is preferred. So we
have xPy and yPz and wish to show that xPz must hold. As
between x and y, the chooser will prefer x, by our first
assumption, so he will not choose y; and as between y and z
he prefers y, by our second assumption, so he will not
choose z; hence he will choose neither y nor z, but rather

x. Thus, in the presence of z, he chooses x over z, so his
behaviour will conform to xPz, Q.E.D.

   Two assumptions are at work in this argument: the first
being that possible incomparability between the extreme
terms, x and z, needs no attention; the second that the addition of further options to the original pair x and y will
not upset the previously established preference between them
(sometimes called the principle of 'independence of irrelevant alternatives'). I hope to have said enough previously
to have made the first assumption seem doubtful. And as for
the second assumption, I refer the reader back to my discussion of the case of the three racehorses which beat one another in dual contests, while the outcome of a race between
all three is indeterminate, to show that this assumption,
too, however plausible it may seem at first sight, need not
be regarded as having universal validity. For the insertion
of new options may well induce a shift of relevant criteria
of preference, as previously explained. Hence, Sen's argument for the derivability of transitivity, though of interest to those theorists who will not seriously entertain incomparability (failure of completeness), cannot be accepted
in the present context.

Questioning Preferential Asymmetry

BDT axioms claim that the preference judgment xPy is incompatible with yPx, unless some change of preference occurs.
This, apparently the least vulnerable of the Bayesian axioms,
is open to some objections similar to those I have already
raised. For it may well occur in real life that somebody
prefers x to y for one good reason and yet also prefers y to
x for another good reason. I may at a given moment genu-
inely prefer to travel to London by car because that would
take less time, but also prefer to go by train because that
would be safer. So we have have here a case, once more, of
'incomparability' or indeterminacy.

   To be sure, if we understand by preference only what is
implied by actually choosing, then xPy will necessarily
exclude yPx: I cannot at the same time go to London by car
and also go by train. But if we were to take 'preference'
in this implausibly behaviouristic fashion, we should have
to conclude in quite realistic cases, such as that of the
choice between car and train, that we could not know hat
our preferences were until we had acted. We should be like

the legendary person who replied to the admonition to 'think
before you speak' by saying 'How do I know what I think
until I hear what I say'? A rigidly behaviouristic approach
to decision theory would play havoc with the use of the
Bayesian system as a normative guide to decisions not yet
implemented.

Ambiguities of 'Inconsistency'

When proponents of BDT claim that violations of the axioms
in the actual behaviour of a would-be rational decision-
maker generate 'inconsistency', they usually mean logical
contradiction. (Hence the tendency to think of a BDT as
articulating a 'logic' of decision.) Whether one agrees
will depend upon the sense attached to the slippery term
'prefers'. In ordinary life, an assertion of the form xPy
is naturally construed as roughly equivalent to something
like 'I am now inclined to choose x rather than y', which is
not yet a logical contradictory of 'I am now inclined also
to choose y rather than x'. And neither assertion is logically incompatible with 'But I fancy I shall in the end do
something quite different'! Similar remarks apply to such
lurking implications as 'I think that x might well be more
worthwhile' (or desirable, sensible, or commendable, etc.).
Any committed behaviourist who wants to reject such statements as unverifiable assertions of intent might well be
asked to consider whether his own preferred interpretation
of xPy as a prediction (as I assumed earlier on for the sake
of argument) must not itself be viewed as an unverifiable
assertion of the speaker or thinker's attitude. For there
is, as it were, a logical gap between any expression of
inclination, desire, choice-worthiness, and the like, and
the final decision.

There is a tendency for committed Bayesians to view any
departure from what I have called the 'Bayesian Code', i.e.,
conformity with the interpreted mathematical model in order
to 'maximise expected utility', as a manifestation of 'inconsistency' or, even more damagingly, as a case of defective rationality. Let us consider the kind of deviation
that may arise.

Imagine that Eligo, in the book-prize example, to have
arranged the set of books available in a single order of
preference, construed as 'present inclination' (but without
having used the preposterously 'conscientious' examination

of all possible pairs to eliminate any lurking cycles). Let
B1 be at the head of the list. When the moment comes to
announce his decision, however, he actually chooses B2. Has
he behaved irrationally? Well, that depends upon his motivation. He might simply have found, at the moment of action, that he then, after all, wanted B2 rather than B1. Or
he might suddenly have remembered that he already possessed
a copy of B1! Or he might suddenly have recalled previous
occasions in which conscientious behaviour like a good Bayesian resulted in choices that he later regretted, his attitude being expressible as 'It pays to behave like a good
Bayesian -- and then to trust last-minute impulse'! Or he
might wish to show his independence as a free agent, by
frustrating the prediction made by an officious friend who
had been privy to his calculations. (Such reasons would be
all the more attractive if Eligo thought that the calculated
advantage of B1 over B2 was slight.) In short, one can
imagine any number of sensible reasons for what might at
first look like a perverse choice. Would Eligo, in any of
these imagined cases, be acting 'irrationally'? I think
not.

An accusation of irrationality would be most plausible
if Eligo were to explain his apparently perverse action by
saying 'I thought B1 was the right book to choose -- and
that's why I didn't choose it'! But even that posture might
be defensible. The great and unjustly neglected Nineteenth
Century writer, Samuel Butler, although a principled athe-
ist, made a point of going to church occasionally, in order
not to behave with rigid uniformity. The implied metaprin-
ciple strikes me as eminently laudable and 'rational'.
(Whether the reader will agree must depend upon his or her
interpretation of that 'essentially contested' concept of
rationality.)

Coping With Cyclicity

A confirmed Bayesian, unshaken, as I would suspect, by the
difficulties raised above, might well challenge me to offer
some promising alternative. I would agree that it is too
easy merely to claim that it is more rational (or reasonable, or intelligent) to take the emergence of cyclicity
seriously than to brush it aside as evidence of the decision-maker's irrationality. How then, should one deal with
such cases of indeterminacy?

Consider the following situation: In search of a new secretary, I have reduced the field of applicants to three persons, whose scores on the relevant criteria (say, accuracy, reliability and skill in human relations) show the same kind of pattern as in the case of the football teams considered above. There are a number of strategies I might pursue to resolve the indeterminacy. For instance: (1) To invoke some extra criterion (perhaps relative need for employment?) which might yield a decisive choice; or (2) toss a coin; or (3) toss a coin only to eliminate one of the candidates, thus leaving me with a modicum of choice; or (4) invite the applicants themselves to make suggestions; or (5) show the dossiers to a respected colleague for an extra opinion; or (6) 'yield to impulse', hoping that my unconscious motivation may serve better than further cogitation; and so forth. Of course, the problem posed may really be insoluble, but the 'cunning of reason' should not be underestimated.

Concluding Remarks

I hope I have said enough to have made a good case for further reconsideration of the alleged usefulness of current versions of the 'Bayesian Code'. Had space and time permitted, I could have strengthened this contention by considering the more complex cases of choice under risk or uncertainty. I would like to have discussed in detail the sorely neglected point, familiar to philosophers but mostly ignored by decision theorists, that the options available in serious decision-making are necessarily expressed in 'intensional' ('with an s') descriptions, and the complexities arising from unconscious or deliberate adoption of favoured aspects of the available options. I hope to discuss these and related matters elsewhere, before long.

REFERENCES

Harsanyi, J.C.: 1977, Rational Behavior and Bargaining Equilibrium in Games and Social Situations, Cambridge University Press, Cambridge, especially chapter 3.

Simon, H.A.: 1978, Reason in Human Affairs, Stanford University Press, Stanford, page 3.

Gardner, M.: 1974, <u>Scientific American</u>, vol. 231, no. 4
    (October), pp. 120-125.

Sen, A.: 1973, 'Behaviour and the Concept of Preference',
    <u>Economica</u>, 40: 241-259.

Robert Sugden

REGRET, RECRIMINATION AND RATIONALITY[1]

In a number of recent papers Graham Loomes and I have
presented a theory of choice under uncertainty which can
explain some frequently observed violations of expected
utility theory (Loomes and Sugden, 1982, 1983a and 1983b;
see also Bell, 1982). Our regret theory starts from the
following idea. Suppose someone has to choose between
two actions, A_1 and A_2, in conditions of uncertainty.
He or she does not know which of a number of states of
the world will occur. In some states of the world A_1
will lead to a better consequence than A_2, while in others
the converse is true. Suppose the individual chooses
A_1 and then, when the uncertainty is resolved, it turns
out that the consequence that actually occurs is worse
than the one that would have occurred, had he or she chosen
A_2. In this event, we suggest, the individual will
experience regret - the painful sensation of recognising
that 'what is' compares unfavourably with 'what might
have been'. Conversely, if 'what is' compares favourably
with 'what might have been', the individual will experience
a pleasurable sensation, which we have called rejoicing.
We assume that when making a choice between two actions,
the individual can foresee the various experiences of
regret and rejoicing to which each action might lead,
and that this foresight can influence the choice that
the individual makes.

Many economists seem to be uneasy about incorporating
regret into a theory of choice - particularly into a theory
of rational choice (which is what Loomes and I have claimed
our theory to be). The source of this uneasiness seems
to be the following line of thought.[2] In the theory of
choice under uncertainty, states of the world are defined
so that which state occurs is completely outside the control
of the individual whose choices are being considered;
if one state occurs rather than another, then as far as
the individual is concerned, this is a matter of pure
chance. In regret theory it is this element of pure chance

L. Daboni et al. (eds.), Recent Developments in the Foundations of Utility and Risk Theory, 67–80.
© *1986 by D. Reidel Publishing Company.*

that determines whether any given action will lead to
regret. Suppose, for example, that I have the opportunity
to bet £10 on a game of roulette. If I am to make a
rational decision, it would seem, I must somehow weigh
the amount I stand to win and the probability of winning
it against the £10 I stand to lose. If I come to the
conclusion that, on balance, it is better to make the
bet, this is a judgement I have made in full knowledge
of the possibility that I may not win. Now suppose I
do bet, and don't win. According to regret theory, I
now experience regret over not having the £10 that I would
have had, had I not bet. Isn't this irrational? My not
having won is a matter of pure chance. If, before the
roulette wheel was spun, I was happy with my decision
to bet, what reason can I now have for regretting that
decision? Notice also that regret theory assumes not
merely that an individual will regret a decision <u>after</u>
it has turned out badly, but that he will foresee the
possibility of such regret <u>before</u> he chooses. In other
words, at the same time as I am choosing to bet on the
spin of the roulette wheel, I am convinced that I shall
regret this choice if I happen to lose. The purpose of
this paper is to enquire into whether such a state of
mind can be regarded as rational.

1. Regret and Self-Recrimination

Regret, as usually understood, seems to have two distinct
components. One component is the simple <u>wish</u> that you
had chosen differently. You now know something that you
didn't know when you made a particular choice (that is,
which state of the world has occurred) and with the benefit
of hindsight you know you would have done better if you
had not made the choice you did. This wish need not involve
any judgement that your original decision was wrong at
the time you made it. For example: you set out on a car
journey at 12.00 and have an accident because a tree has
fallen on the road. If you had set off at 11.50 you would
have avoided the accident. You may wish you had set off
at 11.50 even though you know that there was no way you
could have known that 11.50 was the better time to start.
    The other component of regret is <u>self-recrimination</u>
or <u>repentance</u> or <u>self-blame</u> - the state of mind you have
when you come to believe that a previous decision involved

an error of judgement, that it was wrong at the time you
made it. You may experience this state of mind even when
your decision has turned out well. For example: you choose
to drive home rather than take a taxi after you have had
too much to drink. You don't have an accident and you
are not stopped by the police. Next morning you may regret
the foolish risks you ran, even though you have come to
no harm and saved a taxi fare.

Up to now, Loomes and I have defended the rationality
of the behaviour explained by regret theory by appealing
to the first of these two notions of regret. Regret,
we have suggested, is <u>wishing</u> you had chosen differently.
Wishing that things had been different seems to us to
be a perfectly normal state of mind for human beings;
and for most of us, this state of mind is painful. The
concept of rationality, we have argued, should not be
applied to wishes, or to pleasures and pains. If you
are prone to experience the pain of regret - of wishing
you had chosen differently - this seems to be a fact about
your psychology that you must learn to live with. A theory
of rational choice ought to take such psychological propensities as given.

This argument, I believe, is an adequate defence
against the claim that regret theory is irrational, <u>provided
that the theory can be presented and developed without
any reference to selfrecrimination</u>. However, I am now
beginning to wonder whether it <u>is</u> possible to leave self-
recrimination out of the theory. In the next section
of the paper I shall explain the nature of these doubts.
Then I shall ask whether it is possible to incorporate
self-recrimination within the concept of regret without
undermining the claim that regret theory is a theory of
rational choice.

2.   Some Problems in Regret Theory

Suppose you have a friend who knows a great deal about
horses. From experience you have learned that her tips
are usually well founded, but you also know that the only
sure way to make money out of betting is to be a bookmaker.
Your friend tells you that a certain horse, running in
a particular race the next day, is much more likely to
win than its 50-1 odds suggest. You seriously consider
betting £10 on the horse, but in the end you decide not

to take the risk. Next day the horse wins. You would
probably then feel a great deal of regret about having
missed out on a £500 win.

But now consider a different version of the story.
Your friend knows nothing that suggests the horse is any
better than its odds indicate, and you do not give more
than a moment's thought to the possibility of betting
on it. Nonetheless, it wins the race. You might then
<u>wish</u> you had bet £10 on it; but, I suggest, any regret
you feel will be much less painful in this version of
the story than in the previous one.

Why are these two cases different? The relevant
consequences are the same in each case: you end up with
no change in your wealth, but you <u>could</u> have won £500.
The difference, I suggest, is that you had much more <u>reason</u>
to bet on the horse in the first case. In the second
case, you can tell yourself that, although it would have
been nice if you had bet on the horse, your original
decision was perfectly sensible at the time: how could
you have known that the horse was going to win? It is
much harder to avoid self-recrimination in the first case,
and to suppress the feeling that you ought to have had
more confidence in your friend's judgement.

The point of this example is that the pain you feel
when you compare 'what is' with 'what might have been'
depends on something more than the nature of the two consequences you are comparing. It seems to depend also
on the extent to which you can defend your original decision
to yourself, or, conversely, on the extent to which you
blame yourself for your original decision. This is a
dimension of regret that has no obvious place in the theory
that Loomes and I formulated.

Of course, there is no reason to expect the theory
to take account of every dimension of regret that anyone
could ever experience: all theories are simplifications
of reality. However, this particular simplification does
seem to lead to problems for the development of regret
theory. I shall now describe some of these problems.

CHOICE UNDER UNCERTAINTY

Since certainty is a limiting case of uncertainty, one
might expect a theory of choice under uncertainty to include
a theory of choice under certainty. Regret theory, as

Loomes and I first presented it, _does_ imply a theory of choice under certainty, but one that intuitively seems rather odd.

Suppose you have to choose between two actions, A_1 and A_2. A_1 offers the certainty of £10; A_2 offers £5 if state S_1 occurs and £15 if state S_2 occurs. The probabilities of S_1 and S_2 are p and 1-p. According to regret theory, you will experience rejoicing if you choose A_1 and then S_1 occurs. You will gain some utility in addition to the utility you would have derived if you had simply been given the £10. The psychological intuition here is that you derive some satisfaction from knowing that, as things have turned out, your original decision was the best you could have made.

But suppose that p = 1. In this case, the choice is between £10 for sure and £5 for sure. If you choose the £10, will you experience rejoicing when state S_1 occurs - as it must? Rejoicing seems psychologically out of place here. This is perhaps because, just as regret is linked with self-recrimination, rejoicing is linked with self-congratulation. If you have chosen £10 rather than £5, you have hardly performed a feat worthy of congratulation.

Fortunately, it makes no difference to the _predictions_ of regret theory whether rejoicing is experienced under certainty or not: whichever of the two actions has the higher basic utility will be chosen in either case. However, Loomes and I have claimed - and still wish to claim - that one of the strengths of regret theory lies in the psychological plausibility of its assumptions. It would be inconsistent for us now to take refuge behind the principles of Chicago methodology.

Furthermore, to accept that rejoicing is not experienced when choices are made under certainty is to open the way for more awkward questions about regret theory. Returning to the case of the choice between A_1 and A_2, if rejoicing is not experienced when p is equal to 1.0, is it experienced with full intensity as p _approaches_ 1.0? There seems little cause for selfcongratulation if you choose A_1 when p = 0.9999, and then S_1 occurs. Similarly, if choice under certainty does not lead to rejoicing, what about cases where a choice has to be made between a dominating action and a dominated one? In this case too, it seems quite obvious how you should choose, and there is little reason to feel proud about recognising this.

LIMITED GAMBLING

It is well known that many people are willing to gamble
on terms that are no better than actuarially fair. This
behaviour can be observed in controlled experiments.
For example, Kahneman and Tversky (1979, problem 14) found
that 72 per cent of their subjects preferred a 0.001 chance
of winning 5000 Israeli pounds to the certainty of
winning 5.

Regret theory can explain this by hypothesising that
regret is a non-linear function of the difference between
the 'basic' (or 'choiceless') utilities of 'what is' and
'what might have been'. Provided the non-linearity of
regret outweighs the effect of diminishing marginal (basic)
utility of wealth, an individual will prefer small-stake
large-prize gambles to actuarially equivalent certainties
(Loomes and Sugden, 1982 pp.814-5). Roughly speaking,
the logic behind this prediction is that by choosing the
gamble, the individual avoids the risk of experiencing
intense regret. (In Kahneman and Tversky's example, someone
who chooses the gamble can never regret more than the
loss of 5 Israeli pounds; someone who chooses the certainty
may come to regret having missed out on 4995.)

The problem with this prediction is that, although
most people seem to be inclined to take on occasional
small-stake largeprize gambles, they do so only
occasionally, and usually for stakes that are quite small
in relation to their total wealth. Why is most gambling
on such a limited scale? If someone is occasionally
prepared to bet on an outsider in a horse race, why does
he not bet on an outsider in every race, every day? Such
behaviour would seem to be implied by the logic of regret
theory. Similarly, if someone is willing to pay, say
£5 for a 0.1 chance of winning £50, why is he not willing
to pay £5,000 for a 0.1 chance of winning £50,000? This
second question might be answered by appealing to the
diminishing marginal (basic) utility of wealth, but this
would be a suspiciously ad hoc response. If the individual
takes on the small bet it is (according to regret theory)
because any non-linearity in the basic utility function
is outweighed by the non-linearity of regret. To hypo-
thesise that this position is reversed for the large bet
would seem a rather contrived way of accounting for the
evidence.

Regret theory explains small-stake large-prize gambling as a strategy for avoiding the relatively severe regret associated with not gambling: in terms of regret, one might almost say that the gambler is playing safe. Introspection, however, suggests that this kind of regret causes significant pain only if the individual has seriously considered gambling, and is still unconvinced of the wisdom of his decision not to gamble. (That was the point of the earlier example of the racing tip from the knowledgeable friend.) I can see the danger of circularity here, but I cannot help concluding that regret theory, as originally formulated, applies only to those cases in which the individual has already recognised 'gambling' and 'not gambling' as real options for him - options he can imagine wanting to choose.

NON-PAIRWISE CHOICES

Loomes and I have always acknowledged the difficulty of extending regret theory beyond cases of pairwise choice. In regret theory, in contrast with more conventional theories of choice, actions cannot be evaluated independently of one another: the value of choosing one action depends on the nature of the other action or actions that would consequently be rejected.

The logic of regret theory seems to imply that any rejected action can give rise to regret and rejoicing; there is no reason to suppose that when an individual compares 'what is' with 'what might have been' he considers only one 'might have been'. Returning to the example of the horse race, suppose you have received the tip that the 50-1 outsider is likely to do well. You seriously consider three options: not betting at all, betting £5, and betting £10. In the end you take a middle course and bet £5. The horse wins. Do you feel rejoicing about having won £250, or do you feel regret about having missed out on the extra £250 you would have won if you had bet the full £10? Which of these two emotions predominates may reveal something about your personality, but most people, I suspect, would experience some mixture of the two.

This suggests that the way to generalise regret theory is to evaluate each feasible action in relation to all the other feasible actions - that is, in relation to the

whole set of actions that must be rejected if the action
in question is chosen. This seems to require some way
of weighting the various experiences of regret and
rejoicing. Then the real problem of generalising regret
theory is that of producing a theory of these weights.

Any plausible theory of such weights must, I think,
take some account of the extent to which an action is
a serious candidate for choice or, to put it slightly
differently, of the extent to which the individual could
sensibly blame himself for not having chosen it. Take
the case of the horse race. Suppose it is possible for
you to bet any amount of money (say in multiples of £1)
from zero to the total value of your wealth on the 50-1
horse. If your wealth is £20,000 there are 20,0001 actions
in the feasible set. Whatever you choose, you will have
rejected 20,000 other actions, each of which in principle
could give rise to regret or rejoicing after the race
is over. Some of these actions - perhaps those involving
bets of between nothing and £10 - will have been considered
as serious possibilities before they were rejected. Others
were so out of the question as to be rejected instantly,
or perhaps were never even thought of at all. A theory
of weights that ignores this distinction is, I think,
most unlikely to give satisfactory predictions.

3. Difficult Choices

Throughout the previous section of this paper, I have
spoken of actions as being 'serious candidates' or 'serious
possibilities' or 'real options', and I have argued that
it is only these actions that will be significant as sources
of regret and rejoicing. If only one action is a serious
candidate - if the one that ought to be chosen is 'obvious'
- then regret and rejoicing may not arise at all. But
what do these concepts mean?

It is important to recognise that there is no simple
relationship between 'obviousness' and strength of preference. Consider a one-dimensional choice made under
certainty. Suppose you have to choose between a gift
of £100 and a gift of £50. Presumably it is quite obvious
which you should choose. Now suppose the choice is between
a gift of £100 and a gift of £99.99. In this case your
strength of preference will be much less, but which of
the two you should choose is no less obvious. Conversely,

suppose you have to choose between two very different jobs. Perhaps one will lead to a career as an academic and the other to a career as a civil servant. You may find this choice very difficult, the arguments on each side being finely balanced. But this is not the same thing as the indifference you feel when you choose between two apparently identical tins of baked beans in a super-market.

The idea that a person may come to a choice problem without any pre-existing preference to guide him - that he may not know what he prefers - is so alien to economic theory that it is hard for an economist to formulate it. Nevertheless, not knowing one's own preferences is a common enough state of mind, and one which everyone has surely experienced at some time. The distinction between knowing and not knowing one's preferences - between consulting one's preferences and having to decide what they are to be - is real enough, even if it has no place in the con-ventional theory of rational choice.[3] It is this distinction, I suggest, that lies behind the concept of difficulty - or, conversely, obviousness - of choice.

The evidence that regret theory has attempted to explain is the product of some well-known experimental work (e.g. Allais, 1953; Lichtenstein and Slovic, 1971; Kahneman and Tversky, 1979; Grether and Plott, 1979). These experiments have involved a very special kind of choice problem. I shall suggest that these problems are likely to be seen as difficult in the sense I have been discussing.

Subjects have been asked to choose between pairs of actions involving uncertain consequences. The con-sequences have been one-dimensional, and the dimension (usually money) has been one along which subjects can safely be presumed to prefer more to less. Probabilities have either been given to the subjects as part of the data of the choice problems, or have been readily calculable by applying common-sense rules (such as counting the numbers of different colours of ball in an urn).

In one sense, these features may seem to reduce the difficulty of the choice problem. Certainly this is how it would seem to an expected utility theorist: these are problems that are much simpler to formulate in expected-utility terms than many of the messy choices we meet in everyday life. Nevertheless, it is important to realise that these problems are highly <u>artificial</u>. Apart from

the minority of people who regularly gamble on games of
pure chance, the subjects of these experiments are unlikely
to have had much experience of this sort of choice.   The
choice problems they have tackled in everyday life will
probably have involved ill-defined feasible sets,[4] multidimensional consequences and unknown probabilities.   We
should not therefore expect people to come to these problems
with ready-made preferences of the kind that they have,
for example, between tea and coffee.

The point of most of these experiments has been to
identify predictable patterns of behaviour that violate
expected utility theory.   These violations typically take
the form of 'reversals' of preference between one pairwise
choice and another, when according to expected utility
theory the two choice problems are equivalent to one
another.   It is important to notice, however, that if
either of the two choice problems is taken in isolation,
expected utility theory has nothing to say about which
action should be chosen.   For example, a subject may be
observed to prefer £30 for sure (A) to a 0.8 chance of
£40 (B).   According to expected utility theory, this entails
that he will prefer a 0.25 chance of £30 (C) to a 0.2
chance of £40 (D).   In reality, many people who prefer
A to B also prefer D to C (the common ratio effect).
The conjunction of these two preferences violates the
expected utility theory: but either preference, taken
in isolation, would be consistent with the theory.   In
other words, even for an expected utility theorist, there
is no way in which these problems can be solved by rational
analysis alone; which action is better is ultimately a
matter of taste or personal judgement.

Furthermore, the problems presented to subjects are
often deliberately designed to induce reversals of preference.   For example, the particular consequences and probabilities used to construct the actions A, B, C and D
described in the previous paragraph would induce a reversal
for many subjects.   This would be regarded as an interesting
experimental result.   But suppose that the smaller consequence was £5 rather than £30.   Then almost all subjects
would prefer B to A and D to C.   This pattern of choice
would be consistent with expected utility theory, and
also with common sense: it would be obvious, and therefore
uninteresting.   Similarly, if the smaller consequence
was £39, almost everyone would prefer A to B and C to
D; this too would be an obvious and uninteresting result.

In order to generate preference reversals, it is necessary
to select choice problems in which, for the typical subject,
the merits of the alternatives are quite finely balanced.

So the problems presented to subjects in experiments
are not representative of the choices they confront in
everyday life. They are choices of a kind that the typical
subject has had little experience of dealing with; they
are not susceptible to rational analysis in the sense
that, say, a choice between a dominated and a dominating
action is; and they are finely balanced. In other words,
they are difficult choices.

4.   Regret and Rationality

The thrust of my argument so far has been that regret
and rejoicing are most likely to be significant when a
choice has been difficult. A choice is difficult when
the individual concerned has no preference to 'consult';
he simply <u>does not know</u> which action he prefers. Nevertheless, he has to choose something. Whatever he chooses,
he chooses it without being able to convince himself that
this is the right choice. It is not the logical consequence
of acting on some general principle to which he is committed; it is simply a choice he has had to make. If
the choice is made under uncertainty, he may come to wish
he had chosen differently, because he comes to know that
another choice would have led to a better outcome. This
does not establish that his original choice was <u>wrong</u>
- which state of the world occurred was a matter of chance
- but it was not obviously <u>right</u>. He cannot console himself
with the thought that his original choice was justified:
it wasn't. In this sense, there is an element of self-
recrimination along with the wish that a different choice
had been made. And it is a kind of self-recrimination
that can be <u>foreseen</u>. If a person cannot justify the
choice he is making at the time he makes it, he can foresee
that he will not be able to justify it afterwards.

So the idea of foreseeing self-recrimination is not
a contradiction in terms. Nevertheless, many expected
utility theorists would be unhappy with this argument
as a defence of the rationality of regret theory, for
two main reasons. First, because I have presupposed that
people's preferences may be incomplete: they may come
to choice problems without having preferences to guide

them.   It might be claimed that incomplete preferences
are themselves a form of irrationality.   Second, because
my argument seems to contain a Catch-22 problem, leading
to its self-destruction.   If regret theory is a theory
of rational choice, won't a person who acts in accordance
with the theory be able to justify his choices precisely
because they are in accordance with the theory?

The answer to these problems, I believe, is that
regret theory is not a theory of rational choice in quite
the same sense that expected utility theory is supposed
by its proponents to be.   A person who acts according
to expected utility theory has a complete and internally
consistent pattern of preferences - a master plan - for
dealing with every possible contingency within a very
broad class of choice problems.   If the axioms of that
theory have normative content, it is because they provide
guidance to individuals when drawing up such master plans.
They set out a way (not, of course, the only way) in which
a person might make all his planned choices consistent
with one another; but, at the level of the one-off choice
problem, they have little to say.

Regret theory, in contrast, comes into its own when
people don't have master plans of this kind.   To say this
is to say that the patterns of choices predicted by the
theory are not master plans in their own right.   In other
words, people may repeatedly behave as regret theory
predicts, but they do not do so as part of a conscious
plan.   Regret theory describes some of the regularities
in human behaviour that occur because people sometimes
don't know how they should choose.   If this is so, it
is clear that the people whose choices are being explained
cannot themselves see the theory as a means of completely
justifying their choices; the whole problem is that they
cannot find a course of action that they can completely
justify to themselves.

On this account, then, regret theory is ultimately
descriptive rather than prescriptive.   But to say this
is not to say that the patterns of choice it describes
are irrational.   They are the choices of people who cannot
find sufficient reasons to justify their actions; but
these choices are not contrary to reason.   Regret theory,
I believe, describes the choices of rational people.

It is, of course, open to the expected utility theorist
to insist that any individual who lacks a complete master
plan is necessarily irrational.   In other words, it is

irrational to find choices difficult; it is irrational not to know what one should do. But since we all know that human beings often do find choices difficult, this amounts to saying that homo sapiens is an irrational species. Such a definition of rationality would seem remarkably unhelpful.

Department of Economics
University of Newcastle upon Tyne
Newcastle upon Tyne
NE1 7RU
England

NOTES

1. Needless to say, the problems dealt with in this paper have been the subject of discussion between Graham Loomes and me over several years, and so many of the ideas in the paper may originally have been his. It should not be assumed, however, that he endorses all the arguments I put forward here.

2. In presenting this argument as devil's advocate I am recalling informal comments made by, amongst others, James Buchanan, Michael Jones-Lee, Kevin Keasey, Patrick Minford, John Peirson and Charles Rowley.

3. Compare Amartya Sen's (1982, pp.60-62) discussion of the problem of Buridan's ass.

4. In his paper to the FUR-84 conference, Kenneth MacCrimmon described how the businessmen on whom he experimented got round his attempts to confront them with realistic pairwise choice problems: faced with an apparently stark choice between two options, their first instinct seemed to be to suggest a third option such as compromise or delay.

REFERENCES

Allais, M. (1953) 'Le comportement de l'homme rationnel devant le risque; critique des postulats et axiomes de l'ecole Americaine' Econometrica, Vol.21, pp.503-46.

Bell, D.E. (1982) 'Regret in decision making under uncert-ainty' Operations Research, Vol.30, pp.961-81.

Grether, D.M. and Plott, C.R. (1979) 'Economic theory of choice and the preference reversal phenomenon' American Economic Review, Vol.69, pp.623-38.

Kahneman, D. and Tversky, A. (1979) 'Prospect theory: an analysis of decision under risk' Econometrica, Vol,47, pp.263-91.

Lichtenstein, S. and Slovic, P. (1971) 'Reversals of preference between bids and choices in gambling decisions' Journal of Experimental Psychology, Vol.89, pp.46-55.

Loomes, G. and Sugden, R. (1982) 'Regret theory: an alter-native theory of rational choice under uncertainty' Economic Journal, Vol.92, pp.805-24.

Loomes, G. and Sugden, R. (1983a) 'Regret Theory and measurable utility' Economics Letters, Vol.12, pp.19-21.

Loomes, G. and Sugden, R. (1983b) 'A rationale for prefer-ence reversal' American Economic Review, Vol.73, pp.428-32.

Sen, A.K. (1982) Choice, Welfare and Measurement, London: Blackwell.

PART II

UTILITY AND UNCERTAINTY

Maurice Allais

DETERMINATION OF CARDINAL UTILITY
ACCORDING TO AN INTRINSIC INVARIANT MODEL

ABSTRACT

The purpose of the Paper is to show that it is possible to represent all the empirical data of the 1952 Experiment (19 subjects) and of the 1975 Experiment (8 subjects) by only one model, the same whatever the subjects considered.

An invariant formulation is presented of the generating function $X=f(A)$ corresponding to the condition $\mathcal{A}(U_o+X)=2\mathcal{A}(U_o+A)$ where $\mathcal{A}(U_o + X)$ represents cardinal utility of a given subject, and U_o his psychological assets, that is his psychological estimate of his assets.

The function of cardinal utility of any one subject can be deduced from the knowledge of his generating function. The function of cardinal utility is invariant from one subject to the next once one considers the ratio X/μ , in which μ represents the index of a subject with respect to a reference subject.

All the empirical data can be validly represented by the same generating function and a single function of cardinal utility which together constitute the intrinsic invariant model. This agreement is the more remarkable in that the intrinsic invariant model was deduced from the analysis of the empirical data of the 1952 Experiment alone, and it applies itself as well to the empirical data of the 1975 Experiment.

Not only the preceding analysis gave undeniable evidence of the existence of cardinal utility, but its expression appears effectively to be invariant from one subject to the next both at a given moment and over time, at least as a first approximation.

This conclusion is the more significant in that the expression of cardinal utility as a function of variable X shows a very striking similarity to the expression for psycho-physiological sensation as a function of luminous stimulus determined by Weber's and Fechner's successors.

L. Daboni et al. (eds.), Recent Developments in the Foundations of Utility and Risk Theory, 83–120.

SUMMARY

INTRODUCTION

The purpose of this Paper is to show that it is possible to represent all the empirical data of the 1952 experiment (19 subjects) and of the 1975 experiment (8 subjects) by only one model, the same whatever the subjects considered : *The Intrinsic Invariant Model.*

The 1952 Experiment was organised after the May 1952 Paris International Colloquium. The limited 1975 Experiment was organised to check the main results of the 1974-1975 analysis of the   data of the 1952 Experiment [1].

The present paper is only a very abridged version of my 1984 Memoir *"The Cardinal Utility and its Determination - Hypotheses, Methods and Empirical Results"* [2] in which the reader will find all necessary justifications and appropriate comments.

For sake of brievety the main mathematical formulas and numerical results of the Model considered are presented below on *Tables I to XIII,* the following text being limited to the statement of fundamental properties. All the results obtained are illustrated by *Charts.*

In my (1977) Memoir only the loglinear approximation of the cardinal utility function was used (T II).

1. *THE INTRINSIC INVARIANT CARDINAL UTILITY MODEL* [3]

1.1. *Fundamental Hypotheses of the Invariant Cardinal Utility Model*

The general properties of the Invariant Cardinal Utility Model are derived from very simple Hypotheses on the Cardinal Utility Function (T I and T III).

1.2. *Generating Function of the Invariant Cardinal Utility Model*

The generating function $X = f(A)$ of the Cardinal Utility Model corresponds to the condition $\jmath(U_o + X) = 2\jmath(U_o + A)$ considered by the 1952 and 1975 Experiments with $A \geqslant 0$. For a given subject $\jmath(U)$ represents the cardinal utility function for $U = U_o + X$ where U_o represents his *psychological assets,* that is his *psychological estimate* of his assets, and X a virtual increase of U_o (T I).

For a given subject, his answers X are represented as functions of A by Charts like *Chart I.*

The general properties of the Generating Function are
derived from the general properties of the Cardinal Utility
Function. It has two components f_1 and f_2. The component
f_1, valid for small values of X, is loglinear. The component f_2 can be determined only by the analysis of the empirical data (T IV).

From the invariance of the function of cardinal utility
and of the generating function for all subjects it results
that it is possible to deduce the cardinal utility function
and the generating function of any subject from the knowledge
of the Cardinal Utility Function and the Generating Function
of a particular subject taken as reference. This *Reference
subject* can be defined by the abscissa $K = K_R$ of the vertical
asymptote of the generating function of the reference subject.
Any subject is characterised relatively to the Reference subject by the coefficient $\mu = U_o/U_{oR}$, U_{oR} being the value of U_o
for the Reference subject (T V).

The particular mathematical form of the component f_2
of the Generating Function has been deduced from the *General
properties* of the Generating Function *and* from the *empirical
analysis* of the data of the 1952 Experiment. As a matter of
fact its sole justification is its capacity to represent correctly these data. The generating function so deduced depends
on three parameters α, a and μ (T VI) :
  - α and a are specific parameters common to all the
    the subjects ; they characterize the general Cardinal
    Utility Model
  - the parameter μ characterizes the subject considered
    in relation to the reference subject.

The curves representing the generating functions of the
different subjects are identical within a displacement along
the straight line X = 2A . *They depend only on the coefficients* α , a *and* μ , *and their structure is invariant for
the different subjects* (T VI,5).

For a given series of observations the parameters α ,
a and μ of the generating function can be determined by
very simple processes (T VII).

1.3. *Cardinal Utility Function of the General Model*

The function of cardinal utility $\measuredangle = \measuredangle\left(1 + X/U_o\right)$ of any one
subject can be deduced point by point from the knowledge of
his generating function (T VIII).

The function of cardinal utility is invariant from one
subject to the next once one considers the ratio $X/\mu = X_R$,

in which μ represents the index of the considered subject
with respect to the reference subject. It is remarkable that
the invariant cardinal utility function is *approximately loglinear over a very large domain* (T IX).

1.4. Intrinsic Invariant Model of Cardinal Utility

The Intrinsic Invariant Model is defined by two specific va-
lues α^* and a^* of the coefficients α and a of the *Invariant
Cardinal Utility Model*. The coefficients α^* and a^* are deduced from the sole consideration of the mathematical properties of the Generating Function and the corresponding Cardinal Utility Function of the Invariant Cardinal Utility Model (T X and T XI).

The generating function and the cardinal utility function of the Intrinsic Invariant Cardinal Utility Model are
represented in *Charts VIII and IX*. *Chart IX* shows that the
cardinal utility function is *approximately loglinear over a
very wide range* (T XI,3).

As regards applications, the *Intrinsic Invariant Model*
only comprises *a single arbitrary parameter μ* , the ratio of
the psychological assets of the considered subject to that
of the reference subject (T XI,5).

In last analysis the justification of the particular
choice of the values α^* and a^* for the coefficients α and a
rests essentially on the capacity of the *Intrinsic Invariant
Model* to represent correctly not only the empirical data of
the 1952 Experiment but also those of the 1975 Experiment.

2. EMPIRICAL VERIFICATION OF THE INTRINSIC INVARIANT MODEL [4]

2.1. 1952 Experiment

The agreement of the Intrinsic Invariant Model with the empirical data of the 1952 Experiment is all the more remarkable
as the specific values α^* and a^* of the coefficients α and
a are determined *only from pure mathematical considerations*
and consequently are independent of the empirical data (for
illustration see *T XII,2* , and *Charts XII, XIII, XIV and XV*).

2.2. 1975 Experiment

The agreement of the Intrinsic Invariant Model with the empirical data of the 1975 Experiment appears *all the more significant* in that it relates to a small number of subjects, and

to a wide range of Questions between 1 and 1,000, whereas the
fitting of the Model depends only of one parameter μ (for illustration see *T XII,3 , and Charts XVII and XVIII).*

   This agreement is all the more remarkable in that the
Intrinsic Invariant Model has been deduced *from the sole analysis* of the empirical data of the 1952 Experiment. Indeed
the invariance of the intrinsic invariant Model for very different subjects at very distant epochs is *very striking* (for
illustration see *T XII,4 and Charts XXI and XXII).*

2.3. *Explanation of all the previously observed difficulties*

The Intrinsic Invariant Model explains the deviations observed
in the fit of data relating to the loglinear formulation equally well for the low and high values of the answers X to the
Questions asked.

   It explains in particular why certain subjects were unable to answer certain questions for which the threshold of
satiety is overcrossed (T V,5).

   By admitting a horizontal asymptote corresponding to satiety *(Chart IX),* the curve representing cardinal utility effectively corresponds to the data of our introspection, whereas the loglinear formulation includes no situation of satiety whatever (T II).

3. *INTERPRETATION OF THE RESULTS OBTAINED* [5]

3.1. *Existence of an underlying structural coherence*

The quality of fit of the Intrinsic Invariant Model and the
coherence of the findings show that the intrinsic invariant
generating function should be viewed as covering an *underlying structural reality* that corresponds to intrinsic properties of cardinal utility.

3.2. *Nature of psychological assets*

The analysis which has been carried out shows that the psychological estimates of the subjects' assets do take into
account not only the patrimony assets but also, at least partially, the future incomes. They do take also into account
the specific character of the subjects considered.

   Considering the approximative loglinearity of cardinal
utility over a very wide range $A_2 \leqslant X \leqslant X_2$, i.e. the very

striking approximation $\Delta \backsim m \log(1 + X/W)$ over this range,
the interpretation $W = U_0$ *rests on the hypothesis* that in a
very large domain the cardinal utility function is approximately a linear function of the logarithm $\log U$ of the psychological assets U (T XI , 3-4).

3.3. *Psychological assets and psychological cash balances*

The analysis of the observed data leads to the conclusion that
when a subject appraises the intensity of his preferences,
he behaves *completely differently* depending on whether the
virtual changes in his assets that he can envisage are relatively small or very high. This conclusion emerged as *incon-
trovertible.*

Whereas in the latter case the subject considers his
total psychological assets U_0 , in the former he refers to a
much smaller amount the order of magnitude of which corresponds to his psychological cash balances U_0' , i.e. his psychological estimate of his cash balances.

As for the psychological cash balances U_0' the justification of the estimate $U_0' = W'$ *relies on the hypothesis* that
the cardinal utility function is approximately a linear function of the logarithm $\log U'$ of $U' = U_0' + X$ for the small values of X (T IX,2 and T XI,4).

3.4. *Indexes of psychological indetermination*

On the whole the answers to the different questions are *remarkably* consistent. The deviations from the formulation of the
Intrinsic Invariant Model correspond to *psychological errors*
relating to the intensity of preferences. These errors are
comparable in nature to the errors made by any measuring de-
vice in other domains, whatever the domain considered.

The deviations observed correspond to the subjects' hesi-
tation in determining the values of their answers X ; and the
indexes of psychological indetermination which can be deduced
from the analysis of their answers to the questions asked allow to measure the order of magnitude of the errors made by
the subjects in estimating their intensity of preferences
(T XIII, 1-3).

The deviations observed suggest that the psychological
estimates of cardinal utility are subject to a margin or error of approximately 7 % when they are compared with the total variation M of the function or cardinal utility considered
for positive values of X .

It is particularly significant to observe that the *indexes of psychological indetermination* which can be deduced from the answers of the subjects are all of the same order of magnitude, regardless of the age, profession, social background, ..., of the subjects considered in the 1952 Experiment.

As a matter of fact this analysis allows the determination of the standard psychological error on X corresponding to the psychological indetermination.

This standard psychological error σ_{μ} is of the order of 36.5 % for the considered subjects of the 1952 Experiment when the standard deviation of (log X - log X*) of the corresponding individual fittings is approximately 36.8 %. It should be underlined that the calculus of σ_{μ} is *totally independent* of any hypothesis on the expression of the cardinal utility function (T XIII,4).

4. *OVERALL VIEW* [6]

4.1. *The Intrinsic Invariant Model and the empirical data*

All the empirical data of the 1952 and 1975 Experiments can be validly represented, at least as a first approximation, by the same generating function and a single function of cardinal utility which together constitute the Intrinsic Invariant Model.

This agreement is the more remarkable *in that the Intrinsic Invariant Model was deduced from the analysis of the empirical data of the 1952 Experiment alone, and it applies itself as well to the empirical data of the 1975 Experiment,* whose twelve questions however covered a far wider range between 1 and 1,000   than the four questions asked in 1952 covering only a range of variation of 10 to 100 of A.

4.2. *Existence of a cardinal utility*

The results obtained confirm in a striking and indisputable way the effective existence for each subject considered of a cardinal utility which indeed is real, and not at all metaphysical, as Savage contended in defending his neo-Bernoullian theory and as is still contended by very numerous neo-Bernoullians.

However, the proof of the existence of cardinal utility goes far beyond the debate on neo-Bernoullian theories. In fact this proof fully reinstates in economic theory *a psycho-*

logical concept which has been banished from it after Pareto's time as a result of erroneous analyses and interpretation.

In fact, although this concept *does not need to be considered* in working out the theory of general economic equilibrium and the theory of economic efficiency, or, in a general frame, the general theory of surpluses, it is *indispensable* for establishing any effective theory relating to conflicts opposing economic agents in sharing the obtained surpluses, conflicts whose final settlement depend not only on their preferences, *but basically on the intensity of their preferences*. The consideration of the cardinal utility concept is also indispensable for any comprehensive theory of governmental choices and decisions, in particular regarding their effects on income distribution. The same is also true of the specification of any theory of choice within a family, based on the consideration of the relative intensity of the preferences of its members and on interpersonal comparisons.

4.3. *The cardinal utility function, a psychological invariant*

As regards my previous works, relating to invariants in economic behaviour, especially to invariants in monetary psychology, the intrinsic invariant model of cardinal utility provides a new and striking example of invariance in space and over time. Not only the preceding analysis gave undeniable evidence of the existence of cardinal utility, but its expression appears to be *invariant from one subject to the next both at a given moment and over time, at least as a first approximation*.

This conclusion is the more significant in that the expression of cardinal utility as a function of the variable X shows *a very striking similarity* to the expression for psychophysiological sensation as a function of luminous stimulus, determined by Weber's and Fechner's successors *(Charts XXV and III)*.

As a result it appears that basic principles of the laws of psychophysiology remain valid in the field of economic psychology.

4.4. *The future of the intrinsic invariant formulation*

The present paper *is not presented* as the elaboration of a definitive model of cardinal utility, *but simply* as a stage defining an empirical approach, methods of analysis, guiding principles and hypotheses, and a basis of reflection for the

study of human economic psychology following the path opened
up over a century ago by Weber and Fechner in their psychophysiological analysis of sensations and in the XVIIIth century
by Daniel Bernoulli in his analysis of the Saint Petersburg
Paradox.

As a matter of fact the Intrinsic Invariant Generating
Function which I have derived from the empirical analysis of
the results of the 1952 Experiment has incontestably a *contingent character*. It is thus possible, if not probable, that this
function will be replaced by another sooner or later. However,
if it is, it will be replaced by a *neighbouring* function which
can represent observed data at least as well, and the same will
be true of the corresponding function of cardinal utility.

In any case, three significant conclusions seem to be
established, namely that :
- *the cardinal utility function of any subject has an upper
limit corresponding to satiety ;*
- *the function of cardinal utility of any subject can be represented, at least as a first approximation, by one and only
one function, invariant in space and over time ;*
- *the subjects' behaviour vis-à-vis the intensity of their
preferences differs entirely depending on whether the virtual
changes of their psychological assets are likely to change
their living conditions radically or not.*

NOTES (Text, Tables and Bibliography)

(1) On these experiments see Allais 1952c and Allais 1977 ;
    § 3, p. 447-449 ; § 6, p. 451-454 ; and Appendix C, § C.5-
    C.9, p. 614-620 ; and Charts I to VI, p. 640-645. See
    also Allais, 1984, Appendices II, III and IV.
(2) This Memoir, the french version of which has been distri-
    buted in the Venice Conference, will be published shortly
    in the Review *"Theory and Decision".*
(3) Allais, 1984, Parts II, III, IV and V ; - (4) id. Part VI ;
(5) id., Part VII ;- (6) id., Part VIII ; - (7) id., § 1.4. ;
    - (8) id., § 1.5. ; - (9) id., § 2.2. ; - (10) id., § 2.4.;
    - (11) id., § 2.5. ; - (12) id., § 3.5.-3.6. ; - (13) id.,
    § 3.7. ; - (14) id., § 4.2.
(15) id., § 4.6. ; - (16) id., § 5.1.-5.3. ; - (17) id., § 5.1-
    5.3. ; - (18) id., § 6.1.-6.4. ; - (19) id., § 7.6.
(20) The reader will find an extensive bibliography in Allais
    (1984).

P.S.- Requests for reprints should be sent to ; Allais, Centre
    d'Analyse Economique, 62 Bld St.Michel, 75006, Paris, France.

I. CARDINAL UTILITY ANALYSIS
DEFINITIONS AND NOTATIONS [7]

1. General notation

Δ : cardinal utility
U_o : psychological assets
U_o' : psychological cash balances
X : virtual increase of psychological assets
$U = U_o + X$: virtual psychological assets   (1)
$\Delta(U_o) = 0$ (2)
Unit of value : one million (1952) francs (approximately
         equivalent to 10,000 $ 1983)

2. Psychological equivalent intervals

Psychological intervals (U_o , U_o+A) and (U_o+A , U_o+X) are
equivalent if

$$\Delta(U_o+A) - \Delta(U_o) = \Delta(U_o+X) - \Delta(U_o+A) \qquad (3)$$
i.e.
$$\Delta(U_o+X) = 2\Delta(U_o+A) \qquad (4)$$

3. Generating Function and determination of the cardinal utility function

$$\boxed{\begin{aligned} \frac{X}{U_o} &= f\left(\frac{A}{U_o}\right) \qquad \text{for} \qquad \Delta\left(\frac{X}{U_o}\right) = 2\Delta\left(\frac{A}{U_o}\right) \\[2mm] \Delta\left[f\left(\frac{A}{U_o}\right)\right] &= 2\Delta\left(\frac{A}{U_o}\right) \end{aligned}} \qquad \begin{aligned} (5) \\[4mm] (6) \end{aligned}$$

The knowledge of the generating function f determines the
cardinal utility function Δ by condition (6).

4. Empirical Data

1952 and 1975 Experiments : $A > 0$, $X > 0$
1952 Experiment : 4 Questions : A_i, X_i ; 19 subjects j
1975 Experiment : 12 Questions : A_i, X_i ; 8 subjects j

5. Average subject of a Group of subjects

Geometric averages : $A_i = \overline{A_{ij}}$ \qquad $X_i = \overline{X_{ij}}$ (7)

II. LOGLINEAR MODEL OF CARDINAL UTILITY [8]

1. Hypothesis

$$s = m \log (1 + X/V) \tag{1}$$

2. Generating Function

$$X = A (2 + A/V) \qquad\qquad A \geqslant 0 \tag{2}$$

Logarithmic Graphic Representation :

Asymptote : $\log X = \log A + \log 2 \qquad (X = 2A) \tag{3}$

3. Interpretation of V (estimate of the psychological assets)

$$V = U_o \tag{4}$$

4. Reference Subject

$$V = V_R = 1 \tag{5}$$

5. Invariance Conditions

$$\frac{X}{X_R} = \frac{A}{A_R} = \frac{V}{V_R} = \frac{U_o}{U_{oR}} = \lambda \tag{6}$$

6. Fitting

$$X = A (2 + A/\lambda) \qquad\qquad V = \lambda \tag{7}$$

7. Analysis of the 1952 and 1975 Experiments

The loglinear formulation has been used, as a first approximation, in the analysis of the results of the 1952 and 1975 Experiments in Allais (1977): *Appendix C,* § C5-C9, p. 614-620 ; § C21-C22, p. 632-634 ; and *Charts I to VI,* p. 640-645.

8. Limited validity of the loglinear formulation

The loglinear model is not valid : – for the small values of X ; – for the very large values of X (satiety).

III. INVARIANT CARDINAL UTILITY MODEL
POSTULATES ON THE CARDINAL UTILITY FUNCTION [9]

Postulate I : Invariance

The cardinal utility of a given subject is an *invariant* function of X/U_o .

Postulate II : Continuity

$\triangle$ and $d\triangle/dX$ are continuous functions for every va-lue of X .

Postulate III : Satiety

$$\triangle (X/U_o = \infty) = M \tag{1}$$

Postulate IV : Loglinearity for small values of X

$$\triangle = m' \mu' \qquad \text{for} \qquad X/U_o \leqslant X_1 /U_o' \tag{2}$$

$$\mu' = \log (1 + X/W') \qquad X \geqslant 0 \tag{3}$$

W' = estimate of the psychological cash balances U_o' (4)

Postulate V : Approximate loglinearity over a wide range of X

$$\triangle \curvearrowleft \log (1 + X/W) \qquad \text{for} \qquad A_2 \leqslant X \leqslant X_2 \tag{5}$$

W = estimate of the psychological assets U_o (6)

IV. INVARIANT CARDINAL UTILITY MODEL
GENERATING FUNCTION [10]

1. Fundamental Properties

1.1. Invariance (Consequence of Postulate I)

The function
$$X/U_o = f\ (A/U_o)$$
is the same for all subjects.   (1)

1.2. Satiety - Vertical asymptote $X = K$ (Consequence of Postulate III)

$$X/U_o = f(K/U_o)\ = \infty \qquad (K/U_o) = M/2 \qquad (2)$$

Representative curve of the Generating Function :
vertical asymptote of abscissa K.

1.3. Small values of X/U_o (Consequence of Postulate IV)

$$\frac{X}{U_o} = f_1\left(\frac{A}{U_o}\right) = \frac{A}{U_o}\left(2 + \frac{A/U_o}{W'/U_o}\right) \quad \text{for} \quad \frac{A}{U_o} \leqslant \frac{A_1}{U_o} \qquad (3)$$

Asymptote : $X = 2A$

2. Components of the Generating Function

f_1 : $X/U_o = f(A/U_o) = f_1\ (A/U_o)$ for $A/U_o \leqslant A_1/U_o$	(5)
f_2 : $X/U_o = f(A/U_o) = f_2(A/U_o)$ " $A/U_o \geqslant A_1/U_o$	(6)

Component f_1 : corresponds to Postulate IV
Component f_2 : to be deduced from the analysis of the
empirical data of the 1952 Experiment (T VI below)

3. Continuity conditions of the two components f_1 and f_2 (Consequences of Postulate II)

$$X/U_o = f_1\ (A/U_o) = f_2(A/U_o) \quad \text{for} \quad X=X_1 \quad A=A_1 \qquad (7)$$

$$df_1\ /dA = df_2\ /dA \qquad\qquad " \qquad " \qquad " \qquad (8)$$

V. INVARIANT CARDINAL UTILITY MODEL
REFERENCE SUBJECT [11]

1. Definition

The subject of reference is defined by the condition

$$\boxed{K = K_R}$$ $$(1)$$

2. Generating Function of the Reference Subject

$$\boxed{\begin{array}{lll} f_1 \; : & X_R = A_R(2 + A_R/W'_R) & \text{for} & A_R \leqslant A_{1R} & X_R \leqslant X_{1R} \\ f_2 \; : & X_R/U_{oR} = f_2(A_R/U_{oR}) & " & A_R \geqslant A_{1R} & X_R \geqslant X_{1R} \end{array}}$$ $$\begin{array}{l}(2)\\(3)\end{array}$$

3. Cardinal Utility Function of the Reference Subject

$$\Delta = \Delta \left(X_R / U_{oR} \right)$$

4. Invariance Conditions for a Given Subject

$$\left\{ \begin{array}{lll} K = \mu\, K_R & W' = \mu\, W'_R & U_o = \mu\, U_{oR} \\[2mm] A = \mu\, A_R & X = \mu\, X_R \\[2mm] A_1 = \mu\, A_{1R} & X_1 = \mu\, X_{1R} \end{array} \right. \qquad (4)$$

$$\boxed{\begin{array}{l} \mu = \text{coefficient characterizing the considered subject} \\ \text{relatively to the reference subject} \end{array}}$$

5. Satiety

When $A \geqslant K$ the subject is unable to answer, the corresponding value X being infinite.

VI. INVARIANT CARDINAL UTILITY MODEL
CHARACTERISTIC PARAMETERS
OF THE GENERATING FUNCTION OF THE REFERENCE SUBJECT [12]

1. Definition of the Reference Subject

$$\boxed{K_R \ = \ 1000} \tag{1}$$

2. Generating Function of the Reference Subject

$$
\begin{array}{lll}
f_1 \ : \quad X_R = A_R(2 + A_R/W_R') & \text{for} \quad A_R \leqslant A_{1R} \quad X_R \leqslant X_{1R} & (2) \\[2mm]
f_2 \ : \quad X_R = a\,A_R / \left(\log \dfrac{K_R}{A_R}\right)^{\alpha} & \text{for} \quad A_R \geqslant A_{1R} \quad X_R \geqslant X_{1R} & (3)
\end{array}
$$

The component f_2 is deduced *from the empirical analysis of the 1952 data.*

3. Implications of the continuity conditions (T IV)

$$
W_R' = \frac{\mathfrak{z}'^{(1+\alpha)}}{\alpha\,a\,e^{\mathfrak{z}'}}\,K_R
\qquad
A_{1R} = \frac{K_R}{e^{\mathfrak{z}'}}
\qquad
X_{1R} = \frac{a\,K_R}{\mathfrak{z}'^{\alpha}\,e^{\mathfrak{z}'}}
\tag{4}
$$

$\mathfrak{z}' = $ the greatest root of equation (6) $\qquad\qquad\qquad$ (5)

$$2\,\mathfrak{z}'^{(1+\alpha)} - a\mathfrak{z}' + a\alpha = 0 \tag{6}$$

4. Values of W , A and X corresponding to the smallest root of equation (6)

$$
W_R = \frac{\mathfrak{z}^{(1+\alpha)}}{\alpha\,a\,e^{\mathfrak{z}}}\,K_R
\qquad
A_{2R} = \frac{K_R}{e^{\mathfrak{z}}}
\qquad
X_{2R} = \frac{a\,K_R}{\mathfrak{z}^{\alpha}\,e^{\mathfrak{z}}}
\tag{7}
$$

$\mathfrak{z} = $ the smallest root of equation (6)

5. Generating function of a given subject (Invariance condition)

$$
\begin{array}{lll}
f_1 \ : \quad X = A(2 + A/W') & \text{for} \quad A \leqslant A_1 \quad X \leqslant X_1 & (9) \\[2mm]
f_2 \ : \quad X = a\,A / (\log K/A)^{\alpha} & \text{for} \quad A \geqslant A_1 \quad X \geqslant X_1 & (10) \\[3mm]
\multicolumn{2}{l}{\dfrac{A}{A_R} = \dfrac{X}{X_R} = \dfrac{K}{K_R} = \dfrac{A_1}{A_{1R}} = \dfrac{X_1}{X_{1R}} = \dfrac{A_2}{A_{2R}} = \dfrac{X_2}{X_{2R}} = \mu} & (11)
\end{array}
$$

The Invariant Cardinal Utility Model depends only of two specific parameters α and a , *the same for all subjects.*

VII. INVARIANT CARDINAL UTILITY MODEL FITTING METHODS [13]

1. Structural Relation

$$\boxed{X = a\,A \Big/ \left(\log \frac{\mu K_R}{A}\right)^\alpha}$$

(1)

2. Determination of α, a and μ for a given series of N observations (A_i, X_i)

One considers the correlation :

$$\log X_i/A_i = -\alpha \log\log \mu K_R/A_i + \log a \qquad (K_R = 1000)$$

(2)

μ is chosen to maximize the correlation coefficient R.

3. Determination of a and μ corresponding to a given series of N observations for a given value α^* of α

μ is chosen to minimize σ^2 with

$$\sigma^2 = \sum_i \left(\theta_i - \theta_m\right)^2 / N$$

(3)

$$\theta_i = \log\left(X_i/A_i\right) + \alpha^* \log\log\left(\mu K_R/A_i\right) \qquad (K_R = 1000)$$

(4)

$$\theta_m = \left(\sum_i \theta_i\right) / N \qquad \left(a = e^{\theta_m}\right)$$

(5)

4. Determination of μ corresponding to a series of N observations (A_i, X_i) for given values α^* and a^* of α and a

μ is chosen to minimize E with

$$E = \sum_i \left(\log X_i - \log X_i^*\right)^2 / N$$

(6)

$$X_i^* = a^* A_i \Big/ \left(\log K/A_i\right)^{\alpha^*} \qquad\qquad K = \mu K_R$$

(7)

5. Fittings

For all the considered data one verifies *a posteriori* that it is sufficient to consider only the component f_2 of f (T VI), i.e. relation (1) above of the generating function since we always find for the considered data

$$A_i / \mu \geqslant A_{1R}$$

(8)

VIII. INVARIANT CARDINAL UTILITY MODEL
DETERMINATION OF THE CARDINAL UTILITY FUNCTION
FROM THE GENERATING FUNCTION [14]

1. Hypotheses

(a) $$\delta(X) = 2\,\delta(A) \qquad (1)$$

for

$$X = A(2 + A/W') \qquad \text{for} \quad A \leqslant A_1 \quad X \leqslant X_1 \qquad (2)$$

$$X = a\,A/(\log K/A)^{\alpha} \qquad \text{for} \quad A \geqslant A_1 \quad X \geqslant X_1 \qquad (3)$$

(b) $\quad \delta = m' \log(1 + X/W') \qquad \text{for} \quad X \leqslant X_1 \qquad (4)$

2. Determination of δ for $X \geqslant X_{1R}$ for the Reference Subject

To any point $\widehat{M}_1$

$$\begin{cases} u_1 = \log\left(1 + \widehat{X}_1/W'_R\right) \\ \delta_1 = m'\,u_1 \end{cases} \qquad (5)$$

of the straight line (b) corresponds a series of points $\widehat{M}_n$

$$\begin{cases} \widehat{X}_n = a\,\widehat{X}_{n-1} \Big/ \left(\log K/\widehat{X}_{n-1}\right)^{\alpha} \\ \delta_n = 2^{n-1}\,\delta_1 \end{cases} \qquad (6)$$

Asymptote : $\quad n - 1 = p$

$$\delta_p = M/2 \qquad \text{for} \qquad \widehat{X}_p = K \qquad (7)$$

$$M = 1.9 \qquad 2^p\, m' \log\left(1 + \widehat{X}_1/W'_R\right) = M/2 = 0.95 \qquad (8)$$

where $\widehat{X}_1$ corresponds to $\widehat{X}_p = K$. The coefficient m' results from (8).

IX. INVARIANT CARDINAL UTILITY MODEL
FUNDAMENTAL PROPERTIES OF THE CARDINAL UTILITY FUNCTION [15]

1. *Invariance*

$$\delta = \delta \left(X / U_o \right) = \delta \left(X_R / U_{oR} \right) \tag{1}$$

The function δ is the same for every subject.

2. *Loglinearity for small values of X*

$$\delta = m' u' \qquad \text{for} \qquad X \leqslant X_1 \tag{2}$$

$$u' = \log \left(1 + X/W' \right) = \log \left(1 + X/\mu \, W_R' \right) \tag{3}$$

3. *Approximative loglinearity over a very large domain*

$$\delta \curlywedge m \, u \qquad \text{for} \qquad A_2 \leqslant X \leqslant X_2 \tag{4}$$

$$u = \log \left(1 + X/W \right) = \log \left(1 + X/\mu \, W_R \right) \tag{5}$$

A_2 and X_2 are defined by equations (7) and (11) of T VI.

4. *Interpretation of the parameters W and W' in the framework of the Model*

$$U_o' \; = \; W' \; = \mu \, W_R' \tag{6}$$

$$U_o \; = \; W \; = \mu \, W_R \tag{7}$$

5. *Invariance Conditions*

$$\frac{W'}{W_R'} = \frac{W}{W_R} = \frac{K}{K_R} = \frac{A}{A_R} = \frac{X}{X_R} = \frac{A_1}{A_R} = \frac{X_1}{X_{1R}} = \frac{A_2}{A_{2R}} = \frac{X_2}{X_{2R}} = \mu \tag{8}$$

6. *Characteristic Parameters*

The parameters W_R', W_R, A_{1R}, X_{1R}, A_{2R}, X_{2R} are determinate functions of α, a and K_R (T VI, 3-4).

X. INVARIANT CARDINAL UTILITY MODEL FOR
$$\alpha = \alpha^* = 1 \qquad a = a^* = 21.671$$
INTRINSIC INVARIANT MODEL [16]

1. Generating Function

$$f_1 \; : \quad X = A(2 + A/W') = A(2 + A/\mu W_R') \quad \text{for} \quad A \leqslant A_1 \quad X \leqslant X_1 \quad (1)$$

$$f_2 \; : \quad X = a^* A \Big/ \Big(\log \frac{K}{A}\Big)^{\alpha^*} = a^* A \Big/ \Big(\log \frac{\mu K_R}{A}\Big)^{\alpha^*} \quad \text{for} \quad A \geqslant A_1 \quad X \geqslant X_1 \quad (2)$$

2. Reference Subject

$$\mu = 1 \qquad\qquad K_R = 1000 \qquad\qquad (3)$$

3. Characteristics Coefficients α^* and a^*

- The value $\alpha^* = 1$ corresponds to a mathematical proper-
ty of the Generating Function $\left(\zeta \zeta' = \zeta + \zeta' = a^*/2\right)$

- For $a = a^* = 21.671$ the iteration process (3) of
T VIII (determining the cardinal utility function
from the generating function) leads to
$$\widehat{X}_8 = A_2 \qquad \text{for} \qquad \widehat{X}_1 = A_1 \qquad (4)$$

4. Associated parameters for $\alpha = \alpha^* = 1 \; ; \; a = a^* = 21.671$
$K = K_R = 1000 \; ; \; M = 1.9$ (T VI, 3-4 and T VIII, 2)

$$
\begin{bmatrix}
\zeta' = 9.721 \\
A_{1R} = 0.0600 \\
X_{1R} = 0.1338 \\
W_{1R}' = 0.2617 \\
m' = 0.02636
\end{bmatrix}
\begin{bmatrix}
\zeta = 1.115 \\
A_{2R} = 328.0 \\
X_{2R} = 6377 \\
W_{2R} = 18.81 \\
m = 0.2390
\end{bmatrix}
\begin{bmatrix}
\delta_1 = m \log\left(1 + A_{2R}/W_R\right) = 0.6966 \\
\quad = 2^7 m' \log\left(1 + A_{1R}/W_R'\right) \\
\delta_2 = m \log\left(1 + X_{2R}/W_R\right) = 1.393 \\
\quad = 2\delta_1 = 2^8 m' \log\left(1 + A_{1R}/W_R'\right) \\
(\delta_2 - \delta_1)/M = 36.6 \%
\end{bmatrix}
$$

The values of all these parameters are derived from the
considered values of α , a , K and M (T VI, 3-4).

XI. FUNDAMENTAL PROPERTIES OF THE INTRINSIC INVARIANT MODEL[17]

$$\alpha = \alpha^* = 1 \qquad a = a^* = 21.671$$

1. Components of the Generating Function

Component f_1 : it results from Postulate IV (T III)
Component f_2 : its mathematical form results from the
            empirical analysis of the (1952) data (T VI)

2. Purely Mathematical Definition of α^* and a^*

The coefficients $\alpha = \alpha^*$, $a = a^*$ correspond to purely
mathematical properties of the Generating Function and
of the corresponding Utility Function (T X,3).

3. Approximative loglinearity of the Cardinal Utility Function for $A_2 \leqslant X \leqslant X_2$

$$s \sim m\,u \qquad \text{for} \quad A_2 \leqslant X \leqslant X_2 \quad (s_1 \leqslant s \leqslant s_2) \qquad (1)$$

$$\left| \frac{s}{mu} - 1 \right| \leqslant 0.4\,\% \qquad\qquad " \qquad\qquad " \qquad\qquad (2)$$

$$u = \log(1 + X/W) = \log(1 + X/\mu\,W_R) \qquad (3)$$

4. Interpretation of the parameters W and W' in the framework of the Intrinsic Invariant Model

$$U'_0 = W' = \mu\,W'_R \qquad (4)$$

$$U_0 = W = \mu\,W_R \qquad (5)$$

5. Invariance Conditions

$$\frac{K}{K_R} = \frac{W'}{W'_R} = \frac{W}{W_R} = \frac{A}{A_R} = \frac{X}{X_R} = \mu \qquad (6)$$

$$\frac{A_1}{A_{1R}} = \frac{X_1}{X_{1R}} = \frac{A_2}{A_{2R}} \approx \frac{X_2}{X_{2R}} = \mu \qquad (7)$$

6. Charts

Generating Function of the Reference Subject : Chart VIII
Cardinal Utility Function   "   "   : Chart IX

XII. INTRINSIC INVARIANT MODEL
EMPIRICAL VERIFICATIONS AND ILLUSTRATIVE RESULTS[18]

1. Fittings

The fitting depends only of *one parameter* μ for a given Group of subjects and N observations (T VII,4)

$$e = \sqrt{E} \qquad E = \Sigma \left(\log X_i - \log X_i^* \right)^2 / N \qquad (1)$$

2. Empirical Data of the 1952 Experiment

Group Fittings
Results : *Charts XII and XIII* as illustrations

Group	I	II	III	IV	V	All
Number of subjects n	4	5	3	5	2	19
" " observations N	4	4	4	4	3	
μ	7.2	1.5	0.24	0.14	0.084	
e (%)	11.5	7.9	11.9	15.7	15.9	11.7

Individual Fittings
Value of e corresponding to relations (1) for the 19 subjects = 34.3 %
Illustrative subjects : *Charts XIV and XV*

3. Empirical Data of the 1975 Experiment

Group Fittings
Results : *Charts XVII and XVIII* as illustrations
Group E $n = 5$ N = 10 $\mu = 1.03$ e = 13 %

Individual Fittings
Value of e corresponding to relations (1) for the 6 subjects of Group E = 40.5 %

4. Two illustrative subjects of the 1952 and 1975 Experiments

Results : *Charts XXI and XXII*
Rabussier (1952) (N = 3) $\mu = 0.077$ e = 4.1 %
Anonymous I (1975)(N = 10) $\mu = 4.6$ e = 8.4 %

5. Fittings

As a matter of fact one verifies *a posteriori* that all the fittings depend only of the component f_2 of the Generating Function (T VII,5)

XIII. INDICES OF PSYCHOLOGICAL INDETERMINATION [19]

1. Answers X to the Questions of the Experiments

The answers were "yes" or "no" for different values of
X for each value of A with the following mentions :

> BH   much hesitation
> H   hesitation
> PAH   almost with no hesitation
> AH   without hesitation

2. Index of psychological indetermination

Considering the values X_1 and X_2 separating the mentions
AH or PAH from the mentions H or BH, and

$$\delta s = \frac{ds}{du} \ \frac{\delta X}{U_o + X} = \frac{ds}{du} \ \delta u \qquad (1)$$

$$u = \log\left(1 + X/U_o\right) \qquad \delta u = \log\left(1 + X_2/U_o\right) - \log\left(1 + X_1/U_o\right) \quad (2)$$

the index of psychological indetermination is taken as

$$\pi = \frac{\delta s}{M} = \frac{1}{2M} \frac{ds}{du} \left[\log\left(U_o + X_2\right) - \log\left(U_o + X_1\right) \right] \qquad (3)$$

$$\frac{ds}{du} = \frac{ds}{du}\left(U_o + X\right) \qquad M = 1.9 \qquad (4)$$

3. Results for the 1952 Experiment

For all the 14 subjects j of the 1952 Experiment who
have effectively given indications of § 1 above the
values of π_{ij} for the different Questions i are remarkably consistent and of the same order of magnitude : 7%.

4. Estimate of the standard value $\sigma_{\hat{r}}$ of the Psychological Errors on X

$$\sigma_{\hat{r}} = \frac{1}{1.96} \ \text{average of} \ \left| \frac{1}{2} \log \frac{X_2}{X_1} \right| = 36.5 \ \%$$

This value corresponds to the 14 considered subjects.
The calculation of $\sigma_{\hat{r}}$ is totally independent of any
hypothesis on the cardinal utility function.

CHART I (§9.42)

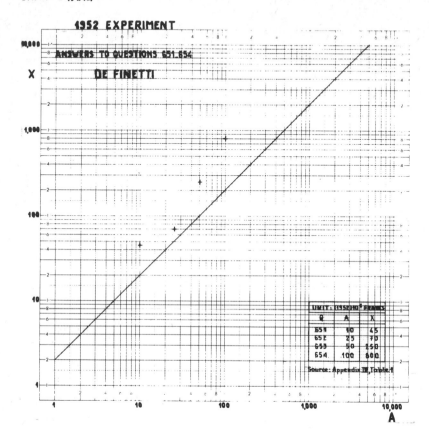

1952 EXPERIMENT

ANSWERS TO QUESTIONS 651-654

DE FINETTI

UNIT: (1952) 10⁵ FRANCS		
Q	A	X
651	50	45
652	25	70
653	50	150
654	100	600

Source: Appendix III, Table 1

CHART Ⅱ (§ 1.5)

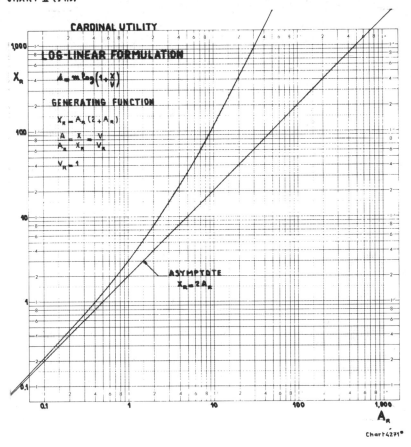

CARDINAL UTILITY

LOG-LINEAR FORMULATION

X_R $A_R = m \log\left(1 + \frac{X}{V}\right)$

GENERATING FUNCTION

$X_R = A_R (2 + A_R)$

$\frac{A}{A_R} = \frac{X}{X_R} = \frac{V}{V_R}$

$V_R = 1$

ASYMPTOTE
$X_R = 2 A_R$

A_R

Chart 4271°

CHART Ⅷ (§5.2, Tables I and Ⅱ, and §5.4)

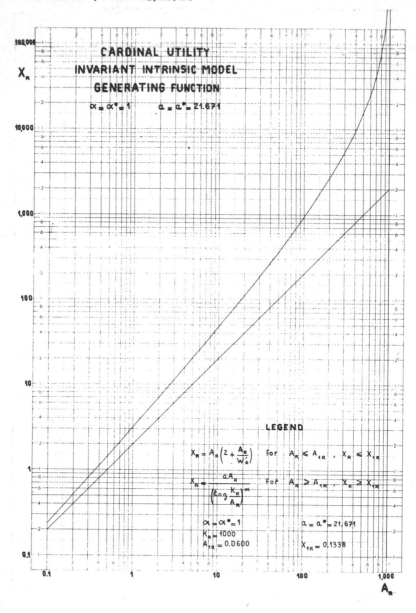

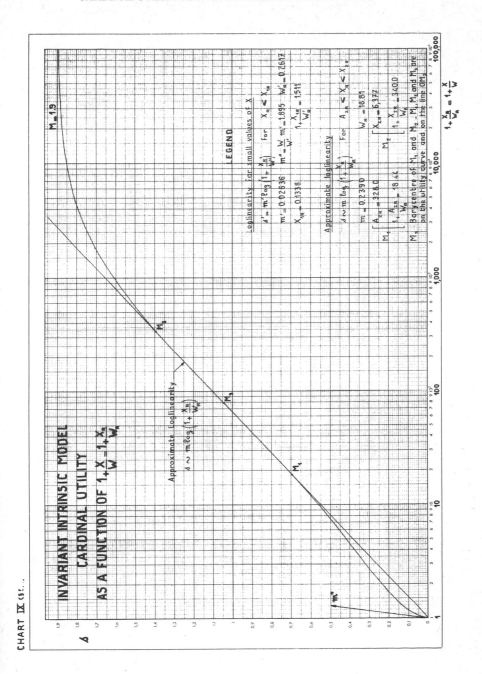

CHART IX (5...

CHART XII (§ 6.11)

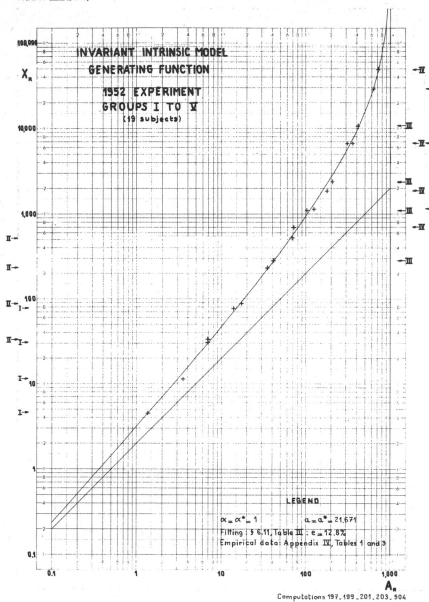

Computations 197_199_201_203_504

CHART XIII (16.14)

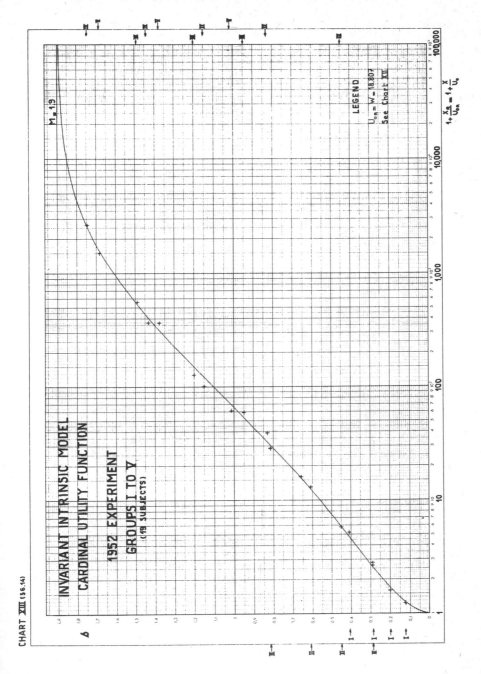

INVARIANT INTRINSIC MODEL
CARDINAL UTILITY FUNCTION

1952 EXPERIMENT
GROUPS I TO V
(19 SUBJECTS)

M = 1.9

LEGEND

$U_{OR} = W = 18.807$

See Chart XII

$1 + \dfrac{X_R}{U_{OR}} = 1 + \dfrac{X}{U_o}$

CHART XIV (§ 6.14)

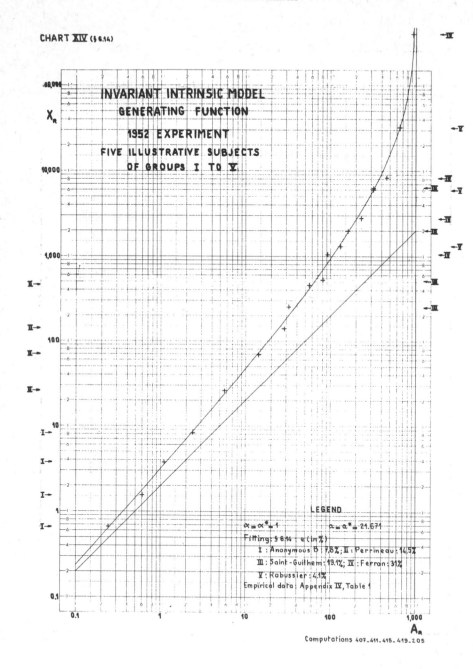

INVARIANT INTRINSIC MODEL
GENERATING FUNCTION
1952 EXPERIMENT
FIVE ILLUSTRATIVE SUBJECTS
OF GROUPS I TO V

LEGEND

$\alpha = \alpha^*= 1$ $\alpha = a^* = 21.671$

Fitting: § 6.14 : e (in %)

I : Anonymous B : 7.8%; II : Perrineau : 14.5%
III : Saint-Guilhem : 19.1%; IV : Ferran : 31%
V : Rabussier : 4.1%
Empirical data : Appendix IV, Table 1

Computations 407_411_415_419_205

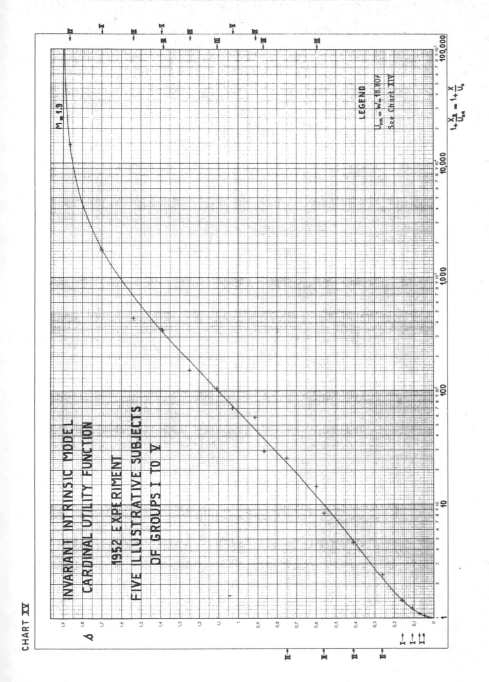

CHART XV

INVARIANT INTRINSIC MODEL
CARDINAL UTILITY FUNCTION

1952 EXPERIMENT
FIVE ILLUSTRATIVE SUBJECTS
OF GROUPS I TO V

LEGEND

$U_{0n} = W = 18.80^{f}$
See chart XIV

$1 + \dfrac{X_a}{U_{0n}} = 1 + \dfrac{X}{U_0}$

CHART XVII (§ 6.2)

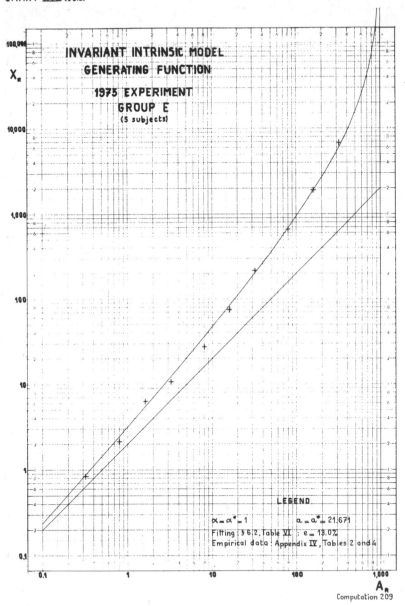

Computation 209

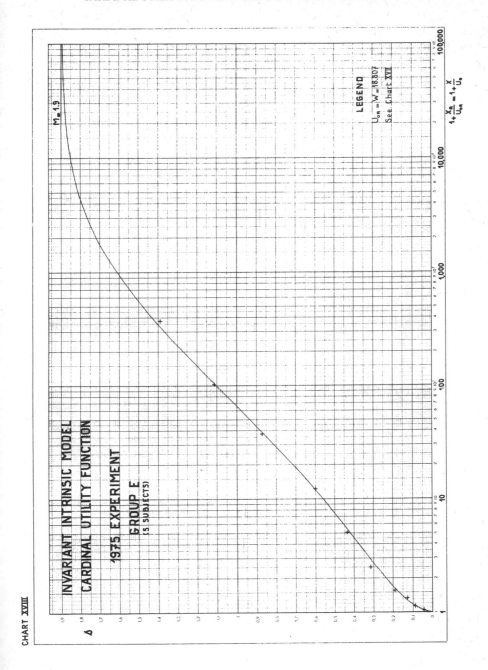

CHART XVIII

INVARIANT INTRINSIC MODEL
CARDINAL UTILITY FUNCTION

1975 EXPERIMENT

GROUP E
(5 SUBJECTS)

$M = 1.9$

LEGEND

$U_{oR} = W = 18.807$
See Chart XVII

$1 + \dfrac{X_R}{U_{oR}} = 1 + \dfrac{X}{U_o}$

CHART **XXI** (§6.3)

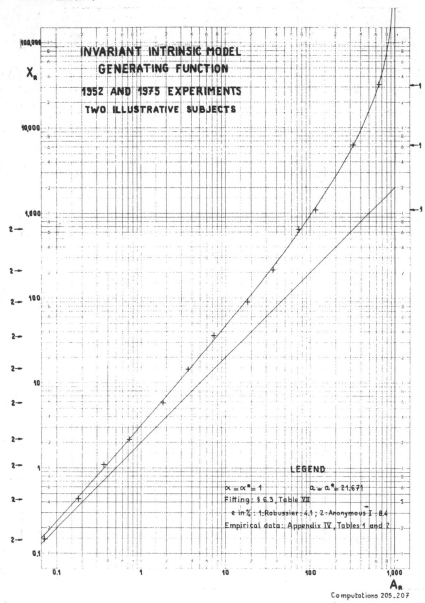

INVARIANT INTRINSIC MODEL
GENERATING FUNCTION

1952 AND 1975 EXPERIMENTS

TWO ILLUSTRATIVE SUBJECTS

LEGEND

$\alpha = \alpha^* = 1$ $a = a^* = 21.671$

Fitting : § 6.3 , Table **VII**

e in % : 1:Robussier : 4.1 ; 2:Anonymous I : 8.4

Empirical data : Appendix **IV** , Tables 1 and 2

Computations 205_207

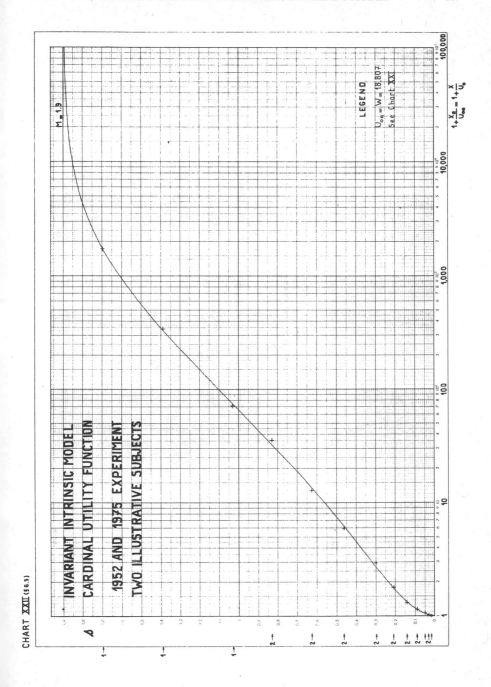

CHART XXII (16.3)

INVARIANT INTRINSIC MODEL
CARDINAL UTILITY FUNCTION

1952 AND 1975 EXPERIMENT
TWO ILLUSTRATIVE SUBJECTS

M = 1.9

LEGEND

$U_{OR} = |W = 18,807$
See Chart XXI

$1 + \dfrac{X_R}{U_{OR}} = 1 + \dfrac{X}{U_O}$

CHART **XXV** (§ 8.3)

CARDINAL UTILITY

AS A FUNCTION OF A VIRTUAL INCREASE X OF THE PSYCHOLOGICAL CAPITAL

ACCORDING TO THE INTRINSIC MODEL

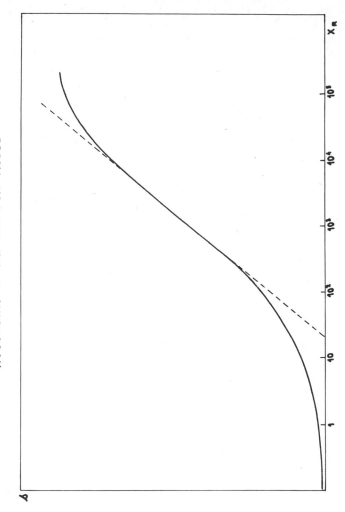

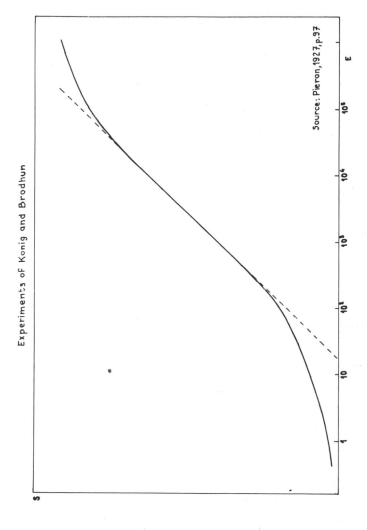

CHART III (§1.56)

PSYCHOPHYSIOLOGICAL SENSATION
AS A FUNCTION OF LUMINOUS STIMULUS

Experiments of König and Brodhun

Source: Piéron, 1927, p. 97

BIBLIOGRAPHY [20]

Allais, Maurice : 1952a, *Fondements d'une Théorie Positive des Choix comportant un Risque et Critique des Postulats et Axiomes de l'Ecole Américaine (Foundations of a Positive Theory of Choice involving Risk, and a Criticism of the Postulates and Axioms of the American School)*, *Econométrie,* Colloques Internationaux du Centre National de la Recherche Scientifique, Vol. XL, Paris, 1953, p.257-332. (See also p. 34-35, 37-39, 40, 47-48, 151-163, 194-197 and 245-247).
  This memoir was republished in Vol. 144 of the *Annales des Mines,* special issue, 1955, and again as a separate volume, under the same title by the Imprimerie Nationale 1955.
—— : 1952b, Le Comportement de l'Homme Rationnel devant le Risque : Critique des Postulats et Axiomes de l'Ecole Américaine (The Behavior of Rational Man facing Risk : Criticism of the Postulates and Axioms of the American School) in *Econometrica,* Vol. 21, n° 4, October 1953, p. 503-546. (Summarised version of the 1952 Memoir).
—— : 1952c, La psychologie de l'homme rationnel devant le risque - La théorie et l'expérience, *Journal de la Société de Statistique de Paris,* January-March 1953, p. 47-73.
—— : 1976, *The Foundations of a Positive Theory of Choice involving Risk and a Criticism of the Postulates and Axioms of the American School,* english translation of the (1952) Memoir, in Allais and Hagen, 1979, p. 27-145.
—— : 1977, *The so-called Allais'Paradox and Rational Decisions under Uncertainty,* in Allais and Hagen, 1979, p. 437-699.
—— : 1983, *The Foundations of the Theory of Utility and Risk Some Central Points of the Discussions at the Oslo Conference* in Hagen and Wenstop, edit., Progress in Decision Theory, Reidel, 1984, p. 3-131.
—— : 1984, The Cardinal Utility and its Determination, Hypotheses, Methods and Empirical Results, *Theory and Decision,* forthcoming.
Allais, Maurice and Hagen, Ole : 1979, *Expected Utility Hypotheses and the Allais' Paradox ; Contemporary Discussions and Rational Decisions under Uncertainty with Allais' Rejoinder,* Reidel, Dordrecht, 1979, 715 p.

Pieron, Henri : 1927, *Psychologie expérimentale,* A. Colin, Paris 220 p.

Georges Bernard

THE PRESENT STATE OF UTILITY THEORY

1. Summary and Conclusion

The present state of the utility theory can be summarized by
four propositions :

1. The utility function u (x) derived from the vNM (von
Neumann & Morgenstern) axiomatics is <u>not</u> the cardinal
utility of the certain outcome x ; this last utility is a
different function v (x).
2. The relation between u and v expresses the utility of
uncertainty. If u = v, as assumed in /14/, the expected
utility, a preference functional among uncertain prospects,
expresses a risk neutral behavior.
3.The axioms of vNM shall be dropped. In particular, single
stage and multiple equivalent bets are not indifferent, i.
e. of equal utility. This proposition, which requires the
abandonment of the independance axiom as expressed by axiom
3:C:b of vNM and by the formulations of Samuelson /2/ and
Malinvaud /3/, is necessary in order to be able to establish
a general utility function of uncertain prospects such that
it covers the intrinsic utility of uncertainty.
4. Such a general utility function is non-linear in proba-
lities.

At present three schools are offered. The first, represented
among others by the three anthors quoted in Section 2 of
this paper, tries to formulate and empirically verify the
points 1 and 2 of this conclusion. The second, of, among
others, the three authors quoted in Section 3 of this paper,
tries to prove conclusions 3 and 4.

My proposal of 1966 - 1974 /19 to 25/ assumes all four conclusions. But it lacks formal proof and is also critized as
it can lead to violations of the principle of dominance. It
is shown in /22/ and recalled here that such violations are
in fact fruitful explanations of possible actual behaviors
and can be considered as rational.

Our younger followers should seek a synthesis of these
schools.

L. Daboni et al. (eds.), Recent Developments in the Foundations of Utility and Risk Theory, 121–138.
© 1986 by D. Reidel Publishing Company.

Introduction

The subject : the utility theory is and has been a most
beaten track. It is and it remains a diffucult theme as its
fundamental character is subjectivity, something quite
strange if not contradictory to a scientific approach. In
consequence, since two centuries or more that it is discussed, utility has arrived at the status of a kind of divi-
nity, protected by priests. An unorthodox opinion was until
quite recently considered a sacrilege. A dogma was taught at
universities all over the world. Since the end of last war
expected utility was such a dogma, its apostles being John
von Neumann and Oscar Morgenstern and its followers
generations of academics.

The situation is now different. Thirty years after the first
blasphemy by M. Allais at the Paris CNRS seminar of 1952,
twenty years after my own effort, the FUR 82 has definitely
cleared the path to new horizons, to a new approach and to
an important progress in our understanding of the problem.

Such an opinion is not only a personal one. At FUR 82 our
distinguished colleague, professor Ole Hagen, stated :
"thirty years ago it was blasphemy and the suicide of an
academic career to hold that the expected utility is unsuf-
ficient. It is today a respectable research effort".

What I will submit here is divided into four sections.

In Section 1 I present a short history of the case. Its
recent period is well illustrated by a list of papers
published in Econometrica /1 to 13/. Of course the
literature on the subject, even if one restricts it to
Econometrica, is not exhausted by my list ; one has only to
refer to the titles found in the references of these
articles.

Sections 2 and 3 describe briefly the first two schools
quoted above. The papers of the six authors are of course
reduced here only to a few sentences each. The interested
readers will find the full texts in /27/,/15/ and /28/.

In Section 4 I recall my own proposal (the "third school")
and its present criticism and draw some economic consequences from its results. The main result is illustrated by an
application of the CEVR utility function. This proposal is
of course subject and open to controversy.

Section 1. History.

It can be dated from Blaise Pascal and the bet of Chevalier de Méré on interrupted dice throws. The story at its beginning is Franco-Swiss, as the Bernoulli family was from Basel. They were the first to formalize the utility of uncertain monetary gains in the St. Petersburg game still now discussed and taught.

Paul Samuelson states in his survey of the St Petersburg paradox /29/ that between 1738, date of the publication of Daniel Bernoulli's memoire and 1934, when Karl Menger published his paper on uncertainty in utility theory, nothing upsetting has been proposed on the subject. In fact in this interval of nearly two hundred years the interested people lived on the distinction between moral and mathematical expectation and also lively participated in the existence quarrel on the cardinality or the ordinality of the utility.

The reference list of Econometrica shows that since 1945 an explosion of new analyses arrived. J. von Neumann and O. Morgenstern publish their Theory of Games in 1944 /14/. In 1952 the French National Research Centre organizes in Paris a seminar on Utility Theory. The sole participant to put to doubt the vNM expected utility is M. Allais and also, to some extent, P. Massé. Allais states and he is perhaps right at the time, that the Franco-Swiss matter of the XVIIIth century has become Franco-American at the beginning of the second half of the XXth. /4/ One can hold that it is today a global one.

Whatever the truth of this last "problem", the dogma of expected utility has been during the thirty years which followed 1945 largely considered as a normative rule of behavior. J. Marschak states : "rationality rules which result in the maximization of expected utility... are as compelling as the rules of arithmetic in numerical calculus or rules of logic in reasoning". Such an opinion is formulated in a commentary of O. Morgenstern's as follows :
"The vNM theory is true in the sense that if somebody's behavior deviates from this rule, he will change his choice when the theory is explained to him".

Outstanding contributions in the literature of this period are those of K.J. Arrow, for instance /1/, W.J. Pratt /6/ as well as two short notes by P. Samuelson /2/and E. Malinvaud /3/ on the independence axiom consistent with the certainty equivalent of a random variable. M. Allais and many others reacted to the reigning theory by counterexamples and bets which they called paradoxes.

They thus followed their ancestors of the XVIIIth century.
M. Allais in particular attached his name to experiments of
choices of extreme values and probabilities or very small
differences in these values or probabilities, which choice
makers often could not grasp. /4/,/15/

The use of paradoxes is quite common and also attractive and
convenient, in many disciplines. The theoretical physics is
full of such cases. They have supplied generations of
academics with easy subjects of manuals, lessons and papers
in journals, so they are quite common in the treatment of
the utility theory, in particular.

Endeavours to prove by experiences the rule of maximization
of expected utility, periodically reported since the Fif-
ties, always failed. In 1979 the group of the Theory & Decision journal published a collective work, edited by M. Allais and O. Hagen /15/. As I wrote in my critique of this
book /24/, its main purpose was the analysis of cases of
non-compliance to the expected utility rule, i. e. of its
axioms, cases continued to be called paradoxes.

The FUR 82 conference, meeting in Norway thirty years after
the French seminar of 1952, was in the mind of its promoters
aimed mainly at the discussion of the Allais - Hagen book.
In fact it brought quite a new and very promising illumina-
tion if not explanation of the difficulties if not inconsis-
tencies of the theory as it stood at its beginning. I called
this conference a watershed event and I do hope that the FUR
84 will be retained as the gusher of a powerful river.

The main result of FUR 82, as I, and I do hope many others
see it, can be spelled out in a few sentences.

vNM formally prove, although in their reasoning there is a
flaw to which we will come later, assumed three sets of
rationality axioms,

(a) the result, known since 200 years, that cardinal utility
of a random variable is measured by the expectation of utilities of the outcomes of this variable :
$$U(X) = \sum pu(x) \quad \text{or} \quad U(X) = \int u(x)\,dF(x)$$
(b) that the function u(x) is a cardinal measure of the utility of the outcome x, defined up to a linear transformation.

We now know that if the second consequence of the vNM
axiomatics is accepted, as the authors of the Theory of
Games have done, the first consequence represents the
behavior (the preference relation on the set of choices) of
a decision maker neutral to risk (or uncertainty, which I
consider identical to risk, see Note in Appendix).

In this case the result is not general but a special one. In the general case u(x) represents in the expression of the utility of a random variable the behavior in the simultaneous presence of the value x and of the uncertainty about its obtaining, i.e. risk aversion or risk love. So in the general case the cardinal utility of the value x is not the function u(x) as specified in the utility U(X) of the random variable, but a distinct function which I will denote, following Krzysztofowicz, v(x). For instance, the measure of risk aversion as proposed by Arrow and Pratt, the relative curvature -u"/u' of the function u, is not a correct one, as this function represents not only the intrinsic utility of risk, such as risk aversion, but also the utility of the value x.

K.J. Arrow formulates this result as follows : (/30/, page 24) : "Suppose the Bernoulli hypothesis is false, but individuals are rational in the weaker sense of Allais and Hicks, there is an ordering of probability distributions. . this means that there is a utility function which depends on x and p and is defined only up to a monotone transformation"

One can add to this formulation that if it is assumed that u≠v, one can continue to accept the expectation of utilities u as the utility of an uncertain prospect. My proposal (/19/ to/25/) does so and proposes as an approximation of the general function u not a linear or quadratic form, as Machina does, but a CEVR function of constant value and risk elasticities. More on my proposal in Section 4.

Those who sticked to the vNM expected utility continued to assert that u is the cardinal utility of the value x, i.e. u=v. They proposed many formulations of this function, such as tha quadratic $u = ax - x^2$ (Markowitz, Borch), exponential $u = 1-e^{-ax}$ (Freund) power $u = x^a$ etc.

But, by confusing u and v, these authors implicitly assumed that the vNM expected utility represented only risk neutral behaviors. By proposing to measure risk aversion (or love) by the analysis of such functions v, they were inconsistent, as v has nothing to do with uncertainty.

Section 2. Empirical Approach.
This approach consists in a definition and measure of the distinct functions u and v and of their relation, by means of experiments on choice-maker samples. A good clarification of this approach is given by A.Camacho /16/. He did not go beyond stating that the mapping of v into u : u = F (v) defines the behaviors in uncertainty. If F is linear, u = v up to a linear transformation.

This is the vNM case and the agent is risk neutral. If F is monotonously increasing and convex, the agent is risk averse if F is concave, he is risk loving .

R. Krzysztofowicz /17/ looks after a theoretical relation between u and v. He writes it u = w (v) and considers the Pratt-Arrow function c (x) = - u"/u' and similar functions m (x) = - v"/v' and n (x) = - w"/w', from which he obtains the mapping function w.
He applies such results to experiments, very illustrating. Few people display risk neutrality, most manifest either risk aversion or risk love ; a person in given circumstances has a stable and consistent behavior.

Mc. Cord & de Neufville /18/ assert that "contrary to vNM axioms utility functions depend on the probability distribution". They obtain experimentally the functions u and v with results quite similar to those of Krzysztofowicz. In a very simple way they assume that the difference u - v defines the intrinsic utility of uncertainty : For u>v the choice maker is risk averse, for u<v he is risk loving and for u = v risk neutral.

Section 3. New Axiomatics.
These axiomatics differ from the one of vNM, as some of their axioms are dropped. It seems useful to reproduce here the three groups of axioms of the Theory of Games, in their original notation (§ 3.6.1 ; page 26 of the paperback edition of 1964, J. Wiley & Sons ; u and v are two utility function of vNM) /14/) :

3 : A Exhaustivity and Transitivity
3 : A : a for any two u, v one and only one of the three following relations holds : > , =, <
3 : A : b   u > v > w ⇒ u > w
3 : B Ordering and Combining, which I would call Convexity
u ≷ v ⇒ u ≷ αu + (1 - α) v
u > w > v ⇒ αu + (1 - α) v > w

3 : C Algebra of Combining
3 : C : b α/βu + (1 - β)v/ + (1 - α)v = γu + (1 - γ)v where
γ = αβ
3:C:b is a formulation of what is called the axiom of independence.

M. Allais is of the opinion that axiom 3 : B excludes the intrinsic utility of uncertainty. We interpret this position as signifying that u = v (in our natation where u is the vNM utility function and v utility in certainty).
But M. Allais on one side drops the axiom 3 :B and on the other states that u = v. This seems to be his disagreement

with what has been described in Section 2, where experiments have shown that u ≠ v. M. Allais further considers that vNM erred when they wrote (page 632 of /14/): "(The axiom 3:C:b) expresses the combination rule for multiple chance alternatives and it is plausible that a specific utility or disutility of gambling can only exist if this simple combination rule is abandonned".
M. Allais retains this axiom 3 : C : b.

It seems to me, considering the present state of the theory, that both axioms 3 : B and 3 : C should be dropped, the group 3 : A remaining, if a consistent theory of utility in uncertainty is to built, including the intrinsic utility of the uncertainty. The conjecture of vNM was, in my opinion, incomplete but correct.

M. Allais in /28/ replaces the axiom 3 : B by a new one, which he calls of "cardinal isovariation" and finally obtains the following expression of the utility of a random variable :

with
$$u (C + V) = \bar{u} + r/\psi(u - \bar{u})/$$
$$\bar{u} = \mu_1 = \int_{-\infty}^{\infty} u \, \psi(u) \, du$$
$$r = f (\mu_2, \mu_3 - - - \mu_n)$$
$$u = u (C + g)$$

where g is the "gain", C is wealth, u is cardinal utility, V the monetary value of the random variable considered, which has the probability density function $\psi(u)$, $\bar{u}$ is the first moment of u and μ_n moments of higher order of u. The function r represents the specific element of risk. For r = 0, the formulation reduces to the vNM expected utility. This last utility thus does not take into account the instrinsic utility of uncertainty.

As I understand this proposal, it amounts to measure the utility of a random variable (of an uncertain prospect...) by the vNM utility, denoted $\bar{u}$, to which is added a function of moments of higher order (greater than one) of the distribution and also of the distribution of the deviations of the cardinal utility u with respect to its expectation.

Ole Hagen (/15/, page 27) postulates that the utility U of a random variable is a function of the expectation of utilities of values (hence u = v in our notation), denoted $\hat{u}$, and of all moments of higher order. This is similar to the formulation of Allais. But Hagen proposes an approximation of the general function by
$$U = \hat{u} + f (s, z) + \varepsilon$$
where f expresses the intrinsic utility of uncertainty by means of s, standard deviation of u and of z = $m_3 : s^2$, the ratio of the third moment to variance.

ε is an error element. So in this approximation Hagen more explicity abandons linearity of utility in probability, i. e. the independence axiom.

Mark Machina, /13/ and /27/, does so in en even more explicit way as his initial contribution at the FUR 82 as well as his Econometrica paper is called "Expected Utility Without the Independence Axiom".

It is not easy to summarize his approach. He starts with a clear opposition to the normative nature which several authors wanted to attach to the expected utility rule. He agrees that in order to include the specific utility of uncertainty it is necessary to establish a non-linear relation between utilities and probabilities of outcomes, which amounts to abandoning the independence axiom.

His proposal consists of a local function of utility, which would retain the linearity in probabilities and would in a sense be tangent to the general function, this last being non-linear, not respecting the independence axiom. The new axiom of Machina is the one of differentiability. He calls it the axiom of "smoothness of preferences over alternative probability distributions".

The Fréchet differentiability of the function U allows Machina to formally obtain an expression of a preference functional V (F) such that a differential variation between utilities of F^+ and F (i. e. the preference of F^+ over F) is

$$V(F^+) - V(F) = \int U(x,F)(dF^+ - dF) + o(\| F^+ - F \|)$$

where U is the local function, linear in probabilities and respecting the vNM axioms.

For an approximation of o Machina proposes the "quadratic form"

$$\frac{1}{2} \left[\int S(x) \, dF(x) \right]^2 = \left[E_F(S(x)) \right]^2$$

This proposal is too not very different from those of Allais and Hagen. But it drops explicitly the independence axiom.

In general the a priori rationality of the new axioms, of "cardinal isovariation" by Allais or of "Fréchet differentiability" by Machina is not clearly perceived, at least by the undersigned.

Section 4. My own proposal and its economic consequences. Risk pooling.

It seems useful to recall here that the understanding of the vNM utility function u as obtained formally from their axioms of rational behavior is equivalent to three conclusions : (a) the utility of a probability distribution (the

preference functional) is apparently, but not really, linear
in probabilities, (b) the vNM utility function u is defined
up to a linear transformation and (c) the rationality axioms
of vNM are respected, in particular the independence axiom
stating indifference between compound and equivalent simple
bets.

There is however a difficulty in the formal deduction of the
function u from the axioms, as done by the authors of the
Theory of Games. They use the certainty aquivalence
principle for the bet$<x_1, p, x_2>$, compared to the certain
value x and write it, as we now understand, in an inconsistent manner :

$$u (x) = pu (x_1) + (1 - p) u (x_2)$$

while it should be written

$$v (x) = pu (x_1) + (1 - p) u (x_2)$$

K.J. Arrow states this difficulty as follows (/30/, page 29)
: "The identification of certainty aquivalents requires
comparison of two alternatives, one risky, one certain,
which are far from each other in any reasonable metric". If,
as the undersigned has proposed twenty years ago and Arrow
now suggests (quoted in Section 1, see /30/ page 24), the
dependence of the function u on probabilities is explicited
by replacing u (x) by u (x, p), formally the three
conclusions hereabove cannot stand, while the principle of
expected utility maximisation does stand.

If, as several authors at FUR 82 have contended explicitly
or implicitly (Allais, Hagen, Machina, Pope and others), the
identity of u and v stands, the certainty equivalence
principle stands but the expected utility cannot represent
all possible behaviors.

To do so, one must abandon some rationality axioms, for
instance the independence axiom. So these authors endeavour
to formulate new axiomatics and new axpression of utilities
of probability distributions, or preference functionals in
uncertainty.

My own proposal (/19/ to /25/) consists in writing u (x) a
priori as u (x, p) and proposing an approximation of this
general function, within the middle range of values and
probabilities, by a CEVR function of constant value and
risk elasticities. This simple and operational proposal
implies the distinction between u and v and also abandons
the rationality axiom of independence. It is thus a synthesis of the two approaches briefly described in Sections 2
and 3 above.

My proposal has been critized by Allais and Machina with
opposite arguments.

These arguments as well as the certainty equivalence principle and the "certainty effect" of Tversky, are conveniently
clarified by recalling § V.1 (page 217) of /22/) which bears
the subscript "The inconsistency of the CEVR function".

A simple bet $\langle x_1, p, x_2, \rangle$ already quoted above, is discussed ; one assumes $x_1 > x_2$ and one can write :
$$u_1 = v\ (x_1)\quad u_2 = v\ (x_2),\quad v\ (x) = p\ u\ (x_1,\ p) + q\ u\ (x_2, q)$$
$(q = 1 - p)$

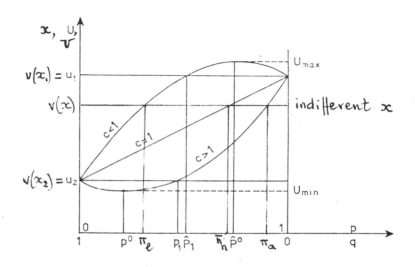

$c < 1$ risk loving
$c = 1$ risk neutral
$c > 1$ risk averse
π_ℓ probability of a bet indiffferent to x for risk loving
π_n the same for risk neutral
π_a the same for risk averse persons

It is clear that (i) for risk loving persons for $\hat{p} < p < 1$ and
for risk averse persons for $0 < p < p^o$ the stochastic
dominance principle is violated. This is the argument of
Machina. But if $x_2 \to 0$, $u_2 \to o$ or if $x_2 < 0$, the gambler pays
a stake, this violation ceases and the dominance principle
is respected. It is shown in /22/ that the range of
violation is in real situations always small if any.
If nevertheless the violation exists, it is also explained
in the paper that such a violation is rational : a strongly
risk averse person can prefer a certain small prize to a

lottery with small positive probability of winning a greater
prize ; a strongly risk loving person can prefer on the
contrary a lottery with a probability less than one of winning the greater prize to the certain gain of this prize.
(ii) If now $x_1 \rightarrow x_2$, $u_1 \rightarrow u_2$, dominance is violated for
smaller risk love or risk aversion. This too is sensible;
but if $x_1 = x_2$, all uncertainty ceases ; the whole picture
is as absurd as dividing a finite number by zero. This is
the argument of Allais.
Fig. 2 shows also the reality of the "certainty effect":
$u(x_1, p) \rightarrow v(x_1)$ when $p \rightarrow 1$ and $u(x_2, q) \rightarrow v(x_2)$ when
$p \rightarrow 0$, $q \rightarrow 1$. If the vNM function is assumed, there is a
discontinuity at these limits. (See/12/)
One can also scale the vertical axis in the "indifferent
certain value x" ; the indifferent bet for this value varies
according to the intrinsic utility of risk, as shown. On can
write $v(x) = pv(x_1) + (1 - p) v(x_2)$ only if the   choice
maker is risk neutral, $u = v$.

The economic consequences of this approach are quite significant. They are the consequence of what Professor Robin
Pope called at the FUR 82 the "Risk Pooling".

I remember that one of my colleagues objected, in 1964, when
I discussed with him the CEVR function, with a following
argument : if the independence axiom is dropped, which
states indifference between one stage and two or more stages
games, then one could obtain fair gains by mere aggregation
of bets. This would be equivalent to bying two dollars with
one. In my opinion this is exactly what happens at horse
races with the pari mutuel or the bookmaker trade ; it is
present in many games against a banker, in lotteries and,
with a much greater economic importance, within the insurance industry. The trade between agents who have different
attitudes towards risk, more formally whose intrinsic risk
utility is different, allows for such fair gains. And this
reality cannot be covered by the expected utility theory,
as, what my colleague correctly expressed, the independence
axiom eliminates any "irrational" trading of one dollar
against two . . .

The simplified example of insurance which I developed in my
1966 and 1974 papers clearly illustrates the point. It
shows by means of the CEVR function how risk pooling by the
insurance company makes its activity profitable while
increasing the utility of the purchaser of insurance. If
they were not rather complicated, the formulations of Allais
Hagen and Machina should be able to present the same results.

My example is a simple case of fire insurance :

Let s be the annual premium and S the probable damage in the same period. S is in reality a random variable of an experimentally known distribution. We will simplify by considering a single loss S, whose probability of obtaining is p, so that this distribution is reduced to : loss S with probability p and loss O with probability q = 1 - p.
Let c and a be the elasticities of the utility with respect to risk and value.

Bying insurance is advantageous for the owner of the asset if disU (s) = s^a $\leqslant$ disU (S) = $S^a p^c$
(the loss of the premium is certain, the loss by fire uncertain)
By taking logarithms : logs $\leqslant$ log S - rc/a, where
  r = - log p is a measure of risk, conveniently made in decibels (dB)
This formula for a "fair" premium differs from the usual "pure" premium s^o in the classical insurance theory
  log S^o $\leqslant$ log S - r
The difference, in logarithms, between a fair premium according to the CEVR utility function and the classical pure premium is log s - log s^o = r (1 - c/a)
Assume c = 1,1, a normal fear of risk, a = 1,222, a high value, indicating that the purchaser of insurance will be almost ruined if his uninsured property burns up. We have c/a = 0,9 and log s - log s^o = 0,1r
Suppose that the probability of fire during the period is 0,001, r = 30 dB, then
          log s = log s^o = 3 dB
The fair premium is twice the pure premium, for our figures, of course made to deliver this result.

The insurance compagny, operating on a large population of customers, has different value and risk elasticities. If we assume that for it a = c = 1, the pure premium (the vNM expected utility) represents for the compagny its pure cost of selling this insurance so that it earns, by risk pooling, a certain gross profit equal to the difference s - s^o in dollars. This profit is equitable, as both sides increase their utility by contracting.
The elasticity a is greater for poorer purchasers of insurance, as ruin is nearer for them. Thus rich people overpay insurance, when they buy it a standard rates, while the poor underpay it. The insurance industry is a positive factor of redistribution of wealth.

The reality just described by this simplified case is an important economic fact.

Such exchanges with significant increases of utility for both trading partners generate savings of the same kind as other price included transfers (PIT's). Risk pooling is an economic phenomenon worth of further study. By the way, it is one of two such effects, essentially due to uncertainty in human activity. The second such effect is well known within the banking industry. Banks consolidate or pool checking and other accounts. Such accounts are redeemable on sight or within a specified delay. But the statistical effect of their large number allows banks to offset a part of this liability in their balance sheets against long term assets, as practically never all creditors will ask to redeem their account at the same time. This elemantary reality creates for the bank a possibility of investment, i. e. a macroeconomic saving in a way quite similar to the effect on insurance companies of the intrinsic utility of uncertainty implied by the non respect of the independence axiom.

APPENDIX

Note.

This paper may puzzle for two reasons : (a) the words uncertainty and risk are used indiscriminately in the text and
(b) no mention is made of the large literature on subjective
probability, for instance the works of Savage, Luce &
Raiffa, Schlaifer, de Finetti and others.

I owe an explanation of these two deficiencies. They are
intentional.

May I quote what I published in the second volume of the
results of FUR 82, under the title "Progress in Utility and
Risk Theory /28, part II/ (quote)

"The distinction between risk and uncertainty, as commonly
met in the literature, since F.H. Knight. . . defines "uncertainty" as absence of knowledge about probability distributions and "risk" as a situation in which such information
is available. In my opinion this distinction is arbitrary
and confusing and does not represent actual states. The
problem is of the amount of information available on uncertainty, a term formally defined as the set of states comple-
mentary to the set of certain states, thus contrary to certainty. There is a scale of possible degrees of information
about uncertainty, by large not a measure nor even a compact
bounded interval, but what one may call a quantification of
some sort . . . What is called "risk" in the literature is
such a degree of information on uncertainty which allows to
assume a probability distribution, more or less objective.
And what is usually called "uncertainty" is unrealistic. In
all cirumstances a choice-maker can bet, i. e. assume a
purely intuitive or subjective probability distribution.
Once such a quantification is made, it should be used in the
same way throughout an application to an utility theory, i.
e. when formalizing preferences over distributions. This
requirement rules out all ways proposed by Savage, Marschak,
de Finetti, Harsanyi and many others. In short, these scho-
lars propose to assume that an educated gambler tossing dice
will change in his mind the probability of obtaining a six
according to his or her aversion or love of winning or
losing or even of the mere act of gambling. Such an assumption hurts common sense. On the contrary, personal utility being subjective per definition, it is not irrational
to include in this subjectivity the behaviors in the presence of uncertainty. Thus it is consistent to assume that

the utility function u, for instance in the vNM expected
utility rule, is dependent not only on the value of the
outcome but also on the probability of its obtaining. In
other terms and in order to drive home the point by repeating it, the probability can be objective, for repeated
events. On the contrary objective personal utility is contradictory, an inconsistent definition. This is why the
approach made by vNM and developed at the FUR 82 - and by
myself since twenty years-is consistent.
The distinction between value and its utility has the same
character. Value can be and most often is objective. Utility
never is. (unquote)

In fact I would like to correct here this last opinion. Only
personal utility is per definition subjective. Social, i. e.
collective utility can in a sense be "objectivized".

I am not going to take on here the quasi philosophical or at
least ethical quarrel about libertarian aggregation of
utilities or the exogeneous character of social utility, but
only show on two examples how such social "objective"
utility can, at least in theory, be measured.

First example : the utility of life (the disutility of
death) is for each human perfectly subjective. This disutility can generally speaking be considered as very great if
not infinite. Now socially the utility of one death can very
well be statisically measured.
Suppose on a road crossing statistics show x fatal accidents
per year. If now this crossing, by an investment of a given
sum of money I is improved, say by an underpass, and the
statistics show a decrease in the x accidents, say to y, by
dividing the investment I by the difference (x-y) a "value
of one death" is obtained ; and it is per definition objective.
Second example : The utility or, better said, the ethics of
abortion and euthanasia (the beginning and the end of life)
are, from the point of individuals concerned, choices of
essentially subjective utility. The woman and the old person
are sole judges. But socially the utility of allowing
abortion is objective with arguments such as preventing
clandestine interventions, promoting or on the contrary
fighting against natality. As regards euthanasia, while
social tabous affect such acts with a strong "objective"
disutility, similar arguments to those of the road accidents
in the first example can eventually be put forward, by ta-
kinginto account the cost of the care of terminal patients.

Such cases occur even now and the subjective utility of
persons incapable of choice is in fact incapable too to
influence the decision. Social or objective utility, based
for instance on religious grounds, must be substituted.

C.N.R.S.
Paris

REFERENCES

A. ECONOMETRICA

1. K.J. ARROW Alternative Approaches to the Theory of Choice in Risk-taking Situations (19), 4, October 1951 404-438
2. P.A. SAMUELSON Probability, Utility and the Independence Axiom (20), 4, October 1952
3. E. MALINVAUD Note on the vNM Strong Independence Axiom (20), 4 October 1952 679-680
4. M. ALLAIS Le Comportement de l'Homme Rationel Devant le Risque (21), Oct 1953 503-546
5. R.J. FREUND The introduction of Risk Into a Programming Model (24), 3, July 1956 253-26
6. J.W. PRATT Risk Aversion in the Small and in the Large (32) 1-2, Jan. Apr. 1964 122-137.
7. G. BERNARD On Utility Functions (35) 5 supp. 1967 24-25
8. J.E. STIGLITZ Behavior Towards Risk With Many Commodities (37), 4 Oct. 1969 660-668
9. E. MALINVAUD First Order Certainty Equivalence (37), 4 Oct. 1969 706-718
10. W.R. RUSSELL & TAE KUN SEO Admissible Sets of Utility Functions in Expected Utility Maximization (46), 1 Jan. 1978 181-184
11. L. SELDEN A New Representation of Preferences Over Certain and Uncertain Consumption Pairs. The Ordinal Certainty Equivalent Hypothesis (46), 5 Sep. 1978 1045-1060
12. D. KAHNEMAN & A TVERSKY An Analysis of Decision Under Risk (47), 2 March 1979 263-292
13. M.J. MACHINA "Expected Utility" Analysis Without the Independence Axiom (50), 2 March 1982 277-324

B. OTHERS

14. J. von NEUMANN & O. MORGENSTERN The Theory of Games and Economic Behavior Princeton 1947
15. M. ALLAIS & O. HAGEN (Eds) Expected Utility Hypotheses and the Allais Paradox 1979 Reidel
16. A. CAMACHO Cardinal Utility and Decision Making Under Uncertainty /27/, pp. 347-371
17. R.KRZYSTOFOWICZ Risk Attitude Hypotheses of Utility Theory /27/ pp. 201-217
18. M. McCORD & R. de NEUFVILLE Fundamental Deficiency of Expected Utility /27/ pp. 181-201
19. G. BERNARD Réduction du paradoxe de St. Petersbourg par la théorie de l'utilité, C.R. de l'Académie des Sciences 1964 (259), 3168-3170

20. G. BERNARD Jeu de St. Petersbourg généralisé C.R. de l'Académie des Sciences 1966 (262) 240-242
21. G. BERNARD Sur les fonctions d'utilité Revue Fse de R.O. 1966 N° 41 323-352
22. G. BERNARD On Utility Functions, Theory & Decision 1974 (5) 205-242
23. G. BERNARD Note on Two Applications of the CEVR Utility Function, Theory & Decision 1978 (9) 199-203
24. G. BERNARD Review of /15/ Kyklos vol 34 1981 Fasc. 1 106-109
25. G. BERNARD Deterrence, Utility and Rational Choice - A Comment Theory & Decision 1982 (14) 89-97
26. G. BERNARD On Utility Functions ; Present State Theory & Decision 1984 (17) 97-100
27. B.P. STIGUM & F. WINSTØP (Eds) Foundations of Utility and Risk Theory With Applications Reidel 1983
28. F. WINSTØP & O. HAGEN Progress in Utility and Risk Theory Reidel 1984
29. P.A. SAMUELSON St. Peterburg Paradoxes . . . Journal of Economic Literature (15) 1977
30. K.J. ARROW in /27/ pp. 19-32 Behavior Under Uncertainty and Its Implications for Policy.

Allan Gibbard

A CHARACTERIZATION OF DECISION MATRICES THAT YIELD INSTRUMENTAL EXPECTED UTILITY*

In this paper, conditions are given under which decision matrices yield the kind of expected utility proposed by Stalnaker (1972). This is the kind of expected utility that Harper and I (1978) called $\mathcal{U}$-utility; in this paper I call it *instrumental expected utility*.

Decision matrices play a central role in Savage's argument (1954, 1972) that rationality involves expected utility maximization. The premises of Savage's argument consist of postulates governing an agent's preference ordering of the acts in a decision matrix. Even a reader skeptical of the notions of subjective probability, utility, and expected utility is supposed to recognize Savage's postulates as requirements of rationality. Understanding Savage's argument, then, must involve understanding decision matrices.

What, then, should Savage's argument be taken to show? Savage speaks at times as if his goal were to provide a behavioristic account of utility and subjective probability. The account he offers, though, is far from behavioristic. His argument invokes an elaborate set of assumptions for which he provides no behavioristic test: that, for instance, the agent identifies each act open to him with a function from states to outcomes (p. 14).

I take the interest of Savage's argument not to be in its behaviorism, but rather to be as follows. The argument is directed to people who are skeptical of the notions of subjective probability and utility, and skeptical of the claim that in all cases, ideal rationality involves expected utility maximization. Subjective probability and utility are quantitative notions— suspiciously quantitative, a non-Bayesian may feel—and it is these quantitative notions Savage's argument is meant to support. His audience is assumed to understand and accept various qualitative notions. One such notion is that of belief with certainty; indeed, the audience is supposed already to understand what it is for the agent to believe that the outcome of act a in state S is O. No behavioristic test for whether the subject has this belief is required for the purposes of such an argument.

The explication of decision matrices in this paper has a dual purpose. One is to explain the role decision matrices play in uncritical calculations of expected utility; the other is to explain the role they play in Savage's

* Earlier versions of this paper were presented at the University of Pittsburgh and the University of Michigan, and I am grateful for the helpful discussion on both occasions.

L. Daboni et al. (eds.), Recent Developments in the Foundations of Utility and Risk Theory, 139–148.
© *1986 by D. Reidel Publishing Company.*

argument. For the latter purpose—if I am right about the force of Savage's argument—decision matrices must be explicated in qualitative terms that could be understood by an audience skeptical of quantitative subjective probability and utility. For the former purpose, quantitative notions may be used: the goal should be to show that if expected utility is calculated from decision matrices as explicated in this paper, then it does indeed capture the quantitative notion of instrumental expected utility. A qualitative notion used for the second purpose may constitute a special, extreme case of a quantitative notion used for the first purpose.

The primitive, qualitative notions I shall use are these. (1) *Belief.* $K(P)$ will mean that the subject believes proposition P with certainty. Its quantitative expression, in terms of the agent's subjective probability measure ρ, is $\rho(P) = 1$. (2) *Conditional belief.* $K(P/Q)$ will mean that the subject is disposed to believe P given Q, in the sense that if he were to learn Q and nothing else, he would then believe P. The quantitative expression of $K(P, Q)$ is $\rho(P/Q) = 1$. (3) *Bringing about* and *instrumental independence*, which will be explicated in terms of a conditional connective '$\square\!\rightarrow$'. A sentence $a\,\square\!\rightarrow P$ is to be read, "If I were now to do a, then P would obtain." I take the moral of a number of recent studies (Lewis, 1976; Gibbard and Harper, 1978) to be that a person's instrumental beliefs cannot be deduced from the subjective probabilities he ascribes to non-causal propositions, so that for purposes of decision theory, an agent's causal beliefs must be represented explicitly. An agent's belief that he is faced with a certain decision matrix is causal: it involves the belief that the states of the matrix are causally independent of what he does, and beliefs about what the causal consequences would be of each act in each state of that matrix. (4) *Basic value.* An agent may care intrinsically whether a given proposition obtains, or he may not. Corresponding to this qualitative notion of intrinsically caring, Harman (1967) has developed a quantitative notion of *basic intrinsic value*, which I shall shorten to *basic value*. That an agent intrinsically cares whether P holds will be expressed quantitatively by saying that P has non-zero basic intrinsic value; in that case, I shall say qualitatively that the proposition is *basically valued*. Section 2 says more about this.

1. Propositions, Acts, and Action Conditionals

The chief tools used to construct the theory of this paper will be *propositions* of various kinds. Propositions in the theory are versatile: they are the bearers of probability, and they are the objects of wanting. When the agent wants something, that is to say, what he wants is that some proposition hold: If I want happiness, I want it to be true that I will be happy. Propositions of certain kinds, moreover, will turn out to constitute the states of the matrix formulation of decision theory, and sets of propositions will constitute the outcomes.

Propositions for our purposes can be identified with sets. The members of these sets are possible worlds, or maximally specific states of affairs; a proposition is identified with the set of possible worlds in which it obtains. "Events" as decision theorists commonly use the term will here be treated as propositions of a certain kind. For any proposition Q and possible world w, either Q obtains in w or $\overline{Q}$ obtains in w. (Here and throughout this paper, a bar indicates negation, so that $\overline{Q}$ is the negation of Q). To say that propostions P *entails* proposition Q, or $P \Rightarrow Q$, is just to say that $P \subseteq Q$.

The *acts* in the matrix formulation will receive little analysis here. A matrix represents a decision problem confronting an agent at a time; the agent and time will be said to constitute an *occasion*. I shall speak of the *alternatives open to* an agent *at* a time, or *open on* an occasion; these alternatives are to be understood as the maximally specific acts which the agent is certain he can perform at that time. The set $\mathcal{A}$ of alternatives open to an agent at a time t, then, has the following properties: For each act a in $\mathcal{A}$, the agent believes he can perform a at t; he believes that at t, he cannot jointly perform any two distinct acts in $\mathcal{A}$; and he believes that at t, he cannot avoid performing some act in $\mathcal{A}$. For the sake of simplicity, I shall assume that $\mathcal{A}$ is finite. Throughout the rest of this paper, the letters 'a' and 'b', with or without subscripts, will be used as variables whose values are acts in the set $\mathcal{A}$, and capital letters will be used for propositions.

I shall write "If I were to do a then P would obtain" as "$a \,\square\!\!\rightarrow P$" (See Stalnaker, 1968). To say that $a \,\square\!\!\rightarrow P$ is not to say that the agent's doing a would bring it about that P. It is rather to say that either his doing a would bring it about that P, or P would hold independently of whether or not he did a. In this way, '$\square\!\!\rightarrow$' is explained in terms of 'bringing about' and 'independence'. In what follows, the direction of explanation will be reversed. Logical properties will be ascribed to $\square\!\!\rightarrow$, and then what it is for P to be a consequence of a, and what it is for P to hold independently of what the agent does, will be put in terms of '$\square\!\!\rightarrow$'. Q is a *consequence* of act a iff $a \,\square\!\!\rightarrow Q$ and for some alternative b to a, $b \,\square\!\!\rightarrow \overline{Q}$. Q is *causally act-independent* iff either for every $a \in \mathcal{A}$, $a \,\square\!\!\rightarrow Q$ or for every $a \in \mathcal{A}$, $a \,\square\!\!\rightarrow \overline{Q}$.

Thus on the view in this paper, an action conditional $a \,\square\!\!\rightarrow Q$ is a proposition of a special kind. We can say the following about the logical properties of '$\square\!\!\rightarrow$'. To each alternative $a \in \mathcal{A}$ is associated a possible world w_a, *the world that would obtain were a performed*. Where $a \in \mathcal{A}$ and Q is a proposition, $a \,\square\!\!\rightarrow Q$ is a proposition which is true iff Q obtains in w_a. I shall suppose (although it is not part of Stalnaker's logic) that where a and b are alternatives open on the same occasion, $b \,\square\!\!\rightarrow (a \,\square\!\!\rightarrow Q)$ is the same proposition as $a \,\square\!\!\rightarrow Q$. The agent believes that he will perform exactly one of the acts in $\mathcal{A}$, and so he believes

$$(\forall a)(a \,\square\!\!\rightarrow Q) \longrightarrow Q, \tag{1}$$

that if Q would obtain whatever he did, then Q is true. Because of this, he believes that

$$(\forall a)(a \,\square\!\!\rightarrow Q) \vee (\forall a)(a \,\square\!\!\rightarrow \overline{Q}) \tag{2}$$

obtains if and only if

$$(\forall a)[(a \,\square\!\!\rightarrow Q) \longleftrightarrow Q] \tag{3}$$

obtains; he can thus regard (2) and (3) as alternative ways of saying that Q is causally act-independent.

Because either Q or $\overline{Q}$ obtains in w_a, we have

$$(a \,\square\!\!\rightarrow \overline{Q}) \longleftrightarrow \neg(a \,\square\!\!\rightarrow Q). \tag{4}$$

Where $\mathcal{Q}$ is a set of propositions, let $\mathbf{aut}\mathcal{Q}$ be the proposition that exactly one member of $\mathcal{Q}$ obtains, and let $\mathbf{aut}_{Q:Q\in\mathcal{Q}}(a \,\square\!\!\rightarrow Q)$ be the proposition that exactly one of the propositions $a \,\square\!\!\rightarrow Q$ with $Q \in \mathcal{Q}$ obtains. Then we have

$$(a \,\square\!\!\rightarrow \mathbf{aut}\mathcal{Q}) \longleftrightarrow \mathbf{aut}_{Q:Q\in\mathcal{Q}}(a \,\square\!\!\rightarrow Q),$$

since each side holds iff $\mathbf{aut}\mathcal{Q}$ obtains in w_a.

Finally, if P entails Q, so that Q holds in every world in which P holds, then $a \,\square\!\!\rightarrow P$ entails $a \,\square\!\!\rightarrow Q$. For let P entail Q, and let $a \,\square\!\!\rightarrow P$ hold in world w. Then P holds in w_a, therefore Q holds in w_a, and hence $a \,\square\!\!\rightarrow Q$ holds in w.

These are all the special properties of '$\square\!\!\rightarrow$' that the agent need accept for what follows. He is supposed to accept all logical consequences of those propositions he accepts, and in any context in which he is supposed to ascribe subjective probabilities to propositions, it is supposed that those ascriptions satisfy the standard laws of probability. That means that the theory is one of ideal rationality, not of humanly attainable rationality.

2. Value

"Value", as I shall be using the term, is a matter of what the agent wants, or what his goals are. The expected utility of an act is, roughly put, the expected degree to which performing the act would bring about the achievement of the agent's goals. The task of this section is to find a system for characterizing an agent's goals that will fit into a formula for expected utility.

One clear, systematic way to represent the goals of an agent is by a function which, for each possible world, gives the degree to which his goals are satisfied in that world. I shall call such a function $\mathcal{V}$ a *world-value function*. To see how such a function might work, suppose that I am an egoistic hedonist: I want as great a balance of pleasure over pain in my life as possible. We can characterize my goals by saying that for any world w, the degree $\mathcal{V}(w)$ to which w satisfies my goals equals the total amount of pleasure I have in w minus the total amount of pain I have in w. When I speak of the *value* of a possible world w for an agent, or simply its *value*, I shall mean this quantity $\mathcal{V}(w)$, the degree to which the agent's goals are satisfied in that world.

If the number of possible worlds is finite, then the world-value function $\mathcal{V}$ gives all the information about the agent's goals that is needed in a theory of expected utility maximization. The *instrumental expected utility* of an act a can then be defined by the formula,

$$\mathcal{U}(a) = \sum_w \rho(a \,\square\!\!\rightarrow w)\mathcal{V}(w). \qquad (5)$$

It remains to be seen whether in the cases I want to consider—cases in which there are an enormous but finite number of possible worlds—the agent's goals can be put in a less global, more perspicuous form than that given by the world-value function $\mathcal{V}$. Now the value of a possible world for an agent presumably depends in some way on the propositions that hold in that world. The agent will value a world to the degree, roughly, that propositions he wants to be true hold in that world and propositions he wants to be false do not. The value of a world for an agent should be, in some sense, the sum of the values of the propositions which hold in that world.

Getting a theory of value for propositions can be a tricky matter, especially if the values of the propositions that hold in any world w are to add up to the value $\mathcal{V}(w)$ of that world. In what follows, I draw heavily on Harman (1967). Take these two propositions.

H : I am happy.

J : The cow jumps over the moon.

Suppose I want H to hold and don't care about J. I then, we might suppose, value the proposition $H\&J$ because it entails H. Let w be a possible world in which both H and J hold. Then the proposition $H\&J$ holds in w, and if I get the value $\mathcal{V}(w)$ of w by adding the values of the propositions that hold in it, I will inclued in the sum both the value of H and the value of $H\&J$. But $H\&J$ has value for me only because it entails h, and so in effect I have counted the value of H twice.

To deal with the problem, Harman proposes a kind of value he calls *basic intrinsic value*, and which I shall call *basic value*. Where the *intrinsic value* of a proposition is the degree to which its holding is valued for its own sake, its *basic value* is the part of its intrinsic value which does not derive from the intrinsic value of propositions which it properly entails—that is to say, which it entails but is not entailed by. In the example, then, the intrinsic value of $H\&J$ does not consist at all of basic value, whereas for all I have said, the intrinsic value of H may.

So far, I have supposed us to have a quantitative notion of *world-value*, the degree to which an agent's goals are satisfied in a possible world. I have then gone on to suppose that world-value could be calculated in terms of a quantitative *basic value* ascribed to propositions. What qualitative notion of value corresponds? For a proposition to have positive basic value is for the agent to want it to hold, for its own sake, apart from any proposition which it properly entails. For it to have negative basic value is for the agent to want it not to hold, with the same qualifications. In either case, I shall say that the proposition is *basically valued*, or that the agent *values* the proposition *basically*. A proposition is basically valued, then, if and only if it has non-zero basic value. Now although what it is for a proposition to be basically valued has been characterized in terms of basic value, which is quantitative, the notion of valuing basically can be understood in a purely qualitative way. For an agent basically to value a proposition is for him to want it to hold, or want it not to hold, apart from considerations of what might bring it about, what evidence it might provide about the truth of other propositions, and what propositions it properly entails.

In what follows, conditions will be put on a decision matrix in terms of the qualitative predicate 'is basically valued'. The quantitative notion of having non-zero basic value will then be used to characterize decision matrices that yield instrumental expected utility.

3. Decision Matrices Characterized

In this Section, both general decision matrices and Savage decision matrices will be characterized in qualitative terms. Savage decision matrices have act-independent states, and it is to them, I am suggesting, that the Savage postulates reasonably apply. They allow calculation of instrumental expected utility by the formula

$$\mathcal{U}(a) = \sum_S \rho(S)\mathcal{D}(O_{aS}),\tag{6}$$

where S ranges over the states of the matrix. General decision matrices, on the other hand, need not have act-independent states. From a general decision matrix, expected utility is calculated by the formula[1]

$$\mathcal{U}(a) = \sum_S \rho(a\,\square\!\!\rightarrow S)\mathcal{D}(O_{aS}).\tag{7}$$

The definitions to follow consist of three conditions on the set S of states and one condition governing the outcomes. Two conditions on S,

---

[1] This formula is due to Stalnaker (1972).

called Partition and Definiteness of Outcome, characterize general decision matrices; an additional condition of Act-Independence characterizes Savage decision matrices.

Equations (2) and (3) allow act-independence of Q to be formulated in two equivalent ways.

$$K\left((\forall a)(a \mathbin{\square\!\!\rightarrow} Q) \vee (\forall a)(a \mathbin{\square\!\!\rightarrow} \overline{Q})\right). \tag{2'}$$

$$K(\forall a)\left((a \mathbin{\square\!\!\rightarrow} Q) \leftrightarrow Q\right). \tag{3'}$$

A *consideration*, then, is defined as a proposition C such that

(i) the agent cares about C, and

(ii) C is not act-independent.

We can now proceed to give a matrix formulation of expected utility. Consider first general decision matrices. Let S be a set of propositions. The first requirement on S will be that S constitute a partition—indeed, not only that the agent believe that one and only one proposition in S obtains, but that he believe that whatever he did, one and only one proposition in S would obtain.

CONDITION 1. *Partition.*

$$(\forall a)K\left(\mathbf{aut}_S(a \mathbin{\square\!\!\rightarrow} S)\right).$$

(In this and all that follows, the variable S takes as its values all members of S, the set of states of the matrix which the conditions govern.)

The condition of Definiteness of Outcome is that for each act a and each proposition $S \in S$, the agent be certain which considerations would obtain were he to perform a in S. To formulate this, we need to explicate what it is for the agent to believe that a consideration C would obtain were he to do a in S. The tools at hand include action conditionals and conditional belief. With them we can say

$$K\left((a \mathbin{\square\!\!\rightarrow} C)/(a \mathbin{\square\!\!\rightarrow} S)\right), \tag{8}$$

that the agent is disposed, on learning that S would obtain were he to do a, to believe that C would obtain were he to do a. I suggest (8) as a rendering of "the agent believes that C would obtain were he to do a in S." Likewise, the agent's believing that C definitely would not obtain were he to do A in S can be expressed

$$K\left((a \mathbin{\square\!\!\rightarrow} \overline{C})/(a \mathbin{\square\!\!\rightarrow} S)\right).$$

The condition of Definiteness of Outcome is that for each act a and proposition $S \in S$, the agent have a definite belief as to which considerations would obtain and which would not were he to do a in S.

CONDITION 2. *Definiteness of Outcome.* For each $a \in A$, $S \in S$, and consideration C, either

$$K\big((a\,\square\!\!\rightarrow C)/(a\,\square\!\!\rightarrow S)\big)$$

or

$$K\big((a\,\square\!\!\rightarrow \overline{C})/(a\,\square\!\!\rightarrow S)\big).$$

We are now in a position to define the outcome of an act in a state. The outcome of an act in a state will be a set of propositions, and it will consist of all the considerations the agent believes would obtain were he to do that act in that state.

DEFINITION O. The *outcome* O_{aS} of act a in state S is the set of all considerations C such that

$$K\big((a\,\square\!\!\rightarrow C)/(a\,\square\!\!\rightarrow S)\big)$$

Formally, we can think of a *general decision matrix* that applies to an occasion as a function whose domain is $A \times S$, where (i) A is the set of acts open on the occasion to which the matrix applies, and (ii) S is a set of propositions satisfying the conditions of *Partition* and *Definiteness of Outcome*. To any $a \in A$ and $S \in S$, this function assigns the set of propositions picked out by Definition O as the outcome of a in S. The term 'general decision matrix', then, has been defined without presupposing the quantitative notions of subjective probability and cardinal utility. If we now introduce quantitative subjective probabilities and basic value, we can define the *value* (or *desirability*) $D(O_{aS})$ of an outcome O_{aS} by the formula

$$D(O_{aS}) = \sum_{C:C\in O_{aS}} B(C), \tag{9}$$

and calculate expected utility from a general decision matrix by the Stalnaker formula (7). It is argued in an expanded version of this paper (Gibbard, 1984) that we should accept (7) as a correct characterization of instrumental expected utility.

A general decision matrix is a *Savage decision matrix* if and only if its states are instrumentally act-independent in the sense already defined.

CONDITION 3. *Instrumental Act-Independence.*

$$(\forall S)K\big((\forall a)(a\,\square\!\!\rightarrow S) \vee (\forall a)(a\,\square\!\!\rightarrow \overline{S})\big). \tag{10}$$

Given this 'condition, Conditions 1 and 2 can be simplified. By the equivalence of (2) and (3), this condition is equivalent to the requirement

$$(\forall S)K(\forall a)\big((a\,\square\!\!\rightarrow S) \longleftrightarrow S\big). \tag{11}$$

For any occurrence of '$a \mathbin{\square\!\!\rightarrow} S$' in Conditions 1 and 2, then, we can substitute S, which yields the following simplified conditions.

CONDITION 1'. *Savage Partition.* $(\forall a)K(\mathbf{aut}\,S)$.

CONDITION 2'. *Savage Definiteness of Outcome.*

$$(\forall a, S, C)\left[K\left((a \mathbin{\square\!\!\rightarrow} C)/S\right) \vee K\left((a \mathbin{\square\!\!\rightarrow} \overline{C})/S\right)\right].$$

Next, we can simplify the definition of 'outcome'. With 'S' substituted for '$a \mathbin{\square\!\!\rightarrow} S$', Definition O becomes:

DEFINITION O'. The *Savage outcome* O_{aS} of act a in state S is the set of all considerations C such that $K\left((a \mathbin{\square\!\!\rightarrow} C)/S\right)$.

Finally, with 'S' again substituted for '$a \mathbin{\square\!\!\rightarrow} S$', formula (7) for calculating expected utility becomes (6).

4. The Point

Formula (5) defined instrumental expected utility without appeal to decision matrices. The characterizations of general and Savage decision matrices that I have given will be adequate if, whenever they are satisfied, formulas (7) and (6) respectively are equivalent to (5). They must be equivalent in the sense that for any two alternatives a and b, $U(a) > U(b)$ holds when U is calculated by (7) or by (6) if and only if it holds when U is calculated by (5). In the longer version of this paper presented in Venice (Gibbard, 1984), it is shown that this adequacy condition is satisfied.

The conditions set on decision matrices in this paper look natural enough; they simply reflect, if I am right, what a skillful user of decision matrices will require of a matrix before he uses it. The point of formulating these conditions explicitly is first, to make explicit what skilful users do implicitly, and second, to illuminate the nature of Savage's argument. Savage can be seen as formulating requirements on rational choice in qualitative terms—in terms of *belief* and a thing's *being of value*—and then showing anyone who accepts those requirements that he is committed to the qualitative notions of *subjective probability* and *instrumental expected utility*. Stalnaker's insight provides the key to viewing Savage's argument in this way.

REFERENCES

Gibbard, Allan and Harper, William L. (1981). "Counterfactuals and Two Kinds of Expected Utility", in Hooker, Leach, and McClennen (eds.), *Foundations and Applications of Decision Theory*, Vol. I (Dordrecht, Holland: Reidel), 125–162. Also in Harper, Stalnaker, and Pearce (1981).

Gibbard, Allan, (1984). "Decision Matrices and Instrumental Expected Utility", full version of paper presented to the Second International Congress on Foundations of Utility and Risk Theory, Venice, June 1984.

Harman, Gilbert H. (1967). "Toward a Theory of Intrinsic Value", *Journal of Philosophy* **64**, 792-804.

Harper, W.L., Stalnaker, R., and Pearce, G. (1981). *Ifs: Conditionals, Belief, Decision, Chance, and Time* (Dordrecht, Holland: Reidel).

Ramsey, Frank Plumpton (1931). "Truth and Probability", in *The Foundations of Mathematics*, (London: Routledge and Kegan Paul).

Savage, Leonard J., (1954). *The Foundations of Statistics* (New York: Wiley).

———, (1972). *The Foundations of Statistics*, 2nd Edition (New York: Dover).

Stalnaker, Robert (1968). "A Theory of Conditionals", in *Studies in Logical Theory, American Philosophical Quarterly* Monograph Series **No. 2** (Oxford: Blackwell).

———, (1972). Letter to David Lewis, exerpted in Harper, Stalnaker, and Pearce (1981).

Luciano Daboni

ASSOCIATIVE MEANS AND UTILITY THEORY

Let C be a set of random payoffs (lotteries) whose outcomes belong to the closed interval $a \leq x \leq b$.

Capital letters X, Y,... will be used to denote both a random payoff and its probability distribution. Degenerate distributions that concentrate the whole probability on the sure payoff x, are denoted by x*.

If X and Y are elements of C, then the (compound) lottery, XPY, whose outcome is the lottery X with probability P, or Y with probability 1-P, belongs to C.

B.de Finetti (1931) has defined the "associative mean" of X, any functional M(X) of the distribution X which satisfies:

  i) $M(x^*) = x$,
 ii) $M(X) = M(Y)$ implies $M(XPZ) = M(YPZ)$ for any $Z \varepsilon C$ and $P \varepsilon [0,1]$,
iii) $M(X) > M(Y)$ if X strictly dominates Y.[1]

The associative property is properly stated by ii) (See de Finetti, 1952). Assume now that

 iv) to any X of C corresponds a (unique) associative mean M(X).

The following fundamental theorem holds (see Nagumo and Kolmogoroff, in Hardy et al., 1931; de Finetti, 1931).

A necessary and sufficient condition for M(X) to be an associative mean of the distribution X is that there exists a continuous and strictly monotonic function $\varphi(x)$ in the closed interval $a \leq x \leq b$ for which

$$M(X) = \varphi^{-1} \left\{ \int_a^b \varphi(x) dF_X(x) \right\} \qquad (1)$$

L. Daboni et al. (eds.), Recent Developments in the Foundations of Utility and Risk Theory, 149–151.
© *1986 by D. Reidel Publishing Company.*

The function φ is unique up to a linear transformation.[2] Hence we can restrict our attention simply to the increasing functions φ(x) and their strictly increasing linear transformations.

It is therefore clearly understood that the function φ plays the role of a <u>utility function</u> and that M(X) is the certainty equivalent of X according to the utility function φ.

The functional M(X) induces on C a complete ordering for the preference among lotteries X of C, coherent - according to iii) - with that based upon stochastic dominance. The complete ordering is that of the expected utility.

Now it is possible to prove that if M(X) is a mean which satisfies properties i) and ii) and

iii) if M(X) > M(Y), for every number m satisfying M(X) ≥ m ≥ M(Y) there is a number με[0,1] such that m = M(XμY),

then M(X) is an (associative) monotonic mean.[3]

That being so we can derive the existence of the utility function from the postulates:

I) To any X of C corresponds a certainty equivalent M(X) such that:
II) M(x*) = x for any sure amount x.
III) if M(X) ≥ M(Y) ≥ M(Z) there exists Pε[0,1] such that M(Y) = M(XPZ),
IV) M(X) ≥ M(Y) implies M(XPZ) ≥ M(YPZ) for any ZεC and Pε[0,1] and vice versa.

It is now interesting to compare these postulates with the postulates of the well known axiomatic approach to the theory of utility proposed by J. von Neumann and O. Morgenstern.

We recall these postulates (suitably reformulated):

i)' a complete preference ordering (≥) exists on C which is coherent with the partial ordering induced by the stochastic dominance relation between the elements of C,
ii)' for any X ≥ Y ≥ Z you can find a number Pε[0,1] such that Y is indifferent to XPZ (analogous to our (III)),
iii)' if X ≥ Y then XPZ ≥ YPZ for any ZεC and Pε[0,1] and

vice versa (analogous to our (IV)[4].

So we can conclude that the approach a la von Neumann-Morgenstern and resorting to the notion of associative means, both lead to the existence of a utility function.

This utility function is a continuous function if originated from the Nagumo - Kolmogoroff - de Finetti theorem. In the classical approach the utility function is continuous if we moreover require the existence of a certainty equivalent for any elementary lottery b*Pa*.

Department of Finance Mathematics
University of Trieste

NOTES

1. We recall that X strictly dominates Y, if $F_X(x) \leq F_Y(x)$ for any x and the strict inequality holds for at least one x.
2. We write (1) in the form $\varphi(M)=E[\varphi(X)]$; then for any real numbers $a \neq 0$, b, we have $a\varphi(M)+b=aE[\varphi(X)]+b= =E[a\varphi(X)+b]$. Denote by $\varphi'(x)$ the function $a\varphi(x)+b$. It is $\varphi'(M)=E|\varphi'(X)|$ and $M=\varphi'^{-1}\{E|\varphi'(X)|\}$.
3. For the proof see: the Appendix in L. Daboni, "On the axiomatic treatment of the utility theory", Metroeconomica 36, 2-3.
4. By axioms ii)' and iii)' we can easily prove that: a) $X \geq Y$ implies $X \geq XPY \geq Y$ for any $P \epsilon [0,1]$ and b) $X \geq Y$ and $0 \leq \mu \leq P \leq 1$ implies $XPY \geq X\mu Y$ and, vice versa, $XPY \geq X\mu Y$ for P, $\mu \epsilon [0,1]$ and $X \geq Y$ implies $\mu \geq P$.

REFERENCES

Daboni, L.: 1984, "On the Axiomatic Treatment of Utility Theory", Metroeconomica 36, 2-3.
de Finetti, B.: 1931, "Sul Concetto di Media", Gior. Ist. It. Attuari.
Hardy, G. H., J. E. Littlewood and G. Polya: 1952, Inequalities, Cambridge University Press, Cambridge.

Guido A. Rossi

ON UTILITY FUNCTIONS IN A FINANCIAL CONTEXT

1. Introduction

1.1. - A financial context is to be defined by means of the
kind of operations we refer to, and the purpose we pursue.

  A utility function is defined with reference to a single
decision (at a time) of a certain kind, and to a decision-
maker and his needs.

  To complete the description, let us note that we consider only the operations which are certain at first, examining the uncertain ones later.

1.2. - We define certain, discrete and finite (1) operations
as a finite sequence of finite money movements, happening at
fixed epochs (2), between the decision-maker and any other
counterpart. Any movement is represented by a real   number,
whose absolute value is the amount of money involved,   and
whose sign is positive if the sum is received by the decision-maker, negative if it is paid by him. The operation hap
pens because of some decision, either present or past, such
as the signing of a contract, but it does not represent the
contract, or anything else: it represents   the money movements only.

  Since any decision happens at some point during a period
of time in which other decisions are taken, we must consider
the possibility of distinct money movements, at the same e-
poch, as the result of distinct decisions; if the operation
registers the real money movements originating or termina-
ting in the decision-maker, it is natural to sum contemporary movements to obtain the resulting movement.

  We consider that the decision-maker is interested in all
operations, defined as above, to make a decision.

  We have, then, real vectors with n components, n arbitra
ry, the i-th component being the movement at the i-th epoch,
constituting an abelian additive group.

1.3. - The purpose we pursue is that of maximizing   wealth.

153

L. Daboni et al. (eds.), Recent Developments in the Foundations of Utility and Risk Theory, 153–160.
© 1986 by D. Reidel Publishing Company.

This notion is rather vague, and we make it precise saying that, in this sense, we consider that decisions are made as a consequence of a preference ordering, of all operations, that, when applied to the choice between single movements, at one and the same epoch, even if this can be set arbitrarily, becomes the ordering given by that very amount of money.

1.4. - The decision is to be made in two steps: in the first step a preference ordering is attributed to the set of all operations, and a representation of this ordering is constructed, then a decision is made that is consistent with the ordering.

The consistency must not be endangered if we take into consideration the operations which are also "differential", (in the usual terminology).

That is, each operation which is the difference between the movements that will happen because of the decision of the decision-maker, and those which would have happened anyway (the latter operation can be called the "situation") (3); or is the difference between alternative operations, one of which is to be chosen.

We assume that if y is preferred to x, it happens because adding $y-x$, to x, causes an upward movement in the preference ordering; so, if adding z to x increases the preference, the same result must be obtained adding z to y.

The assumption is obvious when all the components of z are non-negative; if it is not the case this becomes a true postulate, which we believe is not restrictive: we conjecture it can be proved that it is a consequence of simpler and compelling facts.

For the moment we can sketch a possible reasoning of a decision-maker that endorses the assumption.

Let us suppose that the decision-maker is interested in choosing between one option that will cause the total money movements x and another one that will cause y instead of x, with y preferred to x; then $y=(y-x)+x$, and x is an operation that will happen anyway, so it looks like something irrelevant with regard to any decision based on the preference: comparing y and x becomes, then, equivalent to comparing operations $y-x$ and the null operation 0 (the first giving y and the second x) with the result that the preference depends on both comparisons and must be the same. It is best observable however in the comparison between $y-x$ and 0. Moreover the

same final comparison between y-x and 0 happening on different occasions, being the same, should give the same indiffe
rence, or the same direction of preference;   and,   since two
identical operations are obviously indifferent, any two operations x, y, whose difference y-x is indifferent   to   the
null operation 0, are indifferent themselves.

Finally, under our assumption any comparison of operations, y and x, for the sake of establishing a preference or
dering, is equivalent to comparing the difference y-x   and
the null operation 0.

2.   Statement of the Problem

2.1 - With these basic assumptions about the context, we can
characterize the description of the decision problem as follows.

2.2. - First of all we must observe that   representing   the
above mentioned preference ordering by means of a function
$\phi:R^n \to R$ with arbitrarily large n, is by no means restrictive.

And that is because the image space, R, has the same car
dinality as R^n, and the same ordering type as the one of all
possible money movements at a single epoch, that is again R.

For such reasons any other way of representing the requi
red ordering should be obtained by a function $f \cdot \phi$, where   f
is an order preserving bijection, and the image space is order isomorphic with R; sometimes being also a subset of some
other set.

Considering that ϕ is defined up to a monotonic transfor
mation $R \to R$ we can include any such function in f, in the attempt to find a function ϕ which is also canonical.

2.3. - Therefore we look for a function ϕ that satisfies the
following requirements:
1) $\phi(x)$ is defined over the whole R^n,   for no   x   can be
excluded, is partially (4) continuous because   the   ordering
of R, considered as the space of all possible   money   movements at a single epoch, is continuous.
2) $\phi(x) > \phi(x+z) \to \phi(y) > \phi(y+z)$ because the preference revealed by the decision of passing from situation x to   x+z   depends on z only, and hence the same preference   should   hold
between y and y+z (5).

3) ϕ is canonical in some sense, other then the partial continuity, which will become clear afterwards; in particular it is partially increasing, and in a strict way.

2.4. - The maximum of ϕ should be the decision of the decision-maker when he chooses to make a non-null decision.

2.5. - The above requirements have different origins: 2.2. and 2.3.3) are perhaps the most convenient among many possible ones; 2.3.1) and 2) are derived from the definition of operations and the purpose of maximizing wealth as described before, together with the postulated extension of 2.3.2) to the non-obvious cases; 2.4. is an obvious consequence.

So we do not have all the usual explicit axioms : the real starting point is the definition of the context, augmented by postulate 2.3.2).

3. Solution of the Problem

3.1. - The following theorem holds:
Any partially continuous ψ on R^n that satisfies: (see the appendix)

(*) $\psi(\underline{x}) > \psi(\underline{x}+\underline{z}) \rightarrow \psi(\underline{y}) > \psi(\underline{y}+\underline{z})$ for every $\underline{x}$, $\underline{y}$, $\underline{z}$,

is not constant, and is also either partially constant or partially strictly monotonic, will be continuous and constant or monotonic on any straight line, and its level sets will be linear subspaces of R^n of dimension n-1. Then $\psi(\underline{x}) = f(\underline{b} \cdot \underline{x})$ with f continuous and strictly monotonic.

3.2. - From this we obtain what is useful for our purpose. Eliminating f, to get a canonical ϕ, we have $\phi(\underline{x}) = g(\underline{c} \cdot \underline{x})$, with the additional result that at least one component (say the k-th) of the vector $\underline{c}$ is equal to 1, and g is continuous and strictly increasing. So $\underline{c} > 0$.

Any preference ordering then is canonically represented by a function $g_k(\underline{x}) = \underline{c} \cdot \underline{x}$ which has the meaning of the single sum of money that, subtracted at epoch k from the operation $\underline{x}$ makes the result equivalent to the null operation, or is equivalent, at epoch k, to the whole operation $\underline{x}$. We could deduce some properties of the components of $\underline{c}$ also, but we are not interested in that here (6).

3.3. - This is a canonical representation of the ordering in the sense that any possible monotonic function has been eliminated and the meaning of g_k is particularly interesting. Some authors consider a concave·(or other) monotonic function U to show individual inclinations, some others don't since it is useless for revealing preference and can give some problems (7).

We agree with the latter position, but in either case we can see that we have obtained a function that orders operations according to a rational preference and has two interesting properties: its meaning and the linearity; so we have a canonical utility function, and we can dispense with any such. U.

3.4. - When we turn our attention from certain to uncertain situations and operations, considering operations defined as above, but whose occurrence depends on some event·of a random experiment, we have a very natural way of dealing with them.

A stochastic utility function should be the "certain equivalent" to the whole possibility, and then the expectation or forecast (8), of canonical utilities with the probabilities of the corresponding events, would again be a canonical utility.

At this point it must be remarked that the introduction of a concave monotonic function U, of the canonical utility, is not as devoid of meaning as it was before, especially as it can be used to show risk aversion.

4. Comment

4.1. - From this point on, further reasoning would lead us to say something substantially equivalent to what De Finetti said, in [1] or [2] for instance, as we have proved that passing through a "monetary equivalent" is necessary (and sufficient, save for risk aversion), in the context outlined, where we do not consider the individual psychology of the decision-maker.

We may note that we have not required any archimedean

property, *a priori*, for the ordering, since we have obtained
it from the corresponding property of the sums of money, con
sidered at one and the same epoch. Besides, we did not requi
re any *a priori* property for the coefficients c_i,   so that
their value may be chosen by the decision-maker according to
his needs.

Last but not least, we found an indicator of preference
which is an associative mean, without requiring this property *a priori*.

4.2. - Most interesting is the fact that any index of type
$c \cdot x$ (c with the described properties), being linear, gives
to the set of all x the structure of an   abelian   additive
group, is partially continuous and strictly monotonic and sa
tisfies formula (*) of 3.1.. So it satisfies all the require
ments stemming from the definition of the financial context
augmented by postulate 2.3.2) as previously outlined.

The conclusion is that the use of such an index is equivalent to assuming that one is operating in a context and
with a purpose and a reasoning which are the ones we sketched. Someone may consider that he is indeed in this situation: this is more likely to happen with organisations then
with single individuals.

But many people may not find it possible   to describe
their financial activity by means of operations with the pro
perties we required: then they should not use a linear index
if they still agree on the purpose and the reasoning.   And
anyone who believes it is good to use a linear   index, such
as the discounted cash flow, should ask himself if he is ap
plying it to appropriate operations, lest he maximize, unwil
lingly, someone else's wealth.

In this sense it is clear enough that our basic rationality assumption, of coherence with some defined purpose, can
become very powerful; in some cases, at least.

5. Appendix

5.1. -   Here we will limit ourselves to an outline of the
proof; for further details see [3].

The theorem is proved through the following steps.
The first is to see that if the formula (*) in   3.1.
holds, then similar formulae hold where   we   substitute
$\rightarrow$ with $\leftrightarrow$, we change the direction of both inequalities and,

finally, we substitute $\underline{x}+\underline{z}=\underline{y}$, $\underline{z}=\underline{x}-\underline{y}$ on either side. Using a technique similar to that used to derive the solution of Cauchy's functional equation, we show that any increase or decrease or equality of ψ existing between two points (operations), say $\underline{x}$ and $\underline{y}$, extends to the points of rational abscissa of the straight line passing through $\underline{x}$ and $\underline{y}$; the same property holds on any parallel straight line.

So any level set containing point $\underline{x}_i$ is dense on the linear subspace of R^n determined by the $\underline{x}_i$, and a subset of R^n is a level set for ψ iff it can be obtained from a level set by a translation.

If we require ψ to be partially strictly monotonic, or constant, and continuous, (which is equivalent to saying that is can be used to reveal a preference or indifference of the type required) it can be shown by induction over the dimension n, of R^n, that ψ has the same properties on any straight line and the level sets are linear subspaces of R^n of dimension either n or n-1.

The initial case with n=1 is obvious.

If n=2 the proof is rather complicated.

If n=2 and ψ is partially constant the theorem is again obvious; if it is not so we begin by changing the variables, with a linear transformation such as to obtain a $\psi(x,y)$ that is strictly increasing, as a function of x and y separately. Then we show that $\psi(x,mx)$, m>0 is strictly increasing (obvious) and continuous (by *reductio ad absurdum*) we show that the greatest lower bound of its values for x>0 is equal to $\psi(0,0)$ and extend this argument to all other cases and points of continuity desired). Considering a translation we can repeat the reasoning with any two parallels to the axes, obtaining that $\psi(x, m_o x+n)$, for some m_o>0, n arbitrary, is continuous and increasing; so it assumes the value $\psi(0,0)$ in one and only one point (in the even quadrants), and the set of such points, for all different values of n, is a straight line $y=m_1 x$, m_1<0 giving the required property for level sets. It is easy to complete the proof for the straight lines $y=mx+n$, m<0, $m\neq m_1$, by decomposing any increment along this straight line in two, one along a horizontal line, the other along a level set.

The proof is then obtained by considering the level set containing the origin, and reasoning as for the previous cases on the last one, or two components. For other level sets we use a translation.

Then using the technique involved in deducing the equation of a cylinder we get: $\psi(\underline{x})=f(\underline{b}\cdot\underline{x})$ with f monotonic and continuous.

Institute of Finance Mathematics
University of Turin

NOTES

(1) Hence bounded.
(2) Then possible epochs constitute a sequence which is possibly infinite; the actually used ones are a vector.
(3) We have a null decision then: that of letting things continue as they would have. Besides, nothing that happens can be left out of the description (and perhaps recalled afterwards), such as integrative operations, for instance. We have a null situation also, that in which the movements that will happen are all zero; a situation that is most likely to be changed by a decision.
(4) With respect to every component x_i of $\underline{x}$.
(5) Another interpretation of requirement $\overline{2}$) is this: if the decision leading to the differential operation z is judged convenient by someone, it should be similary judged by anyone else with similar preferences since for both them the increase in ϕ should mean an increase of money in some way.
(6) For a more detailed version, see [3]; there the original assumptions are somewhat less general and more technical. The present paper stems from further discussion on assumptions and results.
(7) See [1].
(8) As may have been noticed, we refer to De Finetti's choice, for vocabulary, when possible.

REFERENCES

[1] B. DE FINETTI, *Sulla preferibilità*, Giornale degli Economisti e Annali di Economia, 1952, 684-709.
[2] B. DE FINETTI and F. EMANUELLI, *Economia delle assicurazioni*, UTET, Torino, 1967.
[3] G.A. ROSSI, *Una disequazione funzionale e le scelte finanziarie*, Istituto di Matematica Finanziaria dell'Università di Torino, Serie III n. 23, Torino, 1980.

Hector A. Munera

THE GENERALIZED MEANS MODEL (GMM) FOR NON—DETERMINISTIC DECISION MAKING:
A UNIFIED TREATMENT FOR THE TWO CONTENDING THEORIES

1.   INTRODUCTION

Two schools of thought have been arguing for more than thirty years about the foundations of the theory of choice under uncertainty, namely:
- The neo-Bernoullian or American school defending an Expected Utility Model (EUM henceforth), and
- The Allais or French school propounding a model based on the moments of the probability distribution over psychological values, or Moments Model (MM hereafter).

There is an ever increasing evidence that the Expected Utility Model can not hold its ground as a normative and descriptive theory universally acceptable to all individuals under all circumstances. It is rather fascinating to witness the efforts made by proponents of the established theory to devise new ideas that would preserve the linear shape of the model, although the contents might not be linear any longer. In a way the present situation reminds the fall of the Ptolemaic astronomical theory: any new finding against it was explained by introducing ever more complicated epicycles. Eventually the simplest Copernican theory succeeded.

Allais (1953) suggested that a reasonable model for non—deterministic decision making should include also the higher moments of the probability distribution over psychological values. Some EUM proponents have remarked that Allais' proposal is non-testable because it is too general (e.g. Amihud, 1979; Chew, 1983). The author exhibited some years back a linearized form of the MM that, fulfilling Allais criterion, is simple enough to be tested (Munera, 1978; Munera and de Neufville, 1983). Taking one step further the main points for an axiomatic derivation are sketched herein.

The sometimes bitter controversy has centered around the <u>acceptability</u> of some of the mathematical assumptions

161

L. Daboni et al. (eds.), Recent Developments in the Foundations of Utility and Risk Theory, 161–184.
© *1986 by D. Reidel Publishing Company.*

used in the axiomatic derivation of the EUM. In this paper
a _novel_ idea is presented, that might bridge the
differences of opinion between proponents and opponents of
the EUM.

It is argued that the crux of the controversy
resides with the _interpretation_ of the mathematical
operations --that is, with the meaning of the axioms
associated with each mathematical condition-- but _not_ with
the mathematical technicalities themselves.

By using the well known concept of generalized means
(also called additive means) it is possible to derive both
contesting theories (i.e. EUM and MM) from the same core of
axioms, that --surprisingly enough-- includes an extended
form of the hotly debated Substitution Principle. In this
sense, the proposed Generalized Means Model is a unified
and unifying theory.

The general concept of MEAN was axiomatically
developed for uniform distributions by Kolmogoroff (1930)
and extended to general probability distributions by de
Finetti (1931). Using these pioneering works, Hardy,
Littlewood and Polya (1934) fully developed the theory. An
axiomatic derivation of the EUM is already implicitly
contained in these early studies, several years in advance
to von Neumann and Morgenstern's (1944) axiomatization of
the EUM.

This paper is organized as follows. Section 2
discusses some conditions that a theory must fulfill to
have _normative_ power, and argues the existence of an
implicit _meta-decision_, or precondition, whereby the axioms
of the theory under consideration are _accepted_ or _rejected_.
Then it continues with the formulation of the general
problem of non-deterministic decision making and defines
some possible _meta-axioms_. A set of axioms for a preference
ordering over alternatives (i.e. over probability
distribution functions) is proposed. This naturally leads
to the more comprehensive Generalized Means Model (GMM,
henceforth).

Section 3 is an informal sketch of the
representation theorem leading to the GMM, and section 4
derives, as a particular case, the Linearized Moments Model
(LMM) formerly proposed by the author (Munera, 1978). This
LMM is also a special form of Allais' MM. The derivation of
the EUM as a particular case of the GMM is included next;
some behavioural assumptions implicit in current
axiomatizations of the EUM, but generally overlooked, are

also discussed in this section. A final section 5 summarizes the main findings and conclusions.

2.   AXIOMS OF THE GENERALIZED MEANS MODEL (GMM)

2.1.   On normativity and axiomatization

The initial success of the EUM was a result of the concurrence of two conditions:
- A set of axioms (or rules) of apparent simplicity and logical appeal, from which the model is derived, and (pressumably) hence its normative power. And,
- A simple linear shape. It may be speculated that linearity exerts a sort of _fascination_ on human mind (the present author is not the exception): Linear models are considered more natural, more "objective", than non-linear models. This is also the case in physics, where the theory of relativity introducing _curved_ spaces was (initially) very difficult to accept.

     It must be remarked, however, that a set of axioms per se is not sufficient to establish the _normative_ power of a theory. Mathematicians rather easily obtain self-consistent constructs, but it does not mean a fortiori that such constructs represent real objects, or, in the case at hand, that some real being must abide by them. The link between the mathematical model and the real world must be stated in a separate, explicit, and unambiguous fashion. This seems to be the real issue in the controversy surrounding the EUM.

     Of course, axioms can not be proved. For _logically self-consistent_ and _free_ individuals (or societies) axioms are just _acceptable_ or _unacceptable_. This is a preliminary _meta-decision_ that must be answered in advance, before claiming that any theory -the EUM in particular- has _normative force_.

     The operational process to find the answer of a given individual to this meta-decision may be either _explicit_ (for instance by direct questioning about the logic appeal of the axioms) or _implicit_ (say, analysis of decisions implied by the model to determine whether such choices are acceptable to that particular individual or not).

     It seems that the majority of proponents of the EUM adopted the _explicit approach,_ although Savage (1972, p.102) also considered viable the implicit method. The meta-decision question is answered by EUM proponents with a cheerful: "Yes, the axioms are acceptable". This answer is, of course, correct. Unfortunately, EUM proponents dismiss as "non-rational" other correct answers, for instance:

  -- "All are acceptable, except one of them",
  -- "Some are acceptable, some unacceptable", or
  -- "None is acceptable".

  For example the author's answer to the meta-decision question is: "All axioms are logically acceptable, except the substitution principle as currently stated".

2.2. The problem of non-deterministic decisions

Many real life problems, e.g. choice between energy systems, may be cast into the following idealized decision tree (figure 1):

- A decision node at t_0 (the present) with several non-deterministic alternatives.[1] Next decision nodes are at t_1 after resolution of uncertainty for the previous period (t_0, t_1). Decision nodes are found again at t_2, t_3,..., after resolution of uncertainty for the immediately preceding period (t_1, t_2), (t_2, t_3),....

- Each alternative leads to non-deterministic consequence vectors C, embedded in a non-deterministic environment E.

- At every decision node it is possible to revise the valuation of the consequences related with each alternative. All new information on both consequences C and the environment E may be used; also, any new alternatives uncovered during the preceding time periods may be added to the analysis.

- For the random subset of non-deterministic consequences, it is possible to establish bona fide probability distributions.[2]

- Always, one possible alternative is: "do nothing". Then, the system stays in a sort of evolving status quo, eventually leading to a new state at the end of the period.

  It should be noted that this formulation with only one chance node between decision nodes does not decrease

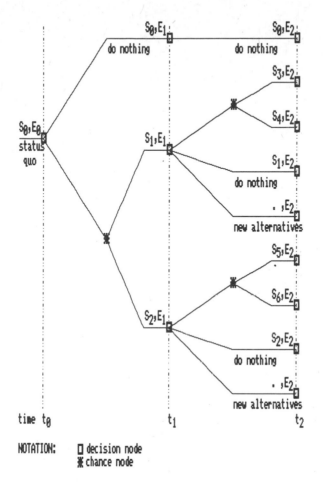

time t_0 t_1 t_2

NOTATION: ☐ decision node
             ✻ chance node

Figure 1. The problem of non-deterministic decisions.
Choices are made sequentially at times t_1, t_2, t_3, ...,
after resolution of non-deterministic conditions in
preceding time-periods. Decisions have direct bearing on
the state of the system S, but no direct influence on the
state of the external environment E. At the moment of the
initial decision t_0 some of the alternatives available in
the future are known, but some other are unknown; the
latter are called "new alternatives". Total information
available at t_0 is, then, lower than at future times t_1,
t_2, ...

the generality of the representation. For compound trees, i.e. when there are chance nodes linked together <u>without intervening decision nodes</u>, the tree may be <u>folded-back</u>, that is, reduced to a simple tree, by using the standard methods of probability theory. This process of formulating and simplifying the tree that best represents the decision problem is somewhat related to the <u>editing</u> process suggested by Kahneman and Tversky (1979).

As argued by the author elsewhere in the context of a flexibility principle (Munera, 1978; Munera and de Neufville, 1983), the derivation of the EUM from its axioms implicitly uses a <u>two-period decision tree</u> (This remark is similar to Pope's (1984) contention that the delay in learning the outcomes should be explicitly considered in the derivation of the EUM). On the other hand, most examples used to test and/or justify the EUM are only one- or, at most, two-period problems. This means that the reasonability of some very basic assumptions of the EUM is never checked. In order to avoid such shortcomings, it is suggested that decision trees are a very useful pictorial representation, even for the theoretical justification of a model.

2.3.   Meta-axioms for non-deterministic decisions

Underlying the meta-decision, there are individual traits that shape the individual's general attitude towards non-deterministic conditions. At least, three different questions --in decreasing order of generality-- must be considered:

- Question 1. Is a <u>sequential</u> decision process (as in Fig. 1) equivalent to a <u>single</u> decision at time $t_0 = 0$, thus commiting the individual for many time-periods into the future? The answer is provided by the <u>Flexibility Principle</u>.

- Question 2. Given that decisions must be taken at $t_0 = 0$ with suitable <u>estimates</u> for <u>future</u> evaluation of consequences, what are the minimum requirements for the decision model? The answer is provided by the <u>Allais-Tintner Principle</u>.

- Question 3. Given a general decision model, what behavioural description of the individual should be used?

The answer is provided by the <u>Attitude Towards Certainty Condition</u>.

2.3.1. The flexibility principle

Informally, the flexibility principle tells whether an individual considers equivalent a <u>sequential decision process</u> with (inasmuch as possible) complete information and uncertainty resolution (as in figure 1) to a <u>puntual decision</u> at time t_0, where future states must be estimated. Individuals may like, dislike, or be indifferent towards flexibility.

Individuals who <u>prefer</u> flexibility will <u>never</u> consider a punctual decision equivalent to a sequential process. For them, decisions taken at $t_0 = 0$ have <u>operational meaning</u> only, as a sort of second-best action, that may be revised when more information becomes available. Normativity must be understood here in the restricted sense of a <u>prescriptive rule</u> for unavoidable operational decisions.

On the other hand, individuals <u>disliking</u> flexibility might tend to give normative value to the prescriptive implications of a model that allows them to make decisions at $t = 0$ once and for all future times.

Finally, individuals <u>indifferent</u> towards flexibility would most likely accept the normativity of the EUM, since such indifference is a pre-condition to the derivation of the EUM (Munera, 1978; Munera and de Neufville, 1983).

2.3.2. The Allais-Tintner Principle

In real life decisions must, of course, be taken at t_0 with whatever information is available at that moment. Individuals may then, quite rightfully, require that the theory of choice should include as much information as possible about the non-deterministic characteristics of the alternative. For this reason it may be argued that a significant number of individuals would find <u>acceptable</u> the following condition suggested by Allais (1953) and, even earlier, by Tintner (1941):

<u>Allais-Tintner Principle</u>: The whole probability distribution function over psychological values must be considered. This may be captured by some function of <u>all</u> the moments of the probability distribution.

Individuals accepting this principle would take decisions according to a Moments Model (MM); a particular form being the Linearized Moments Model (LMM) later developed herein.

Other individuals may find that the <u>first moment</u> suffices to capture the non-deterministic content of the alternative. This group would then accept the EUM as a normative theory.

Furthermore, some other individuals might find that the Allais-Tintner principle does not suffice to capture the non-deterministic content of probability distributions. For them, the LMM is not applicable; perhaps, another form of the GMM with functionals other than the moments could be acceptable.

2.3.3. The attitude towards certainty condition

It has been observed by many authors (e.g. Allais, 1979; Kahnemann and Tversky, 1979) that individuals may exhibit special behaviour in the vicinity of certainty, that is, when the probability of a non-deterministic outcome tends to one. Three different categories of individuals may be recognized, namely:

a. <u>Absolute consistency with certainty</u>

A prospect with one outcome C, whose probability tends to 1, is evaluated in the limit as C. The outcome may be <u>favourable</u> or <u>unfavourable</u> to the individual. The other outcome is the status quo.

Behaviourally, this may be described as: "An almost certain gain is a sure gain, and an almost certain loss is a sure loss".

b. <u>Partial consistency with certainty</u>

Two subgroups are identified:

- <u>Pessimistic individuals</u>: "An almost certain loss is a <u>sure</u> loss, but an almost certain gain is not a <u>sure</u> gain".
- <u>Optimistic individuals</u>: "An almost certain gain is a <u>sure</u> gain, but an almost certain loss is not a sure loss".

c. <u>Inconsistency with certainty</u>

Neither almost sure gains nor almost sure losses are equivalent to the deterministic gains or losses.

Anyone of these three patterns of behaviour may serve as an answer to Question 3 at the beginning of this section. The appicable pattern may be found by direct questioning or, indirectly, by observing actual choices.

The set of answers to the three questions above define a group of axioms <u>acceptable</u> to the decision maker. Once it is done, the model resulting from these axioms should have, for that person, <u>normative force</u> or, at least, <u>prescriptive value</u>.

2.4.   <u>Axioms for non-deterministic decisions</u>

Three groups of rules that might be <u>acceptable</u> to many individuals for non-deterministic decision making are informally stated:

2.4.1. <u>Axiom 1: Complete ordering under certainty</u>
There exists a preference index $h(.)$ mapping the consequences vector C into the real line.[3]

<u>Comments</u>. Since $h(C)$ refers to deterministic objects it should be obtained by deterministic methods, like the value function as used by Kahneman and Tversky (1979) or by Keeney and Raiffa (1976, chapter 3). In some applications $h(C)$ may be a cardinal utility, while in other cases it may be a physical index, say concentration of substances whose optimum is not at one end (like carbon dioxide in the atmosphere). In some cases, if preferred, this first assumption could be derived from other more basic notions in a theory of choice under certainty.

Any alternative with probability distribution F_c over consequences C_j may be converted to an alternative with probability distribution F_h over preference indices h_j.

This first assumption is the only one that is not necessary to derive the EUM by using generalized means. All the other following assumptions are required to derive both the LMM and the EUM.

2.4.2. <u>Axiom 2: Deterministic - Non-deterministic conexion</u>
It ascertains that there exists one deterministic consequence, C_e, equivalent to a given non-deterministic alternative A and that the process to obtain C_e takes into account the entire probability distribution. This assumption effectively assigns a <u>deterministic</u> preference index $h(C_e)$ to the <u>nondeterministic</u> alternative A. Any of the following notations is used: $H(A) = h(C_e) = h_e$.

The main underlying idea is the following: represent any probability distribution function F by a set of deterministic dimensions and, furthermore, require that

such dimensions fulfill some reasonable properties. In this
paper we select as appropriate dimensions a set of n
functions $M_k(F)$, called <u>generalized means</u> and defined by
Eq. 1, section 3. Under such assumptions, the following two
conditions a) and b) imply the axiom:

a. <u>Properties of the generalized means</u>
Each individual dimension M_k must exhibit the following two
properties:
-- <u>Consistency with certainty</u>. Each dimension $M_k(.)$ reduces
   to x for degenerate alternatives producing x with
   probability p = 1.
-- <u>First-degree extended stochastic dominance</u>. Let $F_1 \geq F_2$
   for all x and $F_1 > F_2$ for some x, then each dimension M_k
   obeys $M_k(F_1) \leq M_k(F_2)$.

b. <u>Properties of the certainty equivalent</u>
There exists a certainty equivalent h_e, function of n
independent generalized means M_k. The function h_e also
exhibits the two properties of consistency with certainty
and first-degree stochastic dominance required for the
individual dimensions M_k.
       <u>Comments</u>. Consistency with certainty and first-
degree stochastic dominance are properties generally
present in the EUM, sometimes in the axiomatization proper.
In the GMM proposed herein, they are exhibited by the
majority of decision makers described in section 2.3.3., as
follows:
- Absolutely consistent individuals fulfill the condition
  for <u>all</u> probability distributions;
- Pessimistic individuals fulfill the condition only for
  the limited class of completely unfavourable probability
  distributions (see section 3.1);   .
- Optimistic individuals only obey the condition for
  completely favourable alternatives (see section 3.1).
       For probability distributions other than those
listed above, neither consistency with certainty nor first-
degree stochastic dominance are requirements of the GMM.
       Some axiomatizations of the EUM, e.g. Luce and
Raiffa (1957), are based on assumptions of continuity and
monotonicity defined over two consequences only (typically
the least and the most preferred consequences). It is noted
that, when enforced, our first-degree extended stochastic

dominance is, by far, a more general assumption. For the case of mixed alternatives (see section 3.1), the same monotonicity principle suggested by Luce and Raiffa (1957) may be overlayed on top of the GMM, thus further structuring the model (Munera, 1978 and 1984a).

Finally, the existence of a certainty equivalent effectively defines a common scale for deterministic and non-deterministic objects.

2.4.3. Axiom 3: The extended substitution principle

In a compound decision tree, a probability distribution F may be substituted by another one F^* having the same numerical values on the relevant dimensions, i.e. with the same generalized means. In symbols, consider two alternatives F and F^* such that $M_k(F) = M_k(F^*)$ for all k. Then, $M_k(tF + (1-t)G) = M_k(tF^* + (1-t)G)$ for t $\in$ (0,1) and for all relevant k.

Comments. In agreement with our meta-axioms, the Allais-Tintner Principle in particular, this axiom ascertains that any part of an alternative may be substituted by an equivalent alternative, such that all the relevant generalized means $M_k(.)$ are equal in both alternatives. Note, however, that this does not imply that both probability distributions are identical. It may be remarked that the EUM requires only one generalized mean (the expected value) to be equal for F and F^*.

It is further stressed that in the GMM the substitution is made between two non-degenerate probability distribution functions F and F^*, whereas in the derivation of the EUM one of them is degenerate (a sure outcome). Furthermore, the substitution involves deletion of decision nodes (Munera, 1978); recall also the discussion on the flexibility principle and figure 1.

3.   DERIVATION OF THE GENERALIZED MEANS MODEL

Representation theorem for the GMM. There exist functions H(A) fulfilling axioms 1, 2 and 3 of previous section.

Sketch of proof. To simplify the exposition, discrete alternatives with T consequences C_j, each with probability

p_j will be considered. The preference index for the state of the system resulting from outcome C_j will be denoted by h_j. The extension to continuous probability distributions is straightforward by using Lebesgue-Stiltjes integrals to substitute the discrete summations.

3.1.   Existence of alternatives over preference indices

By using Axiom 1, convert any alternative over consequences C_j to an alternative over preference indices h_j. Order the h_j increasingly such that

$$h_w = h_1 < h_2 < h_3 < \ldots\ldots < h_T = h_b$$

where $h_w = h_1$ is the worst consequence and $h_T = h_b$ is the best possible consequence. If there are ties among the h_j join the probabilities.

It is clear that the alternatives over h described above exist if, and only if, axiom 1 holds.

Let h_0 be the preference index of the (evolving) status-quo, then three cases may be immediately recognized:
a. Favourable alternatives when $h_0 \leq h_w$.
b. Unfavourable alternatives when $h_b \leq h_0$.
c. Mixed alternatives when $h_w \leq h_0 \leq h_b$.

3.2.   Existence of the generalized means

Hardy, Littlewood and Polya (1934, pages 158 ff.) following the line of thought of de Finetti (1931) show the following theorem:

The most general functional of F satisfying axioms 2.a (consistency with certainty and first order extended stochastic dominance) and axiom 3 (extended substitution principle) is the generalized mean $M_k(A)$ defined by

$$M_k(A) = M_Z(F) = Z^{-1}\left[\int_{-\infty}^{\infty} Z(h)dF(h)\right] = Z^{-1}\left[E[Z(h)]\right] \quad (1),$$

where $Z(h)$ is a continuous and strictly increasing function in the interval (h_w, h_b); k represents different valid functions $Z(.)$. In fact Z only needs to be strictly monotonic, since $-Z$ is strictly increasing when Z is strictly decreasing. The integral is understood in the sense of Stieltjes-Lebesgue. As usual, $Z^{-1}(.)$ is the inverse function of $Z(.)$.

The generalized means are unique up to a linear transformation in the function Z as shown by Hardy, Littlewood and Polya (1934, page 66):

"In order that $M_Z(A) = M_X(A)$ for all alternatives A, it is necessary and sufficient that

$$X = aZ + b \qquad\qquad (2)$$

where a and b are constants and $a \neq 0$". It is well known that the property described by Eq. 2 is an important characteristic of the EUM; clearly, it is just a particular case of a property exhibited by all generalized means.

3.3.   Existence of the certainty equivalent

Let n be the minimum number of independent generalized means completely representing the distribution function F, then there exist functions $H(.)$ such that

$$h_e = H(A) = H(M_1(F), M_2(F), \ldots, M_n(F)) \qquad (3)$$

satisfies axiom 2.b (consistency with certainty and first-degree stochastic dominance).

The most general form of the GMM is given by Eq. 3. Additional structure is brought in by the individual attitudes towards certainty (section 2.3.3). The process is illustrated in next section for the simplest $H(A)$: a linear combination of generalized means,

$$h_e = H(A) = \sum_{k=1}^{n} r_k M_k(A) \qquad\qquad (4).$$

4.   THE EUM AND THE LMM AS PARTICULAR CASES OF THE GMM

4.1.   The Linearized Moments Model

The problem of moments has received ample attention in the
mathematical literature. The basic idea is to determine
under what conditions n moments of the probability
distribution completely represent the distribution, and
whether a given set of moments uniquely determine the
probability distribution. For a comprehensive treatment of
the subject see Shohat and Tamarkin (1943).

        In this paper it is assumed that the probability
distribution may be indeed represented by n moments.
Furthermore, accepting the Allais-Tintner Principle, $Z(.)$
in Eq. 1 is defined as $Z(h) = h^k$; thus, $Z^{-1}(z) = z^{1/k}$. In
this fashion the generalized means of Eq. 1 become
linearized moments:

$$M_k(A) = Z^{-1}[E(h^k)] = [E(h^k)]^{1/k} \qquad (5)$$

and the simplest $H(A)$ of Eq. 4 becomes

$$H(A) = \sum_{k=1}^{n} r_k [E(h^k)]^{1/k} \qquad (6),$$

which is precisely the General Risk (or Uncertainty)
Operator formerly proposed by the author (Munera, 1978;
Munera and de Neufville, 1983). This model is renamed here
to become the Linearized Moments Model, LMM.

        Previous derivation is summarized in Figure 2, where
the similar process leading to the EUM (discussed in next
section 4.2) is included as well.

        In order to establish the link with the real world,
it may be speculated that the coefficients r_k of the LMM
capture the individual attitude towards randomness (ATR
henceforth).[4]

        The conditions of consistency with certainty and
first-degree stochastic dominance (axiom 2.b) immediately
limit the potential values of r_k to the positive region as
follows:

$$\sum_{k=1}^{n} r_k = 1, \; r_k \in [0,1] \text{ for } k = 1, 2, .., n \qquad (7)$$

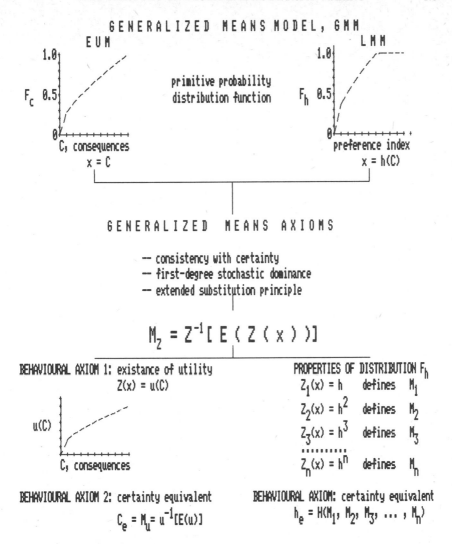

Figure 2. EUM and LMM as particular cases of the GMM.
The properties of the generalized means are common to the
EUM and the LMM. Each model is derived from a different
initial probability distribution, more general in the case
of the LMM. Also, there is difference regarding the
interpretation of the means: the EUM immediately attaches
behavioural meaning to a single M_z; the LMM, on the other
hand, represents the probability distribution F_h as
function of several M_z.

Recalling the attitude towards certainty introduced in section 2.3.3, two forms of the LMM may be recognized as briefly discussed below.

4.1.1. Model for absolute consistency with certainty

Odd moments $Z = h^k$ monotonically increase, regardless of the sign of h. This implies that Eq. 5 is indeed a generalized mean for any alternative A. For individuals exhibiting absolute consistency with certainty, even moments can not enter in Eq. 6, thus obtaining a LMM with odd moments only (Munera, 1984b). In such case coefficients for k even are zero, i.e. $r_k = 0$ for k = 2, 4,..., whereas coefficients for odd k obey Eq. 7. Then from eqs. 5 and 6 the preference index for alternative A is given by

$$H(A) = r_1 M_1(A) + r_3 M_3(A) + r_5 M_5(A) + \cdots \qquad (8)$$

4.1.2. Models for partial consistency with certainty

The partial consistency is induced by the even moments of the probability distribution function. Recalling that h(.) is an index of preference, i.e. that larger numerical values are preferable to the individual, it is obvious that even moments $Z = h^k$ increase monotonically for favourable alternatives and decrease monotonically for unfavourable ones.

By definition, pessimistic individuals must exhibit consistency with certainty for unfavourable alternatives only. From Eqs. 6 and 7 it follows that

$$H(A) = r_1 M_1(A) - r_2 M_2(A) + r_3 M_3(A) - \cdots \qquad (9)$$

Likewise, by definition optimistic individuals exhibit consistency with certainty for favourable alternatives only. Therefore, the certainty equivalent for the alternative is given by

$$H(A) = r_1 M_1(A) + r_2 M_2(A) + r_3 M_3(A) + \cdots \qquad (10)$$

where the coefficients r_k obey Eq. 7. Note that, when k is even, it is mandatory to select the positive sign for $M_k(.)$.

It is the author's opinion that absolute consistency

with certainty is a desirable condition for corporate, regulatory and social decision making. On the other hand, for individual decision making any of the three cases listed in section 2.3.3 may arise. In the context of the EUM, it seems that most individuals exhibit "risk-aversion" for favourable prospects. This feature is somehow similar to pessimism in the LMM.

For descriptive applications it is suggested that the first three terms in Eqs. 8 to 10 are sufficient to capture the main features of the non-deterministic alternatives (this was also suggested by Allais, 1953). The descriptive power of such Three Moments Model (TMM) is demonstrated elsewhere (Munera, 1978; Munera and Yadigaroglu, 1980; Munera and de Neufville, 1983; Munera, 1984a and 1984b).

4.2.   Derivation of the EUM

From the representation theorem sketched in section 3, and, further recalling the comments to the axioms of the GMM in 2.4, it may be inferred that the EUM may be treated as a special case of the general problem, as illustrated in Fig. 2. Some comments to this derivation are in order:

4.2.1. Primitive probability distribution
It is quite clear that an important difference between the EUM and the LMM is the starting probability distribution function:
-- Distribution function F_c over consequences or states in the EUM, and
-- Distribution function F_h over preference indices in the LMM.

4.2.2. Absolute generality of the generalized means
The generalized means are mathematical objects, originally developed in the context of physical applications, that apply to any (probability) distribution function F over a (random) variable C. The functionals $M_z(F)$ as in Eq. 1 exhibit the following three properties:
a) Consistency with certainty (axiom 2.a).
b) First-degree extended stochastic dominance (axiom 2.a).
c) Extended substitution principle (axiom 3).

Conversely, the generalized means are defined by the three properties above.

The continuous monotonic function $Z(C)$ may be anything. For instance, $Z(C)$ may be related to:
- Properties of the (probability) distribution function F, like the moments.
- Physical properties of C, say the mass or the length.
- Psychological perceptions about C, i.e. perceptions of someone pondering C, like, for instance, the utility in the sense of the EUM.

The three basic properties of the generalized means listed above are exhibited both by the EUM and the LMM, thus constituting a core of axioms common to the two models. Notice, however, that a behavioural interpretation for the indices obtained (i.e. of the generalized means) requires some additional assumptions, as discussed in next section.

Although the aspect just mentioned is usually overlooked, it is our claim that leaving out such behavioural assumptions is not a minor point. Indeed, it is easy to construct models with the same properties of the generalized means, but completely devoid of any behavioural content whatsoever. For example, let C be some monetary outcome payable in one-dollar bank-notes and let $Z(C)$ be the area (or, if you prefer, the weight in the Moon) of such outcome. Quite obviously, the behavioural content of an EUM, or of a GMM, based on such $Z(.)$ would be very controversial. Nontheless, such model would be consistent with all axioms of the generalized means.

4.2.3. Behavioural assumptions implicit in the EUM

In Fig. 2 the EUM is derived from five assumptions, three defining the generalized means plus two behavioural conditions:

a) Behavioural assumption 1: Existence of utility

There exists for each individual a unique (up to a linear transformation), monotonic and continuous function $Z(C)$, independent of F_c. This function is called utility $u(C) = Z(C)$.

After introducing this assumption Eq. 1 becomes,

$$M_u(F_c) = u^{-1}[E(u(C))] \tag{11}$$

Note that $u(C)$ is a scale for consequences C, applicable to any F. This includes the particular case of degenerate alternatives, like sure outcomes. Further, recall that generalized means, including the EUM, exhibit consistency with certainty. Then, u(C) must be applicable to both deterministic and non-deterministic consequences. Being so, it is rather surprising that a function that (pressumably) correctly represents deterministic preferences, can, at the same time, correctly and completely represent the non-deterministic preference structure (some proponents of the EUM boldly claim that u(.) represents all individual attitudes towards "risk").

It must be strongly remarked that, even if u(C) exists, there are many other functions Z(C) with the same properties (continuous and monotonous over C), leading therefore to different generalized means.

This means, furthermore, that even after granting the existence of utility for the sake of the discussion, the function u(C) is not unique --i.e. it is not the only one exhibiting the properties of the generalized means-- as claimed by proponents of the EUM.

In the context of the EUM it is usually interpreted that the generalized mean $M_u(F_c)$ is the certainty equivalent C_e of the nondeterministic alternative A by writing

$$u(C_e) = u(M_u) \qquad\qquad (12)$$

and, hence

$$u(C_e) = E[u(C)] \qquad\qquad (13).$$

This innocent looking assignment implies in fact an additional axiom since the left hand side of Eq. 12 is a scale for <u>deterministic</u> quantities (like the certainty equivalent), whereas $M_u(.)$ on the right hand side is a mathematical property associated with $Z(C) = u(C)$ (whose existence is ascertained by previous axiom). Eq. 12 thus further confirms our previous remark that the u(C) of Eq. 11 is a scale for deterministic consequences too, and not merely a scale for uncertain consequences as seems to be the claim of some defenders of the EUM.[5] Furthermore, and as a final confirmation of our remark, by writing the same u(.) on both sides of Eqs. 12 and 13 it is assumed that <u>non-deterministic alternatives</u> are measured on the same scale u(C) as <u>single deterministic consequences</u>.

The foregoing remarks are summarized as:

b) Behavioural assumption 2: Certainty equivalents
There exists a unique deterministic consequence C_e equivalent to every non-deterministic alternative A over consequences C. Furthermore, C and C_e belong to the same scale.

It is the author's contention that behavioural assumptions similar to a) and b) described above must be implicitly present in the axiomatization of the EUM. For instance, Luce and Raiffa (1957) identified utility with a subjective probability making a two-outcome alternative equivalent to a sure consequence C. Giving the name of "utility" to that probability is an innocuous exercise if, and only if, no particular meaning is associated with "utility". However, interpreting u(C) as capturing all individual opinions about the non-deterministic content of the alternative does require some further assumptions. Luce and Raiffa (1957, page 29) were aware of this difficulty when they wrote (after deriving the index u(L) from their axioms of ordering, continuity, substitutibility, transitivity and monotonicity):

"If a person imposes a transitive preference relation over a set of lotteries and if to each lottery L there is assigned a number u(L) such that the magnitudes of the numbers reflect the preferences, i.e. $u(L) \geq u(L')$ if and only if L is preferred or indifferent to L', then we say there exists a utility function u over the lotteries. If, IN ADDITION, the utility function has the property that u[qL, (1-q)L'] = qu(L) + (1-q)u(L'), for all probabilities q and lotteries L and L', then we say the utility function is linear". In a footnote they continued: "Sometimes this property is referred to as the expected utility hupothesis since it asserts that the utility of a lottery is equal to the expected utility of its component prizes" (underlining in the original; capitals added).

4.2.4. Behavioural assumptions in the LMM
In contrast to the previous derivation of the EUM, the LMM does not introduce behavioural assumptions directly into the generalized means. Instead, the Z(h) are identified with properties of F (the moments), and not with individual perceptions regarding the uncertainty content of C (recall that C = h is a preference index under certainty).

The generalized means of Eq. 1 are consistent with

the axioms, <u>independently of any behavioural assumption</u> about the uncertainty content of the alternative under consideration. This is a major difference with the EUM.

The behavioural assumptions for the LMM are contained in axiom 2: the deterministic - non-deterministic conexion. They may be summarized in two points:
- Existence of a certainty equivalent, belonging to the same scale as the deterministic preference index. And,
- Existence of coefficients related to the individual attitude towards randomness.

5.   CONCLUSION

A Generalized Means Model (GMM) for non-deterministic decision making was derived from a set of axioms, whose core is the concept of <u>mean</u> axiomatized in Italy by de Finetti and Kolmogoroff in the very early 1930's. It comes as a surprise, that the axioms of the generalized means include an <u>extended</u> form of the Substitution Principle.

As sketched in the paper, the two contending theories --the Expected Utility Model and some forms of the Moments Model-- may be derived as particular cases of the GMM. This joint derivation allows one to pinpoint the introduction of the behavioural assumptions for both the EUM and the GMM. It turns out that the EUM introduces the behavioural constraints related to uncertainty at an earlier stage. This may account for the reduced capability of the EUM to handle the "risk" content of non-deterministic alternatives.

It was found that the simplest Moments Model consistent with the axioms of the GMM is the Linearized Moments Model (LMM) proposed by the present author in earlier research (Munera, 1978). A simplified model with only three moments (TMM) was suggested for practical applications.

Since the LMM is consistent with a set of reasonable axioms, it may be concluded that the LMM is a <u>normative</u> -- or at least <u>prescriptive</u>-- theory for individuals obeying the axioms of the GMM. For <u>descriptive</u> purposes the simple TMM usually suffices.

Nuclear Engineering Laboratory
Swiss Federal Institute of Technology

ACKNOWLEDGEMENTS

The author whishes to thank Prof. George Yadigaroglu of the Swiss Federal Institute of Technology for his longstanding encouragement and support, and for providing the stimulating working conditions at his Institute that made possible this research.

NOTES

1. The standard words <u>lottery</u>, <u>gamble</u> or <u>game</u> seem to evoke in some people non-relevant social or religious concerns. It might be, therefore, more convenient to use <u>alternatives</u> (as suggested here) or <u>prospects</u> (as proposed by Kahneman and Tversky, 1979).
2. <u>Non-deterministic</u> is used here as a generic expression for consequences whose occurrence can not be predicted in advance, either because they are random, or because they may arise from as yet unknown phenomena, or because they depend of a human future purposeful action. <u>Randomness</u> is meant in the sense of many, small, and complex physical causes compounding together to produce an unknown result in the future.
3. To simplify notation, preferences are related to consequences C of alternative A. Actually, preferences refer to states of the system S, function of both C and the initial state S_0. The functional form of h(.) may depend on the state of the environment E at that particular time. The state of the world W is defined by S and E. Furthermore, there is no need for the preference index h(.) to be monotonic.
4. In his original work the present author referred to r_k as "risk parameters" (Munera, 1978). The word <u>risk</u>, however, evokes <u>danger</u>, which not always is the case. Therefore, it is suggested that the r_k coefficients are more readily linked to randomness or, perhaps more generally, to uncertainty.
5. This observation is related to, but weaker than, Allais' (1979, page 103) claim that when neo-Bernoullian utility exists it merges with cardinal utility.

REFERENCES

Allais, M.: 1953, 'Le Comportement de l'Homme Rationnel Devant le Risque: Critique des Postulats et Axiomes de l'Ecole Americaine', Econometrica 21, 503-546.

Allais, M.: 1979, 'The Foundations of a Positive Theory of Choice involving Risk and a Criticism of the Postulates and Axioms of the American School', 27-145 and 'The So-called Allais Paradox and Rational Decisions Under Uncertainty', 437-681 in M. Allais and O. Hagen (eds.), Expected Utility Hypotheses and the Allais Paradox, D. Reidel Publishing Co, Dordrecht, Holland, 714 pp.

Amihud, Y.: 1979, 'Critical Examination of the New Foundation of Utility', 149-160 in M. Allais and O. Hagen (eds.), Expected Utility Hypotheses and the Allais Paradox, D. Reidel Publishing Co, Dordrecht, Holland, 714 pp.

Chew, S.H.: 1983, 'A Generalization of the Quasilinear Mean with Applications to the Measurement of Income Inequality and Decision Theory Resolving the Allais Paradox', Econometrica 51, 1065-1092.

de Finetti, B.: 1931, 'Sul Concetto di Media', Giornale dell'Istituto Italiano degli Attuari 2, 369-396.

Hardy, G.H., J.E. Littlewood and G. Polya: 1934, Inequalities, Cambridge University Press, Cambridge, U.K., second edition (1952) 324pp.

Kahneman, D. and A. Tversky: 1979, 'Prospect Theory: An Analysis of Decision Under Risk, Econometrica 47, 263-291.

Keeney, R.L. and H. Raiffa: 1976, Decisions with Multiple Objectives: Preferences and Value Tradeoffs, John Wiley, New York, 569 pp.

Kolmogoroff, A.: 1930, 'Sur la Notion de la Moyenne', Atti della Reale Accademia Nazionale dei Lincei, Rendiconti, Serie 6 12, 388-391.

Luce, R.D. and H. Raiffa: 1957, Games and Decisions, John Wiley and Sons, Inc., New York, 509 pp.

Munera, H.A.: 1978, Modeling of Individual Risk Attitudes in Decision Making under Uncertainty: An Application to Nuclear Power, Ph.D. dissertation,Department of Engineering, University of California, Berkeley, California, USA, 266 pp.

Munera, H.A. and G. Yadigaroglu: 1980, 'A New Methodology to Quantify Risk Perception', Nuclear Science and Engineering 75, 211-224.

Munera, H.A. and R. de Neufville: 1983, 'A Decision Analysis Model when the Substitution Principle is not Acceptable', 247–262 in B.P. Stigum and F. Wenstøp (eds.), _Foundations of Utility and Risk Theory with Applications_, D. Reidel Publishing Co., Dordrecht, Holland, 491 pp.

Munera, H.A.: 1984a, 'The Generalized Means Model for Non-deterministic Decision Making: II. Overview of a Unified Theory', submitted to _Theory and Decision_.

Munera, H.A.: 1984b, 'The Generalized Means Model for Non-deterministic Decision Making: III. A Normative Theory when Absolute Consistency with Certainty is Desirable', Working Paper, Institute of Energy Technology, ETH-Zurich, 46 pp.

Pope, R.: 1984, 'The Utility of Gambling and of Outcomes: Inconsistent First Approximations', 251–273 in O. Hagen and F. Wenstop (eds.), _Progress in Utility and Risk Theory_, D. Reidel Publishing Company, Dordrecht, Holland, 279 pp.

Savage, L.J.: 1972, _The Foundations of Statistics_, 2nd. Revised edition, Dover Publications, New York, 310 pp.

Shohat, J.A. and J.D. Tamarkin: 1943, 'The Problem of Moments', _Mathematical Surveys_ 1, The American Mathematical Society, New York, 144 pp.

Tintner, G.: 1941, 'The Theory of Choice under Subjective Risk and Uncertainty', _Econometrica_ 9, 298–304.

von Neumann, J. and O. Morgenstern: 1944, _Theory of Games and Economic Behavior_, Princeton University Press, 3rd. edition, Science Editions, John Wiley, New York (1964) 640 pp.

Antonio Camacho

INDIVIDUAL CARDINAL UTILITY, INTERPERSONAL
COMPARISONS, AND SOCIAL CHOICE

1. Introduction

The problem of <u>Social Choice and Individual Values</u> is the problem of determining a social ordering or social ranking of given <u>states</u> based, or depending, on the individual <u>values</u> with regard to those <u>states</u>.

Aside from the trivial case where there are no conflicts among the values of the different individuals, it implies <u>always</u> making interpersonal comparisons of the individual values. Thus if individual 1 attaches a greater value to <u>state</u> x than to <u>state</u> x' and individual 2 attaches a greater value to <u>state</u> x' than to <u>state</u> x: That <u>state</u> x is ranked socially above <u>state</u> x' means, in some sense, that the gains in value to individual 1 are greater or more important than the losses to individual 2 by having x instead of x'; that <u>state</u> x' is ranked socially above <u>state</u> x, that the losses to individual 1 are smaller than the gains to individual 2 by having x' instead of x; and finally, that x is ranked socially indifferent to x', that the gains to individual 1 are equal to the losses to individual 2 by having x instead of x'.

A <u>social choice mechanism</u>, that is a mechanism or rule to determine a social ordering of given <u>states</u> based on the individual values of those <u>states</u> is, whether we admit it or not, a mechanism to make interpersonal comparisons of values; and vice versa, a rule to make interpersonal comparisons of values can be interpreted as a social choice mechanism. Therefore, to talk of a social choice mechanism that does not make interpersonal comparisons of <u>values</u> appears to be a contradiction.

If social choice is then to make interpersonal comparisons of individual values, how much <u>can</u> and <u>should</u> we know about individual values? Is the individual preference orderings of the given <u>states</u> what

185

L. Daboni et al. (eds.), Recent Developments in the Foundations of Utility and Risk Theory, 185–200.
© *1986 by D. Reidel Publishing Company.*

we can and should know as the ordinalists claim (see for instance Arrow (1963, pp. 10-11), Gärdenfors (1984), Samuelson (1947, pp. 227-8, 1967, 1977). Or, can we and should we know more about individual values in order to arrive at reasonable social choice mechanisms? This paper is devoted, in great part, to a discussion of these questions.

Section 2 will be mainly dedicated to discuss the can we question. The should we question will be taken up in section 3. In section 4, the general problem of social choice will be considered in view of the conclusions arrived at in sections 2 and 3.

2.   The "Can We" Question: Cardinal Utility

In the long controversy in the economic literature of cardinality vs. ordinality, a main issue has been whether or not an individual can go beyond the simple ranking or ordering of alternatives according to his preferences and also rank or compare the intensities of the preferences. This is the classical problem of whether the utility function can be only ordinal, that is, represent only the order of preference of the individual; or whether it can be cardinal and represent not only the order of preference but also the intensity of the preference.

Before proceeding to the discussion of this issue, the following remark seems appropriate. It is universally acknowledged that to make interpersonal comparisons of intensities of preferences is, by an order of magnitude, a more difficult problem than that of making comparisons by a single individual of his intensities of preference. If we deny that an individual say Mr. 1, who prefers x over x' and x' over x'' can assert whether his intensity of preference for x over x' is greater than, equal to, or smaller than, his intensity of preference for x' over x'', how can we then proceed to propose a social choice mechanism which implies, as stated in the introduction, making comparisons of intensities of preferences among different individuals? Suppose that Mr. 1 prefers x over x', and Mr. 2 x' over x. Suppose further that we assert that neither Mr. 1 can make a meaningful statement with regard to his intensity of preference for x over x'; nor Mr. 2 with regard to his intensity of preference for x' over x. How can we then proceed to propose a social choice mechanism to socially rank x and x' if this implies, as stated before, making a comparison between the intensity of preference of Mr. 1 for x over x', and of Mr. 2 for x' over x? It appears, in view of this, that to work on problems of social choice requires, at least, an open mind with regard to the problem of comparisons of intensities of preference by an individual or, as it is more commonly known, cardinal utility.

After this remark, let us proceed now to consider the cardinal utility or intensities of preference problem. But before I present my own approach, to this problem, that I have labeled the repetition approach, I would like to briefly review, and state my reaction to, the most important methods or approaches proposed by other researchers to determine cardinal utilities.[1] More concretely, I will briefly review the expected utility approach formalized by von Neumann and Morgenstern (1947); the utility differences approach formalized, among others, by Frisch (1926), and by Alt (1971); and the minimum perceptible threshold suggested as far back as 1781 by Borda, proposed in 1881 by Edgeworth, and adopted more recently by Ng (1980).

That there are intensities of preference seems to be universally accepted. That if I prefer x over x' and x' over x'', my preference for x over x' may be stronger than my preference for x' over x'' appears to be accepted by almost everybody. The problem then seems to be, how can we make this notion of intensity of preference operational and describe a method to measure it?

The method proposed by what I have called the expected utility approach axiomatized by von Neumann and Morgenstern consists in asking the individual to rank lotteries. Then from the ranking of these lotteries, if it satisfies certain so called rationality axioms, a cardinal utility function, and the intensities of preference implied by this function can be obtained such that the individual ranks the lotteries as if he were maximizing his expected utility. Thus, if an individual prefers x to x' and x' to x'' and then he prefers a lottery where he can win x with probability $\frac{1}{2}$ and x'' with probability $\frac{1}{2}$, to having x' with certainty, this is interpreted as meaning that his intensity of preference for x over x' is greater than his intensity of preference for x' over x''.

Two things should be pointed out with regard to this

method: (1) If intensities of preference exist in any
meaningful way, they should be present even in a world of
certainty and the individual should not have to recur to
play lotteries to measure them. (2) If intensities of
preference exist in a world of certainty, and if they
affect the way an individual ranks lotteries, and if the
way the individual ranks lotteries satisfies the so called
rationality axioms and therefore a cardinal utility
function can be obtained, still the intensities of
preference implied by the obtained cardinal utility
function may not coincide with the intensities of
preference of the individual in a world of certainty. The
individual's intensities of preference in a world of
certainty may have been altered by the uncertainty factor
introduced in the expected utility approach.[2]

The utility differences approach assumes that the
individual is able to rank, according to his preferences,
not only the different alternatives, but also differences
of preference among pairs of alternatives. To determine his
cardinal utility, say, of money, questions like the
following are asked to the individual:[3] "for what value
of i is your intensity of preference for $ i over $ 100
the same as your intensity of preference for $100 over
$50?.

The problem with this approach is that it does not
provide an operational definition of the preference
ordering postulated on pairs of alternatives. If I were
asked the question stated in the previous paragraph, I
would respond by asking what it meant.

The minimum perceptible thresholds approach to
cardinal utility borrows the notion of minimum perceptible
thresholds, developed by Fechner and Weber, from
psychology. According to this approach the intensity of
preference between, say, x and x' is determined by
counting the number of minimum perceptible
thresholds between x and x'. It has the attraction for
some of the researchers working on the problem of
social choice of providing a so called objective
way of determining the unit of measurement for the
individual cardinal utilities and thus facilitating the
interpersonal comparison of these utilities.

The notion of minimum perceptible thresholds, which
appears appropriate in measuring sensation as a function
of the intensity of the stimulus, does not appear
appropriate, in this writer's view, to determine

intensities of preference and cardinal utility; and much
less, to be used in making interpersonal comparisons of
utilities. If I am a diabetic, I may very well strongly
prefer a smaller to a larger amount of sugar in my coffee
even if the difference in sweetness is below the minimum
perceptible threshold. Other similar examples can
easily be suggested by the reader.

In determining preferences and intensities of
preference of alternatives, the individual, again in this
writer's view, takes (or should take) into consideration
not only <u>sensation</u>, whether it is pleasant or unpleasant,
but all the consequences of the alternatives under
consideration. The sensation derived from an
alternative is part of the consequences of the
alternative, but not necessarily all. Therefore,
reference only to minimum perceptible thresholds in
determining intensities of preference and cardinal utility
for an individual seems unsatisfactory.

Let us proceed to present the <u>repetition</u> approach.
Space consideration does not permit to give a detailed
account of the approach. For this the reader is referred
to Camacho (1982), and the references given there. The
basic idea underlying this approach appears, once it is
properly understood, very simple and natural. Therefore,
it is hoped that the condensed version that follows will
suffice to provide the reader with a clear understanding
of the approach.

The notions of <u>choice situation</u> and <u>identical
choice situations</u>, and the consideration of sequences
of identical choice situations, are basic parts in the
approach proposed here to defining <u>intensity of
preference</u> and <u>cardinal utility</u>.

A decision maker facing a set of possible alternatives
and trying to choose one out of this set of possible
alternatives available to him constitutes a <u>choice
situation</u>. Thus an individual after dinner facing a set
of three alternatives x≡ coffee, x'≡ tea, x''≡ camomile
and trying to decide whether to drink coffee or tea or
camomile constitutes a choice situation.

The decision maker can <u>imagine</u> a sequence of
repetitions of the <u>same</u> choice situation and the
corresponding sequence of choices, one choice for each
choice situation, and proceed then to rank the possible
corresponding sequences of choices, according to his
preferences. From the ordering of the corresponding

sequences of choices, which it is assumed satisfies certain natural conditions, the notion of intensity of preference can be precisely stated and a cardinal utility function defined on the choice set, corresponding to the choice situation, derived.

Consider the choice situation described above where an individual after dinner faces a set of three alternatives $x \equiv$ coffee, $x' \equiv$ tea, $x'' \equiv$ camomile. Suppose that, given the choice situation, the individual prefers coffee to tea and tea to camomile, that is the individual prefers x to x' and x' to x''. Suppose further that the decision maker imagines now sequences of three <u>identical</u> choice situations and proceeds to order the 27 possible sequences of three drinks (coffee, coffee, coffee), (coffee, coffee, tea),..., (camomile, camomile, camomile). Then:

(1) If the decision maker ranks the sequence (coffee, tea, camomile) equal to the sequence (tea, tea, tea), then we conclude that his strength of preference for coffee over tea is equal to his strength of preference for tea over camomile: the loss of satisfaction suffered by changing the first entry of the sequence (coffee, tea, camomile) from coffee to tea is equal to the gain in satisfaction obtained by changing the third entry from camomile to tea.

(2) If the decision maker ranks the sequence (coffee, tea, camomile) above the sequence (tea, tea, tea), then we conclude that his strength of preference for coffee over tea is greater than his strength of preference for tea over camomile: the loss of satisfaction suffered by changing the first entry of the sequence (coffee, tea, camomile) from coffee to tea is greater than the gain in satisfaction obtained by changing the third entry from camomile to tea.

(3) If the decision maker ranks the sequence (coffee, tea, camomile) below the sequence (tea, tea, tea), then we conclude that his strength of preference for coffee over tea is smaller than his strength of preference for tea over camomile: the loss of satisfaction suffered by changing the first entry of the sequence (coffee, tea, camomile) from coffee to tea is smaller than the gain in satisfaction obtained by changing the third entry from camomile to tea.

Suppose now as a further illustration that the decision maker ranks the sequence (coffee, camomile, camomile) equal to the sequence (tea, tea, tea), then the conclusion is that his intensity of preference for coffee over tea is twice as much as his intensity of preference for tea over camomile. In general, the strength of preference for coffee over tea is, say, h times the strength of preference for tea over camomile if the decision maker when considering h + 1 identical choice situations is indifferent between the sequence consisting of h + 1 teas and the sequence consisting of 1 coffee and h camomiles.

Let, as above, the action "having coffee" be denoted by x, the action "having tea" by x' and the action "having camomile" by x". Thus the set of available actions, to be denoted by X, is X = {x, x', x"}. Assume, as before, that the decision maker prefers having coffee to having tea and having tea to having camomile. That is he prefers x to x' and x' to x".

The ordinal utility function, as is well know, is an assignment of numbers to actions such that (i) if two actions are indifferent to each other from the decision maker's point of view, the numbers assigned to them must be equal; and (ii) if one action is preferred by the decision maker to another action, the number assigned to the preferred action must be greater than the number assigned to the other action.

Thus, if the decision maker prefers, as stated above, x to x' and x' to x": u(x)= 3, u(x')= 1, u(x")= 0; and v(x)= 2, v(x')= 1, v(x")= 0 are both ordinal utility functions.

But if we want the assignment of numbers to actions, that is the utility function, to represent not only the order of preference of the decision maker but also its strength of preference, and the strength of preference of the decision maker for x over x' is, say, twice as large as his strength of preference for x' over x", then we should require that the difference between the numbers (the utilities) assigned to x and x' be twice as large as the difference between the number (utilities) assigned to x' and x". In this case u(x)= 3, u(x')= 1, u(x")= 0 is a utility function that satisfies such a requirement and is called a _cardinal_ _utility_ _function_. The function v(x)= 2, v(x')= 1, v(x")= 0, that indicates the preference ordering of the actions by the decision maker but not the

strength of his preferences is called an <u>ordinal</u>
<u>utility function</u>. A utility function which is
required to represent <u>only</u> the order of preference is
called an <u>ordinal utility function</u>. A utility function
which is required to represent both the order of preference
and the intensity <u>of</u> preference is called a
<u>cardinal utility function</u>.

3. The "Should We" Question: Unsatisfactoriness of the Ordinal Approach

In the previous <u>section</u> we have argued that we
can know more about individual values than the simple
ranking of <u>states</u>. More concretely, we have argued
that not only preferences but also intensities of
preference can be precisely defined and that each
individual can arrive at his cardinal utility function
representing not only his preference but also the
intensities of his preference.

But even if each individual can have this information
regarding his values, is it necessary to use it in making
social choice decisions? This is the <u>should we</u> question
to which I shall now turn.

To answer this question, we will first try to show the
consequences of not using information regarding the
intensities of preference of the individuals and basing
the social choice decisions only on the individual
rankings o preference orderings of the different
<u>states</u>. More concretely, we will try to show that any
social choice mechanism that is based only on the
individual preference orderings is not Pareto-optimal in
the sense that it may make a sequence of choices which is
not Pareto-optimal, that is such that there is another
sequence which is at least as preferred by every
individual and strictly preferred by at least one.

The complete details of the proof of this theorem
cannot be given here and again the reader is referred to
Camacho, (1982). But the underlying idea is quite simple
and it is hoped that it will be easily understood with the
help of the discussion and example that follows.

Consider two individuals Mr. 1 and Mr. 2, and two
social <u>states</u> x and x'. Consider two situations:
<u>situation</u> 1 and <u>situation</u> 2. Suppose that in
<u>situation</u> 1 Mr. 1 prefers x to x' and Mr. 2, x' to x;

and in situation 2, Mr. 1 prefers x' to x   and Mr. 2, x
to x'.

Consider now a social choice mechanism that chooses x
in situation 1 and x in situation 2. The choosing of x
in situation 1 can be interpreted as considering the
preference of Mr. 1 in this situation for x over x'
stronger or more important than the preference of Mr. 2
for x' over x. The choosing of x in situation 2 can be
interpreted as considering the preference of Mr. 2 in
this situation for x over x' stronger or more important
than the preference of Mr. 1 for x' over x.

But how can we make such comparisons without even
knowing the strength of preference of Mr. 1 for x over x'
in situation 1 as compared to his strength of preference
for x' over x in situation 2; and the strength of
preference of Mr. 2 for x' over x in situation 1 as
compared to his strength of preference for x over x' in
situation 2? It may very well occur that the strength of
preference of Mr. 1 for x over x' in situation 1 is
smaller than his strength of preference in situation 2
for x' over x; and that the strength of preference of Mr.
2 for x' over x in situation 1 is greater than his
strength of preference for x   over x' in situation 2. If
this is the case, then the sequence x' in situation 1
and x' in situation 2 is preferred by both Mr. 1 and Mr.
2 to the sequence x in situation 1 and x in situation 2
generated by the mechanism, which implies that it is not
in fact, Pareto-optimal.

Now that it has been shown that social choice
mechanisms which are based only on the individual
preference orderings are not Pareto-optimal, we should ask
the following question: Can we construct Pareto-optimal
social choice mechanisms, if we also use information
regarding intensities of preference of the individuals?
The answer is yes as it will be indicated below.

The notion of intensity of preference and cardinal
utility discussed in section 2 for the case of a choice
situation can easily be extended to the case of different
choice situations.

If there are k_i different choice situation $E_i^1, \ldots,$
$E_i^j, \ldots, E_i^{k_i}$ for individual i, and the choice set
contains m alternatives $x_1, \ldots x_r, \ldots x_m$, then instead
of a cardinal utility function defined on the choice set,
we have a matrix of cardinal utility indices

$$\underline{u}_i\ (m,k_i) = \begin{bmatrix} u_i(1,1),\ldots u_i(1,j),\ldots,u_i(1,k_i) \\ \cdot \qquad\qquad \cdot \qquad\qquad \cdot \\ \cdot \qquad\qquad \cdot \qquad\qquad \cdot \\ \cdot \qquad\qquad \cdot \qquad\qquad \cdot \\ u_i(r,1),\ldots u_i(r,j),\ldots,u_i(r,k_i) \\ \cdot \qquad\qquad \cdot \qquad\qquad \cdot \\ \cdot \qquad\qquad \cdot \qquad\qquad \cdot \\ \cdot \qquad\qquad \cdot \qquad\qquad \cdot \\ u_i(m,1),\ldots u_i(m,j),\ldots,u_i(m,k_i) \end{bmatrix}$$

where $u_i(r,j)$ represents, for individual i, the cardinal utility index of alternative x_r when choice situation j obtains. These utility indices, which are constant up to transformations of the form $u_i'(r,j) = c \cdot u_i(r,j) + b_j$, where c and b_j are real numbers with $c > 0$, have the property that given a sequence of choice situations $E_i^{j_1},\ldots E_i^{j_h},\ldots,E_i^{j_n}$, the corresponding sequence of actions $x_{r_1}\ldots,x_{r_h},\ldots,x_{r_n}$ is at least as preferred as the corresponding sequence of actions $x_{r_1'},\ldots,x_{r_h'}, \ldots x_{r_n'}$, if and only if

$$\sum_{h=1}^{n} u_i(r_h,j_h) \geq \sum_{h=1}^{n} u_i(r_h',j_h).$$

Now let each individual choose one out of his class of cardinal utility matrices defined above. Define a social choice mechanism by having society select for each situation a state whose sum of the corresponding individual cardinal utility indices is greatest. This social choice mechanism, it can be proved, is Pareto-optimal in the sense that for any finite sequence of situations that may occur, the corresponding sequence of states generated by the mechanism is Pareto-optimal.

By now having the individuals choose matrices out of their corresponding classes of cardinal utility matrices in different ways a class of Pareto-optimal social choice mechanisms can be obtained.

It can be shown also that social choice mechanisms which satisfy a mild anonymity condition and that use less information, in some well defined sense, than that contained in the cardinal utility indices are not, in general, Pareto-optimal.

It should also be noticed that the class of social choice mechanisms just defined, in addition to being

Pareto-optimal, are very attractive from an informational
point of view. For each <u>situation</u> that may occur what
each individual has to reveal to be fed into the mechanism
is only his cardinal utility indices of the different
<u>states</u>, corresponding to the given <u>situation</u>. If we
require that the social choice mechanism use only <u>ordinal</u>
<u>language</u>, that is that the individuals transmit only
messages stating how they rank sequences of <u>states</u>
corresponding to sequences of <u>situations</u> of the same
size, then, to achieve Pareto-optimality, the mechanism
becomes cumbersome from an informational point of view.
Indeed, it can be proved, Camacho, (1982), that
if the mild anonymity condition is required in addition to
the use of only <u>ordinal</u> <u>language</u>, then to achieve
Pareto-optimalily: it is not enough that the individuals
reveal, for each <u>situation</u> that obtains, how they order
the different <u>states</u> in that situation; it is not even
enough that they reveal how they order for any
conceivable <u>finite</u> sequence of <u>situations</u> all the
possible sequences of the same size of <u>states</u>. Thus, if
Pareto-optimality is a property that must be required of
every social choice mechanism, then the <u>minimum</u>
information that we must have with regard to individual
values for each <u>situation</u> is the corresponding cardinal
utility indices of the different <u>states</u> of the
individuals. And the answer to the <u>should we</u> question is
definitely in the affirmative.

4.   The Problem of Social Choice

It has been argued above that to make <u>social</u>
<u>choices</u> is to make interpersonal comparisons of utility
and vice versa. Whether we admit it or not, any social
choice mechanism makes interpersonal comparison of
utility. And any <u>rule</u> to make interpersonal comparisons
of utilities can be viewed as defining a social choice
mechanism. Therefore, to talk of a social choice
mechanism that does not make interpersonal comparisons is
to talk of a <u>logical</u> <u>impossibility</u>. The correctness
of this assertion is corroborated by the fact that most of
the important results presented in the last thirty some
years in the social choice literature are indeed different
formalizations in the form of theorems, and proofs, of
this basic logical impossibility.

It has been argued also that if we are going to deal
with the problem of social choice, that is, if we are
going to deal with the _equivalent_ problem of making
interpersonal comparisons of utility, then individual
intensities of preference must be taken into
consideration. Otherwise, the results generated by the
social choice mechanism may be unsatisfactory. This
argument has been formalized in the form of a theorem that
roughly states that any social choice mechanism that
satisfies a mild anonymity condition, and that uses less
information with regard to individual values than that
contained in their cardinal utility indices is not
Pareto-optimal.

Furthermore, it has been shown that, by using the
cardinal utility indices proposed by this writer, a class
of Pareto-optimal social choice mechanisms can be
defined.

Therefore, if we require, as I think we should, that a
social choice mechanism satisfy, in addition to the mild
anonymity condition, the Pareto-optimality property, then
the _minimal_ information that must be required with
regard to individual values is that provided by cardinal
utility indices of the different individuals.

This is the position held by this writer which is at
variance with the position held by the ordinalists (see
for instance Arrow (1964, pp. 10-11); Gärdenfors (1983);
Samuelson (1947, pp. 227-8, 1967, 1977)) who roughly
assert that the _maximal_ information that must be
required with regard to individual values is that
contained in the individual preference orderings of the
alternative _states_.

But even if we agree on the _minimal_ information that
must be required with regard to individual values, the
problem of how to use this information to determine a
social choice mechanism remains. How should we combine the
cardinal utility indices of the individuals to construct
a social choice mechanism?

The numerical values of the cardinal utility indices
proposed above for an individual depend on the _origin_
to be chosen, that can be different for different
situations, and the units of _measurement_ to be
adopted, that must be the _same_ for all the _situations_.
If we propose as a _rule_, to determine a social ordering of
the different _states_, the maximization of the sum of the
cardinal utility indices of the individuals, the resulting

social ordering is dependent, as is well known, on the units of measurement adopted by each individual. Therefore, a criterion must be provided for determining these units of measurement.

Although such a criterion was provided in Camacho (1982, pp. 82-4), the criterion was presented there only as an example of how the normalization of the cardinal utility indices of different individuals could be achieved before proceeding to add them to obtain the social ranking. It was not presented as a criterion that could be defended on more general ethical grounds.

It is the feeling of this writer that a general criterion for normalizing (fixing the unit of measurement for each individual) the cardinal utility indices of different individuals that could be defended under general ethical grounds, is not known yet.

This does not mean that there are no cases for which there exist sound ethical grounds, and we are willing to make interpersonal comparisons either by fixing the unit of measurement for each individual cardinal utility and then adding the resulting cardinal utility indices to obtain a social ordering, or through some other procedure. What we are asserting is that a general criterion, that is a criterion that could be defended under general ethical grounds, is not known yet.

As an example of a case where we might be willing to prescribe a procedure to determine the unit of measurement, to be used by each individual, and to aggregate the resulting cardinal utility indices that may look acceptable from an ethical point of view, consider the following.

Suppose a social club and its choice problem of accepting or rejecting the applications of membership by outside individuals. Let x represent rejecting a new application, and x' accepting it. The preferences of each member of the club are clearly x' preferred to x (x'> x) if the member likes the applicant, x preferred to x' (x > x') if he doesn't. Suppose further that the intensity of preference of each member, in the sense defined in section 2, for x over x', when he does not like the applicant, with regard to x' over x, when he does like applicant, is a very large number N, which happens to be the same for all members of the club.

In this case it appears appropriate, and defendable from an ethical point of view, to fix the unit of measurement of each member by having his cardinal utility indices be:

u(x')=1, u(x)=0, when the member likes the applicant;
u(x)=N, u(x')=0, when he doesn't.

And recommend as a social choice mechanism the maximization of the sum of the individual cardinal utility indices.

Remark. It should be observed that if N is greater than the number of members of the club minus one, then the social choice mechanism proposed above generates the same social choices as the unanimity rule where an application is accepted if no member objects to it, and rejected even if only a single member objects to it.

An example similar to the one stated above, and others were presented in Camacho (1982, chapter 11), to show that social choice mechanisms used in the real world such as majority rule, unanimity rule, two-thirds majority, Borda count, that "look" ordinal, may indeed be taking into consideration intensities of preference and be cardinal.

These examples seem to indicate not that we should be resigned to use ordinal methods, but that in the real world intensities of preference are indeed taken into consideration in choosing social choice mechanisms. This appears to be contrary to what is done in most of the theoretical literature where consideration of intensities of preference is rejected.

That a theory as the one sketched in this paper can justify many of the social choice mechanisms used in the real world can be viewed as an indication of its usefulness and as an indirect test of its validity. Thus, even if a theory is based on axioms that are difficult or impossible to reject by direct experiments, its validity still can be assessed indirectly. For a somewhat different view, see Sugden (1983).

Department of Economics
University of Illinois
Chicago

NOTES

1. For a more extensive discussion of these approaches, see Camacho (1980).
2. For further elaboration on this point, see Camacho (1979) and (1983).
3. See Allais (1979, pp. 615-19).

REFERENCES

Allais, M.: 1979, "Allais Rejoinder: Theory and Empirical Evidence," in Maurice Allais and O. Hagen (eds.) Expected Utility Hypotheses and the Allais Paradox: Contemporary Discussions with Allais Rejoinder, D. Reidel, Dordrecht, Holland, 437-684.

Alt, F.: 1971, "On the Measurability of Utility," in John S. Chipman, Leonid Hurwicz, Marcel K. Ricter, and Hugo F. Sonneschein (eds.), Preferences Utility and Demand, Harcourt Brace Jovanovich, New York. Translated by Siegfried Schach under the editorship of J. S. Chipman.

Arrow, K. J.: 1963, Social Choice and Individual Values, John Wiley and Sons, New York.

Borda, J. C. de: 1781, "Memoir Sur les Elections au Scrutin," Memoires de l'Academic Royale des Sciences.

Camacho, A.: 1979, "Maximizing Expected Utility and the Rule of Long Run Success," in M. Allais and O. Hagen (eds.), Expected Utility Hypotheses and the Allais Paradox: Contemporary Discussions with Allais Rejoinder, D. Reidel, Dordrecht, Holland, 203-29.

Camacho, A.: 1980, "Approaches to Cardinal Utility," Theory and Decision 12, 359-79.

Camacho, A.: 1982, Societies and Social Decision Functions: A Model with Focus on the Information Problem, D. Reidel, Reidel, Dordrecht, Holland.

Camacho, A.: 1983, "Cardinal Utility and Decision Making under Uncertainty," in B.P. Stigum and F. Wenstøp (eds.), Foundations of Utility and Risk Theory with Applications, D. Reidel, Dordrecht, Holland, 347-70.

Edgeworth, F. Y.: 1881, Mathematical Psychics, Kegan Paul, London.

Frisch, R.: 1926, "Sur un Probleme d'Economie Pure", Norsk Matematisk Forenigns Skrifter, Serie I, No. 16, 1-40.

Gärdenfors, P.: 1984, "On the Information About Individual Individual Utilities Used in Social Choice," Mathematical

Social   Sciences.

Ng, Yew-Kwang: 1980, Welfare Economics: Introduction and
    Development of Basic Concepts, John   Wiley   and   Sons,
    New York.

Samuelson, P.A.: 1947, Foundations of Economic Analysis,
    Harvard University Press, Cambridge, Mass.

Samuelson,   P.A.:   1967, "Arrow's Mathematical Politics,"
    in S. Hook (ed.), Human Values and Economic Policy:
    A Symposium, New   York   University Press, New York.

Samuelson, P.A.: 1977, "Reaffirming the   Existence   of a
    Reasonable   Bergson-Samuelson Social Welfare Function,"
    Economica 44, 81-8.

Sugden, R.: 1983,   "Book Reviews", The Economic Journal
    93, 637-5.

Ole Hagen

SURVIVING IMPLICATIONS OF EXPECTED UTILITY THEORY

1. Introduction

All readers with a scientific training are, of course, aware of the logical fallacy in believing that if proposition A implies proposition B, then B depends on A and/or that verification of B implies verifications of A, or in symbols:
$(A=>B)=>(B=>A)$ (false!).

However, it is my impression that emotional attachment to A can lead even trained researchers into committing such fallacies subconsciously. Maybe those opposed to both A and B can be led into the same trap.
Let us take an example which is emotionally neutral:

Theory: Throughout the universe any unsupported object falls down. Down is everywhere an unambiguously defined direction, so that all free falling objects trace parallel straight lines.

Implica- If anywhere an object is dropped from the top
tion A: of a right circular cone, with the base circle on the surface of quiet water, it will trace a straight line towards the centre of the circle.

So far all is logically consistent and was not contradicted by observable facts, and for centuries this was common belief. Let us look at another implication:

Implica- If the earth were convex, as some ignoramuses
tion B: believe, the great oceans would be drained of water, so, the earth cannot be convex.

Since the Flat Earth Society is now dissolved after the studying of satellite photos, I shall proceed to the field of decision theory.
The pre-Bernoullian theory of expected monetary value (EMV) maximization has many plausible implications, among

L. Daboni et al. (eds.), Recent Developments in the Foundations of Utility and Risk Theory, 201–214.
© *1986 by D. Reidel Publishing Company.*

which are <u>all</u> the axioms and <u>all</u> the implications of
the von Neumann/Morgenstern type of expected utility
theory. These contain no statement on the shape of the
utility function for monetary wealth, so it might well be
linear. In the academic world the EMV-maximization theory
was brought down by the St. Petersburg paradox. The St.
Petersburgh game had infinite EMV, and since no gambler
can pay an infinite price for the game, the EMV theory was
rejected.

Had the EMV theory had defenders as die-hard as the
neo-Bernoullians of later times, they would have rejected
this argument by pointing out that neither can any bank
pay out an infinite prize. This discovery was left to K.
Menger (1934), see also Jeffrey (1965), Hagen (1972) and
Gorovitz in Allais/Hagen (eds.) (1979). Menger did not,
however, revive the EMV theory, because he pointed out
that even if the St. Petersburgh game were truncated to
become finite, it would not be saleable at EMV. So it was
actually Karl Menger who brought the EMV theory down, and
the paradox should really be called a Bernoulli-Menger
Paradox.

Today it is the expected utility maximizing (EUM)
theory which is fighting a rear guard defence against
criticism due to implications contradicted by empirical
evidence, which, it is claimed, also renders its normative
interpretation ambiguous (Hagen 1984). As one of the
"moderate revolutionaries" (Arrow 1983), I feel the need
to reassure the establishment that some of the dear
implications of their theory may not go down with it.

2. Dominance

What is commonly known as stochastic dominance of the
first order is implied in the EUM theory if and only if
it is combined with the tacit assumption that a higher
amount of money has a higher utility. That this is not
accepted by all, is shown by Amihud (1979) in discussing
Allais' "absolute preference": "Consider a man who gambles
against his good friend and wants him to win".

Allais' axiom of absolute preference is formulated in
terms of money and is, therefore, identical with what is
now called stochastic dominance of the first order, which
is generally assumed to be an implication of EUM theory.

In (Hagen 1969) basically the same thought is

expressed in terms of utility. I shall henceforth refer to it as 'utility dominance', and this is directly implied in EUM theory. I intend to show that utility dominance does not depend on EUM theory.

Let us first take the models for ranking of games with state-independent utilities, typically: stochastically independent games (one roulette for each game). Pope (1983, page 260 and note 18) lists the models of Allais, Hagen, the regret theorists and herself as violating "sometimes" stochastic dominance and therefore, according to Machina (1983: 272-3), she says, unacceptable. I have looked up Machina (1983: 272-3) and find only (Edwards 1955) and (Kahneman & Tversky 1979) listed. Much as I appreciate the honour of appearing in this company, this was not Machina's intention. He said so at FUR 84 and added that he had tested my three moments model among others for this and other criteria of rationality, and it had passed. As this is not published, I will show two of my own tests on my three moments model (1969 with revisions 1972, 1979).

In my model the mean, dispersion and skewness effects are represented by defining the utility of a game:

$$U = f(\hat{u}, s, z)$$

where: u = utility of outcome
$\hat{u}$ = expectation of utility of outcome
s = standard deviation in terms of u
z = m_3/s^2, when $s \neq 0$, otherwise $z=0$
m_3 = third moment in terms of u

It is postulated that in unique games

$$\frac{\delta U}{\delta \hat{u}} > 0 \ (=1) \tag{1}$$

$$\frac{\delta U}{\delta s} \leq 0 \ (=0 \text{ when } s=0) \tag{2}$$

$$\frac{\delta^2 U}{\delta s^2} < 0 \tag{3}$$

$$\frac{\delta U}{\delta z} > 0 \tag{4}$$

Let us demonstrate attempts to prove inconsistency between these axioms and the axiom of utility dominance.

Consider the set of games where the two outcomes have the utilities u_0 and u_1, and:

$$u_0 = 0 \tag{5}$$
$$u_1 = 1 \tag{6}$$
$$p = \text{probability of } u_1 \tag{7}$$

It follows that:

$$\hat{u} = p \tag{8}$$
$$s^2 = p(1-p)^2 + p^2(1-p) = p(1-p) \tag{9}$$
$$s = [p(1-p)]^{1/2} \tag{10}$$
$$m_3 = p(1-p)^3 - p^3(1-p) = p(1-p)(1-2p) \tag{11}$$
$$z = 1 - 2p \tag{12}$$

For mathematical convenience we use s^2 instead of s. This means

$$\frac{\delta U}{\delta s^2} < 0 \tag{13}$$

We derivate U, which is now a function of p:

$$\frac{dU}{dp} = \frac{\delta U}{\delta \hat{u}} \cdot \frac{d\hat{u}}{dp} + \frac{\delta U}{\delta s^2} \cdot \frac{ds^2}{dp} + \frac{\delta U}{\delta z} \cdot \frac{dz}{dp} \tag{14}$$

$$\frac{dU}{dp} = 1 + \frac{\delta U}{\delta s^2}(1-2p) - 2\frac{\delta U}{\delta z} \tag{15}$$

If we change p from 0 to a very small amount, so small that the change in u and s^2 is negligible, we have a jump in z from 0 to practically 1. For example: $p = 0$ implies $s = 0$ and by definition $z = 0$. If $p = 0.0001$, then $\hat{u} = 0.0001$, $s \approx 0.01$ and $y = 1 - 2p = 1 - 0.0002 = 0.9998$. So:

$$\Delta U \approx \frac{\delta U}{\delta z} \tag{16}$$

Obviously, this does not jeopardize consistency.
From here on counting as if $p = 0$:

$$\frac{dU}{dp} = 1 + \frac{\delta U}{\delta s^2} - 2\frac{\delta U}{\delta z} \tag{17}$$

$$\frac{dU}{dp} > 0 \Rightarrow \frac{\delta U}{\delta s^2} - 2\frac{\delta U}{\delta z} > -1 \tag{18}$$
(Condition 1)

If $p = 0.5$:

$$\frac{dU}{dp} = 1 - 2\frac{\delta U}{\delta z} \tag{19}$$

$$\frac{dU}{dp} > 0 \Rightarrow \frac{\delta U}{\delta z} < 0.5 \tag{20}$$
(Condition 2)

If $p \approx 1$:

$$\frac{dU}{dp} \approx 1 - \frac{\delta U}{\delta s^2} - 2\frac{\delta U}{\delta z} \tag{21}$$

$$\frac{dU}{dp} > 0 \Rightarrow \frac{\delta U}{\delta s^2} + 2\frac{\delta U}{\delta z} < 1 \tag{22}$$
(Condition 3)

It is easy to see that no inconsistency is implied
when p alone changes. (See <u>figure 1</u>).
Figure 1 shows discontinuities at $p = 0$ and $p = 1$. In
the beginning, U jumps to a higher value than û because z
jumps to its maximum while s remains almost zero. Then U
increases more slowly than û and p, so that when $p = 0.5$
($s = 0.5$, $z = 0$) U is smaller than û. Now, as s decreases,
dU/dp increases. When p becomes unity, U jumps to be equal
to û and unity.
The figure bears some resemblance to the value of a

chance (p_i of winning x_i) in (Tversky and Kahneman
1979: 263-291). Their mistake lies in applying this in n
outcome games (n > 2), which has absurd implications
(Hagen 1983, cfr. 1984).

Let us now consider p and u_o fixed and change u_1. We
have

$$\frac{dU}{du_1} = p + \frac{\delta U}{\delta s} \cdot [p(1-p)]^{1/2} + \frac{\delta U}{\delta z} \cdot (1-2p) \qquad (23)$$

Let us consider alternative values of p

$$p \approx 0 \Rightarrow \frac{dU}{du_1} \approx 0 + \frac{\delta U}{\delta z} > 0 \qquad \begin{array}{l} (24) \\ \text{(Condition 4)} \end{array}$$

$$p = 0.5 \Rightarrow \frac{dU}{du_1} = 0.5 + (0.25)^{1/2} \frac{\delta U}{\delta s} > 0$$

$$\frac{\delta U}{\delta s} > -1 \qquad \begin{array}{l} (25) \\ \text{(Condition 5)} \end{array}$$

$$p \approx 1 \Rightarrow \frac{dU}{du_1} \approx 1 - \frac{\delta U}{\delta z} > 0$$

$$\frac{\delta U}{\delta z} < 1 \qquad \begin{array}{l} (26) \\ \text{(Condition 6)} \end{array}$$

Condition 4 is identical with an axiom. Condition 5 is
obviously plausible, and Condition 6 is implied in
Condition 3.

Changing u_o does not show inconsistency either.
Some years ago, several attempts by a highly qualified
person to show inconsistency in my model came to nothing,
and remain unpublished.

In the case of this model, there is consistency also
with monetary absolute preference.

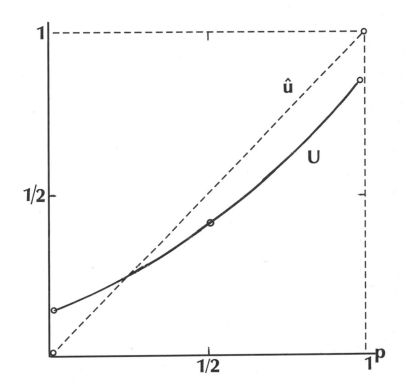

Fig. 1.   Value of <u>one prize</u> game as function of

        p = probability of winning prize
        U = f(û,s,z), where
        û = expected utility
        s = standard deviation in terms of utility
        z = m_3/s^2 = skewness indicator, where
        m_3= third central moment

Generalisation to n outcomes: When one bears in mind that a three statistics model may represent an exact evaluation of two outcome games, but only an aproximative evaluation of games with more outcomes, the generalisation becomes easy: For any logically possible combination of the three statistics one two-outcome game is determined (Hagen 1983). Any game will, in this model, be equivalent to some two outcome game, and the above proof applies.

Let us see what happens if we introduce regret, or even blame (Hagen 1983). (Regret = falling short of the best result by any game in the final state. Blame = falling short of the worst result by any other game, given the final state).

Consider the following three games:

State	1	2	3		
Probability	1/3	1/3	1/3		
Game A	28	20	14		
" B	15	22	30		Utility
" C	29	13	20		
Game A	0	2	16	16	
" B	14	0	0	14	Regret
" C	0	9	10	10*	
Game A	0	0	6	6*	
" B	13	0	0	13	Blame
" C	0	7	0	7	

Assuming utility of wealth to be the usual state independent concept, B dominates C and A. Given the small differences that cause the domination, the difference in the expected utilities of the games or in the utilities of the game by, for example my model, may be so small that the preference is determined by the psychological forces implied in the minimax regret or minimax blame rules. This would lead to preference for C and A respectively.

Now it looks as if the axiom of dominance must be given up if we are to admit regret and similar phenomena into the set of factors determining decisions given the utility of wealth as value.

There is, however, another possibility, as I have

indicated (Hagen 1983). We pick out of prospect theory
(Bernard 1974; Tversky/Kahneman 1979) the sound nucleus
of attaching utilities to the outcome of a game and with
Ståhl (1980), Loomes and Sugden (1982, 1984) and Bell
(1983, 1984) take account of what might have been etc.
(including regret and blame). It is then possible that,
for example the result B,1. will be given a value less
than 10, so that there is no domination. This implies that
the rule of dominance is not violated even if B is not
preferred.

I think that would be a better solution than giving up
domination.

3. Mean—Variance Utility Function

It is a general assumption that the utility of a
probability distribution over money (given EUM) can be
expressed as a function of mean and standard deviation (or
variance) if:

(1) the utility function of wealth is quadratic
or (2) the probability distribution is normal (Gaussian) [1]
This is correct, but the notion that in both (1) and
(2) the EUM is a necessary condition, and that given this
(1) and (2) form a complete list of sufficient conditions,
is false. [2] Proposition (1) is obviously unrealistic, so
it will not be discussed here. But let us see if, with
other utility functions, (2) is a necessary condition.

Any real probability distribution over money can be
approximately expressed by moments:

$$E, \ S^2, \ M_3, \ M_4, \ldots\ldots$$

where E = mean (expected monetary value)
          S^2 = variance
          M_i = i'th central moment

Any continuous probability distribution with an upper
and a lower bound can be approximated by a discreet
probability distribution over n values.

Any discreet probability distribution over n values
can be determined by m statistics, when $m = 2n-1$.
If

$$U = f(u_1, u_2, u_3, \ldots u_n, p_1, p_2, p_3, \ldots p_{n-1}) \tag{27}$$

then

$$U = g(E, S^2, M_3, \ldots M_{2n-1}) \tag{28}$$

This can be transformed into:

$$U = h(E, S^2, S^3 \frac{M_3}{S^3}, S^4 \frac{M_4}{S^4}, \ldots, S^m \frac{M_m}{S^m}) \tag{29}$$

Now the dimensionless moments:

$$\frac{M_i}{S_i} \tag{30}$$

are invariant under a linear transformation of the values of the outcomes so within a set of probability distributions generated in this way, we can write C_i for the dimensionless moments, which are constants, and get:

$$U = h(E, S^2, C_3 S^3, C_4 S^4, \ldots, C_m S^m) \tag{31}$$

and we achieve the radical simplification:

$$U = k(E, S) \tag{32}$$

The assumptions underlying this conclusion do not draw anything from any utility model. It is also of practical relevance. One example is risk sharing. In the case of risk sharing in contracting, I have myself applied the expected utility model (Hagen 1966), but this was not necessary[3]. The above model can be used, and the problem for both parties is the tradeoff between E and S in negotiating the contract.

If the problem of portfolio composition can be split in (1) determining the relative composition of a riskbearing part, and (2) the allocation between this and riskless assets, then the above will imply in both cases: the degree of risk is now reduced to deciding the size of S.

Now we have

$$\frac{dk}{dS} = \frac{\delta h}{\delta S} \cdot 2S + \frac{\delta h}{\delta M_3} \cdot 3C_3 S^2 + \frac{\delta h}{\delta M_4} \cdot 4C_4 S^3 + \frac{\delta h}{\delta M_5} \cdot 5C_5 S^4 \qquad (33)$$

and so on.

If the partial derivatives of h w.r.t. even number moments (dispersion) are all negative, and w.r.t. odd number moments (skewness) are all positive, then

$$C_3, C_5, \ldots < 0 \Rightarrow \frac{dk}{ds} < 0 \qquad (34)$$

On the other hand

$$\frac{dk}{dS} > 0 \Rightarrow \text{ some } C_i \text{ (i odd)} > 0 \qquad (35)$$

Roughly speaking: Negative skewness implies, and even some degree of positive skewness allows us to assume, without contradiction, that a decision maker is averse to risk as expressed by S.

We have then proved more than is necessary to accept Markowitz' E-S decision rule, which I have stated before as being compatible with my 3 moments model (Hagen 1969).

4. Maximizing Logarithmic Expectation in Repeatable Variable Games

Allais (1952/79, p.71) points out that there is little consolation in the thought that I am able to participate in a large number of games with positive monetary expectation if I go broke after a few rounds, or, I would add, if I go broke at all.

There is one way of avoiding this with certainty: Suppose you can participate by various degrees (proportionate amounts of gains and losses) in a game with positive monetary expectation. It is then possible to preclude bankruptcy by reducing/increasing the degree of participation when total wealth reduces/increases.

A simple strategy is to maximize the expectation of the logarithm of wealth in each game.

In (Hagen 1972) I showed that this strategy implied that the probability of coming out with wealth above a minimum wealth level would at some number of games exceed any minimum probability level, and then increase with the number of games.

This can apply to portfolio management, since the market prices of each asset may change each day and in Wall Street almost continuously.

To interpret this as a return to expected utility theory would be basically wrong. According to von Neumann/Morgenstern's axiom 3:C.b, the end result must be compared to the end result of any other strategy. If this strategy dominates the others, neither the expected utility theory nor any other utility theory is called upon.

Assume that we are considering participation in two symmetric two-outcome games with possible gain greater than loss. If the "logarithmic" strategy is compared to a strategy of repeating the first game in the logarithmic strategy each time, the logarithmic strategy will dominate the repetition of the first game, and this latter strategy may lead to bankruptcy no matter how small the stakes of the repeated games are.

5.   Conclusions

We have seen that many decision rules which are intuitively and/or empirically supported and compatible with MEU, are compatible with it but not dependent on it.

There are of course rules of behavior which are implied in MEU and also depend on it like this:

If the hope of winning any of the prizes in a lottery motivates you to buy a ticket, and if you win half the amount of the highest prize, you should pay double or nothing with your prize. See Friedmann-Savage (1948).

The fact that people do not behave this way contradicts the descriptive EUM theory. So does the now very large family of Allais Paradoxes.

Norwegian School of Management.
N - 1340 Bekkestua

NOTES

1. It may surprise some readers that this was used as an example by Allais already in 1952. See Allais (1979).
2. This false notion is the original contribution of many of those who fail to refer to Allais (see note 1).
3. The technique I used in the theoretical appendix can be described as an additive shift in the mean and one multiplicative shift in all differences from mean. This idea was first presented in Arrow (1965; 1971). My result was that if E(S) is a function of S that leaves U constant, and u"<0, then:

$$1 > E''(S)>0$$

This does not depend on the expected utility assumption (U=u), but the conclusion

$$E'(0)=0$$

does. However, if as I would have said today:

$$E'(0)\leq 0$$

the practical implications would be the same: the Pareto-optimal risk sharing will never give full certainty to any one of the negotiating parties, contractor or principal.

REFERENCES

Allais, M.: 1979, "The Foundations of a Positive Theory of Choice Involving Risk and a Criticism of the Postulates and Axioms of the American School", M. Allais and O. Hagen (eds.), Expected Utility Hypotheses and the Allais Paradox, D. Reidel, Dordrecht, (French original 1953).

Allais, M. and O. Hagen, (eds.): 1979, Expected Utility Hypotheses and the Allais Paradox, D. Reidel, Dordrecht.

Amihud, Y.: 1979, "Critical Examination of the New Foundation of Utility", in M. Allais and O. Hagen (eds.), Expected Utility Hypotheses and the Allais Paradox, D. Reidel, Dordrecht.

Arrow, K.J.: 1965, Aspects of the Theory of Risk-Bearing, (Lecture 2), Yrjö Jahnsonen sääto.

Arrow, K.J.: 1971 Essays in the Theory of Risk-Bearing, (Lecture 3), Markhan Publishing Company.

Arrow, K.J.: 1983, "Behaviour under Uncertainty and Its Implications for Policy", in B.P. Stigum and

F.Wenstøp (eds.), Foundations of Utility and Risk Theory with Applications, D. Reidel, Dordrecht.

Bell. D.E.: 1983, "Risk Premiums for Decision Regret", Management Science 10.

Bernard, G.: 1974, "On Utility Functions", Theory and Decision, 205-242.

Edwards, W.: 1955, "The Prediction of Decisions among Bets", Journal of Experimental Psychology.

Friedman, M and J. Savage: 1968, "The Utility Analysis of Choices Involving Risk", The Journal of Political Economy LVI, 279-304.

Hagen, O.: 1966, "Risk Aversion and Incentive Contracting", The Economic Record.

Hagen, O.: 1969, "Separation of Cardinal Utility and Specific Utility of Risk in Theory of Choices under Uncertainty", Statsøkonomisk Tidsskrift 3.

Hagen, O.: 1972, "A New Axiomatization of Utility under Risk", Teorie A Metoda IV/2.

Hagen, O.: 1979, "Towards a Positive Theory of Decisions under Risk", in M. Allais and O. Hagen (eds.).

Hagen, O.: 1983, "Paradoxes and Their Solutions", in B.P. Stigum and F. Wenstøp (eds.) Foundations of Utility and Risk Theory with Applications, D. Reidel, Dordrecht.

Hagen, O.: 1984, "Relativity in Utility Theory" in O. Hagen and F. Wenstøp (eds.): 1984, Progress in Utility and Risk Theory. D. Reidel, Dordrecht.

Hagen, O. and F. Wenstøp: 1984, Progress in Utility and Risk Theory, D. Reidel, Dordrecht.

Loomes, G. and R. Sugden: 1982, "Regret Theory: An Alternative Theory of Rational Choice under Uncertainty", The Economic Journal, 805-824.

Loomes, G. and R. Sugden: 1984, "The Importance of What Might Have Been", in O. Hagen and F. Wenstøp (eds.), Progress in Utility and Risk Theory, D. Reidel, Dordrecht.

Samuelson, P.A.: 1983, Foundations of Economic Analysis, Enlarged Edition, Harvard University Press.

Stigum, B.P. and F. Wenstøp: 1983, Foundations of Utility and Risk Theory with Applications, D. Reidel, Dordrecht.

Ståhl, I.: 1980, "Review of Allais and Hagen's Expected Utility Hypotheses and the Allais Paradox", Scandinavian Journal of Economics, 413-417.

Tversky, A. and D. Kahneman: 1979, "Prospect Theory: An Analysis of Decisions under Risk", Econometrica 47.

Robin Pope

CONSISTENCY AND EXPECTED UTILITY THEORY

1. INTRODUCTION

To disobey expected utility theory is to behave
inconsistently because of framing illusions. Any other
decision procedure would

> "be inconsistent in the sense that it violated
> the laws of preference between options ... If
> anyone's mental condition violated these laws,
> his choice would depend on the precise form in
> which the options were offered him, which
> would be absurd".   Ramsey 1950, p.182.

In 1952 Allais tested this claim at an international
colloquium on risk in Paris by asking Savage to choose
between some simple options, and then proceeded to convince
him that his answers disobeyed expected utility theory.
Surely, said Allais, Savage would choose consistently between
simple options and therefore his answers disconfirmed
Ramsey's claim.

Soon after the tables were turned on Allais. Savage
announced that he had made an "error". Savage said that he
had really wanted to obey expected utility theory but had
been thwarted by framing illusions. Savage used such a
telling numerical example to "prove" his "error" that almost
all economists and psychologists accepted Ramsey's sweeping
claim and placed expected utility theory on a pedestal as the
only consistent decision model. This paper shows that
Savage's proof implies irrational behaviour and traces the
error in Savage's proof to a logical contradiction in von
Neumann and Morgenstern's postulates about when events occur.

My thanks go to Maurice Allais, Ken Arrow, John Blatt, John
Harsanyi, Paul Samuelson, to members of the philosophy
seminar series, Australian National University including Fred
d'Agostino, Richard Routley and Jack Smart, and to many
others. Any remaining errors are my own. The unabridged 40
page version of the paper is available from the author.

L. Daboni et al. (eds.), Recent Developments in the Foundations of Utility and Risk Theory, 215–229.
© *1986 by D. Reidel Publishing Company.*

2. SAVAGE'S SURE-THING PROOF

Allais had asked Savage whether he preferred A to B, and C to
D, where A was a gift of $1m with certainty, B was $5m with
probability 0.10 and $1m with probability 0.89, C was $1m
with probability 0.11 and D was $5m with probability 0.10.[1]
To obey expected utility theory, people who prefer A to B
must also prefer C to D.[2] Savage initially told Allais that
he preferred A to B and D to C.

Savage was dismayed when Allais pointed out to him that
he had disobeyed expected utility theory and decided to apply
his sure-thing principle.to see whether he had made an
"error" in saying that he preferred D to C. The purpose of
the sure-thing principle said Savage is to convert a pair of
<u>simple</u> options into a pair of <u>time sequenced</u> ones with the
same probabilities of final outcomes. This helps a person
"clarify the matter for himself" in choosing between the pair
of simple options, Savage 1954, pp.17, 21 and 23. Savage
duly converted Allais's <u>simple</u> options C and D into <u>time</u>
<u>sequenced</u> ones, $\tilde{C}$ and $\tilde{D}$, by inserting a subsidiary decision,
and reported:

> "I still feel an intuitive attraction [for D
> over C]. But I have since accepted the
> following way of looking at the situation ...
> <u>which amounts to repeated use of the</u>
> <u>sure-thing principle</u> ... [Suppose C and D] are
> realized by a lottery with a hundred numbered
> tickets and with prizes according to the
> schedule shown ...

Ticket Number

...	1	2-11	12-100
C	1	1	0
D	0	5	0

> Now, if one of the tickets numbered from 12
> through 100 is drawn, it will not matter ...
> which ... I choose. I therefore focus on the
> possibility that one of the tickets numbered
> from 1 through 11 will be drawn ... The
> subsidiary decision [is] ... whether I would
> sell an outright gift of $1m for a 10-to-1
> chance to win $5m ... I find that I would

prefer the gift of $1m ... that I prefer ...
(contrary to my initial reaction) C to D ...
in reversing my preference between C and D I
have corrected an error."
                    Savage 1954, p.103, emphasis added.

Let D_1 denote the <u>simple</u> gamble: $0 with probability 0.89
and a subsidiary decision with probability 0.11. Let D_2
denote the <u>simple</u> gamble: $5m (with 10 to 1 odds and so) with
probability 10/11 and $0 with probability 1/11. Let C_2
denote the certain option of an outright gift of $1m. Let $\tilde{C}$
denote the <u>time sequenced</u> gamble: D_1 followed by $0 with a
probability of 0.89 and by C_2 with a probability of 0.11.
Let $\tilde{D}$ denote the <u>time sequenced or compound</u> gamble: D_1
followed by $0 with a probability of 0.89 and by D_2 with a
probability of 0.11. Then Savage's sure-thing proof has the
following format:

(i) $\tilde{C}$ is the same as C and $\tilde{D}$ is the same as D so it is
       inconsistent to prefer D to C and $\tilde{C}$ to $\tilde{D}$; and
(ii) framing the options with a subsidiary decision node, as
       <u>time sequenced</u> ($\tilde{C}$, $\tilde{D}$) instead of as <u>simple</u> gambles
       (C, D), enables a correct perception of what the
       alternatives are, so those people who choose
       inconsistently really prefer C to D and obey expected
       utility theory when not thwarted by framing illusions.

Savage's sure-thing proof is false if proposition (i) is
false. Savage thinks that (i) is true because he thinks that
people should use a form of comparative static analysis to
decide whether options are the same:
       "a <u>chain</u> of decisions, <u>one leading to the other</u>
       <u>in time,</u> is in the formal description proposed
       here regarded as a <u>single</u> decision ... [such
       that] acts and decisions, like events, are
       <u>timeless</u>".
                    Savage 1954, pp.15 and 17, emphasis added.

This critical comparative statics postulate means that Savage
can convert the "<u>temporally</u> described situation" of the
"<u>chain</u> of decisions", the compound gambles $\tilde{C}$ and $\tilde{D}$ into a
<u>single</u> decision, an "<u>atemporal</u>" or "<u>timeless</u>" snapshot, the
snapshots being taken at some point in time after all
component outcomes of $\tilde{C}$ and $\tilde{D}$ have been received, Savage
1954, pp.12, 23 and 103, emphasis added. Snapshots are also

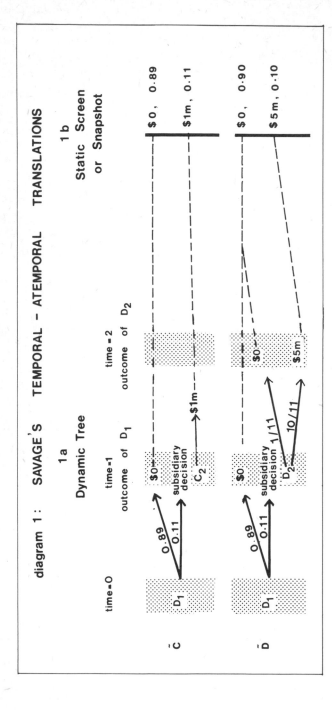

diagram 1 : SAVAGE'S TEMPORAL – ATEMPORAL TRANSLATIONS

1 a
Dynamic Tree

1 b
Static Screen
or Snapshot

Note: In the published accounts of Savage's proof that time sequencing C and D highlights the "real problem" via a "Choice" or "subsidiary decision" node, the prizes are usually converted from Allais's original francs into dollars. The actual dollar amounts most often used in this conversion are those of Diagram 1, e.g. in Karl Borch 1968, p.64 and Markowitz 1970, p.222, or half those of Diagram 1, e.g. Savage 1954, p.103, where C_2 is "an outright gift of $500,000", and D_2 "a 10-to-11 chance of $2,500,000".

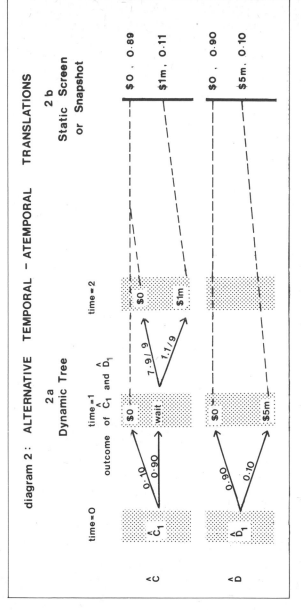

diagram 2 : ALTERNATIVE TEMPORAL – ATEMPORAL TRANSLATIONS

2a
Dynamic Tree

2b
Static Screen
or Snapshot

Source: Derived from Hagen's critical re-organisation of another published version of Savage's proof (in which the prizes are quoted in old French Francs):

"Savage's two games over 100 numbers ... I rearranged in this manner ...

X : No. 1-89 : Nothing.   No. 90-100 : 100 million
Y : No. 1-10 : 500 million.   No. 11-100 : nothing

If the sure thing principle is applied, we ignore No. 11-89 and reduce to 21 events:

Y" : No. 1-10 : Nothing   No. 11-21 : 100 million
X" : No. 1-10 : 500 million   No. 11-21 : nothing

Most people will find Y more attractive in this arrangement." Ole Hagen 1983, pp. 11-12.
See also Hagen 1972, and Kenneth R. MacCrimmon and Stig Larsson 1979, pp. 360-369.

taken of Allais's simple gambles C and D. As the snapshots
of C and $\widetilde{C}$ are the same, and the snapshots of D and $\widetilde{D}$ are the
same, Savage concludes that for C and $\widetilde{C}$, and for D and $\widetilde{D}$, the
probabilities of the final outcomes are the same, and hence
that (i) is true. See Diagram 1.

Now besides Savage's ($\widetilde{C}$, $\widetilde{D}$), there are many other pairs
of options $\hat{C}$, $\hat{D}$ that involve some time sequencing, and for
which $\hat{C}$ and $\hat{D}$ have the same snapshot representation as
Allais's C and D. By Savage's own procedure of "what amounts
to repeated use of the sure-thing principle", these could be
seen as providing alternative ways of enabling a person to
"clarify the matter for himself", Savage 1954, p.21. But
then, as Diagram 2 shows, it is easy to choose a $\hat{C}$ and $\hat{D}$
leading to the conclusion that most people really prefer D
over C, thereby contradicting Savage's Proposition (ii). This
suggests that Savage's comparative static analysis is vague,
informal and even arbitrary.

In fact Savage's comparative statics postulate would
result in people regularly choosing options that do not
maximize their expected utils. The postulate only seems
plausible because Savage's examples are vague, and without
being exact about the details of a particular case, it is
easy to miss irrational implications of a postulate. To see
this, consider a more detailed example.

Virginia is faced with two options, d and $\widetilde{d}$, where d is a
particular instance of Allais's simple gamble D, and $\widetilde{d}$ a
particular instance of Savage's compound gamble $\widetilde{D}$. She must
choose between these one week from now:

    option d - a wheel will be spun one year and one week from
      now with a 10% chance of receiving $5m at that moment
      and a 90% chance of receiving nothing; and

    option $\widetilde{d}$ - a wheel will be spun one year and one week from
      now with an 89% chance of receiving nothing and an 11%
      chance that the wheel will be spun a second time, two
      years and one week from now with a 10/11 chance of
      receiving $5m at that moment and a 1/11 chance of
      receiving nothing.

Virginia risks a longer period of uncertainty should she
choose the compound gamble $\widetilde{d}$. See Figure 1.

A rational choice depends on Virginia's time horizon, the
expected time path of her level of utility within that
horizon, her time preference rate and her maximand. Assume

Figure 1: VIRGINIA'S UNCERTAINTY

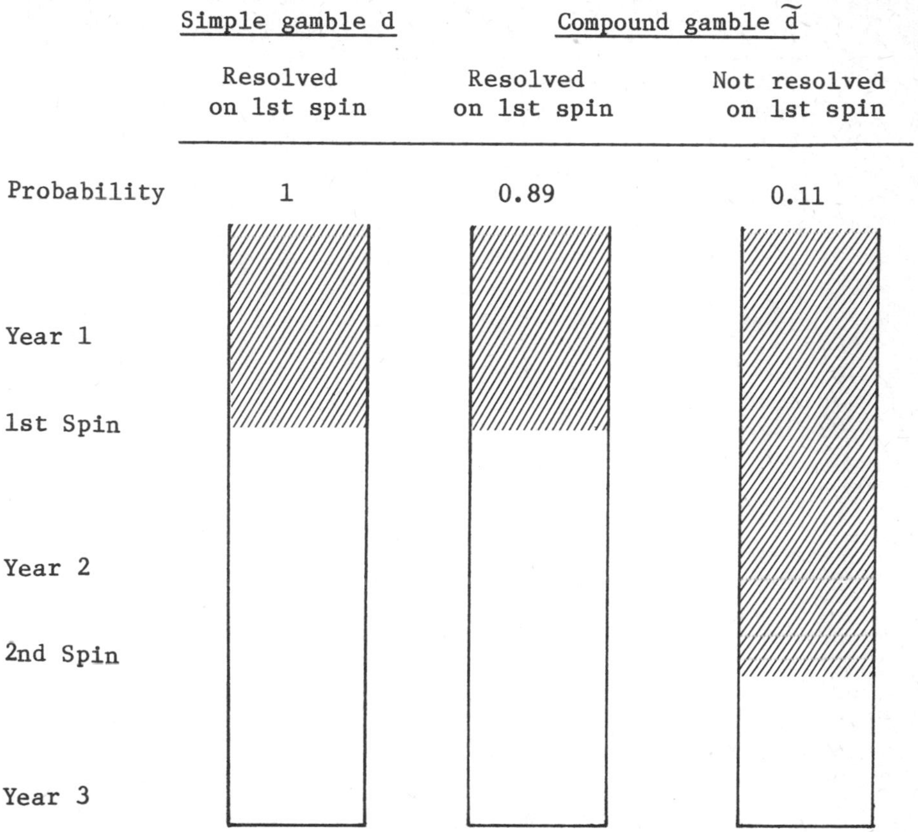

	Simple gamble d	Compound gamble $\tilde{d}$	
	Resolved on 1st spin	Resolved on 1st spin	Not resolved on 1st spin
Probability	1	0.89	0.11

Year 1

1st Spin

Year 2

2nd Spin

Year 3

initial uncertain period: <u>before</u> the outcome of a simple gamble d, is known, or <u>before</u> all relevant outcomes of the compound gamble $\tilde{d}$ are known. It is the period when fear may be experienced.

subsequent certain period: <u>after</u> the outcome of a simple gamble d, is known, or <u>after</u> all relevant outcomes of a compound gamble $\tilde{d}$, are known. It is the period when there is no scope for fear.

that Virginia knows that:
(1) she will die in just over three years and one week from
    now;
(2) her welfare would be 70 utils above its normal level of
    30 utils in a year in which she wins;
(3) as she dislikes shouldering an <u>avoidable risk</u> of a <u>longer
    period of uncertainty</u>, she would incur immediately a fear
    disutility of 20 utils if she were to choose $\tilde{d}$ and so
    risk a longer expected period of uncertainty;
(4) Virginia has a zero time preference rate between utils
    received in year t and year t + 1; and
(5) her maximand is her total expected welfare from and
    including the point of her gambling decision at the
    beginning of year t = 1.

From the last row of Table 1, it can be seen that for
Virginia the difference in her total expected welfare under d
and $\tilde{d}$ is the cost of her fear under the latter, 20 utils.[3]

Table 1: VIRGINIA'S WELFARE IN UTILS

	Simple gamble d		Compound gamble $\tilde{d}$		
Year 1	30		10		
1st Spin	Choice	No choice	Choice	No choice	
Year 2	30	100	30	30	
2nd Spin	irrelevant		irrelevant	relevant	
Year 3	30	30	30	30	100
Total	90	160	70	70	140
Probability	0.9	0.1	0.89	0.01	0.10
Expectation	97.0		77.0		

Virginia therefore rejects Savage's comparative statics
postulate and decides that the simple gamble, d, and the time
sequenced one, $\tilde{d}$, are different options. Option d yields her
higher expected utils than does $\tilde{d}$ and so she rationally
prefers d.

3. OBJECTIONS

Readers may be tempted to make one of four rejoinders. The
first is to contend that the example of Virginia is
irrelevant because her gambles differ as regards the <u>timing
of the future</u> outcomes, whereas Savage's gambles could be
restricted to <u>coincident future</u> outcomes. This rejoinder is
an attempt to defy the laws of physics. In Savage's pair of
gambles D and $\tilde{D}$, all future outcomes cannot occur at the same
future time. For in the time sequenced gamble, $\tilde{D}$, that is
the simple gamble D_1 conditionally <u>followed</u> by another
simple gamble D_2, the future outcomes of D_1 and D_2 cannot
coincide with each other and hence cannot both coincide with
that of D.

   This begs the second rejoinder that in Savage's compound
gamble $\tilde{D}$, the outcome of D_1 need not lead D_2 in time because
<u>no</u> time need elapse between deciding on $\tilde{D}$ and learning the
outcomes of D_1 and D_2. This second rejoinder is incompatible
with the definition of a gamble. Call the pre-outcome period
the period that begins at the point of choosing an option and
continues until people believe that they have learned the
outcome of their choice. Let N denote the length of the
pre-outcome period. Then <u>N defines whether the option is
certain or uncertain.</u> If people choose a certain option,
they believe that they know the outcome of their option at
the point of choice. In their eyes the possible outcome has
a probability of one, and so N = 0. Conversely, if people
choose an uncertain option, i.e. a gamble, they believe that
they do not know the outcome at the point of choice. Hence,

> an option is certain   <u>if and only if</u>   N = 0;
> an option is a gamble   <u>if and only if</u>   N > 0.

   With regard to Savage's compound gamble $\tilde{D}$, D_1 followed
by D_2, if the outcome of D_1 is the subsidiary decision,
let N_1, N_2 and N be the lengths of the pre-outcome period
with regard to D_1, D_2 and $\tilde{D}$ respectively. Assume that no
time elapses between the outcome of D_1 and the commencement
of D_2, nor between outcomes and people learning of these
outcomes. Then if the outcome of D_1 is the subsidiary
decision, D_2 is played and hence

$$N = N_1 + N_2.$$

Otherwise

$$N = N_1,$$

that is,

$$N_1 \leq N \leq N_2.$$

Since D_1 and D_2 are uncertain options,

$$N_1 > 0, \text{ and } N_2 > 0.$$

Hence

$$N > 0.$$

Thus the resolution of Savage's <u>time sequenced</u> gamble $\widetilde{D}$ is
also necessarily non-instantaneous, and not merely
non-instantaneous in some situations such as Virginia's.

The third possible rejoinder is that although the time
profile of the probabilities of the final outcomes of D and $\widetilde{D}$
are different, in the case of Savage's proof, the differences
can be ignored as follows.[4] Let $\widetilde{U}$ denote the (positive or
negative) utils experienced <u>per unit of time</u> throughout the
pre-outcome period of length N. Then the <u>total</u> utils
experienced during the pre-outcome period, $N\widetilde{U}$, can be made
arbitrarily small by making N appropriately small, in which
case the associated differences between simple and compound
gambles will be small enough to be ignorable.

Savage is trying to prove that <u>anybody</u> who disobeys
expected utility theory is behaving inconsistently. So this
rejoinder is only a valid way of retrieving Savage's proof if
for <u>anybody</u> a sufficiently small N can be found such that the
product $N\widetilde{U} \longrightarrow 0$. This is not the case. For N is not an
arbitrary abstract quantity, indefinitely reducible relative
to any given $\widetilde{U}$. To see this, suppose that a moment is the
finite minimal division of time in the discrete (quantum
physics) world. Then N cannot be less than a moment, i.e.
$N \geq 1$. Let the unit of time used in specifying $\widetilde{U}$ be a moment
and let $\widetilde{U}(1)$ denote the (positive or negative) utils
experienced during the first moment. Then $N\widetilde{U} \geq \widetilde{U}(1)$. Hence
for persons for whom $\widetilde{U}(1)$ is sizable, $N\widetilde{U}$ is sizable even when
N is minimized.[5]

The fourth possible rejoinder is that Savage's proof
could be retrieved by making the timing differences in
learning sequential outcomes slight, and that rational people
ignore slight timing differences. This objection is also
invalid. It cannot be contended that people who prefer a
shorter duration of uncertainty – even if only a slightly
shorter duration – are thereby either inconsistent or
irrational in the sense of not maximizing their expected
utility.

4. VON NEUMANN AND MORGENSTERN

The contradictions concerning N that led to Savage's
inappropriate application of the sure-thing principle to time
sequenced gambles, arose because expected utility theory
inadvertently omits the pre-outcome period; and so
inadvertently omits the first row in Virginia's Table 1
above. The error in Savage's proof is a direct consequence
of a timing inconsistency in von Neumann and Morgenstern's
set of axioms. It was their axiomisation that created
Savage's interest in Ramsey's sweeping claims on behalf of
expected utility theory. They located all "events" at a
single future date:

> "events ... are conceived as future events so
> as to make all logically possible alternatives
> equally admissible ... difficulties can be
> obviated by locating all events ... at one and
> the same, standard moment, preferably in the
> immediate future."
> von Neumann and Morgenstern 1947, p.19.

Since the logically possible alternatives are equally
admissible if and only if people do not know the outcome of
their decision,[6] von Neumann and Morgenstern were here
using the word "event" for when people learn the outcome of
their decision. This means that in locating all "events" at
a standard future moment they have assumed that people learn
the outcomes of their decisions at a single future date. In
other words, von Neumann and Morgenstern have restricted
their model to one in which if N is the delay between a
decision and learning its outcome (the length of the
pre-outcome period), and $\bar{N}$ is a constant, $N = \bar{N} > 0$.

Thereby they have excluded:

(i)   <u>certain options,</u> since their outcomes, known at the
        point of choice, are not future "events", but ones
        for which N = 0; and
(ii) <u>time sequenced options,</u> since their sequential
        possible outcomes are non-coincident "events" that
        do not share a common N = $\overline{N}$.

But von Neumann and Morgenstern themselves gave a "certainty
equivalent" interpretation of one of their operations, 1947,
pp.16-17 and 26, and did not exclude a compound gamble
interpretation of their equation of the "Algebra of
Combining", 1947, pp.26-27.[7]

These two contradictions of their timing assumption that
all "events" occur at the <u>same future</u> date crept in because
von Neumann and Morgenstern described probabilities in an
atemporal context, introducing the concept of probability as
a "combination", and continuing in further analysis of their
postulates to describe each probability, as a "combination",
1947, p.27.   Indeed for them the concepts "combination" and
"fraction" corresponded so well with the concept of
probability that they suggested using preferences for a 50-50
probability of receiving either B or C to infer preferences
for receiving a 50-50 combination of B or C for certain,
1947, pp.20-21.   Savage's atemporal treatment of time
sequenced gambles as "mixtures" of simple gambles is thus
derived from von Neumann and Morgenstern's timeless treatment
of probabilities, Savage 1954, p.71.

Even those who examine the implications of N > 0 describe
N > 0 as an optional complication.[8]   Thus according to Allais
and Markowitz, N > 0 is a complication that, "at least as a
first approximation ... can be neglected in the pure theory
of random choice",[9] if there "are no intervening decisions".[10]
Similar sentiments are to be found in Kreps and Porteus, Bell,
Machina and other contributors to dynamic choice theory.[11]
None of these writers, therefore, perceives that N > 0 is the
necessary and sufficient condition for distinguishing an
uncertain from a certain option.   They have thereby helped to
maintain the illusion that there is a non-empty set of risky
choice problems for which Savage's sure-thing proof is
valid.[12]   They have helped to maintain the <u>illusion</u> that
for expected utility theory:

"we have established a set of axioms ... For
these axioms we have carefully shown that
they are free of contradictions".
                    Morgenstern 1974, p.175.

A sister paper examines the consequences of dropping this
illusion, Pope 1984.

Department of Economics,
The University of New South Wales.

NOTES

1. See Markowitz 1970, p.222, for the proof.
2. I have taken the liberty of substituting "C" and "D" for
    what Savage called "gamble 3" and "gamble 4" and of
    doubling the dollar prizes. Allais's original lotteries
    were in French Francs. See Allais's account, Allais
    1979, p.534, and Markowitz's account, Markowitz 1970,
    pp.220-224.
3. See Pope 1983, p.141 ff for a discussion of fear.
4. This might be inferred as the position of Samuelson
    1952, pp.667-678. It is also my recollection of
    Allais's verbal elaboration to me in 1979 of why he
    himself ignores N as a first approximation.
5. For instance if under the compound gamble $\tilde{d}$, the large
    negative component of Virginia's total pre-outcome
    utility, the sum equivalent to minus 20 utils per annum,
    is located <u>entirely</u> in the first moment of N, Virginia
    would still have a sizable difference between her
    expected utils under d and $\tilde{d}$ even if N were minimized
    and she were to learn the outcomes of the first and
    second spins in a moment or two.
6. The logically possible alternatives that are <u>equally
    admissible</u> before decision makers learn the outcome
    become <u>mutually exclusive</u> after they learn the outcome
    and their uncertainty has been resolved.
7. In their equation of the "Algebra of Combining", let
    $g_2 = \beta u + (1-\beta)\underline{v}$, and let $g_1 = \alpha g_2 + (1-\alpha)\underline{v}$, then to
    exclude a compound gamble interpretation, von Neumann
    and Morgenstern needed to stipulate that decision makers
    do not learn the outcome of g_1 prior to learning the
    outcome of g_2.

8. A refreshing exception that has recently come to my
    attention is Peirson 1983.
9. Allais 1984, p.56.
10. Markowitz 1970, p.211.
11. Descriptions of "timeless" or "atemporal" as distinct
    from "delayed" or "temporal" gambles occur in Mossin
    1969, p.174, Drèze and Modigliani 1972, p.309, Kreps and
    Porteus 1979, pp.81-82, Bell 1981, p.238 and Machina
    forthcoming p.4. Note that in Arrow 1983, p.25, the
    delays do not refer to N, the delay between deciding on
    a gamble and learning its outcome. They refer rather to
    delays in receiving prizes and/or embarking on a second
    gamble. See also Arrow 1982, pp.7-9.
12. See von Neumann and Morgenstern 1947, p.28, pp.628-630,
    Morgenstern 1974, p.181 and Pope 1983 and 1984.

REFERENCES

Allais, M.: 1979, "The So-Called Allais Paradox and
  Rational Decisions under Uncertainty", in M. Allais &
  O. Hagen, (eds), Expected Utility Hypotheses and the Allais
  Paradox: Contemporary Discussions of Decisions Under
  Uncertainty with Allais' Rejoinder, Reidel Dordrecht,
  437-681.
Allais, M.: 1984, "The Foundations of the Theory of
  Utility and Risk. Some Central Points of the
  Discussions at the Oslo Conference", in O. Hagen &
  F. Wenstøp (eds), Progress in Utility and Risk Theory,
  Reidel, Dordrecht, 3-131.
Arrow, K.: 1982, "Risk Perception in Psychology and
  Economics", Economic Inquiry, 20, 1-9.
Arrow, K.: 1983, "Behavior under Uncertainty and its
  Implications for Policy", in B. Stigum and F. Wenstøp
  (eds), Foundations of Utility and Risk Theory with
  Applications, Reidel, Dordrecht, 19-32.
Bell, D.: 1981, "Components of Risk Aversion", in J. Brans
  (ed), Operational Research '81, North Holland, Amsterdam,
  235-242.
Borch, K.: 1968, The Economics of Uncertainty, Princeton
  University Press, Princeton, New Jersey.
Drèze, J.& F. Modigliani: 1972, "Consumption Decisions
  under Uncertainty", Journal of Economic Theory, 5,
  308-335.
Hagen, O.: 1972, "A New Axiomization of Utility Under Risk",
  Teorie A Metoda, IV/2, 55-80.

Hagen, O.: 1983, "Paradoxes and their Solutions", in
B. Stigum and F. Wenstøp (eds), Foundations of Utility
and Risk Theory with Applications, Reidel, Dordrecht, 5-17.

Kreps, D.& E. Porteus: 1979, "Temporal von
Neumann-Morgenstern and Induced Preferences", Journal of
Economic Theory, 20, 81-109.

MacCrimmon, K. & S. Larsson.: 1979, 'Utility Theory: Axioms
versus "Paradoxes"', in M. Allais and O. Hagen (eds),
Expected Utility Hypotheses and the Allais Paradox:
Contemporary Discussions of Decisions under Uncertainty
with Allais' Rejoinder, Reidel, Dordrecht, 333-409.

Machina, M.: "Temporal Risk and the Nature of Induced
Preferences", Journal of Economic Theory, Forthcoming.

Markowitz, H.: 1970, Portfolio Selection: Efficient
Diversification of Investment, first edition, second
printing, Yale University Press, New Haven.

Morgenstern, O.: 1974, "Some Reflections on Utility",
posthumously published in M. Allais & O. Hagen (eds),
Expected Utility Hypotheses and the Allais Paradox:
Contemporary Discussions of Decisions Under Uncertainty
with Allais' Rejoinder, Reidel, Dordrecht, 1979, 175-183.

Mossin, J.: 1969, "A Note on Uncertainty and Preferences
in a Temporal Context", American Economic Review, 59(1),
172-174.

Peirson, J.: 1983, "Decision Making Under Risk and Across
Time", Discussion Paper 83.2, Division of Economic
Studies, University of Sheffield, Sheffield.

Pope, R.: 1983, "The Pre-Outcome Period and the Utility of
Gambling", in B. Stigum & F. Wenstøp (eds), Foundations
of Utility and Risk Theory with Applications, Reidel,
Dordrecht, 137-177.

Pope, R.: 1984, "The Utility of Gambling and the Utility
of the Outcome: Inconsistent First Approximations", in
O. Hagen & F. Wenstøp (eds), Progress in Utility and
Risk Theory, Reidel, Dordrecht, 251-273.

Ramsey, F.: 1950, "Truth and Probability", in
R. Braithwaite (ed), The Foundations of Mathematics and
Other Logical Essays, Humanities Press, New York.

Samuelson, P.: 1952, "Probability, Utility and the
Independence Axiom", Econometrica, 20, 670-678.

Savage, L.: 1954, The Foundations of Statistics,
John Wiley & Sons, Inc., New York.

Von Neumann, J. & O. Morgenstern: 1947, Theory of Games
and Economic Behavior, Princeton University Press,
Princeton, New Jersey.

G. Leonardi, E.F. Arcangeli, A. Reggiani

AGGREGATE REVEALED PREFERENCES
AND RANDOM UTILITY THEORY

1. Introduction

The first aim of this paper is to propose a new axiomatic reconstruction of "random utility" models, a rather more general one compared to the former axiomatization developed by Luce and McFadden. The second aim is to show how the resulting theory could solve at least some of the methodological weaknesses of standard Ordinal Utility and Revealed Preference theories in their deterministic version. No attempt will be made here to deal with "non-standard" behavioural hypotheses; we only want to show that, when standard ones are assumed , observation of aggregate choice and demand patterns can be a more realistic but nonetheless rigorous way to give semantic truth to the axioms of Hicks and Allen's Ordinal Utility theory (that is, to play the role that can be attributed to Samuelson's Test on coherence of individual choice).

Under well-known hypotheses from the unified "Ordinal Utility-Revealed Preference" paradigm (Hicks 1956; Wong 1978), one can derive the following basic theorems:

(A) first substitution theorem: when we do not allow for the income-effects,the total pure substitution effect is negative; in vector terms:

$$(p^1-p^0)'(q^1-q^0) = S \leq 0$$

(B) reciprocity theorem:

$$(p^2-p^0)'(q^1-q^0) = (p^1-p^0)'(q^2-q^0) = R$$

(C) second substitution theorem: the cross-effect must not be greater, in size, than the geometric mean of the direct substitution effects, or

$$R^2 \leq [(p^1-p^0)'(q^1-q^0)] [(p^2-p^0)'(q^2-q^0)],$$

231

L. Daboni et al. (eds.), Recent Developments in the Foundations of Utility and Risk Theory, 231–248.
© 1986 by D. Reidel Publishing Company.

where (p^i, q^i) are the price and quantity vectors characterizing choice situation i.

With some loss of generality one obtains also conditions of validity (I≤-S) for the "generalized law of demand" (S+I≤0), where I is the product of price and quantity variations for the income effect.

Among the large set of critical arguments to the standard theory we select here only the most relevant ones for the new approach to "Ordinal Random Utility" described in this paper. Some of the objections can be summarized in short as follows:

    (1) the "Consistency Test" on revealed preference must assume unchanged preferences, with loss of generality or perhaps tautology;

    (2) operationalism in the definition of relevant concepts is not consistent with a deterministic approach;

    (3) finally, we seldom see individual behaviour (and individual tests are indeed an exception in the economic literature).

This is why an aggregate and probabilistic approach seems to be a more reasonable one in order to play the role of the Samuelson's test on Revealed Preference.

This was the contention of McFadden, when speaking of his results on Random Utility Models (RUM) as a "population analog of the conventional theory of revealed preference for individual consumers" (McFadden 1974, p. 108).

The starting point of econometric applications and developments of random utility models, after pioneering psychometric contributions (starting with Thurstone 1927), was Luce's axiom, which states that: (i) choice ratios between any couple of alternatives are independent from the choice set; (ii) they are also independent from irrelevant or zero probability alternatives (Luce, 1959; Debreu, 1960).

Under assumption of empirical validity of this axiom, and for a finite set of N alternatives, one can derive the representability of choice odds as:

$$P_j = \exp \beta v_j \left(\sum_j \exp \beta v_j \right)^{-1} \qquad j = 1, \ldots, N \qquad (1)$$

where v_j is an index of attractiveness of choice j for an "average" choice maker (see section 2). Hence it follows that for any couple of alternatives:

$$\frac{P_i}{P_j} = f(v_i - v_j) = \exp \beta(v_i - v_j) \qquad \forall i, j.$$

This is a particular restriction of the more general case of interdependency of choice probabilities:

$$P_j = h(v_1, \ldots, v_n) \qquad\qquad j = 1, \ldots, N.$$

The fundamental result for the development of the multinomial logit (MNL) model is due to McFadden (1974) and can be restated as follows:

MCFADDEN EQUIVALENCE. THEOREM
"A random utility model of the MNL type, characterized by choice probabilities (1), can be equally produced: (i) by deduction from Luce's axiom, if one specifies the Lemma on choice ratios:

$$\frac{P_i}{P_j} = f(v_i - v_j) \qquad\qquad \forall i, j = 1, \ldots, N.$$

in the exponential form:

$$\frac{P_i}{P_j} = \exp \beta(v_i - v_j) \qquad\qquad \forall i, j = 1, \ldots, N.$$

(ii) by induction from a set of observed aggregate choice patterns in a population, assuming that:
(ii.a) each member of a population of utility-maximizing consumers has a utility function $u(\Theta, z) = v(\Theta, z) + e(\Theta, z)$;
(ii.b) $e(\Theta, z)$ are I.I.D. (independently and identically distributed),
(ii.c) with the Gumbel distribution

$$\Pr \{e(\Theta, z) \le x\} = \exp (-e^{-\beta(x + \gamma)});$$

(see Section 2 for notations)."

In the following Sections we will restate axiom (ii.a) and show that only this assumption is necessary in order to derive the basic theorems (A), (B), and (C).
In Section 5 we will show that the restrictive

hypothesis (ii.b) can generally be relaxed, without the
need to be replaced by any other very restrictive
hypothesis (like the assumption of a multivariate normal
distribution in the alternative Probit approach). The substitution of (ii.b) with a deFinetti representation of
non-independent but "exchangeable" functions will throw
new light on the economic interpretation of Luce's axiom,
which should be relevant both for theory and econometric
applications. Finally, some recent results by one of the
authors of this paper show that also (ii.c) can be somewhat relaxed in asymptotic terms (Leonardi, 1984; Bertuglia
et al., 1984).

2. An Introduction to Random Utility Theory

2.1. DEFINITIONS AND BASIC AXIOMS.

Let : Ω be a finite n-dimension vector space: of
alternatives; Γ a finite m-dimension vector space: of actor
types.
    Let each $z\epsilon\Omega$ identify an alternative by means of its
attributes, i.e. $z = (z_1,\ldots,z_n)$, while each $\Theta\epsilon\Gamma$ identifies
an actor type by means of its attributes, i.e. $\Theta=(\Theta_1,\ldots,\Theta_m)$
    Let us assume that:
    (A.1) each actor is free to choose the alternative
          he prefers and only one alternative for each
          realization,
    (A.2) each actor has a complete order on Ω,
    (A.3) each $z\epsilon\Omega$ is observable,
    (A.4) each $\Theta\epsilon\Gamma$ is not observable,
    (A.5) a probability measure μ is defined on Γ.
Assumption (A.2) implies that for each $\Theta\epsilon\Gamma$ there is at
least one function u_Θ, which maps Ω into the reals, i.e.:

$$u_\Theta: \Omega => R \qquad\qquad\qquad \forall\Theta\epsilon\Gamma.$$

    This mapping defines a function, whose specific value
for any $\Theta\epsilon\Gamma$, $z\epsilon\Omega$ will be written as $u(\Theta,z)$ and called the
utility of an alternative z for an actor Θ. For what
concerns the market mechanism or other allocative
processes which could be at work, no explicit mention is
introduced now, although one could include prices among
attributes of alternatives, and incomes among attributes
of actors.

2.2. REPRESENTABILITY AS AN ADDITIVE RANDOM UTILITY MODEL (ARUM).

Let the means:

$$v(z) = \int_{\Theta \epsilon \Gamma} u(\Theta,z) \, d\mu(\Theta) \qquad\qquad z \epsilon \Omega$$

be finite, and define the random variables:

$$e(\Theta,z) = u(\Theta,z) - v(z). \tag{2}$$

Then from (2):

$$u(\Theta,z) = v(z) + e(\Theta,z).$$

The function $v(z)$, which is a function of observable attributes only, will be called the <u>deterministic utility</u> of z. The random variable $e(\Theta,z)$ will be called the <u>random utility</u>. The distribution of $e(\Theta,z)$ can be defined in terms of the measure μ as follows. Let $\Gamma(z,x) \subseteq \Gamma$ be the subset of $\Theta \epsilon \Gamma$ satisfying the inequality:

$$u(\Theta,z) - v(z) \leq x. \tag{3}$$

Then, from (2), $e(\Theta,z) \leq x$ iff $\Theta \epsilon \Gamma(z,x)$ or:

$$F(x|z) = \Pr\{e(\Theta,z) \leq x\} =$$

$$= \Pr\{\Theta \epsilon \Gamma(z,x)\} = \int_{\Theta \epsilon \Gamma(z,x)} d\mu(\Theta). \tag{4}$$

Thus $F(x|z)$ is the marginal distribution of $e(\Theta,z)$. The joint distribution of any finite countable sequence of alternatives $\{e(\Theta,z_j): z_j \epsilon \Omega, j=1,\ldots,N\}$ can be defined as follows.

Let $x \epsilon R^N$ be an N-dimensional real vector $\{x_1,\ldots,x_N\}$ and define:

$$\Gamma(x) = \bigcap_{j=1}^{N} \Gamma(z_j,x_j) \tag{5}$$

then, from (2):

$$e(\Theta,z_j) \leq x_j \qquad \forall_j, \text{ iff } \Theta \epsilon \Gamma(x)$$

or:

$$\begin{aligned}
F(x) &= \Pr\{e(\Theta,z_1) \leq x_1,\ldots,e(\Theta,z_N) \leq x_N\} \\
&= \Pr\{\Theta \epsilon \Gamma(x)\} \\
&= \int_{\Theta \epsilon \Gamma(x)} d\mu(\Theta).
\end{aligned} \qquad (6)$$

where $F(x)$ is the joint distribution of $\{e(\Theta,z_j): z_j \epsilon \Omega, \ j=1,\ldots,N\}$.

It is easily checked that the distributions $F(x_j|z_j)$ are proper marginals of $F(x)$. From (3) and the definition of $\Gamma(z,x)$ it is true that $\Gamma(z,\infty)=\Gamma$, for all $z\epsilon\Omega$. Hence

$$\bigcap_{k \neq j} \Gamma(z_k,\infty) = \bigcap_{k \neq j} \Gamma = \Gamma$$

and

$$\Gamma(z_j,x_j) \cap_{k \neq j} \Gamma(z_k,\infty) = \Gamma(z_j,x_j) \cap \Gamma = \Gamma(z_j,x_j)$$

By letting all x_k except x_j go to infinity in (6) and substituting the above result:

$$F(\infty,\ldots,x_j,\ldots,\infty) = \int_{\Theta \epsilon \Gamma(\infty,\ldots,x_j,\ldots,\infty)} d\mu(\Theta)$$

$$= \int_{\substack{\Theta \epsilon \Gamma(z_j,x_j) \cap \Gamma(z_k,\infty) \\ k \neq j}} d\mu(\Theta) \qquad = \int_{\Theta \epsilon \Gamma(z_j,x_j)} d\mu(\Theta)$$

$$= F(x_j|z_j);$$

(definition (5) and equation (4) have been used).

3. Main Properties of the General Random Utility Model

3.1. BASIC PROPERTIES OF THE ARU REPRESENTATION.

Short notation: let $\{z_j: z_j \varepsilon \Omega, j=1,\ldots,N\}$ be a finite sequence of alternatives. The following definitions will be used:

$$v_j = v(z_j)$$
$$e_j = e(\Theta, z_j)$$

$$F(x_1,\ldots,x_N) = \int_{\Theta \varepsilon \Gamma(x_i,\ldots,x_N)} d\mu (\Theta) = Pr \{e_1 \leq x_1,\ldots e_N \leq x_N\}$$

$$u_j = v_j + e_j.$$

Maximum utility distribution. The maximum utility is the random variable:

$$u = \max_{1 \leq j \leq N} (v_j + e_j).$$

Its distribution is derived by observing the equivalence between the event:

$$\max_{1 \leq j \leq N} (v_j + e_j) \leq x$$

and the joint occurrence of the events:

$$(v_j + e_j) \leq x \qquad\qquad \forall j.$$

Therefore, if we define:

$$G(x|v_1,\ldots,v_N) = Pr \{u \leq x\}$$

it follows:

$$G(x|v_1,\ldots,v_N) = Pr \{ \max_j (v_j + e_j) \leq x\}$$
$$= Pr \{v_1+e_1 \leq x,\ldots,v_N + e_N \leq x\}$$
$$= Pr \{e_1 \leq x-v_1,\ldots,e_N \leq x - v_N\}$$
$$= F (x-v_1,\ldots,x-v_N). \qquad\qquad (7)$$

Expected maximum utility. The expected maximum utility,

or the expected utility associated with the most attractive alternative within the choice set z_j, is the first moment of $G(x)$ and can be defined:

$$V(v_1,\ldots,v_N) = \int_{-\infty}^{\infty} x \; dG(x|v_1,\ldots,v_N). \tag{8}$$

The following proposition holds:

PROPOSITION 1. The function $V : R^N \Rightarrow R$ is convex.

Proof. For a given sequence $\{e_1,\ldots,e_N\}$, the function $u_e : R^N \Rightarrow R$, defined by

$$u_e(v) = \max_{1\le j \le N} (v_j + e_j) \qquad\qquad v \varepsilon R^N$$

is convex since for any $0\le\alpha\le 1$ and $x,y\varepsilon R^N$:

$$u_e[\alpha x + (1-\alpha)y] = \max_{1\le j \le N} [\alpha x_j + (1-\alpha)y_j + e_j]$$

$$= \max_{1\le j \le N} [\alpha(x_j + e_j) + (1-\alpha)(y_j + e_j)]$$

$$\le \alpha \max_{1\le j \le N} (x_j + e_j) + (1-\alpha) \max_{1\le j \le N} (y_j + e_j)$$

$$= \alpha u_e(x) + (1-\alpha) u_e(y).$$

Therefore the function $V : R^N \Rightarrow R$ is from (8) a convex combination (through the probability distribution G) of convex functions, hence a convex function. Q.E.D.

COROLLARY 1. The Hessian matrix of V is positive semidefinite. Proof. The function V is differentiable by contruction; it is also convex from proposition 1, then the corollary follows. Q.E.D..

In the next section we will show that the basic demand theorems can be derived by this convexity property of the potential function of aggregate choice V, which is defined in utilities (and in prices). The conjugate of V in quantities will be concave (and its Hessian matrix negative semidefinite), hence there is a correspondence between the aggregate choice problem and conventional theory of demand for the individual consumer. Note also that aggregate choice could be interpreted as a sample of different choice situations for the same actor, moving in the actor space through time (but with constant choice set z_j). Following this interpretation the fundamental results of Demand Theory are maintained without ruling out the changing tastes of a consumer, as well as taking into account idiosyncrasies and differences of tastes among individuals.

3.2. CHOICE PROBABILITIES.

The choice probability P_j of alternative j (for i=1,...N) is the probability of occurrence of the event: $u_j > u_k$, $\forall k \neq j$. Let us assume that:

(A.6) $F(x_1,...,x_N)$ is absolutely continuous.
The partial derivatives:

$$F_j(x_1,...,x_N) = \frac{\partial}{\partial x_j} F(x_1,...,x_N)$$

are well defined and P_j is given by

$$P_j = Pr\{u_j > u_k, \forall k \neq j\} =$$

$$= \int_{-\infty}^{\infty} Pr\{v_1+e_1 \leq x,...,x<v_j+e_j \leq x+dx,...,v_N+e_N \leq x\}$$

$$= \int_{-\infty}^{\infty} Pr\{e_1 \leq x-v_1,...,x-v_j<e_j \leq x-v_j+dx,...,e_N \leq x-v_N\}$$

$$= \int_{-\infty}^{\infty} F_j(x-v_1,...,x-v_N) \, dx. \qquad (9)$$

One can easily check that P_j, $\forall j$, is a proper probability distribution: from (9) $P_j \geq 0$. Moreover, from (7):

$$dG(x|v_1,...,v_N) = \sum_j F_j(x-v_1,...,x-v_N) \, dx$$

hence:

$$\sum_j P_j = \int_{-\infty}^{\infty} \sum_j F_j(x-v_1,...,x-v_N) \, dx$$

$$= \int_{-\infty}^{\infty} dG\ (x|v_1,\ldots,v_N) = 1 \qquad\qquad (10)$$

(since G is a probability distribution).
The following proposition holds:
PROPOSITION 2.

$$P_j = \frac{\partial V}{\partial v_j} \qquad\qquad\qquad j = 1,\ldots,N.$$

Proof.
From equations (7) and (8):

$$\frac{\partial V}{\partial v_j} = \int_{-\infty}^{\infty} x\ d[\ \frac{\partial}{\partial v_j}\ G(x|v_1,\ldots,v_N)]$$

$$= -\int_{-\infty}^{\infty} x\ dF_j(x-v_1,\ldots,x-v_N).$$

Integration by parts yields:

$$\frac{\partial V}{\partial v_j} = -\ x\ F_j(x-v_1,\ldots,x-v_N)\ \Big|_{-\infty}^{\infty} +$$

$$+ \int_{-\infty}^{\infty} F_j(x-v_1,\ldots,x-v_n)dx$$

and since the first term on the right vanishes for x=∞ and x=-∞

$$\frac{\partial V}{\partial v_j} = \int_{-\infty}^{\infty} F_j(x-v_1,\ldots,x-v_N)\ dx = P_j$$

because of (9).Q.E.D.
     One can easily show that this proposition doesn't hold for any representation u=u[v(z),e(z)], as it holds for the additive one. Hence, proposition 2 states that the integrability condition for choice probabilities is always satisfied for RUM in additive form (see also Williams, 1977;

Leonardi, 1983). Moreover, an easy corollary follows on symmetry of the Hessian of V or:

COROLLARY 2. The matrix of partial derivatives of the choice probabilities with respect to the deterministic utilities is symmetric, i.e.

$$\frac{\partial P_j}{\partial v_k} = \frac{\partial P_k}{\partial v_j} \qquad\qquad \forall j,k.$$

Proof. From proposition 2.:

$$\frac{\partial}{\partial v_k} P_j = \frac{\partial^2 V}{\partial v_k \partial v_j} = \frac{\partial^2 V}{\partial v_j \partial v_k} = \frac{\partial}{\partial v_j} P_k \qquad \underline{Q.E.D.}$$

3.3. STRICT ORDINALITY OF UTILITY IN ARUM.

The ARU representation has the property of strict ordinality in utilities, which is implied by axiom (A.2). In order to check this property, let us introduce a monotonically increasing transformation which is differentiable.
Let:

$$\underline{u}(\Theta,z) = \beta[u(\Theta,z] \qquad\qquad \beta'> 0 \quad (11)$$

then:

$$\underline{v}(z) = \int_{\Theta\epsilon\Gamma} \underline{u}(\Theta,z)\ d\mu(\Theta) \qquad\qquad (12)$$

$$\underline{e}(\Theta,z) = \underline{u}(\Theta,z) - \underline{v}(z).$$

PROPOSITION 3. When definitions (11) and (12) hold:

$$P_j(v_1,\ldots,v_N) = P_j\ (\underline{v}_1,\ldots,\underline{v}_N) \qquad \forall j$$

is true for any monotonically increasing function β.
Proof. The event:

$$\underline{e}(\Theta,z) \leq \underline{x} = \beta(x)$$

has probability

$$\underline{F}(\underline{x}|z)= \Pr \{\underline{e}(\Theta,z) \leq \underline{x}\} = \int_{\Theta\epsilon\Gamma(z,\underline{x})} d\mu(\Theta).$$

where $\underline{F}(\underline{x}|z)$ is the marginal distribution of $\underline{e}(\Theta,z)$.
    Then for N alternatives in each choice set z_j the joint distribution is, for $\underline{x}= \{\underline{x}_1,\dots,\underline{x}_N\}$, $\underline{v} = \{\underline{v}_1,\dots,\underline{v}_N\}$:

$$\underline{F}(\underline{x}) = \Pr \{\underline{e}(z_j) \leq \underline{x}_j\colon z_j\epsilon\Omega,\ j = 1,\dots,N\}.$$

But, by definition:

$$\underline{F}(\underline{x}) = F(x)$$

so that:

$$\underline{V}(\underline{v}) = \int_{-\infty}^{\infty} d\underline{F}(\underline{x}-\underline{v}) = \int_{-\infty}^{\infty} dF(x-v) = V(v)$$

$$\frac{\partial \underline{V}}{\partial \underline{v}_j} = \frac{\partial V}{\partial v_j} = P_j \qquad\qquad \forall j.\underline{Q.E.D.}$$

4. An Alternative Derivation of Basic Propositions in Demand Theory

For derivation of theorems (A), (B) and (C) of Section 1 in the analog case when one can observe only aggregate choice patterns for samples of population, we make use of Corollaries 1 and 2 above, together with the assumption:
    (A.7) prices are "negative" attributes of alternatives, they are observable and relevant for the average choice maker, so that at least at the aggregate level:

$$\frac{\partial v_j}{\partial \pi_j} < 0 \qquad\qquad \forall j \quad (13)$$

holds, where π_j is the cost associated with alternative j.
(A') FIRST SUBSTITUTION THEOREM:

$$\frac{\partial P_j}{\partial \pi_j} = \frac{\partial P_j}{\partial v_j} \cdot \frac{\partial v_j}{\partial \pi_j} \leq 0 \qquad\qquad \forall j$$

This follows immediately by the non-negativity of the first term (from Corollary 1) and negativity of the second.

One could interpret also alternatives as bundles of commodities, so that prices would be total budgets: in this case, when a dearer alternative has a higher frequency we can define this situation as an aggregate revealed preference $\varphi_r =_{def}$ "If $P_i > P_j$ and $\pi_i \geq \pi_j$ then $z_i \varphi_r z_j$".

We shall assume here Parametric prices, allowing neither for interaction of demand upon prices nor between demand and supply conditions: for an introduction of price formation and market mechanism in RUM one can see applications to transportation and housing market issues in Daganzo (1979), Anas (1982), and Leonardi (1984).Under some restrictions, the effect of a general and proportional variation in parametric prices will change the position of the V function without affecting its shape. Let us consider the rather simpler case when assumption:

$$(A.8) \qquad \frac{\partial v_j}{\partial \pi_j} = \frac{\alpha_n}{\pi_j} \qquad\qquad \forall j;$$

holds, where $\alpha_n < 0$ is a constant among all alternatives. This restriction is satisfied only when a given rate of change in prices has the same effect on "deterministic utilities" for all alternatives. Moreover, let us assume, as in econometric applications:

(A.9) an additive specification of the mapping from attributes to deterministic utilities, with a logarithmic transformation of the attribute "price"; and that:

(A.10) the attractiveness v_j, $\forall j$, of an alternative j is affected by only one price attribute, i.e. its own cost π_j.

We can assume (A.10) because interdependencies and cross-effects between alternatives have been already represented through the mapping from the v_j's to the P_j's (with no logit-like restrictive assumption on this interaction, until now), so that there is no particular reason to take them into account again in the following function:

$$v_j = \sum_{k=1}^{n-1} \alpha_k z_{jk} + \alpha_n \ln \pi_j \qquad\qquad \forall j \qquad\qquad (14)$$

where α_k are known or estimated parameters and z_{jk} values of attribute k for alternative j. This function follows from (A.9) and (A.10) and satisfies (A.8) as well as (A.7) for $\alpha_n < 0$.

PROPOSITION 4. When assumptions from (A.1) to (A.10) hold, then there is zero-degree homogeneity of demand in prices.
Proof. Let $\pi'_j = \tau\pi_j$, $\sigma = \alpha_n \ln\tau$, $y-x = \sigma$ then from (14):

$$v'_j(\pi'_j) = v_j + \alpha_n \ln\tau = v_j + \sigma \qquad \forall j$$

$$V(v'_1,\ldots,v'_n) = V(v_1+\sigma,\ldots,v_n+\sigma)$$

$$= \int_{-\infty}^{\infty} x \; dF(x-v_1-\sigma,\ldots,x-v_n-\sigma)$$

$$= \int_{-\infty}^{\infty} y \; dF(y-v_1,\ldots,y-v_n) + \sigma\int_{-\infty}^{\infty} dF(y-v_1,\ldots,y-v_n)$$

$$= V(v_1,\ldots,v_n) + \sigma.$$

(equations 7, 8 and 10 have been used). Hence it follows:

$$P_j = \frac{\partial V}{\partial v_j} = \frac{\partial V}{\partial v'_j} \qquad\qquad\qquad \forall j. \quad \underline{Q.E.D}$$

Moreover, when the same axioms hold, then from Corollary 2 we derive the:
(B') RECIPROCITY THEOREM:

$$\pi_k \frac{\partial P_j}{\partial \pi_k} = \pi_j \frac{\partial P_k}{\partial \pi_j} = \alpha_n H_{jk}$$

where H_{jk} is the element of the symmetric Hessian H of V.
Finally, we know from Corollary 1 that each principal minor of H must be non-negative; hence we derive the (C') SECOND SUBSTITUTION THEOREM, as follows:

$$H_{jj} H_{kk} - H^2_{jk} \geq 0$$

$$H^2_{jk} \alpha^2_n \leq (\alpha_n H_{jj})(\alpha_n H_{kk})$$

$$\frac{(\partial P_j)^2}{(\partial \pi_k / \pi_k)^2} \leq \frac{\partial P_j}{\partial \pi_j / \pi_j} \cdot \frac{\partial P_k}{\partial \pi_k / \pi_k} \qquad \forall j,k.$$

We cannot introduce in this paper the generalized law of demand in a probabilistic and aggregate version, because we have not yet introduced an explicit income constraint on the choice set of each actor (although we have specified from the beginning that such a constraint can be conceived as one of the m attributes identifying an actor type).

5. A Special Form of an Additive Random Utility Model

5.1. EXCHANGEABILITY: DE FINETTI REPRESENTATION.

Let us assume $z_j = z$, $j=1,\ldots,N$. For such a particular sequence of alternatives we have: $v_j = v$, $\forall j$. Since utilities are defined up to an additive constant, one can arbitrarily set $v=0$, so that $v_j=0$, $\forall j$. The total utility of each alternative is thus just made of the random part, i.e. $u_j = e_j$, $\forall j$.

The joint distribution of utilities is now:

$$\Pr \{u_1 \leq x_1, \ldots, u_n \leq x_n\} = F(x_1, \ldots, x_n) \qquad (15)$$

and obviously coincides with the joint distribution of the random terms. Since the alternatives have equal attributes, it is reasonable to assume that exchanging their order will not change their joint utility distribution. This and (15) imply that the sequence of random terms $\{e_j: j=1,\ldots,N\}$ is exchangeable. The property is stated in the following axiom:

(A.11) Exchangeability of random terms.
"Let $(i_1,\ldots,i_N)$ be any permutation of the subscripts $(1,\ldots,N)$. Then:

$$\Pr \{e_{i_1} \leq x_1, \ldots, e_{i_N} \leq x_N\} \equiv \Pr \{e_1 \leq x_1, \ldots, e_N \leq x_N\}$$

$$\equiv F(x_1,\ldots,x_N)."$$

If the axiom holds, the following theorem, originally due to de Finetti (1930), provides a special representation for $F(x_1,\ldots,x_N)$:

THEOREM D. (De Finetti representation)

"Let $\{e_1,\ldots,e_N\}$ be a sequence of random variables satisfying axiom 11, i.e. exchangeable. Then there is a family of univariate distributions $F(x,y)$ with parameter $y\epsilon Y$, and a distribution $H(y)$ on the parameter space, such that:

$$F(x_1,\ldots,x_N) = \int_{y\epsilon Y} \prod_{j=1}^{n} F(x_j,y) \; dH(y)." \qquad (16)$$

Intuitively, representation (16) splits randomness into two parts. One is associated with the parameters y of the distribution $F(x,y)$, and it does not depend on the alternatives. It thus represents an heterogeneity of individuals: each individual or group has a different distribution $F(x,y)$. The other, conditional on the parameter y, is associated with the alternatives, but for a given y is the same for all alternatives. To summarize, individuals have different parameters, but each of them has random terms independently and identically distributed (i.i.d.). Equation (16) can thus be thought of as an i.i.d. random variable distribution, averaged over a population heterogeneous in their parameters.

5.2. ASYMPTOTIC APPROXIMATION FOR EXCHANGEABLE RANDOM TERMS.

Let the sequence of alternatives become very large, or the discrete choice situation initially assumed tend to be a continuous one: $N \Rightarrow \infty$. Then, since for given y the random terms are i.i.d., the asymptotic results proved in Leonardi (1984a) hold. In particular, under the assumption:

$$(A.12) \quad \lim_{z \Rightarrow \infty} \frac{1 - F(x+z,y)}{1 - F(z,y)} = \exp -\beta(y)x$$

(i.e., let $F(x,y)$ belong to the domain of attraction of the Gumbel or extreme value distribution), it is proved that:

$$P_j(y) = \lim_{N \Rightarrow \infty} P_j(y,N) = \frac{\exp \beta(y)v_j}{\sum_j \exp \beta(y)v_j} \qquad \forall j \quad (17)$$

where $P_j(y)$ is the asymptotic choice probability, conditional on y. The unconditional choice probability is:

$$P_j = \int_{y \epsilon Y} P_j(y) \, dH(y) \qquad \forall j \quad (18)$$

and, by defining the distribution

$$B(x) = Pr \{\beta(y) \leq x\} = \int_{y \epsilon Y(x)} dH(y)$$

where $Y(x)$ is the set of y solving the inequality $\beta(y) \leq x$, equation (18) becomes:

$$P_j = \int_{x=0}^{\infty} \frac{\exp xv_j}{\sum_j \exp xv_j} \, dB(x) \qquad \forall j \quad (19)$$

Equation (19) states that under assumption (A.11) and (A.12), the choice probabilities converge asymptotically towards a mixture of logit models for a heterogeneous population. Only when $\beta(y)$ degenerates to a constant, equation (19) reduces to the standard Logit form (1) and Luce's axiom holds. Let (A.13) be such an assumption: $\beta(y)=\beta$. Then an alternative foundation of the MNL model can be given by axioms (A.1) to (A.5) characterizing any ARUM, plus axioms (A.11) to (A.13) introducing the logit form in more general terms than those of McFadden.

Leonardi - I.I.A.S.A.
Laxenburg, Austria

Arcangeli, Reggiani
D.A.E.S.T.
Venezia, Italy

REFERENCES

Anas, A.: 1982, Residential Location Markets and Urban Transportation, Academic Press, New York.

Bertuglia,C.S., G. Leonardi, S. Occelli, G.A. Rabino and R. Tadei.: 1984, "Location-Transport Relationships: State-of the-Art, Unifying Efforts and Future Developments.", IRES, WP 32, Torino.

Daganzo, C.: 1979, Multinomial Probit (The Theory and Its Application to Demand Forecasting), Academic Press, New York.

Debreu, G.: 1960, "Review of R.D. Luce (1959)." American Economic Review 50, 186-8.

De Finetti, B.: 1930, "Funzione caratteristica di un fenomeno aleatorio", in Atti Accademia Nazionale Lincei Rend. (Cl.Sci.Fis.Mat. Nat.) 4, 86-133.

Hicks, J.R.: 1965, A Revision of Demand Theory, Clarendon Press, Oxford.

Leonardi, G.: 1983, "The Use of Random-Utility Theory in Building Location-Allocation Models", in J.F. Thisse and H.G. Zolled (eds.), Locational Analysis of Public Facilities, North Holland, Amsterdam, pp. 357-383.

Leonardi, G.: 1985, "Equivalenza asintotica tra la teoria delle utilità casuali e la massimizzazione dell'entropia" in A. Reggiani (ed.), Territorio e Trasporti. Modelli matematici per l'Analisi e la Pianificazione, Angeli, Milano.

Luce, R.D.: 1959, Individual Choice Behaviour: A Theoretical Analysis, Wiley, New York.

Thurstone, L.: 1927, "A Law of Comparative Judgment", Psycological Review 37, 273-286.

Williams, H.C.W.L.: 1977, "On the Formation of Travel Demand Models and Economic Evaluation Measures of User Benefit", Environnement and Planning A 9, 285-344.

Wong, S.: 1978, The Foundations of P. Samuelson's Revealed Preference Theory, Routledge & Kegan, London.

Peter Wakker

CONCAVE ADDITIVELY DECOMPOSABLE REPRESENTING FUNCTIONS AND RISK AVERSION

1. Introduction

We study preference relations on sets that are finite-fold cartesian products. Elements of these sets will be called alternatives. The preference relation represents the opinion of a decision maker.

Examples are consumer demand theory, where alternatives are "commodity bundles"; and decision making under uncertainty, where alternatives are "acts".

Our purpose is to characterize (i.e. give properties of the preference relation, necessary and sufficient to guarantee) the existence of special kinds of representing functions, mainly continuous concave functions that are additively decomposable.

An often used property of preference relations is known under various names such as (strong/strict) separability, (preferential) independence, the sure-thing principle. We shall use the term "coordinate independence" (CI) for it. The property was introduced in Sono (1945, 1961) and Leontief (1947a, 1947b) in terms of derivatives of a (presupposed) representing function. See also Samuelson (1947, pp. 174-180). In Debreu (1960) it was formulated in its present, more appealing, form, in terms of the preference relation, without differentiability assumptions. Before, Savage (1954) had introduced the "sure-thing principle" for DMUU. This in fact is identical to CI, as is well known nowadays. It can be seen to underly the "likelihood principle" in statistics, thus should be fruitful there too. See Birnbaum (1962, 1972), Savage (1962), Berger (1980, 1.6.2), or Barnard & Godambe (1982). For an extensive study of generalizations of CI, see Blackorby, Primont and Russell (1978).

In this paper we shall characterize, under a continuity and nontriviality assumption, the existence of concave additively decomposable representing functions. It is known that the combination of CI and convexity for

249

L. Daboni et al. (eds.), Recent Developments in the Foundations of Utility and Risk Theory, 249–262.
© 1986 by D. Reidel Publishing Company.

the preference relation does not suffice for this, see
section 4. We shall introduce a property for preference
relations, the "concavity assumption", that achieves the
desired characterization. It is an extension of "axiom Q"
of Yaari (1978), which there is not studied for its own
sake, but only as an intermediate between a stronger and
weaker property, and concerns the case where every
component equals R_+.

For continuity and concavity to have meaning, at
least some topological and convexity structure is
required. A reader, not interested in these notions in
full generality, may simply assume that the coordinates
refer to convex subsets of Euclidean spaces, and skip over
the specific details of mixture spaces in section 2. Our
notation is chosen such that this can be done without any
problem. Note that we do not assume monotonicity, to
achieve maximal generality.

In section 5 we consider the case where all
components of the cartesian product are identical. The
main application for this is DMUU, with a finite state
space. First the characterization of continuous expected
utility maximization, provided in Wakker (1984a) for a set
of consequences that is a convex open subset of R, is
extended to the case where the set of consequences is any
topologically connected space. Next it is combined with the
concavity assumption, thus characterizing continuous
expected utility maximization with risk aversion. In this
we do not need differentiability assumptions or methods. A
result, using differentiability assumptions, is Stigum
(1972).

The existence of special kinds of representing
(="utility") functions can be verified/justified
(falsified/criticized) if and only if the involved
characterizing properties can be verified/justified
(falsified/criticized). Thus characterization results are
central for the discussion on the foundations of utility.

Proofs are given or referenced in the Appendix.

2.   Product Topological Mixture Spaces

First we introduce "mixture spaces", i.e. sets with a
"mixture operation" on them. These were already used by von
Neumann and Morgenstern (1944) and Herstein and Milnor
(1953). There the mixture operation mainly served as a

generalization of lotteries. Extensive use of mixture spaces is made in Fishburn (1982). See also Luce & Suppes (1965). The applicability of mixture operations to fields such as quantum mechanics, and colour perception in psychology, is indicated in Gudder (1977) and Gudder and Schroeck (1980). Our main intended application is that a mixture operation is a generalization of the convex combination operation in linear spaces.

DEFINITION 2.1: A function $\Theta : C \times [0,1] \times C \Rightarrow C$, where C is a nonempty set, and where we write $p\alpha + (1-p)\beta$ for $\Theta(\alpha,p,\beta)$, is a _mixture operation_ (_on_ C) if the following i, ii, and iii are satisfied for all $\alpha,\beta \in C$; and $p,\mu, \in [0,1]$:
i   : commutativity $p\alpha + (1-p)\beta = (1-p)\beta + p\alpha$.
ii : associativity $\mu(p\alpha+(1-p)\beta)+(1-\mu)\beta = (\mu p)\alpha+(1-(\mu p))\beta$.
iii: identity $1\alpha + 0\beta = \alpha$.
Here (C,Θ), or simply C, is called a _mixture space_.

     It may be argued that ii could be called "distributivity" instead of "associativity". We write α/μ for $(1/\mu)\alpha$, and $p\alpha/\mu$ for $(p/\mu)\alpha$. We say "_y is between α and β_" if $p \in [0,1]$ exists such that $y = p\alpha + (1-p)\beta$. The definitions of convex sets, and affine/convex/concave/ quasiconcave functions, are as in Euclidean spaces.

LEMMA 2.1: If C is a mixture space, then for all $\alpha,\beta \in C$; $p,\mu \in [0,1]$:
iv: $\mu\alpha + (1-\mu)\alpha = \alpha$.
v : $p(\mu\alpha + (1-\mu)\beta) + (1-p)(v\alpha + (1-v)\beta) =$
    $= (p\mu + (1-p)v)\alpha + (p(1-\mu) + (1-p)(1-v)\beta)$.

DEFINITION 2.2: (C,T,Θ), also denoted as C, is a _topological mixture space_ if T is a topology on C, Θ a mixture operation on C, and $\Theta: C \times [0,1] \times C$ (with the product topology) $\Rightarrow$ C is continuous.

LEMMA 2.2: A topological mixture space C is topologically connected.

LEMMA 2.3: Let V from a topological mixture space $(C,T,\Theta) \Rightarrow \dot{R}$ be continuous. The following propositions are equivalent:
i   : There exists $\pi > 0$ such that $V[(\alpha/2) + (\beta/2)] \geq [V(\alpha) + V(\beta)]/2$ whenever $0 \leq V(\alpha)-V(\beta) \leq \pi$.
ii : $V(\alpha/2 + \beta/2) \geq [V(\alpha) + V(\beta)]/2$ for all α,β.

iii: V is concave.

DEFINITION 2.3: For a sequence of mixture spaces $(C_i, \Theta_i)_{i=1}^n$, the <u>product mixture operation</u>
$\Theta : (X_{i=1}^n C_i) \times [0,1] \times (X_{i=1}^n C_i) \Rightarrow X_{i=1}^n C_i$
assigns to every $(x,p,y) = [(x_1,\ldots,x_n),p,(y_1,\ldots,y_n)]$, the image element $(px_1 + (1-p)y_1,\ldots,px_n + (1-p)y_n)$, also denoted as $p(x_1,\ldots,x_n) + (1-p)(y_1,\ldots,y_n)$, or $px + (1-p)y$. We then call $(X_{i=1}^n C_i, \Theta)$, or simply $X_{i=1}^n C_i$, the <u>product mixture space</u>. If the C_i's are topological mixture spaces, then we endow $X_{i=1}^n C_i$ with the product topology and call it a <u>product topological mixture space</u>.

For the above definitions to be suited the following:

THEOREM 2.1: A product mixture operation is a mixture operation. A product topological mixture space is a topological mixture space.

3. The Concavity Assumption

Throughout this section $C = X_{i=1}^n C_i$ is a product topological mixture space. For instance any C_i may be (a convex subset of) R^{m_i}. Elements of C, called <u>alternatives</u>, are denoted by x,y,v, etc., with coordinates x_1, v_2, etc. Elements of $U_{i=1}^n C_i$ are also denoted by α,β,Γ, etc. Less standard is the following notation: $x_{-i}\alpha$ is the alternative with i-th coordinate α, other coordinates equal to those of x.

The decision maker is denoted by T, his preference relation on the set of alternatives by $\succcurlyeq$. We write $x \succcurlyeq y$ if T thinks x at least as good as y. We write $x \preccurlyeq y$ if $y \succcurlyeq x$, $x \prec y$ if not $x \succcurlyeq y$, $x \succ y$ if not $y \succcurlyeq x$, and $x \approx y$ if $x \succcurlyeq y$ and $y \succcurlyeq x$. A <u>weak order</u> $\succcurlyeq$ is <u>complete</u> and <u>transitive</u>, i.e. $[x \succcurlyeq y$ or $y \succcurlyeq x]$, and $[x \succcurlyeq y \& y \succcurlyeq z \Rightarrow x \succcurlyeq z]$ for all $x,y,z \in C$; thus it induces an "equivalence relation", $\approx$. A preference relation $\succcurlyeq$ is <u>convex</u> if $\{x|x \succcurlyeq y\}$ is convex for all alternatives y, and <u>continuous</u> if $\{x|x \succcurlyeq y\}$ and $\{x|x \preccurlyeq y\}$ are closed for all y. Coordinate i is <u>essential</u> (w.r.t. $\succcurlyeq$) if $x_{-i}\alpha \succ x$ for some $x \in C$, $\alpha \in C_i$. A function $V : C \Rightarrow R$ <u>represents</u> $\succcurlyeq$ if $x \succcurlyeq y \Leftrightarrow V(x) \geq V(y)$ for all $x,y \in C$.

LEMMA 3.1: If $\succeq$ is a weak order, then $x \approx y$ whenever $x_j = y_j$ for all essential j.

The above Lemma shows that, for a weak order $\succeq$, the inessential coordinates do not affect $\succeq$. Hence they can be left out, as will be used in Definition 3.2.

LEMMA 3.2: Let $\succeq$ be a weak order on a topological mixture space C. Then the following propositions are equivalent:
i : $x \succeq y \Rightarrow px + (1-p)y \succeq y$ for all x,y; $p \in [0,1]$.
ii: $\succeq$ is convex.
If $\succeq$ is continuous, then a further equivalent proposition is:
iii: $x \succeq y \Rightarrow x/2 + y/2 \succeq y$ for all x,y.

DEFINITION 3.1: We say $\succeq$ is <u>coordinate independent (CI)</u> if $(x_{-i}\alpha) \succeq (y_{-i}\alpha) \Rightarrow (x_{-i}\beta) \succeq (y_{-i}\beta)$ for all x,y,i,α,β.

For the case of exactly two essential coordinates we shall need one more property:

DEFINITION 3.2: Let exactly two coordinates be essential. We say a weak order $\succeq$ satisfies the <u>Thomsen condition</u> if, after removal of the inessential coordinates, $(\alpha,\mu) \approx (\Gamma,\nu)$ & $(\Gamma,\sigma) \approx (\beta,\mu)$ imply $(\alpha,\sigma) \approx (\beta,\nu)$ for all $\alpha,\ldots,\nu$.

The following property is a generalization of "Axiom Q" in Yaari (1978), which is formulated for the case where $C_i = R_+$ for all i, and for this case by some elementary calculus can be seen to be equivalent to our present definition.

DEFINITION 3.3: We say $\succeq$ satisfies the <u>concavity assumption</u> if $x_{-i}\Gamma \succeq y_{-i}\delta$ whenever $x_{-i}\alpha \succeq y_{-i}\beta$ and $\beta = p\alpha + (1-p)\delta$, $\Gamma = p\delta + (1-p)\alpha$ for some $p \in [0,1]$.

A way to see the meaning of this is by substitution in Theorem 3.1.i. The following Lemmas adapt to the present context the Remark at section 4, and the Lemma 2 of section 5 and by that the implication of axiom D through axiom Q, of Yaari (1978).

LEMMA 3.3: The concavity assumption implies CI.

LEMMA 3.4: If $\succeq$ is a continuous weak order that satisfies the concavity assumption, then $\succeq$ is convex.

If three or more coordinates are essential, the above lemma can also be obtained as a corollary of Theorem 3.1 below.

DEFINITION 3.4: $(V_j)_{j=1}^n$ is an <u>array of additive value functions for</u> $\succeq$ if $[x \succeq y <=> \Sigma_{j=1}^n V_j(x_j) \geq \Sigma_{j=1}^n V_j(y_j)]$ for all $x,y \in X_{j=1}^n C_j$. With then $V(x) := \Sigma_{j=1}^n V_j(x_j)$, V is called <u>additively decomposable</u>.

Now we are ready for our main result:

THEOREM 3.1: Let $\succeq$ be a binary relation on a product topological mixture space $X_{i=1}^n C_i$ (e.g. $X_{i=1}^n R^{m_i}$). Let at least two coordinates be essential. Then the following propositions are equivalent:
i : There exists an array of continuous concave additive value functions $(V_j)_{j=1}^n$ for $\succeq$.
ii: The binary relation $\succeq$ is a continuous weak order that satisfies the concavity assumption; if exactly two coordinates are essential, then furthermore $\succeq$ satisfies the Thomsen condition.
Furthermore, if i applies, then $(W_j)_{j=1}^n$ is an array of additive value functions for $\succeq$ if and only if $(\mu_j)_{j=1}^n$ exist, and positive k, such that $W_j = kV_j + \mu_j$ for all j.

The following Corollary applies the above result to a common context, where $C = R_{++}^n$ ($R_{++} = \{\alpha \in R | \alpha > 0\}$), $\succeq$ is <u>monotone</u> ($x_j \geq y_j$ for all j => $x \succeq y$). The property after "furthermore" in ii below, simply is a reformulation of the concavity assumption, so of Yaari's axiom Q. It reflects the idea of nonincreasing marginal utility.

COROLLARY 3.1: Let $\succeq$ be a binary relation on $(R_{++})^n$, $n \geq 3$. Then the following propositions are equivalent:
i : There exist concave (thus continuous) nondecreasing nonconstant functions $V_j : R_{++} => R$, $j = 1,...,n$, such that $[x \succeq y <=> \Sigma_{j=1}^n V_j(x_j) \geq \Sigma_{j=1}^n V_j(y_j)$ for all x,y].
ii: $\succeq$ is a continuous weak order, it is monotone, every coordinate is essential, and furthermore $x_{-i}\alpha \succeq y_{-i}\beta$ => $x_{-i}(\alpha-e) \succeq y_{-i}(\beta-e)$ whenever $(\alpha-\beta)e \geq 0$.

4. Completion of Logical Relations

Throughout this section $\succeq$ is a continuous weak order on a

product topological mixture space $X_{i=1}^{m}\ C_i$, and $n \le m$ is the
number of _essential_ coordinates. In figure 1 we have
indicated the logical relations between the propositions,
numbered 4.1 - 4.4 there.

FIGURE I: (for continuous weak order $\ge$)

There exists an array of continuous concave   (4.1)
additive value functions for $\ge$

n=1: counterexample V = f^5	by	
n=2: counterexample V = f^2	Th.	
n≥3: correct by Theorem 3.1	3.1	

$\ge$ satisfies the concavity assumption   (4.2)

n=1: counterexample V=f^1	by	
n=2: counterexample V=f^3	Lemma	
n≥3: counterexample V=f^3	3.3 & 3.4	

$\ge$ is convex and CI   (4.3)

n=1: correct		
n=2: counterexample V=f^4	direct	
n≥3: counterexample V=f^2		

$\ge$ is convex   (4.4)

n: number of essential coordinates;
V: function, representing $\ge$;
f^j : R_{++}^m => R for all $1 \le j \le 5$; with $f^1(x) = 1$ if
$x_1 \le 1$, $f^1(x) = x_1$ if $x_1 \ge 1$; $f^2(x) = \Sigma_{j=1}^{m} x_j$
$+ \min\{x_j : 1 \le j \le m\}$; $f^3(x) = (m-1)e^{x_1} + \Sigma_{j=2}^{m} \log x_j$;
$f^4(x) = -(\Sigma_{j=1}^{m} (x_j-2))^2$; $f^5(x) = x_1-1$
for $0 < x_1 < 1$, $f^5(x) = (x_1-1)^2$ for $1 \le x_1 < 2$,
$f^5(x) = 3-x_1$ for $x_1 \ge 2$.

For n=1, proposition 4.2 in figure 1 does not imply
4.1, even if a representing function V exists. This
follows from Kannai (1977, p. 17), or from f^5 in figure 1.
This, and f^2, can be seen to represent a $\ge$, that
satisfies the concavity assumption. f^5 is a minor
variation on the example of Artstein in Kannai (1981, p.
562), where it is shown not to be "concavifiable". For
n=2, 4.2 does imply 4.1 iff $\ge$ satisfies the Thomsen

condition.   That $\succeq$, represented by f^2, does not satisfy
this for n=2, and has no additive value functions, can be
seen   from $(1,4,9,\ldots,9) \approx (2,2,9,\ldots,9)$, $(2,8,9,\ldots,9)$
$\approx (4,4,9,\ldots,9)$, $(1,8,9,\ldots,9) \succ (4,2,9,\ldots,9)$.

That $\succeq$, represented by f^1, does not satisfy the conc-
cavity assumption, follows from $(1/2,1,\ldots,1) \succeq (1,\ldots,1)$
$\prec (3/2,1,\ldots,1)$. That f^3 is quasiconcave, thus represents a
convex $\succeq$, can be derived from 6.28 of Arrow and   Enthoven
(1961). For $\succeq$, represented by f^3, by the "furthermore"-
statement of Theorem 3.1, no <u>concave</u> additive value
functions exist, if n≥2: $\succeq$ must violate the concavity
assumption. The observation that 4.3 does not imply 4.2,
for n≥2, is closely related to the observation   that
quasiconcavity and additive decomposability of V do not
imply 4.1, i.e. concavity of V. This latter observation has
been made some times in the literature. The earliest
reference to this, given in Debreu and Koopmans (1982), is
Slutsky (1915).

That $\succeq$, represented by f^4, is not CI for n≥2,
follows from $(2,\ldots,2) \succ (2,3,2,\ldots,2)$ and $(1,2,\ldots,2) \prec$
$(1,3,2,\ldots,2)$. Finally, that for n≥3 $\succeq$, represented by
f^2, is not CI, follows from $(1,6,1,\ldots,1) \succ (3,3,1,\ldots,1)$,
$(1,6,3,\ldots,3) \prec (3,3,\ldots,3)$.

5.   Expected Utility with Risk Aversion

Let $S = \{s_1,\ldots,s_n\}$ be a finite <u>state   space</u>.   Its
elements are <u>(possible) states (of nature)</u>.   Exactly one
is the true state, the other states are not true.   The
decision maker T is uncertain about which of the states
is   true.   C   is   the   set   of   <u>consequences</u>,   and
$x = (x_1,\ldots,x_n) \in C^n$ is the <u>act</u> (= alternative) yielding
consequence x_j if s_j is true.

DEFINITION 5.1: We say $\succeq$ <u>maximizes   subjective expected</u>
<u>utility</u> (SEU) w.r.t. $(P_j)_{j=1}^n$, U if U : C => R, $P_j \geq 0$,
$\Sigma_{j=1}^n P_j = 1$, and $[x \succeq y <=> \Sigma_{j=1}^n P_j U(x_j) \geq \Sigma_{j=1}^n P_j U(y_j)]$
for all x,y. (Here U is the "<u>utility function</u>").

The results of Wakker (1984a), formulated for the
special case that C is a convex open subset of R, are
generalized in the sequel to the case where C is any
connected topological space, e.g. a topological mixture
space, such as a (convex subset of) R^m.

DEFINITION 5.2:   We say $\succeq$ is   cardinally coordinate
independent (CCI)   if $v_{-j}\Gamma \succeq w_{-j}\delta$ whenever $x_{-i}\alpha \preccurlyeq y_{-i}\beta$,
$x_{-i}\Gamma \succeq y_{-i}\delta$, $v_{-j}\alpha \succeq w_{-j}\beta$, and i essential.

THEOREM 5.1: Let $\succeq$ be a binary relation on C^n where $n\epsilon N$,
and C a connected topological space (e.g. R_+^m or R). Let
C be topologically separable if exactly one coordinate is
essential. Then the following propositions are equivalent:
i : $\succeq$ maximizes SEU w.r.t. some $(P_j)_{j=1}^n$, U, where U is
   continuous.
ii: $\succeq$ is a continuous weak order that is CCI.

     The concavity assumption and CCI can be combined
as follows, to give in Theorem 5.2. iii a very concise
characterization of SEU maximization with risk aversion,
i.e. concavity of U.

DEFINITION 5.3: Let $\succeq$ be a binary relation on a product
topological mixture space C^n. We say $\succeq$ is concavely
cardinally coordinate independent (CCCI) if $v_{-j}\sigma \succeq w_{-j}\tau$
whenever $x_{-i}\alpha \preccurlyeq y_{-i}\beta$, $x_{-i}\Gamma \succeq y_{-i}\delta$, $v_{-j}\alpha \succeq w_{-j}\beta$, i is
essential, and $p \epsilon [0,1]$ exists such that $\sigma = p\tau + (1-p)\Gamma$,
$\delta = p\Gamma + (1-p)\tau$.

THEOREM 5.2: Let $\succeq$ be a binary relation on a product
topological mixture space C^n (e.g. $(R_+^m)^n$ or R^n).   Let
at least two coordinates be essential. Then the following propositions are equivalent:
i: $\succeq$ maximizes SEU w.r.t. some $(P_j)_{j=1}^n$, U, where U is
   concave and continuous.
ii: $\succeq$ is a continuous weak order that is CCI, and satisfies
    the concavity assumption or is convex.
iii: $\succeq$ is a continuous weak order that is CCCI.

            APPENDIX: PROOFS

The proof of Lemma 2.1 is in Fishburn (1970, section 8.4).
Lemmas 2.3 and 3.2 are as in Euclidean spaces, Theorem 2.1
is elementary topology. Proofs for these are given in
Wakker (1984b).

PROOF OF LEMMA 2.2: Suppose $A \subset C$ is open and nonempty, say $x \in A$, and A^c is open and nonempty, say $y \in A^c$. Then by elementary topology (by Lemma A1 in Wakker, 1984b) the set $\{p \in [0,1] : px + (1-p)y \in A\}$ and its complement $\{p \in [0,1] : px + (1-p)y \in A^c\}$ are open. But one contains $p = 1$, the other $p = 0$, so both are nonempty, contradicting connectedness of $[0,1]$.

PROOF OF LEMMA 3.1: As an example, let 1,2,3 be not essential, $x_j = y_j$ for all $j \geq 4$. Then $x \approx x_{-1}y_1 \approx (x_{-1}y_1)_{-2}y_2 \approx ((x_{-1}y_1)_{-2}y_2)_{-3}y_3 = y$.

PROOF OF LEMMA 3.3: Let $\alpha = \beta, \Gamma = \delta, p = 1$ in Definition 3.3.

PROOF OF LEMMA 3.4: By Lemma 3.2 we only have to prove that $v \succeq w \Rightarrow v/2 + w/2 \succeq w$. It is sufficient to suppose $v/2 + w/2 \preceq w \preceq v$, and then to derive $v \preceq v/2 + w/2$. We define, inductively, for all $0 \leq j \leq n$, v^j and w^j by $v^0 = v/2 + w/2$, $w^0 = w$, $v^j = v^{j-1}_{-j}v_j$, $w^j = w^{j-1}_{-j}(v_j/2 + w_j/2)$, thus getting $v^n = v$, $w^n = v/2^{j+j}w/2$. For $j = 0$ we have, by assumption, $v^0 \preceq w^0$. Suppose now for some $1 \leq j \leq n$, that $v^{j-1} \preceq w^{j-1}$. Then we apply the concavity assumption with $i = j$, $p = 1/2$, $x = w^{j-1}$, $y = v^{j-1}$, $\alpha = w_j$, $\beta = \Gamma = v_j/2 + w_j/2$, $\delta = v_j$ to obtain $v^j \preceq w^j$. Now by induction $v^n \preceq w^n$, i.e. $v \preceq v/2 + w/2$.

PROOF OF THEOREM 3.1: i => ii is straightforward. So we assume ii, and derive i. By Lemma 3.1 the inessential coordinates do not affect $\succeq$. Hence they can be left out. The additive value functions, to be constructed in the sequel, simply are to be taken constant for these coordinates. So we assume in the sequel that all coordinates are essential.
By Lemma 2.2 every C_i is topologically connected.
By Lemma 3.3 we get CI for $\succeq$. Hence, if $n \geq 3$, then everything of i, except concavity of the V_j's, follows from Theorem 14 of section 6.11.1 of Krantz et al (1971). This theorem is a strenghtening of Theorem 3 of Debreu (1960) because no topological separability of the C_i's is required. If $n = 2$ the same as above (so without the demand of topological separability for the components) can be derived from Theorem 2 of section 6.2.4 of Krantz et al. (1971), the same way as their Theorem 14 of section 6.11.1 is derived from their Theorem 13 there. Their reasoning of section 6.12.3 applies literally for $n = 2$. (See also their exercise 34 of Chapter 6.) These theorems

of Krantz et al. also guarantee the assertion "Furthermore...". So all that remains is concavity of the V_j's. We show concavity of V_1.

Since coordinate 2 is essential, x_2 and y_2 in C_2 exist with $V_2(x_2) - V_2(y_2) = \pi > 0$. V_2 is continuous, and C_2 connected, so $V_2(C_2)$ is connected too. Thus for any $0 \leq \Phi \leq \pi$ there exists z_2 in C_2 such that $V_2(z_2) - V_2(y_2) = \Phi$. By Lemma 2.3, concavity of V_1 is guaranteed if we show that $V_1(\beta) \geq [V_1(\alpha) + V_1(\Gamma)]/2$ for any $\alpha, \beta, \Gamma \in C_1$ such that $\beta = \alpha/2 + \Gamma/2$, and $0 \leq V_1(\alpha) - V_1(\Gamma) \leq \pi$. To this end let $z_2 \in C_2$ be such that $V_2(z_2) - V_2(y_2) = [V_1(\alpha) - V_1(\Gamma)]/2$. We apply, for arbitrary v, the concavity assumption, to obtain $(v_{-1}\alpha)_{-2}y_2 \succeq (v_{-1}\beta)_{-2}z_2 \Rightarrow (v_{-1}\beta)_{-2}v_2 \succeq (v_{-1}\Gamma)_{-2}z_2$, i.e.: $V_1(\alpha) - V_1(\beta) \geq V_2(z_2) - V_2(y_2) \Rightarrow V_1(\beta) - V_1(\Gamma) \geq V_2(z_2) - V_2(y_2)$.

This shows:
$V_1(\alpha) - V_1(\beta) \geq [V_1(\alpha) - V_1(\Gamma)]/2 \Rightarrow V_1(\beta) - V_1(\Gamma) \geq [V_1(\alpha) - V_1(\Gamma)]/2$.
This can only be if $V_1(\beta) \geq [V_1(\alpha) + v_1(\Gamma)]/2$.

PROOF OF THEOREM 5.1: i => ii is straightforward. So we assume ii, and derive i. The cases of one or no essential coordinates are treated as in Wakker (1984a, proof of Theorem 2.1). Taking $\alpha = \beta$, $\Gamma = \delta$, $x = y$ in Definition 5.2 shows that CCI implies CI. Thus, if three or more coordinates are essential, then existence of an array of continuous additive value functions $(V_j)_{j=1}^n$ follows as in the proof of Theorem 3.1. If exactly two coordinates are essential, then we first observe that CCI implies "triple cancellation", i.e. $v_{-j}\Gamma \succeq w_{-j}\delta$ whenever $x_{-j}\alpha \preceq y_{-j}\beta$, $x_{-j}\Gamma \succeq y_{-j}\delta$, $v_{-j}\alpha \succeq w_{-j}\beta$. If j is essential this follows from CCI by taking $i = j$, if j is inessential it is direct. An array of continuous additive value functions $(V_j)_{j=1}^n$ for $\succeq$ is constructed, but now with triple cancellation instead of the Thomsen condition, the same way as was indicated in the proof of Theorem 3.1. See the end of section 6.2.4 of Krantz et al. (1971).

The demonstration that $V_j = p_j U$, for some nonnegative $(p_j)_{j=1}^n$, and continuous U: $C \Rightarrow R$, is performed the same way as in Wakker (1984 a, proof of Theorem 2.1). If no coordinate is essential, we now take $P_j = 1/n$ for all j, and U constant; if one coordinate i is essential we take $P_i = 1$, $P_j = 0$ for all $j \neq i$. If two or more coordinates are essential, then with p_j as above, at least two p_j's are nonzero, so we can take $P_i = p_i/\Sigma_{j=1}^n p_j$ for all i. Thus $\Sigma_{i=1}^n P_i = 1$ is always satisfied.

PROOF OF THEOREM 5.2: i => ii and i => iii are straightforward, so we only prove ii => i and iii => ii. First we assume ii, and derive i. By Theorem 5.1 we see $\succeq$ maximizes SEU w.r.t. some $(P_j)_{j=1}^n$, and continuous U. Thus $(P_j U)_{j=1}^n$ is an array of additive value functions for $\succeq$. This implies that $\succeq$ satisfies the TB-condition if exactly two coordinates are essential. If now $\succeq$ satisfies the concavity assumption, then concavity of U, thus i, follows from Theorem 3.1 and the substitution $W_j = P_j U$. That concavity of U is also implied by convexity of $\succeq$, is well-known.

Now finally we assume iii, and derive ii. CCI for $\succeq$ is straightforward, set p = 0 in Definition 5.3. So only the concavity assumption remains to be derived. Let $x_{-j}\Gamma \succeq y_{-j}\delta$, and $\sigma = p\tau + (1-p)\Gamma$, $\delta = p\Gamma + (1-p)\tau$, for some p ϵ [0,1], σ,τ ϵ C. To prove is that $x_{-j}\sigma \succeq y_{-j}\tau$. If j is not essential this is direct. So let j be essential. If no π,Θ ϵ C exist such that $x_{-j}\pi \prec y_{-j}\Theta$, then $x_{-j}\sigma \succeq y_{-j}\tau$, as desired. So suppose $x_{-j}\pi \prec y_{-j}\Theta$ for some π, Θ. We now first construct α, β such that $x_{-j}\alpha \approx y_{-j}\beta$. To this end, first suppose $y_{-j}\delta \succeq x_{-j}\pi$. Then we have $x_{-j}\Gamma \succeq y_{-j}\delta \succeq x_{-j}\pi$. Thus $\{w \epsilon C \mid x_{-j}w \succeq y_{-j}\delta\}$ and $\{w \epsilon C \mid x_{-j}w \preceq y_{-j}\delta\}$ are both nonempty. Also they are closed, by continuity of $\succeq$, and Wakker (1984b, Lemma A1 applied to complements). By connectedness of C, the intersection of the above two subsets of C is nonempty: it contains some α with $x_{-j}\alpha \approx y_{-j}\delta$. Finally, take $\beta = \delta$.

Remains the construction of α, β as above for the case where $y_{-j}\delta \prec x_{-j}\pi$. Then we have $y_{-j}\delta \prec x_{-j}\pi \prec y_{-j}\Theta$. The same way as above now β is found such that $x_{-j}\pi \approx y_{-j}\beta$. Now finally take $\alpha = \pi$.

We thus always have α,β such that $x_{-j}\alpha \approx y_{-j}\beta$. We can now apply CCCI as in Definition 5.3, with i = j, v = x, w = y, to obtain $x_{-j}\sigma \succeq y_{-j}\tau$.

Peter Wakker
University of Nijmegen

REFERENCES

Arrow, K.J. and A.C. Enthoven: 1961, "Quasi-concave Programming", Econometrica 29, 779-800.

Barnard, G.A. and V.P. Godambe: 1982, Allan Birnbaum, Memorial Article, The Annals of Statistics 10, 1033-1039.

Berger, J.O.: 1980, Statistical Decision Theory, Springer, New York.

Birnbaum, A.: 1962, "On the Foundations of Statistical Inference", Journal of the American Statistical Association 57, 269-326.

Birnbaum, A.: 1972, "More on Concepts of Statistical Evidence", Journal of the American Statistical Association 67, 858-861.

Blackorby, C., D. Primont, and R.R. Russell: 1978, Duality, Separability, and Functional Structure: Theory and Economic Applications, North Holland, New York.

Debreu, G.: 1960, "Topological Methods in Cardinal Utility Theory", in K.J. Arrow, S.Karlin and P. Suppes, (eds.), Mathematical Methods in the Social Sciences, Stanford University Press, Stanford, pp. 16-26.

Debreu, G. and T.C. Koopmans: 1982, "Additively Decomposed Quasiconvex Functions", Mathematical Programming 24, 1-38.

Fishburn, P.C.: 1970, Utility Theory for Decision Making, Wiley, New York.

Fishburn, P.C.: 1982, The Foundations of Expected Utility, Reidel, Dordrecht.

Gudder, S.P.: 1977, "Convexity and Mixtures", SIAM Review 19, 221-240.

Gudder, S.P., and F. Schroeck: 1980, "Generalized Convexity", Siam Journal on Mathematical Analysis 11, 984-1001.

Herstein, I.N. and J. Milnor: 1953, "An Axiomatic Approach to Measurable Utility", Econometrica 21, 291-297.

Kannai, Y.: 1977, "Concavifiability and Constructions of Concave Utility Functions, Journal of Mathematical Economics 4, 1-56.

Kannai, Y.: 1981, "Concave Utility Functions, Existence, Constructions and Cardinality, in S. Schaible and W.T. Ziemba (eds.), Generalized Concavity in Optimization and Economics, Academic Press, New York, pp. 543-611.

Krantz, D.H., R.D. Luce, P. Suppes and A. Tversky: 1971,

Foundations of Measurement, Vol. I, Academic Press, New York.

Leontief, W.W.: 1947a, "A Note on the Interrelation of Subsets of Independent Variables of a Continuous Function with Continuous First Derivatives", _Bulletin of the American Mathematical Society_ 53, 343-350.

Leontief, W.W.: 1947b, "Introduction to a Theory of the Internal Structure of Functional Relationships". _Econometrica_ 15, 361-373.

Luce, R.D. and P. Suppes: 1965, "Preference, Utility, and Subjective Probability", in R.D. Luce, R.R. Bush, and E. Galanter (eds.), _Handbook of Mathematical Psychology_, III. Wiley, New York.

Samuelson, P.A.: 1947, _Foundations of Economic Analysis_, Harvard University Press, Cambridge, Mass.

Savage, L.J.: 1954, _Foundations of Statistics_, Wiley, New York.

Savage, L.J.: 1962, _The Foundations of Statistical Inference_, Wiley, New York.

Slutsky, E.E.: 1915, "Sulla Teoria del Bilancio del Consumatore", _Giornale degli Economisti_ 51, 1-26. Translated into English as: "On the Theory of the Budget of the Consumer", in R. Irwin (1952) _Readings in Price Theory_, American Economic Association, pp. 27-56.

Sono, M.: 1945, "The Effect of Price Changes on the Demand and Supply of Separable Goods" (in Japanese), _Kokumin Keisai Zasshi_ 74, 1-51.

Sono, M.: 1961, "The Effect of Price Changes on the Demand and Supply of Separable Goods", _International Economic Review_ 2, 239-271.

Stigum, B.P.: 1972, "Finite State Space and ExpectedUtility Maximization", _Econometrica_ 40, 253-259.

von Neumann, and O. Morgenstern: 1944, _Theory of Games and Economic Behavior_, Princeton University Press, Princeton.

Wakker, P.P.: 1984a, "Cardinal Coordinate Independence for ExpectedUtility", _Journal of Mathematical Psychology_ 28, 110-117.

Wakker, P.P.: 1984b, "A Characterization of Concave Additively Decomposable Representing Functions and Expected Utility with RiskAversion", Report 8419, Department of Mathematics, University of Nijmegen.

Yaari, M.E.: 1978, "Separable Concave Utilities or the Principle of Diminishing Eagerness to Trade", _Journal of Economic Theory_ 18, 102-118.

PART III

INFORMATION AND UTILITY

Morris H. DeGroot

CONCEPTS OF INFORMATION BASED ON UTILITY

1. Introduction

The central topic of this paper is the measurement of the
amount of information about some parameter θ that is present in a set of data X. The parameter θ can be any quantity such that a decision maker (DM) is uncertain about
its value. We follow a Bayesian approach and assume that
the DM can represent his uncertainty at any stage of the
learning process in terms of a subjective probability distribution over the parameter space Ω of all possible values
of θ. This distribution, in turn, will be represented by
a generalized probability density function (gpdf) ξ with
respect to some fixed σ-finite measure λ on Ω.

Furthermore, we assume that X is a random variable or
random vector taking values in some sample space X.
Uncertainty about X is represented, as in the usual statistical models, in terms of a family of conditional distributions indexed by the parameter θ. Again, these conditional distributions are represented by their gpdf's
$\{f(\cdot|\theta), \theta\epsilon\Omega\}$ with respect to some fixed σ-finite measure
ν on X.

The purpose of this paper is to discuss the basic
concept of the information I(x) about θ in the observation
X = x, and to introduce a new concept of retrospective
information. The relationship between the measure of
information and the choice of a utility function is
emphasized.

In Section 2, the definition of expected information
and its properties are introduced. In Section 3, the
observed or actual information in an observation is discussed, and the additivity of expected information is
described. In Section 4, the distribution of information
is studied. Finally, in Section 5 the concept of retrospective information is defined and its role in sequential
experimentation is described. A more detailed treatment
of the topics covered in this paper is presented in
DeGroot (1985).

265

L. Daboni et al. (eds.), Recent Developments in the Foundations of Utility and Risk Theory, 265–275.
© *1986 by D. Reidel Publishing Company.*

2. Expected Information

We shall begin by reviewing the definition of the expected
information $E[I(X)]$. Consider a decision problem involving
θ in which a DM must choose a decision d from some given
set D. For each $\theta \in \Omega$ and $d \in D$, let $U(\theta,d)$ denote the
utility of the DM if he chooses decision d when the value
of the parameter is θ. For any gpdf $\xi(\theta)$, define

$$V(\xi) = \sup_{d \in D} \int_\Omega U(\theta,d)\xi(\theta)d\lambda(\theta)$$

$$= \sup_{d \in D} E_\theta[U(\theta,d)]. \tag{2.1}$$

Throughout this paper we shall assume that all required
integrals and expectations exist.

The quantity $V(\xi)$ can be regarded as the expected
utility to the DM when his distribution of θ is ξ. Now
let ξ_0 denote the prior gpdf of θ and let $\xi_0(\cdot|x)$ denote
the posterior gpdf given $X = x$. Then the expected information $E[I(X)]$ is defined as follows:

$$E[I(X)] = E_X\{V[\xi_0(\cdot|X)]\} - V(\xi_0). \tag{2.2}$$

In words, $E[I(X)]$ is the expected gain in utility from X.
It can be shown that $E[I(X)] \geq 0$.

A basic property of the function V is that it is con-
vex; i.e., for any two distributions ξ_1 and ξ_2 of θ and
$0 < \alpha < 1$,

$$V[\alpha\xi_1 + (1-\alpha)\xi_2] \leq \alpha V(\xi_1) + (1-\alpha)V(\xi_2). \tag{2.3}$$

Three of the most well-known and most widely-used examples
of such convex functions V are

$$V_1(\xi) = - \text{Var}_\xi(\theta), \text{ for a real-valued parameter } \theta; \tag{2.4}$$

$$V_2(\xi) = \int_\Omega \xi(\theta) \log\xi(\theta) d\lambda(\theta); \tag{2.5}$$

$$V_3(\xi) = \max_i \xi(\theta_i), \text{ for } \Omega = \{\theta_1,\theta_2,\ldots\} \tag{2.6}$$

The function V_1 arises from a decision problem in which
a real-valued parameter θ must be estimated with squared-
error loss. The function V_2 arises from a decision problem in which the DM must specify a gpdf ϕ with respect to

the measure λ, and $U(\theta,\phi) = \log \phi(\theta)$. This example has been discussed by Good (1969) and Bernardo (1979). The function V_3 arises from a decision problem in which the DM must choose one of the finite or countable possible values of θ, and

$$U(\theta,d) = \begin{cases} 1 & \text{if } d = \theta \\ 0 & \text{if } d \neq \theta. \end{cases} \qquad (2.7)$$

It follows from this discussion that expected information can be defined directly in terms of a convex utility function V on the space of distributions of θ. It is not necessary to begin with the specification of a decision problem with a decision space D and utility function $U(\theta,d)$. This topic is discussed further for finite Ω in DeGroot (1962).

3. Observed Information

It should be noted that we have defined the expected information in X before we have defined the observed or actual information in a realization $X = x$. One natural way to define the observed information $I(x)$ is simply to consider the observed change in utility.

$$I(x) = V[\xi_0(\cdot|x)] - V(\xi_0). \qquad (3.1)$$

It follows immediately that the expected information $E[I(X)]$ will then be as we have defined it in (2.2). However, the information $I(x)$, as defined by (3.1), might be negative since it is quite possible for the posterior distribution to leave the DM with more uncertainty and smaller expected utility than he had under his prior distribution. Since we believe that the data always carry positive, or at least non-negative, information for the DM, this approach is unsuitable. The correct definition of $I(x)$ proceeds as follows.

For any distribution ξ and any decision d in a given decision problem, let

$$U(\xi,d) = E_\xi[U(\theta,d)] = \int_\Omega U(\theta,d)\xi(\theta) \, d\lambda(\theta). \qquad (3.2)$$

Also, let d_0 denote the Bayes decision with respect to the prior distribution ξ_0, so

$$U(\xi_0, d_0) = \sup_{d \in D} U(\xi_0, d) = V(\xi_0).$$ (3.3)

We assume the existence and uniqueness of d_0. Then

$$I(x) = V[\xi_0(\cdot|x)] - U[\xi_0(\cdot|x), d_0].$$ (3.4)

In words, $I(x)$ is the expected difference, calculated with respect to the posterior distribution, between the utility from the Bayes decision and the utility from the decision d_0 that would have been chosen if the observation x had not been available. If the decision d_0 does not exist or is not unique then Eq. (3.4) must be modified by means of some convention, but we shall not consider such modifications in this paper.

It follows from the definition (3.4) that $I(x) \geq 0$ for every value of x. Furthermore, $E[I(X)]$ will satisfy Eq. (2.2). Raiffa and Schlaifer (1961), Chapter 4, refer to $I(x)$ as the conditional value of sample information and to $E[I(X)]$ as the expected value of sample information.

There is a helpful geometric interpretation of $I(x)$. Suppose that we want to define the information $I(\xi_0 \to \xi_1)$ in going from one distribution ξ_0 to another distribution ξ_1, based on a given convex utility function $V(\xi)$. For simplicity, assume for the moment that Ω contains just a finite number of possible values of θ, so each distribution ξ on Ω can be regarded as a point in a finite-dimensional Euclidean space. Let $L(\xi|\xi_0)$ be the supporting hyperplane to the function $V(\xi)$ at the point $\xi = \xi_0$, which we assume to exist and be unique. Then

$$I(\xi_0 \to \xi_1) = V(\xi_1) - L(\xi_1|\xi_0) \geq 0.$$ (3.5)

Note that the definition of $I(\xi_0 \to \xi_1)$ in (3.6) is given directly in terms of the function V without any reference to an underlying decision problem or utility function U. Thus, the distinction made by some authors between measures of information that are based on both the DM's distribution ξ and his utility function U, and measures that are based only on ξ is not very clear.

In general, we shall replace the definition of $I(x)$ given in (3.4) by the more general definition

$$I(\xi_0 \to \xi_1) = V(\xi_1) - U(\xi_1, d_0),$$ (3.6)

where d_0 is the Bayes decision with respect to the distribution ξ_0. We now reconsider the examples $V_i (i=1,2,3)$ given by (2.4) - (2.6). The derivations and proofs of these and the other results in this paper are given in DeGroot (1985).

Proposition 1. If $V(\xi) = V_1(\xi)$, as given by (2.4), then

$$I_1(\xi_0 \to \xi_1) = (\mu_1 - \mu_0)^2, \tag{3.7}$$

where μ_i is the mean of the distribution $\xi_i (i=0,1)$.

Proposition 2. If $V(\xi) = V_2(\xi)$, as given by (2.5), then

$$I_2(\xi_0 \to \xi_1) = \int_\Omega \xi_1(\theta) \log \frac{\xi_1(\theta)}{\xi_0(\theta)} d\lambda(\theta). \tag{3.8}$$

The function I_2 is called the expected weight of evidence in favor of ξ_1 against ξ_0 [Good (1950)]or the Kullback-Leibler information for discriminating between ξ_1 and ξ_0 [see, e.g., Kullback (1968), Chap. 1, or Goel and DeGroot (1979)]. An important feature of I_2 is that it is invariant under any one-to-one differentiable transformation of the parameter θ. This property is not shared by the measure I_1.

Proposition 3. If $V(\xi) = V_3(\xi)$, as given by (2.6), then

$$I_3(\xi_0 \to \xi_1) = \xi_1(\theta^1) - \xi_1(\theta^0), \tag{3.9}$$

where θ^i is the mode of the distribution $\xi_i (i=0,1)$.

We also record here the value of $I_2(\xi_0 \to \xi_1)$ for normal distributions of θ.

Proposition 4. Suppose that ξ_i is a normal distribution with mean μ_i and variance $\sigma_i^2 (i=0,1)$. Then

$$I_2(\xi_0 \to \xi_1) = \frac{1}{2}\left[\log \frac{\sigma_0^2}{\sigma_1^2} + \frac{\sigma_1^2}{\sigma_0^2} - 1 + \frac{(\mu_1-\mu_0)^2}{\sigma_0^2}\right]. \tag{3.10}$$

We conclude this section with a basic result regarding the additivity of expected information.

Theorem 1. Let ξ_0 denote the prior distribution of θ, let X and Y be any observations, and let $\xi_1(\cdot) = \xi_0(\cdot|X)$ and $\xi_2(\cdot) = \xi_0(\cdot|X,Y)$. Then

$$E[I(\xi_0 \to \xi_2)] = E[I(\xi_0 \to \xi_1)] + E[I(\xi_1 \to \xi_2)], \tag{3.11}$$

where each of the expectations is taken with respect to
the prior predictive distribution of X and Y.

It has been stated in the literature [see, e.g.,
Lindley (1956)] that the relation (3.11) characterizes the
information measure I_2 as given by (3.9). In fact, however, as Theorem 1 states, (3.11) holds for all information
measures.

4. The Distribution of Information

Essentially all previous work on the subject of statistical
information has been restricted to the study of expected
information, since the maximization of expected utility is
equivalent to the maximization of expected information.
However, there are at least two circumstances under which
the DM is interested in the entire distribution of information: (i) If the DM finds that he has obtained much
more or much less information than he expected, he may
wish to study the distribution of information in order to
evaluate how unusual his data are and decide whether his
model was reasonable. (ii) If the DM has a choice among
different experiments to be performed at varying costs,
where the overall utility of each experiment is not simply
a linear function of the utility of the decision problem
and the cost of experimentation, he may wish to study the
distribution in order to choose an appropriate experiment.

We shall now show that for normal distributions, the
calculation of the distribution of $I_1(\xi_0 \rightarrow \xi_1)$ and the
distribution of $I_2(\xi_0 \rightarrow \xi_1)$, as defined by (3.7) and (3.8),
is essentially the same. Suppose that the prior distribu-
tion ξ_0 of θ is normal with mean μ_0 and precision τ_0,
where the precision of a normal distribution is defined to
be the reciprocal of its variance. Suppose also that an
observation X is to be obtained such that the conditional
distribution of X given θ is normal with mean θ and known
precision r. In general, X might be the sample mean of a
random sample of n observations. Then [see, e.g., DeGroot
(1970), Sec. 9.5] the posterior distribution ξ_1 of θ given
X is normal with mean

$$\mu_1 = \frac{\tau_0 \mu_0 + rX}{\tau_0 + r} \qquad\qquad (4.1)$$

and precision

$$\tau_1 = \tau_0 + r. \tag{4.2}$$

It now follows from (3.7) and (3.10) that

$$I_2(\xi_0 \rightarrow \xi_1) = a_1 + a_2 I_1(\xi_0 \rightarrow \xi_1), \tag{4.3}$$

where a_1 and a_2 are constants depending on τ_0 and r, but not depending on either μ_0 or the observation X. Thus, studying the distribution of either I_1 or I_2 reduces to studying the distribution of $(\mu_1 - \mu_0)^2$.

It follows from the conditions of this example that the prior predictive distribution of X is normal with mean μ_0 and variance $(\tau_0 + r)/\tau_0 r$. Hence, from (4.1), the prior predictive distribution of $\mu_1 - \mu_0$ is normal with mean 0 and variance $r/[\tau_0(\tau_0 + r)]$ and, therefore, the random variable

$$\frac{\tau_0(\tau_0 + r)}{r} (\mu_1 - \mu_0)^2 \tag{4.4}$$

has a χ^2 distribution with one degree of freedom. It should be noted that the distributions of $I_1(\xi_0 \rightarrow \xi_1)$ and $I_2(\xi_0 \rightarrow \xi_1)$ do not depend on μ_0. Also,

$$E[I_1(\xi_0 \rightarrow \xi_1)] = \frac{r}{\tau_0(\tau_0 + r)} . \tag{4.5}$$

An unusually small value or large value of I_1 reflects a value of X that was unusually close to or far from μ_0.

We shall conclude this section with some comments regarding the relationship between sufficient experiments in the sense of Blackwell (1951, 1953) and the distribution of information. It is known that if some observation or experiment X is sufficient for another observation or experiment Y, then $E[I(X)] \geq E[I(Y)]$ for every convex function V and every prior distribution ξ_0 [see, e.g., DeGroot (1962)]. It might be anticipated from this result that if X is sufficient for Y, then the random variable $I(X)$ must be stochastically larger than the random variable $I(Y)$ for every convex function V and prior distribution ξ_0. However, that conclusion is not correct. A simple counterexample is given in DeGroot (1985).

5. Retrospective Information

With just a single observation X or a single change in the
distribution of θ from ξ_0 to ξ_1, it is not possible to
determine whether an unusual value of $I(\xi_0 \to \xi_1)$ is due to
an "inappropriate" prior distribution, i.e., an unlikely
value of θ, or an "inappropriate" likelihood function,
i.e., an incorrect model of the sampling process. In this
section we shall introduce new concepts of information
that are relevant in problems of sequential analysis.

Consider a prior distribution ξ_0 of θ and a finite
sequence of observations $X_1, X_2,\ldots,X_n$ leading successively
to the sequence of posterior distributions $\xi_1,\ldots,\xi_n$.
Thus, ξ_j is the posterior distribution of θ given $X_1,\ldots,$
X_j ($j = 1,\ldots,n$). For a given decision problem, let d_j
denote the Bayes decision with respect to ξ_j ($j = 0, 1,\ldots,$
n). As before, we assume that d_j exists and is unique.

Now, for $i < j \leq k$, we define the information in
changing from ξ_i to ξ_j, evaluated from the perspective of
ξ_k, to be

$$I(\xi_i \to \xi_j | \xi_k) = U(\xi_k, d_j) - U(\xi_k, d_i). \qquad (5.1)$$

We refer to the information defined by (5.1) as retrospective information because it represents information
that we seem to have obtained at an earlier stage of the
sequential process as evaluated with respect to a posterior
distribution that we have reached at a later stage of the
process. It is possible that $I(\xi_i \to \xi_j | \xi_k) < 0$. Roughly
speaking, a negative value of this retrospective information will be obtained if, viewed from our current posterior
distribution, the change from ξ_i to ξ_j moved us away from
the values of θ that we now regard to be the most likely.

Retrospective information is an extension of the concept of information defined by (3.7) since, in our present
notation, $I(\xi_i \to \xi_j) = I(\xi_i \to \xi_j | \xi_j)$. The following
additivity property of retrospective information follows
immediately from (5.1):

$$\sum_{i=0}^{n-1} I(\xi_i \to \xi_{i+1} | \xi_n) = I(\xi_0 \to \xi_n). \qquad (5.2)$$

The pattern of information that is obtained from a
sequential sample can be analyzed in a variety of ways.
For example, each of the following measures of information
can be studied over an appropriate sequence of values of i:

$\{I(\xi_i \to \xi_{i+1})\}$, $\{I(\xi_i \to \xi_{i+1}|\xi_n)\}$, and $\{I(\xi_0 \to \xi_1|\xi_i)\}$.

We shall now present the exact form of retrospective information for the functions $V_i (i = 1, 2, 3)$ given by (2.4) - (2.6).

Proposition 5. If $V(\xi) = V_1(\xi)$, as given by (2.4), then

$$I_1(\xi_i \to \xi_j|\xi_k) = (\mu_k - \mu_i)^2 - (\mu_k - \mu_j)^2, \qquad (5.3)$$

where μ_i, μ_j, and μ_k are the means of the distributions ξ_i, ξ_j, and ξ_k.

Proposition 6. If $V(\xi) = V_2(\xi)$, as given by (2.5), then

$$I_2(\xi_i \to \xi_j|\xi_k) = \int_{\Omega} \xi_k(\theta) \, \log \frac{\xi_j(\theta)}{\xi_i(\theta)} \, d\lambda(\theta). \qquad (5.4)$$

Proposition 7. If $V(\xi) = V_3(\xi)$, as given by (2.6), then

$$I_3(\xi_i \to \xi_j|\xi_k) = \xi_k(\theta^j) - \xi_k(\theta^i), \qquad (5.5)$$

where θ^r is the mode of ξ_r ($r = i, j$).

We conclude with the calculation of three different types of expectations of retrospective information. For $r = 1, \ldots, n$, we shall use the notation E_r to denote a conditional expectation that is calculated given the observations $X_1, \ldots, X_r$.

Theorem 2. For $i < j \leq k \leq n$,

$$E_k[I(\xi_i \to \xi_j|\xi_n)] = I(\xi_i \to \xi_j|\xi_k). \qquad (5.6)$$

In words, Theorem 2 states that if we ask at a given stage k how we expect to evaluate, at some future stage n, a past change in information from ξ_i to ξ_j, the answer is that we expect to evaluate that change exactly as we presently evaluate it at stage k. The answer does not depend on n.

Theorem 3. For $i \leq j \leq k < n$,

$$E_j[I(\xi_i \to \xi_k|\xi_n)] = E_j[V(\xi_k)] - U(\xi_j, d_i). \qquad (5.7)$$

This result has an interpretation in words similar to that given for Theorem 2. Again it can be seen that the expectation in (5.7) does not depend on n.

Theorem 4. For $i \leq j < k < n$,

$$E_i[I(\xi_j \to \xi_k|\xi_n)] = E_i[I(\xi_j \to \xi_k)]. \tag{5.8}$$

In words, Theorem 4 states that if we ask at the beginning of the process how we expect to view a future change from ξ_j to ξ_k from the perspective of the final stage n of the process, the answer is that we expect our final retrospective evaluation to be precisely the same as our prior expectation of that information. Again, the result does not depend on n.

Acknowledgment

This research was supported in part by the National Science Foundation under grant DMS-8320618. I am indebted to John Bacon-Shone of the University of Hong Kong and Richard Barlow of the University of California, Berkeley, with whom the concept of retrospective information discussed in this paper, and its basic properties, were jointly developed.

References

Bernardo, J. M. (1979). Expected information as expected utility. *Ann. Statist.* **7**, 686-690.

Blackwell, D. (1951). Comparison of experiments. *Proc. Second Berkeley Symp. Math. Statist. Probability.* Berkeley: University of California Press, 93-102.

Blackwell, D. (1953). Equivalent comparison of experiments. *Ann. Math. Statist.* **24**, 265-272.

DeGroot, M. H. (1962). Uncertainty, information and sequential experiments. *Ann. Math. Statist.* **33**, 404-419.

DeGroot, M. H. (1970). *Optimal Statistical Decisions.* New York: McGraw-Hill Book Company.

DeGroot, M. H. (1985). Concepts of information based on utility. To appear in *Theory and Decision.*

Goel, P. K., and DeGroot, M. H. (1979). Comparison of experiments' and information measures. *Ann. Statist.* **7**, 1066-1077.

Good, I. J. (1950). *Probability and the Weighing of Evidence.* London: Charles Griffin.

Good, I. J. (1969). What is the use of a distribution? *Multivariate Analysis II* (ed. by P. R. Krishnaiah). New York: Academic Press, 183-203.

Kullback, S. (1968). *Information Theory and Statistics*. New York: Dover Publications.

Lindley, D. V. (1956). On a measure of the information provided by an experiment. *Ann. Math. Statist.* **27**, 986–1005.

Raiffa, H., and Schlaifer, R. (1961). *Applied Statistical Decision Theory*. Boston: Division of Research, Graduate School of Business Administration, Harvard University.

Anio O. Arigoni

INFORMATION UTILITY
- STATISTICAL AND SEMANTICAL FEATURES -

Abstract – The present paper deals with the use of informational criteria in analyzing the utility of formal descriptions of facts. Descriptions' statistical and semantical
features are considered jointly. The ending purpose is at-
taining to a quantitative evaluation of the informational
utility of linguistic variables performing the descriptions
themselves.

1. INFORMATIONAL EXPECTED UTILITY

By 'informational expected utility' we mean the differential informativity   of   variables describing facts;
that is, the amount of uncertainty, about specific facts,
each of said variables can dissipate in a user, when describes facts in cooperation with others.

Besides the statistical uncertainty about the values
taken by such variables, there is a number of other different cathegories of uncertainty   relative to the descriptions the variables themselves perform, which   may
bedevil the use of multivariate data: complexity; factual-
ity —adherence to reality—; up-to-dateness; semantical relevance and others. Within these, the latter playes a fundamental role. By the present paper, the essential basis
for the convolution of the latter itself with the statistical aspects of the variables are set forth.

We consider single variables X_h that together with $\ell-1$
others $(h=1,2,\ldots,\ell)$ perform the mentioned descriptions.

The utility herein considered is expressed by the average information, or entropy, $H(X_h^{*})$: that which one X_h
gives when its as   well statistical as semantical va-
riabilities, with respect to the fact in description, are
taken into analysis.

L. Daboni et al. (eds.), Recent Developments in the Foundations of Utility and Risk Theory, 277–288.
© *1986 by D. Reidel Publishing Company.*

2. STATISTICAL AND SEMANTICAL VARIABILITY

An early attempt of introducing informational criteria   in
multivariate techniques had been made Hirano [10] ;   this
scholar obtained reasonable results in evaluating   variables' significance by applying Shannons' Theory of Information [13] to the maximum likelihood principle proposed by
Akaike [1] and Edwards [7]. Another relevant contribution
to the subject has been recently given by Gokhale [8].

The main features of the subject treated herein are: 1st)
the above mentioned principle is taken into consideration
as for factor analysis; 2nd) information theory results as
extended to the semantical aspects of data. Said extension
is realized by applying formal developments such as alge-
braic structure of formal languages [2], linguistic transformation of descriptions of properties [3], probability
of fuzzy causes and pragmatical informayivity of data [4].
Definitively, in   the analysis we perform of the descriptions, although their information remains of statistical
type, the semantics of the considered data get involved,so
that the true informativity of the descriptions themselves
is retained.

The paradigm followed to develop the subject is based on
descriptions of facts of different levels of complexity;
that is to say, respectively, of *atomic, elementary,*   and
composite facts. More in detail, the possible descriptions
of elementary facts (EF) performable through variables X_h
($h=1,2,\ldots,\ell$) denoting the states —either occurrence   or
not— of one same number of atomic facts (AF) are taken into consideration. Thus, one composite fact (CF) results as
the occurrence of two or more EFs one exchangeably with the
others.

In this manner, the considered varaiables describe, by
the values they take to denote the EFs relative to one CF,
factors of the CF itself.

The values by which each X_h denotes the state of the homologous factor —the h-th AF— forming one same EF is indicated by x_h, the description of the EF itself by X_i; therefore, the description of every EF consists of an ordered
tuple, i.e. $X_i = (x_{1i}, x_{2i}, \ldots, x_{\ell i})$ with $i = 1, 2, \ldots, n = 2^\ell$.

3. SEMANTICAL RELEVANCE OF ATOMIC FACTS

Observations on the occurrence of CFs are generally   unfit

for explaining the reasons of said occurrence as well as
for evaluating causal connections between the occurrence
itself and the state every single factor takes. To the end
of accomplishing the mentioned evaluation, the statistical
variability of said factors as related to the variability
of the CFs can be analysed. When this is performed by considering statistical parameters of both the factors and the
CFs brought about by the factors themselves, as standardized random variables, then the developed mathematical model
is said to be for factor analysis [9]. In Fig.1, a schema-
tization of such a model is shown; in this, circles represent variables, arrows relations determinant-determinated.

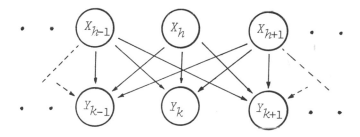

Fig. 1

The variability of factors and of CFs is ascertained by
'reading' the variables X_h and the others, those Y_k describing the same CFs. The observations thusly performed are ar-
raied as rows of a matrix, so that homologous values x_{hi} appear on one same h-th column. Said matrix is called *multivariate data matrix*.

Since the model for canonical factor analysis comes down
from operations on multivariate data matrix, such a model
is framed in multivariate analysis [9]. Therefore, as for
every statistical technique, the relative study is a branch
of applied mathematics. Thus, factor analysis itself is not
a separate technique. In multivariate analysis, in fact:
(1) the model relative to factor analysis can be recognized easily as that of other multivariate techniques (as an
example, the scheme of Fig. 1 can be the same, *mutatis mutan-*

dis, as the one for canonical correlation analysis $|^{14}|$; (2)
for factor analysis, as for most multivariate techniques,
the operated matrices' elements are in every case columns
and, currently, the relative analysis is focused on the variance of the variables whose values form the columns themselves $[^{11}]$. However, a relevant dimension of data is neglected, which thus remains a not inherent part of the obtained results. This is *semantical relevance* of the described AFs, with respect to the CFs' variability, when such AFs
are considered jointly with those ℓ-1 others forming the
specific EFs relative to one same CF.

A model of statistical inference is envisaged herein, in
which statistical data and those semantical above mentioned are convolved.

4. FEATURES OF THE PRESENTED MODEL

The model presented herein is one in which the Y_ks to be explained are *dummy variables*, i.e. are such that the values
they take code for subsets of observations. Likewise, also
the observed variables X_h are so; this because of the different treatment —experimental condictions— under which
such variables in general are read.

Further, whereas in canonical factor analysis the scrutiny is focused on the considered variables' statistical
variablity exclusively, in the model in subject said variability is exchanged with 'entropy'. This last concerns the
relevant information that each of said variables, X_h, gives
about the variability itself: amount of average information
that X_h brings of the variability in explanation, information obtained by taking into account as well statisticalas
semantical characteristics of X_h and that result from the
values simultaneously taken by the observed variables other
than X_h itself —*ceteris variabilibus*— $[^5]$. The conceptuali-
zation of the model is schematized in Fig. 2. In this feeding back arrows are set to signify the influence the values
taken by the Y_ks can have on the relevance of those of the
X_hs; dotted arrows, instead, indicate the consequent mutual
semantical influence among the X_hs, via the values of those
Y_ks.

In the presented model, rather than operating uniquely
on the columns of the matrices, as generally is done in canonical multivariate techniques, also, and overall, rows
are the operated elements. Herein, without loss of gener-

ality, to simplify the argumentation, only binary independent variables X_h are considered. Moreover, the CFs are described by a unique variable Y which, too, is binary.

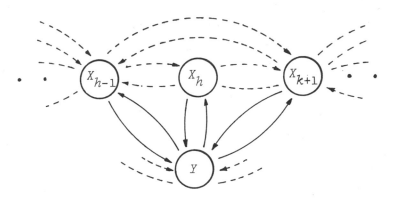

Fig. 2

For confering statistical validity to the inferences feasible through the model, a sufficiently large number N of observations is hypothesized are performed. Each one of these consists in measuring, for N distinct EFs, the ℓ variables X_h contemporaneously. Hence a multinomial data matrix $\mathcal{X}$ can be formed. This last, which is represented in Fig. 3 a, is subseuqently columns-wise transformed into that X appearing in the part b of the same figure. Said matrix X is drawn from $\mathcal{X}$ by gathering together all the identical rows of this —description of identical EFs, i.e. X_is : $\forall h$ $x_{hi} = x_{hj}$, $i \neq j$— to give place to others indicated by X_α and which are such that $\forall h\ x_{h\alpha} = x_{h\alpha}$ $(\alpha=1,2,\ldots,n)$. Thus, by denoting with $|\alpha|$ the number of X_is by which every X_α has been made up:

$$|1| + |2| + \ldots + |n| = \sum_{\alpha=1}^{n} |\alpha| = N \qquad (1)$$

$$
x =
\begin{array}{c}
\\
\mathsf{x}_1 \\
\mathsf{x}_2 \\
\mathsf{x}_3 \\
\\
\\
\mathsf{x}_i \\
\\
\\
\mathsf{x}_{N-1} \\
\mathsf{x}_N
\end{array}
\begin{array}{cccccc}
X_1 & & X_h & & X_\ell \\
\begin{bmatrix} x_{11} & \cdots & x_{h1} & \cdots & x_{\ell 1} \\ x_{12} & \cdots & x_{h2} & \cdots & x_{\ell 2} \\ x_{13} & \cdots & x_{h3} & \cdots & x_{\ell 3} \\ \cdot & & \cdot & & \cdot \\ \cdot & & \cdot & & \cdot \\ x_{1i} & \cdots & x_{hi} & \cdots & x_{\ell i} \\ \cdot & & \cdot & & \cdot \\ \cdot & & \cdot & & \cdot \\ x_{1N-1} & \cdots & x_{hN-1} & \cdots & x_{\ell N-1} \\ x_{1N} & \cdots & x_{hN} & \cdots & x_{\ell N} \end{bmatrix}
\end{array}
\qquad a)
$$

$$
X =
\begin{array}{c}
\\
\mathsf{x}_1 \\
\mathsf{x}_2 \\
\\
\\
\mathsf{x}_\alpha \\
\\
\\
\mathsf{x}_n
\end{array}
\begin{bmatrix} x_{11} & \cdots & x_{h1} & \cdots & x_{\ell 1} \\ x_{12} & \cdots & x_{h2} & \cdots & x_{\ell 2} \\ \cdot & & \cdot & & \cdot \\ \cdot & & \cdot & & \cdot \\ x_{1\alpha} & \cdots & x_{h\alpha} & \cdots & x_{\ell\alpha} \\ \cdot & & \cdot & & \cdot \\ \cdot & & \cdot & & \cdot \\ x_{1n} & \cdots & x_{hn} & \cdots & x_{\ell n} \end{bmatrix}
\qquad b)
$$

Fig. 3

The apriori probability of each one of the achieved X_αs
is noted; its value is:

$$P(X_\alpha) = \sum_{\{i:\ \nabla h\ x_{hi}=x_{ha}\}} P(X_i) \quad = \quad |\alpha|\ /\ N \qquad (2)$$

Subsequently, the descriptions X_α are discriminated according to the function $f(X): X \to Y$ through which all those
X_αs that can exchangeably describe one same CF —indicated
by y_j— are mapped into y_j itself.

Thereby, the presented model constitutes an informational interpretation of discriminant factor analysis, so that
it can be defined as for *informational discriminant factor
analysis* (IDFA).

5. OPERATIONS ON IDFA'S ELEMENTS

By applying function f on X, two subsets S_j ($j = 0, 1$) of
X itself result. Each of these corresponds to one value
$y_j \in \{0, 1\}$ of the unique variable Y by which the CFs are
denoted in IDFA.

The assignation $f(X)$ made of every X_α to one of the y_js
and thusly to one S_j, can be estabilished on the basis
of empirical observations or from mathematical procedures
as, for example, that Bayesian. Of course, for every X_α
assigned to S_j the condictional probability $P(X_\alpha|y_j)$ is a
strictly positive number; in addition:

$$P(S_j) = \sum_{\{\alpha:\ X_\alpha \in S_j\}} P(X_\alpha) \qquad (3)$$

As a further essential step, each subset S_j has to be
semiotically synthetized [2]: integration of the X_αs of
S_j, pair-wise taken, in function of the eventual differentiation of the values of one same variable X_h when the
homologous values of the $\ell-1$ others are correspondently
identical —*ceteris paribus*— [3]. By so doing, another
subset is achieved. The elements forming the latter, although are equivalent to those of S_j in the description
they are performing of a CF, are such that those values
which are irrelevant in the description itself are evin-
ced. Said irrelevant values are indicated by the symbol
*, instead of the binary value either 0 or 1.

The algoritm followed in carring out the above described synthesis is given in every detail in $|3|$; an its outline is sketched below.

Let an S be given; being every X_α of X an ordered ℓ-tuple of values $x_{h\alpha}$, when one pair of *equivalent* descriptions X_α, X_β —both included in S_j— perform the condiction according to which

$$\exists! k: \quad x_{k\alpha} \neq x_{k\beta} \text{ and } \quad h \neq k \quad x_{h\alpha} = x_{h\beta}, \tag{4}$$

then the k-th values $x_{k\alpha}$ and $x_{k\beta}$ are *irrelevant* in the descriptions X_α and X_β are performing in the j-th S, and so is also the homologous k-th factor, with respect to the described j-th CP. Such two descriptions of EFs, X_α and X_β, can therefore be synthetized through a binary operation which is indicated by '$\boxplus$'$[2]$. The obtained result is still a description like those given; precisely it can be written

$$X_\alpha \boxplus X_\beta = X_\chi: \quad \forall h \neq k \quad x_{h\alpha} = x_{h\beta} \text{ and } x_{k\chi} = * \tag{5}$$

The subset deriving directly from synthetizing semiotically S_j is indicated by S_j^k, where $k = 1$. From such an S_j^1 another subset, S_j^2, may be derived likewise. By iterating exhaustively the operated synthesis on the ensuing S_j^ks ($k=1,2,\ldots$), finally a subset S^k such that $S_j^k = S_j^{k+1},\ldots$ is attained inasmuch as no other pairs of descriptions performing (4) can be formed in S_j^k itself; that which indicates that the S_j^k in subject represents the most synthetic form sought for S_j. Said form is indicated by S_j^*.

In so far as the stochastic dimension of the X_χ drawn as above described is concerned, this is computed in function of (1) the probability of X_α and X_β which X_χ derives from (2) the probability distribution on the other descriptions of S_j^k that have to be synthetized to x_α and x_β themselves additionally, via one same number of distinct $\boxplus$s $[4]$.

When the case in which one X_α of an S_j^k has to be synthetized simultaneously to q_α (>1) other descriptions of the same S_j^k presents itself, then said X_α must be disintegrated into q_α elements $X_\alpha i$ ($i=1,2,\ldots,q_\alpha$). These are called *virtual descriptions*; their single probability, $P(X_\alpha i)$: 1st) depends on the probability of the description with which $X_\alpha i$ will be synthetized; 2nd) must be such that $\Sigma P(X_\alpha i) = P(X_\alpha)$. The theoretical development of said disintegration had been considered by utilizing criteria of Non-standard Analysis in Statisticas $[12,6]$.

By carring out all the possible semiotic synthesis feasible on any given S_0 and on the relative complent S_1 (S_0
$\cup S_1 = X$), the two S_j^* thusly deriving give place to $X_j^* =$
$S_0^* \cup S_1^*$ (the indicating by j also X^* stands to denote that
the eventual   irrelevance of values appearing in the descriptions of X^* itself are relative to the descriptions
performed by all the X_αs of X when these are mapped by f
into the subsets S_j $-j = 0$, $1-$) .

6. THE VARIABLES' EXPECTED INFORMATIONAL UTILITY

Let one CF and the partition of X performed for the relative description be given. Every X_h can explain, potentially, the variability of the (unique) Y. This in that, every occurrence in which one value $x_{h\alpha}$ results as relevant
in any virtual description $X_{\alpha i}$ appearing in the X_j^*'s elements, consitutes a contribution to the informativity of
the considered h-th variable; further, the information per-
taining said value represents the measure of the contribution itself. Thus, the differential informativity of every
variable X_h may be considered as the average uncertainty
(entropy), $H(X_h^*)$, that the variable itself dissipates a-
bout the CF in subject, through the relevant values that
X_h takes in the descriptions forming X_j^*.
Such an entropy in IDFA is determined on the basis of
the argumentation that follow.
The Shannon' entropy associated to the probability distribution on the X_αs of X is, by assuming the independence among the X_hs:

$$H(X) = - \sum_{\alpha = 1}^{n} p_\alpha \log p_\alpha = \sum_{\alpha = 1}^{n} p_\alpha I_\alpha \qquad (6)$$

where: $I_\alpha = -\log p_\alpha$ is the purely statistical information
of every X_α and p_α the probability $P(X_\alpha)$ resulting from
the productory

$$p_\alpha = \prod_{h = 1}^{\ell} p_{h\alpha} \qquad (p_{h\alpha} = \text{probability of the va-} \qquad (7)$$
$$\text{lue taken by } X_h \text{ in } X_\alpha)$$

By (7), (6) may be rewritten as

$$H(X) = - \sum_{\alpha = 1}^{n} P_\alpha \log \prod_{h = 1}^{\ell} p_{h\alpha} =$$

$$= - \sum_{\alpha = 1}^{n} P_\alpha \prod_{h = 1}^{\ell} \log p_{h\alpha} = - \sum_{h = 1}^{\ell} \sum_{\alpha = 1}^{n} P_\alpha \log p_{h\alpha} \quad (8)$$

The terms $-(p_\alpha \log p_{h\alpha})$ appearing in (8) are here disintegrated into those conserning the different virtual descriptions $x_{\alpha i}$. This because: lst) the disintegration that the X_αs of each S_j^k ($k=1,2,\ldots$) are eventually required to undergo for being semiotically synthetized, so that the corresponding S_j^* can be derived; 2nd) the possible different relevance —either irrelevant or not— that the distinct $x_{h\alpha}$s may have in the X_αs forming S_j^*.

Thus, the following ewpression for the entropy of X is achieved:

$$H(X) = - \sum_{h = 1}^{\ell} \left(\sum_{\alpha = 1}^{n} \sum_{i = 1}^{q_\alpha} p_{\alpha i} \log p_{h\alpha} \right) \quad (9)$$

In (9), the duble summation inside parenthesis gives the statistical average information relative to every single variable X_h, $H(X_h)$ (each coefficient '$-\log p_{h\alpha}$' appearing in the same summation being the statistical informa- tion given by the value of the h-th variable in each α-th virtual description). Said information, when x_h may in- diffently be either 0 or 1, whichever the probability of such an $x_{h\alpha}$ is becomes:

$$I_{h\alpha}^* = o \quad (10)$$

Consequently, firstly by deriving from (9) the following

$$H(X_h) = \sum_{\alpha = 1}^{n} \sum_{i = 1}^{q_\alpha} p_{\alpha i} \, I_{h\alpha} \quad (11)$$

hence, by taking into account the relevance of the dis- tinct $x_{h\alpha}$s appearing in the virtual descriptions forming as well S_0^* as S_1^*, the differential informativity sought for each variable X_h results to be:

$$H(X_h^*) = \sum_{\alpha = 1}^{n} \sum_{\alpha = 1}^{q_\alpha} p_{\alpha i} \log p_h^* \qquad \sum_{\alpha = 1}^{n} \sum_{i = 1}^{q_\alpha} p_{\alpha i} \, I_{h\alpha}^* \quad (12)$$

In (10), $p_{h\alpha}$ and $I^{*}_{h\alpha}$ denote, respectively: the former, the probability of $x_{h\alpha i}$ whose eventual being irrelevant in the virtual description $X_{\alpha i}$ included in one of the S^{*}_{j}s, i. e. irrelevant with respect to X_{j}, is taken into account; the latter, the information relative to the value $x_{h\alpha}$ it-self.

It is stressed that although (12) comes down from Shannon' formula, (6), the two values of probability appearing in the former are not equal one to another as it is in the latter. This is so in that, in (12), $p_{h\alpha}$ is relative to the information that X_{h} gives by being either '0', '1' or '*', whereas $p_{\alpha i}$ concerns the relative frequency, $|\alpha| / N$, with which X_{h} supplyes the information itself. In (6), instead, not being the eventual irrelevance the values of each X_{h} can take in the distinct X_{α}s accounted, the two considered probabilities are identical.

In addition, notwithstanding the information that $x_{h\alpha i} = *$ supplyes is zero, (10), the equality $P(x_{h\alpha}) = 1$ is not implied said null informaiton follows, in fact, from the lack any semantical thikness deriving to the value in subject from the irrelevance of X_{h} in the virtual description $X_{\alpha i}$.

7. CONCLUDING REMARKS

The factors of composite facts are analyzed, through IDFA, as derived from informational compound of observed varia-bles X_{h} whose variablity is finalized to explain the varia-bilty of the same facts. Consequently, the informational expected utlity of said variables results as a function, not only of the statistical variability of the variables them-selves, but also of the relevance the states of said fac-tors assume, with respect to the considered fact's variabi-ty; states which are described by the values of said X_{h}.

REFERENCES

[1] Akaike, H., Information Theory and the extension of the maximum likelihood principle, in: B.M. Petrov and F. Csaki, 2nd Int. Sym. on Information Theory, (Aka-demykiato, Budapest, 1973), 167-281.

[2] Arigoni, A.O., Mathematical developments arising from 'Semantical Implication', Fuzzy Sets and Systems, 4

(1980), 167-181.

[3] Arigoni, A.O.,"Transformational-generative grammar for description of formal properties,' Fuzzy Sets and Systems, 8, (1982), 311-322.

[4] Arigoni, A.O.,"On the probability of fuzzy causes", Statistica, 4, (1983), 287-297.

[5] Arigoni, A.O.,"Heuristic Information" (submitted to Cybernetics and Systems).

[6] Arigoni, A.O.,"An application of Non-standard Analysis in Statistics", IFAC Int. Sym. on Knowledge Reprentation and Decision Analysis, Univ. of Marseille, July 1983.

[7] Edwards, A.W.F., Likelihood, (Cambridge University Press, 1972).

[8] Gokhable, D.V.,"On entropy based goodness-of-fit tests", Statistics and Data Analysis, 1, (1983), 157-165.

[9] Harman, H.H., Modern Factor Analysis, (The University of Chicago Presses, 1977).

[10] Hirano, K.,"On the best estimator for estimating variance of normal distributions", in: K. Natusita, Recent developments in Statistical Inferences and Data Analysis, (North-Holland, Amsterdam, 1980).

[11] Karshirsagar, A.M., Multivariate Analysis, (Marcel Dekker, N. Y., 1972).

[12] Robinson, A., Non-standard Analysis, (North-Holland, Amsterdam, 1966).

[13] Vann der Geer, J.P., Introduction to Multivariate Analysis, (Freeman and Co., S. Francisco, 1971).

PART IV

RISK PROPENSITY AND DECISION

Kenneth R. MacCrimmon and Donald A. Wehrung

ASSESSING RISK PROPENSITY

1. INTRODUCTION

The most accepted theory of risk is based on utility theory, as developed by von Neumann-Morgenstern (1947), Arrow (1971), and others. If the decision maker obeys the utility axioms, he acts as if he maximizes expected utility. The proof of the expected utility theorem suggests how to construct the utility function that reflects his risk attitudes.

The simplest situation in which to study risk through utility functions requires one sure alternative and another alternative that yields one of two uncertain outcomes. One of the uncertain outcomes is preferred to the sure outcome and one is dispreferred. The probability of receiving each outcome is known. This very simple choice situation is called the "basic risk paradigm". Either this simple paradigm or an extension of it forms the basis for most studies of risk. In the "choice mode", all four factors (certain outcome, gain outcome, loss outcome and probability) are specified, and the person's choice tells us something about his risk propensity. In the "equivalence mode", only three of the factors are specified and the person sets the value of the fourth factor to make the two alternatives indifferent in preference for him. The factor that is left to be specified provides the name (i.e., it is called the gain equivalence method if the gain outcome is left to be specified).

While considerable theoretical work has been done on risk, there have been few major studies directed at assessing people's risk propensity. In the 1960s, Grayson (1960) and Swalm (1966) obtained utility functions of managers. About the same time, Slovic (1964), using a variety of ad hoc methods for assessing risk, found that different methods gave different risk propensities. In one of the few large empirical studies, Kunreuther et al. (1978) studied risk-taking for insurance decisions involving

291

L. Daboni et al. (eds.), Recent Developments in the Foundations of Utility and Risk Theory, 291–309.
© *1986 by D. Reidel Publishing Company.*

natural disasters such as floods and earthquakes. He found that the usual choice models were inadequate to model people's risk behavior.

Risk theory stems from choice theory. As a result, in studying risk-taking the focus has been almost solely on the choices made by a decision maker from among the alternatives presented to him. Yet when we observe actual decision makers, they seldom end up choosing among the original alternatives. They almost always try to modify the alternatives. We need to learn more about how people deal with risk and about the effects of different methods for assessing risk propensity.

In 1972 we began a large-scale study to assess the risk propensity of practicing decision makers. In the process we have studied the risk-taking behavior of over 500 top-level business executives as well as hundreds of students. Here we will report on some key parts of a study involving 509 top-level business executives. The typical executive was a 47 year old vice-president who had been with his firm 15 years and earned $160,000 (in 1984 dollars). The firms were based either in the United States or Canada. All major functional areas of specialization were represented as were over 25 different industries including banking, primary resources, manufacturing, and chemical.

We developed a very elaborate portfolio of risk instruments and risk-related questions. In this paper we will first describe the results of the utility theory instruments. Starting with 50-50 gain equivalences for personal investments, we move on to other probability levels, to business investments, to followups a year later, and to different equivalence methods. Then we extend the basic risk paradigm into several other standardized instruments. We will focus on the extent to which one obtains the same risk propensity from different instruments. We conclude by briefly discussing the broader context including risk measures derived from natural situations and attitudes, as well as the relationship between the various risk measures and key risk-related characteristics. See MacCrimmon and Wehrung (1985) for a description of the complete study.

2. ASSESSING RISK WITH UTILITY-RELATED QUESTIONS

2.1 UTILITY FUNCTIONS BASED ON 50-50 PERSONAL GAIN EQUIVALENCES

We asked each executive to consider an investment of half his net personal wealth.   While the investment was hypothetical, the question was worded to try to get him to think carefully.   We asked him to specify the gain outcome that would make him indifferent between keeping his current net wealth and taking the risky venture in which he could lose half his net wealth with probability 0.50 or win the amount he specified with probability 0.50.

With just a single response, we can only obtain a one-parameter utility function.   Since the question dealt with relative levels of wealth, we assumed a constant relative risk aversion (Arrow, 1971; Pratt, 1964).   Of 484 executives for whom we had data, only 7 were risk seeking and only 15 were risk neutral.   The remaining 95% were risk averse.   This supports the usual assumptions made in economic analysis.

2.2 UTILITY FUNCTIONS BASED ON PERSONAL GAIN EQUIVALENCES: MULTIPLE PROBABILITY LEVELS

By varying the probability level (to 0.6, 0.7, and 0.9), we obtain a basis for a more complex utility function.   As a first step we simply drew a smooth curve through the two fixed points and the four responses.   Two basic shapes emerged: overall concave (with perhaps a small intermediate convex region) and concave for losses and low payoffs and convex for large payoffs (with occasionally small intermediate anomolies). See Figure 1 for some examples.

We next used curve fitting procedures to obtain a three parameter utility function.   We assumed a sumex function (Schlaifer, 1971) which we fit with a least squares criterion using various search techniques, including the Hooke-Jeeves method (Bassler, 1976).

We found a quite consistent picture from both types of curve-fitting analyses of the gain equivalences.   The

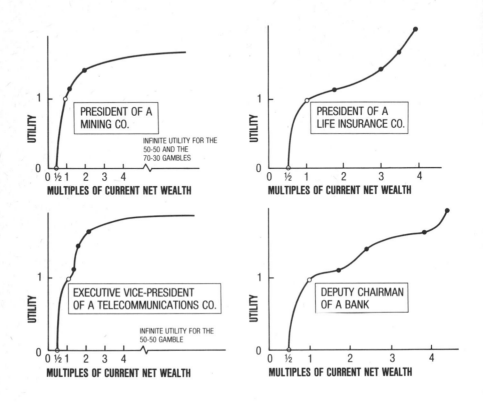

Figure 1   Utility Curves for Selected Executives

managers were risk averse for losses and small gains. Some were risk averse over the whole domain. Others were risk seeking for large gains. Thus we obtained empirical support for the traditional hypotheses that individuals are risk averse over losses.

At this point, we have presented new empirical evidence on risk propensity based on utility functions. Let us go on though to consider other utility-related issues that tend to be neglected in risk studies.

2.3   UTILITY FUNCTIONS FOR BUSINESS GAIN EQUIVALENCES

Do people have the same risk propensity in different domains? More specifically, do they show the same risk propensity in business decisions as they do in personal decisions? If they do not, how can we account for this in our theories?

We asked business utility questions that were the counterpart of the personal wealth utility questions. We will restrict our focus here to the 50-50 equivalence questions. The executives were asked to assume that they could reallocate half of their capital expenditure budget, away from standard projects, paying their usual rate of return, to a new opportunity with uncertain outcomes. The new project had a 0.50 probability of yielding a zero return and a 0.50 probability of yielding the return to be specified by the executive.

The same assumption of constant relative risk aversion was made for business investment as was made for personal investment. Of the 395 executives who had complete answers, 26 executives were risk seeking and 39 were risk neutral. The remaining eighty-three.percent were risk averse. Hence here too we found considerable risk aversion.

But how do personal risk propensity and business risk propensity compare? As we can see in the above numbers, three times as many executives were risk seeking or risk neutral for business investments than for personal investments. In addition, twice as many (106 to 56) were extremely risk averse for personal investments than for business. There is, of course, some arbitrariness in establishing the relevant levels of investment to make a particular risk parameter comparable in the two cases. A sensitivity analysis confirmed the robustness of the results we are describing.

Looking at the differences on a person-by-person basis, we found that two-thirds (259) were more risk averse for personal investments than for business, while the remaining one-third were about equally split between having the same risk propensity in both domains (59) and being more risk averse for business investments (64). In making these intra-person comparisons, we found that the personal and business risk propensities were related. The correlation between these measures was 0.43 (significant at 0.001).

We conclude that business executives are more risk averse for their personal investments than for business investments. It would seem dubious to use a single assessment of risk propensity to apply across these different contexts. At the very least, risk propensity for business-related decisions should be assessed from a business context and personal risk propensities should be assessed from a personal context.

2.4   STABILITY OF UTILITY FUNCTIONS

Do people have the same risk propensity at different time periods? If not why not? How can we develop theories to account for changes, if there are changes?

To find out if utility functions are stable over time, we asked the same questions about personal and business investments to a subset of 100 executives one year later. There were differences. Personal risk propensity seems more stable than business risk propensity. Over a one year period, there was a correlation of 0.36 (significant at 0.001) between the 50-50 personal gain equivalences (n=84). The correlation between the 50-50 business gain equivalences was insignificant at the 0.01 level (n=57).

Hence there is evidence that the utility functions were not stable over time. Since there was change over time we need to investigate the possible reasons for change. If the change was due to a change in wealth, then the assumption of

constant relative risk aversion over wealth is in doubt.
Various analyses showed that the minor wealth changes did
not account for the differences. It would seem then that
there may be some basic instability in the utility-based
equivalence assessments over time.

2.5 UTILITY FUNCTIONS BASED ON DIFFERENT EQUIVALENCE METHODS

Do people exhibit the same utility function and hence the
same risk propensity if they are asked to respond using
different elicitation techniques? Specifically, do gain
equivalences, certainty equivalences, and probability
equivalences yield the same utility function as expected
utility theory would require?

The answer is no. Both our pilot study and the
followup study showed differences. Earlier results from a
pilot study of 40 executives had suggested differences
between certainty equivalences, gain equivalences, and
probability equivalences (Bassler, MacCrimmon, and Stanbury,
1973). In our followup study we obtained gain equivalences
and certainty equivalences for both personal and business
investments. The correlation among the risk propensities
for personal investments was 0.38 (n=53). For business
investments the correlation between the risk propensities
based on the two equivalence methods was only 0.20 (n=37).
Thus different equivalence methods seem to give different
assessments of risk propensity. Similar differences in risk
propensity from different equivalence methods were found by
Hershey, Kunreuther, and Schoemaker (1982). The theory
requires that these different equivalence methods yield the
same utility function. Yet the questions seem to be
perceived and processed in different ways.

2.6 SUMMARY OF RISK ASSESSMENT BASED ON UTILITY FUNCTIONS

Figure 2 summarizes the findings that we have reported on
context, stability, and equivalence method. More detail is
provided in Wehrung, MacCrimmon, and Brothers (1984). Our
conclusion is that context matters, time period matters, and
response mode matters. Yet theories of risk tend to ignore

these factors.   Some new theories can account for some
differences. For example, weighted utility theory (Chew and
MacCrimmon, 1979; Chew, 1981) is consistent with the
differences found in certainty equivalences and gain
equivalences.   However, other new theories which are more
congruent with the whole range of observed behaviors are
needed.

In comparisons to be made in the next section, we need
single numerical measures for risk propensity.   For risk
measures from the utility questions we converted the gain
equivalences into probability premiums. For example, in the
personal   decisions,   the   probability   premium   is
1-p-[1/(2k-1)], where k is the gain equivalence (as a
multiple of current wealth) provided by the subject and p is
the probability of loss. The risk measures for the personal
investment are denoted PGAMBLE50% and PGAMBLE10% for the
gambles with 50% and 10% chance of loss, respectively.   For
the business situation, the risk measures are denoted
BGAMBLE50% and BGAMBLE10%.

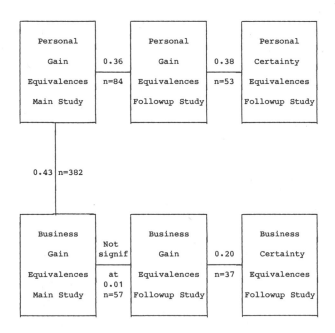

Figure 2   Correlations among Utility-Based Measures

3. ASSESSING RISK WITH OTHER STANDARDIZED INSTRUMENTS

At this point, we have described one of the largest
empirical studies yet undertaken on risk-taking based on
utility-type questions. Yet utility questions are just one
part of our risk portfolio. We developed three other
standardized instruments that are extensions of the basic
risk paradigm. The risk propensity measures from two of
these instruments will be compared to those from the utility
questions.

3.1 THE RISK IN-BASKET

The utility questions are abstract and by their nature do
not allow a study of context. One can, however, embed the
basic risk paradigm in various contexts. We designed a Risk
In-Basket in which the basic risk paradigm was the basis for
four risky business situations: a lawsuit, a customer
threat, a union dispute, and a joint venture. In each
situation there were two alternatives with the same expected
value. One of the alternatives had a sure outcome and the
other had two possible outcomes with specified
probabilities. The executive was asked to respond in three
ways: (a) to write a memo outlining what actions should be
taken, (b) to indicate, on an 11-point scale, his
inclination to take the risky action, and (c) to specify the
probability of the preferred outcome for which he would be
indifferent between the two alternatives.

The memo responses are the richest as a source of data
because they provide information on how business executives
try to modify risky situations (see MacCrimmon and Wehrung,
1984). The rating scales seem the least useful but were
included because ratings are a standard method used in
psychological studies. Here we will focus on the
probability equivalences. For example, in the lawsuit, the
executive was asked to state the smallest chance of winning
the lawsuit that he would require to take the case to court
in lieu of accepting a riskless out-of-court settlement.
For the joint venture, he was asked to state the smallest
chance of capturing the large market share that he would
require to "go it alone" in lieu of the riskless joint
venture.

From these equivalence responses, we derived probability premiums (by subtracting the expected value equilibrating probability). The probability premium will be used as a risk measure. Higher values imply more risk aversion. Attention will be limited to only two of the situations, the lawsuit and the joint venture. The risk measures will be denoted IB:LAWSUIT and IB:VENTURE, respectively. The underlying situations are summarized in the top part of Figure 3.

3.2   RISK-RETURN RANKINGS

The basic risk paradigm can be extended to more than two alternatives and to continuous, rather than discrete, outcomes. In the Risk-Return Rankings instrument we presented a set of nine personal investment alternatives, each described by an expected rate of return and a standard deviation of return. These two parameters defined a normal distribution over returns for a hypothetical investment of 10% of the executive's net wealth. To help an executive understand the significance of the two parameters, six cumulative probabilities for key outcomes (such as breaking even, losing half the stake, etc.) were provided. The executive ranked all nine alternatives in order of his preferences. The riskiest alternative (in terms of having the highest variance as well as the highest probability of loss of various amounts such as the loss of 10%, 50%, or 100% of his stake) was the alternative with an expected return of 25% and a standard deviation of 80%. The safest alternative had an expected return of 15% and a standard deviation of 20%. See the bottom of Figure 3 for a summary of the Risk-Return Rankings instrument.

This instrument can be used to study the perceptions and focus of decision makers faced with such risky alternatives. See Basşler, MacCrimmon, Stanbury, and Wehrung (1978) for some details on this focus. In the present paper, though, we will only consider the risk measures derived from this instrument. For risk measures we use the difference between the preference ranks given to these two alternatives and the ranks these alternatives would receive if all nine alternatives were ordered solely by expected value. The measures were then rescaled so that higher values corresponded to risk aversion. The two risk

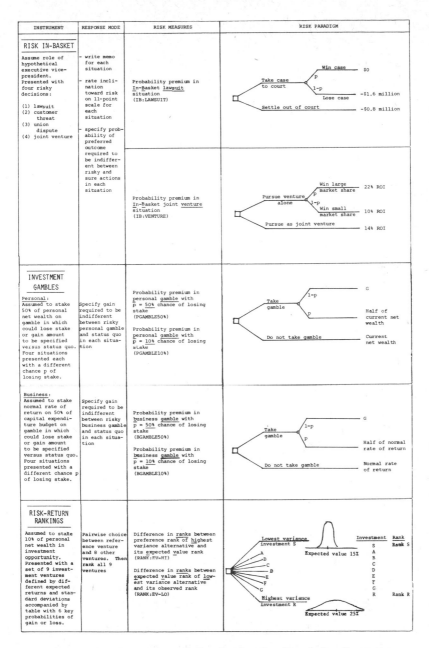

INSTRUMENT	RESPONSE MODE	RISK MEASURES	RISK PARADIGM

Figure 3   Summary of Instruments Used to Measure
Risks in Standardized Situations

measures are called RANK:EV-HI and RANK:EV-LO for the
riskiest and the safest alternatives, respectively.

3.3 REAL MONEY WAGERS

We also studied the risk propensity that could be inferred
from rankings in another instrument called Real Money
Wagers. In this instrument, the subjects could win as much
as $414 or lose as much as $274 of real money on a single
choice. Three sets of five wagers each were presented to
each executive and he was asked to rank the five
alternatives in order of his preference. One alternative in
each set offered a sure gain of $10 while the other four
uncertain binary wagers each had an expected value of $10.
In the first set, the maximum loss ($20) was constant across
all wagers, in the second set the maximum gain ($40) was
constant across all wagers, while in the third set the
probability of loss (0.38) was constant across all wagers.

This format allowed us to study choices when the payoff
context changed. Few executives preferred the sure $10 in
any of the three sets. The most risk averse responses were
given in the set in which the chance of loss was fixed (and
hence the magnitude of loss could vary). The most risk
seeking responses were given in the set where the magnitude
of the maximum loss was fixed. One executive actually won
the maximum amount, $414, and was paid by us; no one lost
the maximum $274, but we were prepared to collect if anyone
had. See MacCrimmon, Stanbury, and Wehrung (1980) for more
details.

Although all the instruments are based on the basic
risk paradigm, we will not include risk measures derived
from the Real Money Wagers instrument in the comparison
(with the risk measures from the other three instruments)
because this instrument was used only in the followup study
and not in the main study.

3.4 COMPARISON AMONG STANDARDIZED RISK MEASURES

As a group, the executives displayed almost the full range
of risk-taking and risk-averting responses on the Risk
In-Basket and Risk-Return Rankings instruments. In the

Investment Gambles (i.e., utility questions), however, risk-taking responses were almost non-existent and extreme risk avoidance was common. This was true for the personal and business situations. When faced with losing half of personal wealth (or the normal rate of return on half of the capital expenditure budget) in return for substantial gains, no more than 4% of the executives gave risk-taking responses. Risk-taking occurred much more frequently (39-68%) in the Risk In-Basket and Risk-Return Rankings instruments.

To what extent can these differences in risk propensity be explained by differences in the domains from which the measures were derived? We will consider this issue by investigating both the personal vs. business domain and a threat versus opportunity domain. This latter domain will be examined by classifying the risky situations within each instrument as relative threats or opportunities. For example, the personal investment gamble having a 50% chance of losing half of net wealth (PGAMBLE50%) was considered a relative threat and the gamble with a 10% chance of loss (PGAMBLE10%) was considered a relative opportunity (because it offered a 90% chance of significant gain). The relative threats for the other instruments were BGAMBLE50%, IB:LAWSUIT, and RANK:EV-HI while the relative opportunities were BGAMBLE10%, IB:VENTURE, and RANK:EV-LO.

Using our four measures of personal risk propensity and our four measures of business risk propensity, there was no apparent trend toward greater risk-taking in either domain. However, when we restricted attention to the four measures derived from the Investment Gambles where the personal and business situations are comparable, there was evidence for greater risk-taking in the business domain than in the personal domain. Not only were the percentages of risk-takers higher in the business gambles than in the personal gambles, but the median probability premiums were significantly lower in the business domain than in the personal domain.

Comparing the threat and opportunity within each instrument, we found greater risk-taking in the threat situation three times out of four. Risk-taking was more frequent in situations involving only losses than in those involving only gains (IB:LAWSUIT vs. IB:VENTURE) and in

situations having higher rather than lower chances of major
losses (PGAMBLE50% vs. PGAMBLE10% and BGAMBLE50% vs.
BGAMBLE10%). This greater risk-taking in threat situations
was supported by significantly lower average probability
premiums in the threat situation compared with the
opportunity situation within the Investment Gambles and Risk
In-Basket instruments.

The two situations within the personal threat domain
are also comparable because both involve investments of
personal wealth. The substantially greater risk-taking in
the Risk-Return Rankings measure RANK:EV-HI (39%) than in
the Investment Gambles measure PGAMBLE50% (under 1%) is
likely a result of the difference in the percentage of
personal wealth at risk. Putting 50% of one's personal
wealth at risk is much more threatening than putting 10% at
risk. In this comparison the executives showed greater
risk-taking in the less threatening situation. Similarly
within the personal opportunity domain there was
substantially greater risk-taking when a smaller percentage
of personal wealth was at stake.

The same type of reasoning can be used to compare the
situations within the business threat domain and within the
business opportunity domain, although the comparability
between situations is not as great as in the personal
cases. The business Investment Gambles involve risking the
normal rate of return on half the capital expenditure
budget, whereas the situations in the Risk In-Basket involve
either gains only or a possible one-time major loss that
could be attributed to parties other than the executive (the
litigant, courts, or prior management). The business
gambles seem much more threatening than the in-basket
situations, and they evoked much less risk-taking (2% to 4%
versus 44% to 53%).

The substantially lower risk-taking in the Investment
Gambles than in the Risk-Return Rankings and Risk In-Basket
could be due to differences in the phase of risk being
examined rather than to differences in the degree of threat
involved. The interpretation of differences in phase
indicates the executives were less willing to take risks
when faced with entering a risky situation than once in it.
Moreover, they were less willing to take risks when faced
with choosing within a risky situation than when recognizing
or adjusting the risks.

3.5 RELATIONSHIPS AMONG THE RISK MEASURES: ENTIRE RISK DISTRIBUTION

In this section we will examine the relationships among the eight risk measures using their entire risk distributions. There are two key questions: (1) do different instruments yield the same assessment of risk propensity for a given person? and (2) if there are differences in risk propensity assessed in different situations, do the different domains of risk (i.e., personal versus business and threat versus opportunity) emerge distinctly?

As a first step in examining the relationship among the measures, we looked at their pairwise Pearson correlation coefficients. In these computations the sample size varied from 285 to 464, since not all measures could be derived for all managers. The highest correlations 0.68, 0.67, and 0.54, occurred between pairs of measures obtained from the same instrument (business Investment Gambles, personal Investment Gambles, and Risk-Return Rankings, respectively). The next highest correlations were obtained for measures derived from threat-threat questions and opportunity-opportunity questions on the two Investment Gambles instruments, i.e., 0.42 (PGAMBLE50%, BGAMBLE50%) and 0.33 (PGAMBLE10%, BGAMBLE10%). The next level of coefficients 0.26 (PGAMBLE50%, BGAMBLE10%) and 0.24 (PGAMBLE10%, BGAMBLE50%) came from "mixed" questions on the Investment Gambles instruments. All these coefficients were significantly different from zero beyond the 0.0001 level (two-tailed test).

The next level of correlation coefficients were obtained from various pairs of measures: 0.19 (BGAMBLE10%, RANK:EV-HI), 0.17 (PGAMBLE10%, RANK:EV-LO), 0.16 (IB:LAWSUIT, IB:VENTURE), and 0.15 (PGAMBLE10%, RANK:EV-HI). All these correlations were significant at the 0.001 level.

In summary, eleven of the twenty-eight correlation coefficients were very significant. All of these coefficients were positive as would be expected by our scaling of all risk measures to have higher values correspond to risk aversion. We conclude that one's propensity to take risks does transfer across some situations. However, the magnitudes of the significant correlations and the existence of the non-significant correlations suggest that there may be important domain effects on risk propensity.

Rather than forcing our dimensions of personal vs. business and threat vs. opportunity upon the analysis, we next did a principal components analysis to determine whether the risk measures, considered as independent variables, could be linearly combined into a smaller number of principal components. This analysis was dominated by a strong instrument effect with measures from different instruments loading heavily on different components. No clear domain effect emerged.

To help determine whether the measures do exhibit a domain effect for either personal versus business or threat versus opportunity, we need to avoid having the results swamped by similarity among questions from the same instrument. Hence it is useful to examine a spatial representation of the measures. A Guttman-Lingoes smallest space analysis for two dimensions did show the closeness among measures derived from the same instrument compared with the distances between measures derived from different instruments. More importantly, it revealed a strong personal versus business horizontal dimension and a vertical dimension that could be interpreted as degree of threat in the risky situation. All four business measures were located to the right of any personal measure. All four threat measures were not located above all the opportunity measures. However among the four personal measures the more threatening Investment Gambles measures both were located far above the less threatening Risk-Return Rankings measures. Within both of these instruments the threat measure was above the opportunity measure. On the business side the threat measure was above the opportunity measure in both Investment Gambles and the Risk In-Basket.

These three sets of analyses (i.e., correlation, principal components, and smallest space) thus provide slightly different views of the same picture. The main relationship among the eight risk measures occurred between measures derived from the same instrument. There did, however, seem to be a domain effect. The four measures of personal risk were internally congruent. This leads to a relatively clear-cut distinction between personal and business risk-taking. There was also evidence for a risk propensity distinction depending upon how threatening the risky situation was. This latter domain effect only emerged once the instrument effect and the personal vs. business effect had been removed.

4. SUMMARY

Assessing risk-taking with a portfolio of instruments raises a number of important questions for further research. Can risk theories be developed to account for differences in risk propensity in personal versus business decisions, in threats versus opportunities, in type of response mode, and over time? Can such theories be extended to incorporate how people recognize, evaluate, and adjust the risky situations they face as well as how they choose within them? One recent step in this direction is Fishburn's (1984) axiomatization of risk perception incorporating the probability of loss.

One can extend the risk portfolio to include nonstandard situations. In the study described here, we also obtained measures of risk propensity from naturally-occurring situations and from attitudes. In addition, we obtained information about many personal, financial, and business characteristics (such as age, wealth, and managerial position) that have been postulated to relate to risk. An analysis of all these factors and their relationships to the measures discussed in this paper is presented in MacCrimmon and Wehrung (1985).

University of British Columbia

REFERENCES

Arrow, K.J., Essays in the Theory of Risk-Bearing, Markham Publishing Company, Chicago, 1971.

Bassler, J.F., "Managerial Risk Attitudes: Utility Function Assessment Analysis", unpublished note, 1976, 8 pages.

Bassler, J.F., MacCrimmon, K.R., Stanbury, W.T., and Wehrung, D.A., "Multiple Criteria Dominance Models: An Empirical Study of Investment Preferences", in Multiple Criteria Problem Solving, S. Zionts (ed.), Springer-Verlag, Berlin, 1978.

Bassler, J.F., MacCrimmon, K.R., and Stanbury, W.T., "Risk Attitudes of Business Executives", paper presented at the Fourth International Conference on Subjective Probability, Utility, and Decision Making, Rome, Italy, 1973.

Chew, S.H. and MacCrimmon, K.R., "Alpha-Nu Choice Theory: A Generalization of Expected Utility Theory", Working Paper, University of British Columbia, July 1979, 30 pages.

Chew, S.H., Two Representation Theorems, Ph.D. thesis, University of British Columbia, 1981.

Fishburn, P.C., "Foundations of Risk Measurement. I: Risk as Probable Loss", Management Science, Vol. 30, No.4, April 1984, pp. 396-406.

Grayson, C.J., Decisions under Uncertainty: Drilling Decisions by Oil and Gas Operators, Harvard University, Boston, 1960.

Hershey, J.C., Kunreuther, H.C. and Schoemaker, P.J.H., "Sources of Bias in Assessment Procedures for Utility Functions," Management Science, Vol. 28, No. 8, August 1982, pp. 936-954.

Kunreuther, H., Ginsbey, R., Miller, L., Sagi, P., Slovic, P., Borkan, B. and Katz, N., Disaster Insurance Protection: Policy Lessons, Wiley, New York, 1978.

MacCrimmon, K.R., Stanbury, W.T. and Wehrung, D.A., "Real Money Lotteries: A Study of Ideal Risk, Context Effects, and Simple Processes," in Cognitive Processes in Choice and Decision Behavior, Thomas S. Wallsten (ed.), Erlbaum, Hillsdale, N.J., 1980.

MacCrimmon, K.R. and Wehrung, D.A., Taking Risks: The Management of Uncertainty, Free Press, New York, 1985.

MacCrimmon, K.R. and Wehrung, D.A., "The Risk In-Basket," Journal of Business, Vol. 57, No. 5, July 1984, pp. 367-387.

Pratt, J.W., "Risk Aversion in the Small and in the Large," Econometrica, Vol. 32, Nos. 1-2, Jan-April 1964, pp. 122-136.

Schlaifer, R., Computer Programs for Elementary Decision Analysis, Harvard University, Boston, 1971.

Slovic, P., "Assessment of Risk Taking Behavior," Psychological Bulletin, Vol. 64, No. 3, (1964), pp. 220-233.

Swalm, R.O., "Utility Theory--Insights into Risk Taking," Harvard Business Review, Vol. 44, No. 6, Nov.-Dec. 1966, pp. 123-136.

Von Neumann, J. and Morgenstern, O., Theory of Games and Economic Behavior, Princeton University Press, Princeton, 1947.

Wehrung, D.A., MacCrimmon, K.R. and Brothers, K.M., "Utility Assessment: Domains, Stability, and Equivalence Procedures," INFOR, Vol. 22, No. 2, May 1984, pp. 98-115.

Lola Lopes

WHAT NAIVE DECISION MAKERS CAN TELL US ABOUT RISK

1. Views of the Decision Maker

During the last 100 years, there have been many changes of fashion concerning the proper relation between the psychologist, the subject, and the subject matter. In the early days, subjects were trained in the techniques of introspection in the hope that they would be able to look beyond the products of higher mental processes and report back on sensation, itself. For reasons that now seem obvious, this program failed and psychological fashion swung to behaviorism, in which the scientific goal was to map directly from observable stimuli onto observable responses. The subject, therefore, came to be treated as a "black box" whose contents were theoretically inconsequential. Since World War II, however, behaviorism has been steadily losing ground to a newer approach, variously called "human information processing psychology" or "cognitive psychology." This approach uses the subject as a "window" on the flow of information through consciousness. Thus, verbal reports are becoming part of the database on which theory is built and for which explanation is required.

In the case of the psychology of risk, one can find illustrations of both the behavioristic and the cognitive approaches to subjects. The most important early studies of risk grew directly out of interest in von Neumann and Morgenstern's (1947) axiomatization of expected utility theory. Among the earliest studies were some aimed at the measurement of utility (Davidson, Suppes, & Siegel, 1957; Mosteller & Nogee, 1951) and others aimed at discovering how distributional factors influence risky choice (Edwards, 1953, 1954a,b,c). In these experiments subjects' responses were typically limited to simple choices, a response mode that reflected not only prevailing conceptions of what might legitimately be construed as data, but also admiration for the minimal assumptions that von Neumann and Morgenstern had chosen to make about the informational content of data.

311

L. Daboni et al. (eds.), Recent Developments in the Foundations of Utility and Risk Theory, 311–326.
© *1986 by D. Reidel Publishing Company.*

In 1968, however, Slovic and Lichtenstein (1968; Lichtenstein & Slovic, 1971, 1973) published the first of a series of studies demonstrating the startling fact that subjects' preferences for risks could be reversed by changes in the <u>response</u> <u>mode</u>. These studies were important in several ways, but for present purposes I will focus on one feature that distinguished them from what had gone before. This was the inclusion in the published reports of verbal statements given by subjects describing how they evaluated the attractiveness of the bets. These reports, which were corroborated by the statistical analysis, suggested that subjects go about the gamble evaluation process in ways that differ profoundly from what would be required under expected utility theory.

Slovic and Lichtenstein (1968) interpreted their results in terms of the information processing limitations of human subjects. As they put it, "the picture of the decision-making process that emerges...is one of a person struggling to integrate several sources of information into a single choice or judgment. The decision maker is guided by certain beliefs...which he combines with strategies designed to make his task less complex" (p.15).

In the years since, it has become increasingly common to find verbal accounts of subjects' decision-making processes rendered as part of experimental reports, accounts that continue to differ both operationally and logically from normative theories. Continuing, also, is the tendency of decision researchers to automatically ascribe these processing differences to human limitations. In essence, the dominant view is that people violate normative principles only because they must. As Slovic, Fischhoff, and Lichtenstein (1977) recently put it, "A coherent picture emerges....Because of limited information-processing capacity and ignorance of the rules for optimal information processing and decision making, people's judgments are subject to various systematic biases" (p. 14).

It is this view of the decision maker that I wish to challenge. Although I am not blind to processing limitations in the human system, I do not see that the evidence supports the claim that people act primarily out of confusion and ignorance. On the contrary, I will argue that the evidence suggests that people do what they do because they <u>choose</u> to do so, having based their choices not only on matters of efficiency and convenience, but also on matters of value on which they knowingly and, in many cases, eloquently disagree with normative theory.

I will present my argument as a set of four propositions about how people process risks. In each case, I will attempt to bridge the gap between behavioral phenomena and theory by using explanations given by naive subjects. Then I will close by relating these propositions to issues in the debate between the French and the American schools of risk theory.

Proposition 1: Risks are represented and processed psychologically in terms of the cumulative probabilities of the possible outcomes.

When people talk about risks, the expressions they use, terms like long shot, almost sure thing, all or nothing, and so forth, typically refer to the shape of distributions. Why shape? Because shape conveys, in an efficent way, the relative probabilities of the possible outcomes. Formal attempts at capturing the essence of this distributional information have generally centered on the higher order moments of the probability distributions, particularly variance and skewness. In psychology, these attempts have been largely axiomatic in spirit (cf. Coombs & Huang, 1970a,b; Coombs and Lehner, 1981; Luce, 1980; Pollatsek & Tversky, 1970) and have tended to ignore the psychological issues of why and how moments come to have their effects. In economics, on the other hand, the psychological issues have received some attention, particularly from Hagen (1969, 1979), who links the moments to emotional states such as hope, fear, and unpleasant levels of uncertainty.

In my recent research on risk (Lopes, 1984), I have attempted to characterize how people think about distributions. My results have tended to confirm Hagen's (1969, 1979) predictions about people's responses to distributions of different shapes, but because my emphasis has been on psychological process, I have worked in a somewhat different framework.

My experimental lotteries have multiple outcomes ranging from 7 to 31 equally spaced prize levels. Two examples are given in Figure 1. Each of the number signs represents a lottery ticket, and the number beside each row represents the prize that is won by each of the tickets in the row. For example, lottery 1a has 10 tickets that win no prize, 9 tickets that win $10, and so forth. Each lottery

```
                              $343     #
                              $331     #
                              $320     #
                              $309     #
                              $297     #
                              $285     #
                              $274     #
                              $263     #
                              $251     #
                              $239     ##
                              $228     ##
                              $217     ##
                              $205     ##
                              $193     ##
                              $182     ##
                              $171     ##
                              $159     ###
                              $147     ###               1a
                              $136     ###
                              $125     ###
                              $113     ###
                              $101     ####
                              $ 90     ####
                              $ 79     ####
                              $ 67     #####
                              $ 55     #####
                              $ 44     ######
                              $ 33     #######
                              $ 21     ########
                              $ 10     #########
                              ZERO     ##########
```

```
       $130     ##############################
       $115     #####################
       $101     ###############
       $ 86     ##########
       $ 71     #######                          1b
       $ 57     #####
       $ 43     ####
       $ 28     ###
       $ 13     ##
       ZERO     #
```

Figure 1.   Example of pair of stimulus lotteries.

has exactly 100 tickets, and the expected value of each is
$100.

Most people, when shown this pair of lotteries, know
exactly which one they would prefer given a free choice of
either. The overwhelming preference is for lottery 1b, a
result which is perfectly compatible with the notion of
marginally decreasing utility. However, when people are
asked why their preferences are as they are, the
explanations focus on the cumulative probability that they
will exceed particular prize levels or ranges. For
illustration, consider this statement given by a female
subject: "I'd pick [1b]. Although the top prize is not
nearly as high as in [1a], it seems one would have a greater
chance of winning a 'worthwhile' amount (i.e., something
over $100)."

Notice that the subject speaks in terms of an
inequality, the likelihood of winning "something over $100."
In my view, this tendency of subjects to describe gambles in
terms of inequalities reflects a more fundamental tendency
to process gambles in terms of their cumulative properties.
In particular, I propose that it is the cumulative
properties of gambles that mediate between the actual
psychological processes of people and the empirical
description of their preferences in terms of variance and
skewness.

Proposition 2: Judgments of risk are functionally and
psychologically analogous to judgments of distributional
inequality.

In their dealings with risky distributions, psychologists
and economists have generally hastened to compress these
multidimensional structures into simpler point descriptions.
My tack has been the opposite, to try to keep my thinking as
close as possible for as long as possible to the actual
shapes of distributions. However, in keeping with the
beliefs expressed in Proposition 1, I opted for a
representation of shape that is cumulative.

For illustration, consider Figure 2. Here are three
lotteries, each with the same number of outcomes and the
same probability levels, and each with the same expected
value. Lottery 2a has high variance and positive skewness.
Lotteries 2b and 2c have the same lower variance, but differ
in skewness. Most subjects like 2a least well for reasons

```
$439    #
$390    ##
$341    ###
$292    ####
$244    #####
$195    #######                          2a
$146    #########
$ 98    ##############
$ 49    #####################
ZERO    ##############################
```

```
$130    ################################
$115    #####################
$101    ###############
$ 86    ##########
$ 71    #######                          2b
$ 57    #####
$ 43    ####
$ 28    ###
$ 13    ##
ZERO    #
```

```
$200    #
$187    ##
$172    ###
$157    ####
$143    #####
$129    #######                          2c
$114    ##########
$ 99    ###############
$ 85    #####################
$ 70    ##############################
```

Figure 2.   Three stimulus lotteries.

that are similar to those given previously.   Of the
remaining two lotteries, subjects who tend to be risk-averse
prefer 2c.   Here, for example, is the reasoning given by the
previous subject: "I'd pick [2c] here. Not only are [its]
highest possible winnings greater than [for 2b], but the
lowest winnings are also quite a bit higher....I'd go with a
sure thing."

Preferences like these should be of no surprise, for
they are exactly what would be expected given either Hagen's
(1969, 1979) distributional model of utility or, for that
matter, given a standard Bernoullian model with marginally
decreasing utility.   However, it seems to me that neither of
these models relates well to people's explanations of their
choices.   To see why not, consider what these   distributions
would look like if they were plotted cumulatively.   Figure 3
gives the three distributions plotted as Lorenz curves.   The
data are simply cumulated on both axes, with cumulative
probability on the abscissa and cumulative gain on the
ordinate.

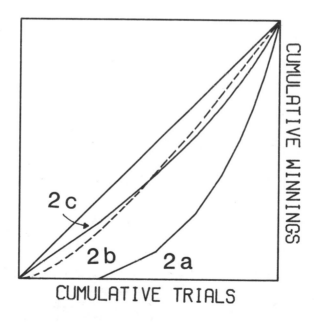

Figure 3.   Lorenz curves for lotteries in figure 2.

In welfare economics, curves like this are used to elucidate inequality in income distributions. Curves that bow far from the main diagonal are generally considered to have greater inequality than curves lying nearer the diagonal. In the case of lotteries, the interpretation is just the same except that, in my view, it is distributional inequality that constitutes the substrate for perceived risk.

Consider, for example, lotteries 2a and 2b. Notice that the positively skewed, high-variance gamble, the one which, recall, most subjects liked least, bows far from the diagonal. Generally speaking, high variance gambles of any kind, symmetric or asymmetric, will show this pattern. More interesting, however, is the comparison of the two gambles having equal variance. Note that the curves cross over one another, so that one curve lies nearer the main diagonal at the low end of the distribution and the other lies nearer the main diagonal at the high end. Which distribution is least risky? According to Hagen's (1969, 1979) model, it is 2c. According to my risk-averse subjects (Lopes, 1984), it is also 2c. In terms of the Lorenz curves, it is the lottery whose distribution lies nearer the diagonal at the low end.

Considerable controversy has raged in welfare economics over the issue of how inequality should be indexed. A. B. Atkinson (1975) has taken the position that seemingly "neutral" statistical measures such as the variance and the Gini coefficient will not suffice because "they embody implicit judgments about the weight to be attached to inequality at different points on the income scale" (p. 47). In his view, the better option is to consider these values explicitly by incorporating into the measure of inequality the distributional objectives that are being pursued.

The measure that Atkinson suggests includes a parameter that allows the user to choose from weighting schemes that range from equal weights for all groups, through various levels of enhanced weighting of the lower income groups, to the extreme position advocated by Rawls (1971) in which nothing is considered except the condition of the lowest income group. In terms of Lorenz curves, the effect of such weights is to favor distributions whose curves lie nearer the diagonal at the low end.

In my view, this kind of weighting, when it is applied to risky distributions, is equivalent to risk aversion as it is displayed in people's preferences and as it is approximated mathematically by models such as Hagen's (1969, 1979) which incorporate variance and skewness into the index of utility. However, the cumulative formulation seems preferable for psychological purposes because it suggests how these statistical moments actually do their work. That is, by thinking of the person as weighting different portions of the distribution unequally, a path is cleared to formulating the psychological process in terms of the attention that people pay to outcomes with differing magnitude.

Proposition 3:   Preferences among risks reflect the likelihood that, in choosing a particular distribution, the decision maker will satisfy one or more goals.

It's a stock observation that goals or aspiration levels are important in risky decision making.   Even naive decision makers would agree, as can be seen in this definition of risk produced by a business executive in a study run by Mao (1970): "Risk is the prospect of not meeting a target rate of return. That is the risk, isn't it? If you are one hundred percent sure of making the target return, then it is a zero risk proposition."
     Given this fact, one would expect that major research effort would have been directed at discovering where aspiration levels come from and how they work. But this is not the case. Instead, the aspiration level has typically been assumed to be either at the status quo (e.g., Kahneman & Tversky, 1979; Payne, Laughhunn, & Crum, 1980) or at some specified level that has been "set" by verbal instructions given to the subject (Laughhunn, Payne, & Crum, 1980).
     In the real world, aspiration levels are much more complex. At a minimum, they reflect both the immediate demands of the decision making situation and the decision maker's dispositional values concerning the trade-off between risk and return. For illustration, consider again lotteries 2b and 2c. When I first began my experiments, I expected that there would be a simple relationship between the preference orderings given by risk-averse subjects and the overall ordering of the lotteries on judged riskiness. This turned out to be correct for most of the lotteries I

used. However, preferences and judgments of risk did not
match up for lottery pairs that differed only in skewness.
Although risk-averse subjects did tend, as I have said
before, to prefer positively skewed lotteries like 2c,
subjects were split right down the middle in their judgments
of relative riskiness: half judged lotteries like 2b to be
the riskier and half judged the opposite (Lopes, 1984).
Furthermore, the views of both groups were strongly held,
and therefore were not likely to have been due to
indifference or unreliability in the judgment process.

On reflection it seemed that the disagreements might be
due to differences in aspiration level. For example,
considering lottery 2c, subjects who aspire to win, say,
$100 or more will judge it to be risky since the probability
of winning that much is small. On the other hand, subjects
who are satisfied to win $70 will consider it to be riskless
since it guarantees that the aspiration level will be met.
This possibility was tested by running the experiment over
and asking subjects to say which lottery it would be more
risky to pay $100 to play (Lopes, 1984). Under this new
instructional set, most subjects agreed that 2c was, indeed,
the risker of the two.

Another possibility that researchers tend to overlook
is that aspiration levels may not always be set before the
choice set is known. Instead, they may be based on an
assessment of what is available. For example, a few years
back, Fryback, Goodman, and Edwards (1973) ran a study in
the Four Queens Casino in Las Vegas in which they tested the
hypothesis that people have preferences for absolute levels
of variance. To their surprise, they found that groups of
subjects choosing from different sets of gambles preferred
greatly different absolute levels of variance, but had
similar preferences for level of variance relative to their
respective stimulus sets. The authors concluded that
"concepts analogous to anchoring, adaptation, assimilation,
and contrast can no longer be ignored by any theory that
attempts to describe human decision making" (p. 278). I
certainly agree, but would add to the list aspiration level,
since it is likely that the subjects set their aspiration
levels only after seeing what outcomes were reasonably
likely to occur given the choice set. Indeed, it is hard to
imagine otherwise, since it would be quite maladaptive for
people not to bring their aspirations into line with the
continually shifting opportunities offered by the
environment.

<u>Proposition 4</u>:   Behaviors that seem anomalous from the expected utility perspective appear sensible when viewed as attempts by the decision maker to achieve goals.

The notion of aspiration level leads naturally to the view that decision making is a future-oriented activity, directed at the achievement of goals. When goals are ignored, however, or when they are captured only indirectly by theories that are inappropriate, human decision making can appear to be strange or even deficient in its rationality.

For example, consider Kahneman and Tversky's (1979) finding that people are ordinarily risk averse in the domain of gains and risk seeking in the domain of losses. This result, which they term the "reflection effect," deviates from the commonly accepted economic view that risk aversion ought to hold for both gains and losses (Arrow, 1971; Pratt, 1964). On the face of it, the economic viewpoint seems apt. After all, what is the sense of avoiding risk in the relatively benign domain of gains and then seeking it in the more perilous domain of losses?

Kahneman and Tversky (1979) answer this question by suggesting that people respond to <u>changes</u> in assets rather than to final asset positions. This corresponds to the theoretical proposal that people have a value function that is concave for gains and convex for losses, sort of a psychophysical function for absolute magnitudes of change. This is certainly sensible psychologically. But I lean toward Allais' (1952/1979, p. 55) view that distributional factors exert greater influence on choices involving risk than do nonlinearities in either the functions for subjective value or subjective probability.

To illustrate, consider again the subject whose preferences were described earlier. Of the lotteries in Figure 2, she preferred <u>2c</u> because it guaranteed the higher minimum while also offering the possibility of a higher maximum. When the prizes were changed to losses, however, her preferences switched: "I'd choose [2b]. I couldn't lose as much as in [2c] and I might lose quite a bit less. (Although I realize [2b] gives a greater chance of losing more than $100.)"

Her preferences did not, however, always switch. For example, of the lotteries in Figure 1, she preferred <u>1b</u> since it gave her a better chance of winning a worthwhile

amount. When the gains were changed to losses, she stuck by
her original preference ordering, saying "I'd choose [1b].
I'd lose a fair amount most likely, but not nearly as much
as I might lose on [1a]. In [1a] I have approximatedly a 1
in 3 chance of losing more than $130."

What is most important here is that the subject's
statements do not suggest different attitudes toward risk
for the domains of loss and gain, nor do they support the
premise that the reflectance effect constitutes a curious,
but unintended, byproduct of the way that people think about
magnitudes. Instead, the switches in preference seem to
come about, when they do, as an expression of the same goal-
directed mechanisms that the subject used for evaluating
positive risks.

Another seeming instance of irrational behavior under
risk concerns subsistence farmers with limited land holdings
who must decide what proportions of their land to devote to
food crops (which generally have lower expected return and
also lower variance of return) and to cash crops (which
generally have higher expected return as well as higher
variance). According to conventional wisdom, the smaller
the farmer, the larger should be the proportion of land
devoted to the "less risky" crop. However, Kunreuther and
Wright (1979) showed that "in many cases, farmers with the
smallest holdings of land plant a larger percentage of their
land with cash crops than those with somewhat larger farms,
often a percentage comparable to that of the very largest
enterprises" (p. 215). Why are these poor farmers willing
to gamble?

Kunreuther and Wright suggest that the nonmonotonicity
occurs because farmers use a lexicographic preference order
for processing risks. Thus, a farmer may wish to maximize
expected return, but he must first satisfy the minimum
requirement of being able to plan on feeding his family.
This requirement is easily met by the high income farmer who
can, therefore, afford to plant lots of the cash crop. The
middle income farmer can also meet the requirement, but only
at the expense of planting less of the cash crop and,
thereby, sacrificing some degree of expected return. For
the poor farmer, however, there is no plan that guarantees
satisfaction of the requirement even if nothing but food
crops are planted. Thus, he must accept an objectively
higher level of risk and grow more of the cash crop.

The farmer's situation is like that of the traveler
described by Allais (1952/1979) who winds up in Marseilles

low in funds and must, at all costs, get back to Paris. This circumstance constrains him to accept whatever gamble offers the greatest chance of winning the price of a ticket. Although one might rationalize the behavior of either the farmer or the traveler within the expected utility model by supposing that the utility function is distorted in the region of these critical requirements, the maneuver seems quite unnecessary in light of the fact that the person has, on the odds alone, taken the proper course of action.

Explanation and Insight

Expected utility theory has assumed many forms since being enunciated by Bernoulli. But one element has remained constant, the view that decision making under risk can be adequately characterized as a process of maximizing a measure that is analogous to mathematical expectation. The alternative view, expressed originally by Allais (1952/1979), is that such a single measure is insufficient for this purpose. Instead, the most critical element is "the dispersion (i.e., the second-order moment) and, generally,...the overall shape of the probability distribution of psychological values" (p. 33).

The lines between these positions have been drawn for more than 30 years, but one can hardly say that the debate has since raged. In psychology, at least, the neo-Bernoullian "American school" has dominated research not only in terms of the constructs and processes that are presumed to underlie risky choice, but also in terms of the implicit norms for rationality that are imposed on the decision maker. This is a pity because the views of the "French school" constitute what is necessary to good science, a viable alternative hypothesis.

If, however, the two viewpoints constitute competing hypotheses, the question arises as to what data can distinguish between them. Probably preferences will not, as is so cogently illustrated by the recent flowering of modifications to the neo-Bernoullian model that rationalize the behavior of subjects in the Allais paradox (cf. Kahneman & Tversky, 1979; Machina, 1982). To the extent, however, that self-reports given by subjects are taken as data, the theories can be distinguished, for they are theories not only about the final behavior in a choice task, but also theories about people's underlying representations

of risks, their goals in risky settings, and the procedures
they use for meeting these goals.

No self-report of risky choice is better known than
Savage's (1954) response to Allais' survey.   Unfortunately,
Savage set a bad precedent in how to deal with introspective
data, for when his intuitions failed to confirm his theory,
he simply changed the intuitions. Altering data to fit a
theory is ordinarily frowned on by scientists, but something
similar tends to be done with self-reports given by naive
subjects in risky decision tasks. This is to assume that
subjects deviate from the neo-Bernoullian ideal because they
are confused and overwhelmed by the difficulty of the task
and   the   inadequacy   of   their information processing
capacities.

Such interpretations are not bourne out by the self-
reports. Subjects do not hem and haw, they do not struggle
and grope.   On the contrary, they ordinarily produce
reasoned accounts that, although they may deviate from the
neo-Bernoullian norms,   accord   with other   intuitively
acceptable objectives.   To me, at least, the conclusion
seems inescapable that experimenters schooled in   the
American viewpoint are listening to their subjects in the
wrong theoretical language, for the subjects appear to be
speaking French.

Department of Psychology
University of Wisconsin

References

Allais, M. (1979a). The foundations of a positive theory
    of choice involving risk and a criticism of the
    postulates and axioms of the American School. In M.
    Allais & O. Hagen (Eds.), Expected utility hypotheses
    and the Allais Paradox (pp.   27-145).   Dordrecht,
    Holland: Reidel. (Original work published 1952)
Arrow, K. J. (1971). Essays in the theory of risk-bearing.
    Chicago: Markham.
Atkinson, A. B. (1975).   The economics of inequality.
    Oxford: Clarendon Press.
Coombs, C. H., & Huang, L.   (1970a).   Polynomial
    psychophysics of risk.   Journal of Mathematical

Psychology, 7, 317-338.

Coombs, C. H., & Huang, L. (1970b). Tests of a portfolio theory of risk preference. Journal of Experimental Psychology, 85, 23-29.

Coombs, C. H., & Lehner, P. E. (1981). Evaluation of two alternative models of a theory of risk: I. Are moments of distributions useful in assessing risk? Journal of Experimental Psychology: Human Perception and Performance, 7, 1110-1123.

Davidson, D., Suppes, P., & Siegel, S. (1957). Decision-making: An experimental approach. Palo Alto: Stanford University.

Edwards, W. (1953). Probability-preferences in gambling. American Journal of Psychology, 66, 349-364.

Edwards, W. (1954a). Probability-preferences among bets with differing expected values. American Journal of Psychology, 67, 56-67.

Edwards, W. (1954b). The reliability of probability preferences. American Journal of Psychology, 67, 68-95.

Edwards, W. (1954c). Variance preferences in gambling. American Journal of Psychology, 67, 441-452.

Fryback, D. G., Goodman, B. C., & Edwards, W. (1973). Choices among bets by Las Vegas gamblers: Absolute and contextual effects. Journal of Experimental Psychology, 98, 271-278.

Hagen, O. (1969). Separation of cardinal utility and specific utility of risk in theory of choices under uncertainty. Saertrykk av Statsokonomisk Tidsskrift, 3, 81-107.

Hagen, O. (1979). Towards a positive theory of preferences under risk. In M. Allais & O. Hagen (Eds.), Expected utility hypotheses and the Allais paradox (pp. 271-302). Dordrecht, Holland: Reidel.

Kahneman, D., & Tversky, A. (1979). Prospect theory: An analysis of decision under risk. Econometrica, 47, 263-291.

Kunreuther, H., & Wright, G. (1979). Safety-first, gambling, and the subsistence farmer. In J. A. Roumasset, J.-M. Boussard, & I. Singh (Eds.), Risk, uncertainty, and agricultural development (pp. 213-230). New York: Agricultural Development Council.

Laughhunn, D. J., Payne, J. W., & Crum, R. (1980). Managerial risk preferences for below-target returns. Management Science, 26, 1238-1249.

Lichtenstein, S., & Slovic, P.   (1971).   Reversals of
    preference between bids and   choices   in gambling
    decisions. Journal of Experimental Psychology, 89, 46-
    55.
Lichtenstein, S., & Slovic, P.   (1973).   Response-induced
    reversals of preference in gambling: An extended
    replication in Las Vegas.   Journal of Experimental
    Psychology, 101, 16-20.
Lopes, L. L.   (1984). Risk and distributional inequality.
    Journal of Experimental Psychology: Human Perception
    and Performance, 10, 465-485.
Luce, R. D.   (1980).   Several possible measures of risk.
    Theory and Decision 12, 217-228.
Machina, M.   J.   (1982). "Expected utility" analysis
    without the independence axiom. Econometrica, 50, 277-
    323.
Mao, J. C. T. (1970). Survey of capital budgeting: Theory
    and practice. Journal of Finance, 25, 349-360.
Mosteller, F., & Nogee, P.   (1951).   An experimental
    measurement of utility. Journal of Political Economy,
    59, 371-404.
Payne, J. W., Laughhunn, D. J., & Crum, R.   (1980).
    Translation of gambles and aspiration level effects in
    risky choice behavior. Management Science, 26, 1039-
    1060.
Pollatsek, A., & Tversky, A.   (1970). A theory of risk.
    Journal of Mathematical Psychology, 7, 540-553.
Pratt, J. W. (1964). Risk aversion in the small and in
    the large. Econometrica, 32, 122-135.
Rawls, J. (1971). A theory of justice. Cambridge, MA:
    Belknap.
Savage, L. J. (1954). The foundations of statistics. New
    York: Wiley.
Slovic, P., Fischhoff, B., & Lichtenstein, S. (1977).
    Behavioral decision theory.   Annual   Review   of
    Psychology, 28, 1-39.
Slovic, P., & Lichtenstein, S. (1968). Relative importance
    of probabilities and payoffs in risk taking. Journal
    of Experimental Psychology Monograph, 78(3, Pt. 2).
von Neumann, J. & Morgenstern, O. (1947). Theory of games
    and economic behavior.   (2nd ed.).   Princeton:
    Princeton University.

Aldo Montesano

A MEASURE OF RISK AVERSION IN
TERMS OF PREFERENCES

1. Introduction

The measure of risk aversion is usually given by the Arrow-Pratt index, which is referred to the neo-Bernoullian utility. But a more general measure is necessary if we accept that a preference model can be considered without assuming, for instance, the independence axiom. A new index of risk aversion is proposed in this paper. It requires only the existence of a certainty equivalent for each action. This index turns out to be zero when the von Neumann-Morgenstern axioms hold and its derivative to be proportional to the Arrow-Pratt index.

It is also shown that the measure of risk aversion can be positive if the von Neumann-Morgenstern axioms are not all assumed.

2. The Measure of Risk Aversion in
Terms of Preferences

The Arrow-Pratt measure of risk aversion (Pratt, 1964; Arrow 1965) is

$$r(c) = - \frac{U''_{NM}(c)}{U'_{NM}(c)}$$

where $c \varepsilon Re^+$ is normally defined as agent's wealth and U_{NM} is the von Neumann-Morgenstern utility index, the existence of which is obviously assumed. Now the measure of risk aversion can be defined without assuming that all the preference axioms of the von Neumann-Morgestern theory hold, but only assuming that the preference model $\langle A, R \rangle$ (where A is the set of actions and R is a preference system on the actions) admits, for any action with two possible consequences, a certainty equivalent, i.e., a

327

L. Daboni et al. (eds.), Recent Developments in the Foundations of Utility and Risk Theory, 327–335.
© *1986 by D. Reidel Publishing Company.*

consequence x which is indifferent to the action. In this case, for any action with the possible consequences c_1 and c_2

$$a(c) = \begin{cases} p & \text{for } c = c_1 \\ 1 - p & \text{for } c = c_2 \end{cases}$$

we can draw (see Fig. 1) the curve c_2SQ, which represents function $x(p)$, and we can define the ratio of area c_2SQ to area c_2c_1Q as the measure of risk aversion between c_1 and c_2.

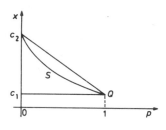

Fig. 1

That is, consequently,

$$\mu(c_1,c_2) = \frac{c_2 + c_1}{c_2 - c_1} - \frac{2}{c_2 - c_1} \int_0^1 x(p)dp.$$

A   positive   value of $\mu(c_1,c_2)$ means risk aversion while   a   negative value means   risk attraction. An equivalent   expression   of $\mu(c_1,c_2)$, when $x(p)$ is a decreasing function, is

$$\mu(c_1,c_2) = 1 - \frac{2}{c_2 - c_1} \int_{c_1}^{c_2} p(x)dx,$$

where $p(x)$ is the inverse function of $x(p)$.
      The   measure   of the local risk aversion in the point

c_1 can be defined considering the limit

$$\mu(c_1) = \lim_{c_2 \to c_1} \mu(c_1, c_2),$$

If this limit is zero, then we can consider the limit

$$\sigma(c_1) = \lim_{c_2 \to c_1} \frac{1}{c_2 - c_1} \mu(c_1, c_2),$$

which represents the velocity by which $\mu(c_1, c_2)$ tends to zero when c_2 approaches to c_1, i.e.,

$$\sigma(c_1) = \lim_{dc \to o} \frac{\mu(c_1, c_1 + dc)}{dc}.$$

3. The Risk Aversion Measure, when the von Neumann–Morgenstern Axioms Hold, and its Connection with the Arrow–Pratt Index

THEOREM 1. If the von Neumann-Morgenstern utility index exists, then $\mu(c_1)=0$ and

$$\sigma(c_1) = - \frac{1}{6} \frac{U''_{NM}(c_1)}{U'_{NM}(c_1)},$$

i.e., $\sigma(c_1)$ is proportional (by factor 1/6) to the Arrow-Pratt measure of local risk aversion.
Proof. Since

$$U_{NM}(x) = p(x)U_{NM}(c_1) + (1-p(x))U_{NM}(c_2),$$

i.e.,

$$p(x) = \frac{U_{NM}(c_2) - U_{NM}(x)}{U_{NM}(c_2) - U_{NM}(c_1)},$$

which is a continuously decreasing function of x, we have

$$\mu(c_1,c_2) = 1 - \frac{2}{c_2 - c_1} \frac{1}{U_{NM}(c_2)-U_{NM}(c_1)} \ x$$

$$x \ [(c_2-c_1) \ U_{NM}(c_2) - \int_{c_1}^{c_2} U_{NM}(x) \ dx].$$

Then, using l'Hospital's rule

$$\mu(c_1) = \lim_{c_2 \to c_1} \frac{-(c_2-c_1)(U_{NM}(c_2)+U_{NM}(c_1))+2\int_{c_1}^{c_2} U_{NM}(x)dx}{(c_2-c_1)(U_{NM}(c_2)-U_{NM}(c_1))} =$$

$$= \lim_{c_2 \to c_1} \frac{U_{NM}(c_2)-U_{NM}(c_1)-(c_2-c_1)U'_{NM}(c_2)}{U_{NM}(c_2)-U_{NM}(c_1)+(c_2-c_1)U'_{NM}(c_2)} =$$

$$= \lim_{c_2 \to c_1} \frac{-(c_2-c_1)U''_{NM}(c_2)}{2U'_{NM}(c_2)+(c_2-c_1)U''_{NM}(c_2)} = 0$$

and

$$\sigma(c_1) = \lim_{c_2 \to c_1} \frac{-(c_2-c_1)(U_{NM}(c_2)+U_{NM}(c_1))+2\int_{c_1}^{c_2} U_{NM}(x)dx}{(c_2-c_1)^2(U_{NM}(c_2)-U_{NM}(c_1))} =$$

$$= \lim_{c_2 \to c_1} \frac{U_{NM}(c_2)-U_{NM}(c_1)-(c_2-c_1)U'_{NM}(c_2)}{2(c_2-c_1)(U_{NM}(c_2)-U_{NM}(c_1))+(c_2-c_1)^2U'_{NM}(c_2)} =$$

$$= \lim_{c_2 \to c_1} \frac{-(c_2-c_1)U''_{NM}(c_2)}{2U_{NM}(c_2)-2U_{NM}(c_1)+4(c_2-c_1)U'_{NM}(c_2)+(c_2-c_1)^2U''_{NM}(c_2)}$$

$$= \lim_{c_2 \to c_1} \frac{-U''_{NM}(c_2)-(c_2-c_1)U'''_{NM}(c_2)}{6U'_{NM}(c_2)+6(c_2-c_1)U''_{NM}(c_2)+(c_2-c_1)^2U'''_{NM}(c_2)} =$$

$$= -\frac{1}{6}\frac{U''_{NM}(c_1)}{U'_{NM}(c_1)}$$

COROLLARY 2. If, instead of the von Neumann-Morgenstern index, another index of utility is used, the measure of local risk aversion is

$$\sigma(c_1) = -\frac{1}{6}\frac{U''_{NM}(c_1)}{U'_{NM}(c_1)} = -\frac{1}{6}\left(\frac{U''(c_1)}{U'(c_1)} + U'(c_1)\frac{F''(U)}{F'(U)}\right)$$

where the utility index U is such that $U_{NM} = F(U)$. Consequently, if $F''<0$ (and $F'>0$), we find $-U''(c_1)/U'(c_1)< -U''_{NM}(c_1)/U'_{NM}(c_1)$, without meaning any difference in risk aversion.

4.   The Risk Aversion Measure when the Independence
Axiom does not Hold

COROLLARY 3. If the preference model $<A,R>$ does not admit the von Neumann-Morgenstern index (for instance, since the independence axiom does not hold), then the measure of risk aversion $\mu(c_1,c_2)$ does not tend necessarily to zero when c_2 tends to c_1. (In this way Corollary 3 justifies Allais's opinion that the von Neumann-Morgenstern theory excludes risk aversion. See Allais (1979), pp. 597-598).

Example. Let us assume a preference model $<A,R>$ represented by the utility index

$$U(a) = \max \{\tfrac{1}{2}(M + U(c_m)), 2M - U(c_M)\},$$

where $M=\Sigma_{c\epsilon C}a(c)U(c)$, $c_m=\min\{c\epsilon Re^+:a(c)>0\}$ and $c_M=\max\{c\epsilon Re+: a(c)>0\}$. This preference model implies that the agent is influenced more by the less good consequences than by the better ones.

The preference model represented by this utility index does not obey the preference axioms of the von Neumann-Morgenstern theory. In particular, von Neumann-Morgenstern's axiom (3:B:a) (ee von Neumann-Morgenstern (1953), p. 26) is not satisfied exactly in the same manner as considered by Allais (1979): for instance, actions

$$a_1 = \begin{cases} 1/3 \text{ for } c = 1 \\ 2/3 \text{ for } c = 3 \end{cases} \qquad a_2 = \{1 \text{ for } c = 2$$

$$a_3 = \begin{cases} 1/2 \text{ for } a_1 \\ 1/2 \text{ for } a_2 \end{cases} \quad \text{i.e., } a_3 = \begin{cases} 1/6 \text{ for } c = 1 \\ 1/2 \text{ for } c = 2 \\ 1/3 \text{ for } c = 3 \end{cases}$$

have utilities $U(a_1)=2/3U(1)+1/3U(3)$, $U(a_2)=U(2)$ and $U(a_3) = \max \{1/12[7U(1)+3U(2)+2U(3), 1/3(U(1)+3U(2)-U(3)]\}$, so that, if $2U(1)+U(3)<3U(2)$ and $U(1)+2U(3)>3U(2)$, we find $U(a_2)>U(a_1)>U(a_3)$ while axiom (3:B:a) would require $U(a_1)<U(a_3)$. (The preceding condition is satisfied, for instance, by functions $U(c)=k+c$ and $U(c)=\log(k+c)$ for any $k\geq0$.)

Considering the measure of risk aversion for this preference model, the utility of the certainty equivalent for action

$$a(c) = \begin{cases} p \text{ for } c = c_1 \\ 1-p \text{ for } c = c_2, \end{cases}$$

where $c_2 > c_1$, is

$$U(x) = \max \left\{ \frac{1+p}{2} U(c_1) + \frac{1-p}{2} U(c_2), \quad 2pU(c_1)-(1-2p)U(c_2) \right\},$$

i.e.

$$U(x) = \begin{cases} 2pU(c_1) + (1-2p)U(c_2) \quad \text{for } 0\leq p\leq 1/3 \\[2mm] \dfrac{1+p}{2} U(c_1) + \dfrac{1-p}{2} U(c_2) \text{ for } 1/3\leq p\leq 1, \end{cases}$$

or

$$
p(x) = \begin{cases} \dfrac{U(c_1)+U(c_2)-2U(x)}{U(c_2)-U(c_1)} & \text{for } U(c_1) \le U(x) \le 2/3U(c_1)+1/3U(c_2) \\[2em] \dfrac{1}{2} \dfrac{U(c_2)-U(x)}{U(c_2)-U(c_1)} & \text{for } 2/3U(c_1)+1/3U(c_2) \le U(x) \le U(c_2). \end{cases}
$$

Since

$$
\frac{1-\mu(c_1)}{2} = \lim_{c_2 \to c_1} \frac{1}{c_2-c_1} \int_{c_1}^{c_2} p(x)dx,
$$

we find

$$
\frac{1-\mu(c_1)}{2} =
$$

$$
= \lim_{c_2 \to c_1} \frac{(U(c_1)+U(c_2))(\hat{c}-c_1)-2\int_{c_1}^{\hat{c}} U(x)dx+\tfrac{1}{2}U(c_2)(c_2-\hat{c})-\tfrac{1}{2}\int_{\hat{c}}^{c_2} U(x)dx}{(c_2-c_1)(U(c_2)-U(c_1))},
$$

where

$$
U(\hat{c}) = 2/3\ U(c_1) + 1/3U(c_2),
$$

thus with

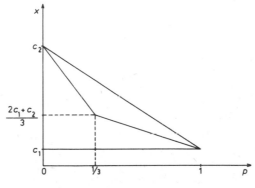

Fig. 2

$$U'(\hat{c}) \frac{d\hat{c}}{dc_2} = 1/3 \ U'(c_2).$$

Then we have

$$\frac{1-\mu(c_1)}{2} = \lim_{c_2 \to c_1} \frac{(\tfrac{1}{2}c_2+\tfrac{1}{2}\hat{c}-c_1)U'(c_2)}{U(c_2)+U(c_1)+(c_2-c_1)U'(c_2)} =$$

$$= \lim_{c_2 \to c_1} \frac{\left(\dfrac{1}{2} + \dfrac{1}{2}\dfrac{d\hat{c}}{dc_2}\right)U'(c_2)+(\tfrac{1}{2}c_2+\tfrac{1}{2}\hat{c}-c_1)U''(c_2)}{2U'(c_2)+(c_2-c_1)U''(c_2)}$$

and consequently

$$\frac{1-\mu(c_1)}{2} = \lim_{c_2 \to c_1} \frac{1}{4} + \frac{1}{4}\frac{d\hat{c}}{dc_2} = \frac{1}{3}$$

i.e., $\mu(c_1)=1/3$ for any smooth function $U(c)$. For instance, if $U(c)=c$, we have the function $x(p)$ of Figure 2, for which

$$\mu(c_1,c_2) = \frac{1}{c_2-c_1} \begin{vmatrix} 1 & c_1 & 1 \\ 0 & c_2 & 1 \\ \dfrac{1}{3} & \dfrac{2c_1+c_2}{3} & 1 \end{vmatrix} = \frac{1}{3}$$

University of Milan
Milan

REFERENCES

Allais, M.: 1979, "The So-Called Allais Paradox and Rational Decision under Uncertainty", in M. Allais and O. Hagen (eds.), Expected Utility Hypotheses and the Allais Paradox, D. Reidel, Dordrecht (Holland).
Arrow, K.J.: 1965, Aspects of the Theory of Risk Bearing,

Yrjo Jahnssonian Saatio, Helsinki.

von Neumann, J. and Morgenstern, O.: 1953, <u>Theory of Games and Economic Behavior</u>, 3rd ed., Princeton University Press, Princeton.

Pratt, J.W.: 1964, "Risk Aversion in the Small and in the Large", <u>Econometrica</u> 32, 122-135.

Gerald L. Nordquist

STATE-DEPENDENT UTILITY AND RISK AVERSION

1. Introduction

We consider here the problem of how to measure risk aversion in the case of state-dependent utility. As is now well recognized, to assume that an individual's utility function is state-dependent is warranted if not required in situations where decisions have uncertain consequences not only for income or wealth but for such things as life and health. Several studies have appeared in the past twenty years which have addressed the reasonableness of this assumption, probed its behavioral implications, and searched for a satisfactory axiomatization.[1] But there has been a noticeable gap in the literature dealing with risk aversion measures for state-dependent utility, analogous to those suggested by Arrow (1971) and Pratt (1964) for the case of state-independent preferences.

In a recent paper, Karni (1983) has shown that the family of strictly concave, state-dependent utility functions can be ordered by means of a risk aversion measure of the Arrow-Pratt type if the functions have the same "reference set". As defined by Karni, the reference set of a utility function is the subset of all points in the domain of expected utility for which the marginal utility of wealth is the same across states. When utility is independent of the state of nature, then the reference set for the utility function is simply the set of secure (sure) wealths. However if the utility function is state-dependent, then at least some the reference points thus defined will have payoffs that are not the same in all states.

The comparability condition suggested by Karni turns out to be fairly restrictive for important applications of the theory. One of the most interesting involves the irreplaceable loss of something of

337

L. Daboni et al. (eds.), Recent Developments in the Foundations of Utility and Risk Theory, 337–351.
© *1986 by D. Reidel Publishing Company.*

great significance, such as life and basic health. In matters so vital, we should not think it at all rare to find individuals for whom cross-state differences in the marginal utility of wealth are very large. Then the subset of wealths defined by the equal-marginal-utility condition is apt to be small, quite possibly empty. In these instances we might very well conclude that there is little or no basis for comparing the risk attitudes of individuals. But this is not necessarily so as we shall endeavor to reveal.

The purpose of this paper is to extend the development of risk aversion measures for state-dependent utility functions. We establish the existence of a class of utility functions that can be compared for risk attitude when the reference is to equal wealth in each and every state of nature. The condition that admits the comparability of two utility functions by means of the Arrow-Pratt concepts is equality in the marginal rate of substitution on the set of sure wealths. With this criterion, no special limits are placed on the curvature of the functions. We also examine measurablilty based on the equal marginal utility condition suggested by Karni and show that it is applicable to functions that are strictly convex in wealth as well as to those that are strictly concave. Finally, the relationship between the measures is studied. We prove that the sets of utility functions that are orderable by means of these two criteria have a nonempty intersection, but neither one is contained in the other.

2. Preliminaries

Suppose there are two states of nature indexed by s = 1, 2. Let X represent a gamble with payoff x_s (a scalar) and probability $P(X = x_s) = p_s$. A state-dependent utility function is a vector-valued function $U(x) = (u_1(x), u_2(x))$ which assigns the value $u_s(x)$ to each and every x in an interval I. Throughout it is assumed that $U(x)$ is strictly increasing and twice-continuously differentiable. The first- and second-order derivatives of U are denoted by $U'(x)$ and $U''(x)$, respectively. The state-dependent coefficient of risk aversion is also a vector-valued function of x: $R(x) = (r_1(x), r_2(x))$, where $r_s(x) = - u_s''(x)/u_s'(x)$. For the utility of a gamble X we write $E[U(X)] = p_1 u_1(x_1) + p_2 u_2(x_2)$, and if wealth is the same in both states, i.e. if $x_1 = x_2 = x$, we write $E[U(x)] = p_1 u_1(x) + p_2 u_2(x)$. Finally, we denote the vector of state probabilities as $p = (p_1, p_2)$.

Consider now a gamble $X = x + Z$ with payoff $x + z_s$ in state s. Assume that $E(Z) = 0$ so that $E(X) = x$. The risk premium π for utility function U is defined by the equation $E[U(x + Z)] = E[U(x - \pi)]$, or written out it is:

$$(1) \quad p_1 u_1(x + z_1) + p_2 u_2(x + z_2) = p_1 u_1(x - \pi) + p_2 u_2(x - \pi),$$

where we understand that both $x + z_s$ and $x - \pi$ are in the interval I. After expanding both sides of (1) and solving we get:

$$(2) \quad \pi(x, Z, p) = p_1 z_1 \left[\frac{-(u_1'(x) - u_2'(x))}{p_1 u_1'(x + \mu_1) + p_2 u_2'(x + \mu_2)} \right]$$

$$+ \frac{1}{2} \frac{p_1}{p_2} z_1^2 \left[\frac{-(p_2 u_1''(x + \nu_1) + p_1 u_2''(x + \nu_2))}{p_1 u_1'(x + \mu_1) + p_2 u_2'(x + \mu_2)} \right],$$

where $x + \mu_s$ and $x + \nu_s$ are in the interval $[x, x + z_s]$, and where we have made use of $E(Z) = 0$. For small gambles we can use the mean $E(X) = x$ to get an approximate value for π:

$$(3) \quad \pi(x, Z, p) \approx p_1 z_1 \left[\frac{- (u_1'(x) - u_2'(x))}{E[U'(x)]} \right]$$

$$+ \frac{1}{2} \frac{p_1}{p_2} z_1^2 \left[\frac{- (p_2 u_1''(x) + p_1 u_2''(x))}{E[U'(x)]} \right].$$

From (3) it is evident that when utility is state-dependent the simple proportionality found in the state-independent case between the risk premium and the coefficient of absolute risk aversion does not hold. The aversion to risk implied by a state-dependent utility function U does involve the ratio of first- and second-order derivatives of u_s at a point x, but the ratio turns out to be $- u_s''(x)/E[U'(x)]$ rather than $- u_s''(x)/u_s'(x)$ as might have been anticipated. Moreover, the risk premium π contains an additional part with coefficient $- (u_1'(x) - u_2'(x))/E[U'(x)]$, which reflects the separate influence of the cross-state difference in the marginal utility of wealth. Of course this term vanishes identically when utility is state-independent. But in the case of state dependence it is not zero everywhere, and its presence in the risk premium is more than a little troublesome. For one thing, π is not necessarily zero if $u_s''(x) = 0$ for both $s = 1$ and $s = 2$ in some neighborhood. For another, π is no longer invariant to a symmetric switch in a gamble from $x + Z$ to $x - Z$.

3. Comparative Risk Aversion with Reference to Secure Wealth

In this section we show that a simple and natural restriction on cross-state marginal utilities permits global comparisons of risk attitudes when the reference point for a gamble is secure wealth. We will make use of the following two definitions:

DEFINITION 1. Two state-dependent utility functions U(x) and V(x) are said to be <u>risk-aversion comparable</u> on interval I if $u_1'(x)/u_2'(x) = v_1'(x)/v_2'(x)$ for all x in I.

DEFINITION 2. Let U(x) and V(x) be two comparable utility functions in the sense of Definition 1, and let $\pi^U(x, Z, p)$ and $\pi^V(x, Z, p)$ be the associated risk premiums. Then U is said to be <u>more risk averse</u> than V if, and only if, $\pi^U(x, Z, p) \geq \pi^V(x, Z, p)$ for all x, Z, and p.

The following two lemmas are used in the proof of Theorem 1.

LEMMA 1. <u>Let U and V be two comparable state-dependent utility functions according to Definition 1. Then</u> $(u_1'(x) - u_2'(x))/E[U'(x)] = (v_1'(x) - v_2'(x))/E[V'(x)]$ <u>for all</u> x <u>and</u> p.

PROOF: Note that the first term in the squared brackets on the RHS of (3) can be written for h = u, v as:

$$(4) \quad \frac{h_1'(x) - h_2'(x)}{p_1 h_1'(x) + p_2 h_2'(x)} = \left[\frac{h_1'(x)}{h_2'(x)} - 1\right] \cdot \left[p_1 \frac{h_1'(x)}{h_2'(x)} + p_2\right]^{-1}.$$

Since comparison of U and V requires $u_1'(x)/u_2'(x) = v_1'(x)/v_2'(x)$, the conclusion follows immediately upon substitution into (4).

LEMMA 2. <u>Let U and V be comparable state-dependent utility functions in the sense of Definition 1. Then</u> $r_1^U(x) - r_1^V(x) = r_2^U(x) - r_2^V(x)$ <u>for all</u> x.

PROOF: The comparability condition of Definition 1 can be expressed as $-(\ln u_1'(x) - \ln v_1'(x)) = -(\ln u_2'(x) - \ln v_2'(x))$. Differentiation of both sides of this equation yields:

$$(5) \quad -\left[\frac{u_1''(x)}{u_1'(x)} - \frac{v_1''(x)}{v_1'(x)}\right] = -\left[\frac{u_2''(x)}{u_2'(x)} - \frac{v_2''(x)}{v_2'(x)}\right],$$

which is the claimed result.

THEOREM 1. <u>Let U and V be comparable utility functions according to Definition 1. Then the following conditions are equivalent:</u>

(i) $R^U(x) \geq R^V(x)$ <u>for all</u> x.

(ii)   <u>There exists a strictly increasing, concave function</u> ϕ <u>such that</u> $\phi\{E[V(x)]\} = E[U(x)]$ <u>for all</u> x <u>and</u> p.

(iii) $\pi^U(x, Z, p) \geq \pi^V(x, Z, p)$ <u>for all</u> x, Z, <u>and</u> p.

PROOF: (i) $\Longrightarrow$ (ii). By hypothesis the functions U and V are strictly increasing in x, therefore so are the functions $E[U(x)]$ and $E[V(x)]$. Thus both E(U) and E(V) have inverses, and there exists a function $\phi = E[U\{E(V)^{-1}\}]$ such that $E[U(x)] = \phi\{[V(x)]\}$. Next we show that ϕ is strictly increasing and concave in x. After differentiating $\phi\{\cdot\}$, and making use of the comparability condition and Lemma 2 we derive:

$$(6) \quad \phi'\{E[V(x)]\} = \frac{E[U'(x)]}{E[V'(x)]}$$

$$= \frac{u_1'(x)}{v_1'(x)} \left[\frac{p_1 + p_2 \dfrac{u_2'(x)}{u_1'(x)}}{p_1 + p_2 \dfrac{v_2'(x)}{v_1'(x)}} \right] = \frac{u_1'(x)}{v_1'(x)} = \frac{u_2'(x)}{v_2'(x)}.$$

In (6) it is clear that $\phi'\{\cdot\}$ is positive since we have assumed that U and V are strictly increasing. Note also that the value of ϕ is independent of p. Next, differentiate $- \ln \phi'\{\cdot\}$ to obtain:

$$(7) \quad - \frac{\phi''\{\cdot\}}{\phi'\{\cdot\}} E[V'(x)] = - \left[\frac{u_s''(x)}{u_s'(x)} - \frac{v_s''(x)}{v_s'(x)} \right],$$

for s = 1, 2. But from (i), $- u_s''(x)/u_s'(x) \geq - v_s''(x)/v_s'(x)$, so (7) is nonnegative. Therefore, $\phi''\{\cdot\} \leq 0$ as claimed.

(ii) $\Longrightarrow$ (iii). Since ϕ is concave in its argument, then for any gamble x + Z where E(Z) = 0 we find $E\{\phi[V(x + Z)]\} \leq \phi\{E[V(x + Z)]\}$ by Jensen's inequality. Also for p = (1, 0) and p = (0, 1) we must have, respectively, $u_1(x + z_1) = \phi[v_1(x + z_1)]$ and $u_2(x + z_2) = \phi[v_2(x + z_2)]$. Then from the last statement we find $E[U(x + Z)] = E\{\phi[V(x + Z)]\}$, and thus:

$$E[U(x - \pi^U)] = E[U(x + Z)] = E\{\phi[V(x + Z)]\}$$

$$\leq \phi\{E[V(x + Z)]\} = \phi\{E[V(x - \pi^V)]\} = E[U(x - \overset{V}{\pi})].$$

Since $E(U)$ is strictly increasing in x, we conclude $\pi^U(x, Z, p) \geq \pi^V(x, Z, p)$ for all x, Z, and p.

(iii)$\Longrightarrow$(i). Suppose not. Then by Lemma 2 there exists an x in the domain of U and V such that $r_s^U(x) < r_s^V(x)$ for s = 1, 2. From (2) we find that the difference between π^U and π^V for any gamble x + Z can be written as:

$$(8) \quad \pi^U - \pi^V = p_1 z_1 \left[\frac{-(u_1'(x) - u_2'(x))}{E[U'(x + M^U)]} - \frac{-(v_1'(x) - v_2'(x))}{E[V'(x + M^V)]} \right]$$

$$+ \frac{1}{2} \frac{p_1}{p_2} z_1^2 \left\{ - \left[\frac{p_2 u_1''(x + v_1^U) + p_1 u_2''(x + v_2^U)}{E[U'(x + M^U)]} \right] \right.$$

$$\left. - \left[\frac{p_2 v_1''(x + v_1^V) + p_1 v_2''(x + v_2^V)}{E[V'(x + M^V)]} \right] \right\},$$

where $M^i = (\mu_1^i, \mu_2^i)$ for i = U, V, and $x + \mu_s^i$ and $x + v_s^i$ are in the interval $[x, x + z_s]$, s = 1,2. If $z_1 = 0$, then the first-order term in the squared brackets on the RHS of (8) is equal to $(u_1'(x) - u_2'(x))/ E[U'(x)] - (v_1'(x) - v_2'(x))/E[V'(x)]$, which is identically zero by application of Lemma 1. Also, by making use of the comparability condition and Lemma 2 we find that the second-order term in the braces can be written as:

$$(9) \quad (r_s^U(x) - r_s^V(x)) \left\{ \left[\frac{p_2}{p_1 + p_2 \frac{u_2'(x)}{u_1'(x)}} + \frac{p_1}{p_1 \frac{u_1'(x)}{u_2'(x)} + p_2} \right] \right\},$$

for s = 1, 2 if $z_1 = 0$. The functions r_s^U, r_s^V, u_2'/u_1' and $[u_2'/u_1']^{-1}$ are continuous, since U and V are assumed to be twice-continuously differentiable functions. Note that the terms in the squared brackets of (9) are never negative, and at least one of them is positive for any p. Then $r_s^U(x) < r_s^V(x)$ implies that (9) is definitely negative. Therefore by continuity there exists some $z_1 \neq 0$ such that (8) is definitely negative, which is a contradiction. Q.E.D.

It should be evident also that Theorem 1 has the effect of limiting the comparisons of risk aversion to individuals who have the same _ordinal_ preferences for wealth across states. Observe that Condition (ii) asserts the existence of a monotone increasing function $E(U) = \phi[E(V)]$. Since this transformation holds for all p, it must hold in the particular cases of p = (1, 0) and p = (0, 1). Thus, $u_s(x) = \phi[v_s(x)]$ for s = 1, 2, and it is clear that U and V are equivalent ordinal representations. This finding should come as no great surprise. The restriction is very natural, and it has been found to be useful in other extensions of Arrow-Pratt theory.[2]

4. Comparative Risk Aversion with Reference to Equal Marginal Utility

We turn now to an examination of the comparability criterion proposed by Kárni, based on equal marginal utility of wealth in each state of nature. In the process we show that the class of utility functions which can be ranked by this criterion includes those that are strictly convex as well as those that are strictly concave (Karni's assumption).

Let U be a state-dependent utility function defined on an interval I, and let $D = I^2$ be the domain of expected utility. Now consider the subset of D for which the marginal utility of wealth in state 1 is equal to the marginal utility of wealth in state 2, i.e. we focus our attention on the set $\tilde{X} = \{(x_1, x_2) \in D: u_1'(x_1) = u_2'(x_2)\}$. Of course, this set may be empty for any given utility function. A simple example is provided by: $U(x) = (ax + 2x^{\frac{1}{2}}, ax + c)$ defined on $(0, +\infty)$, where a and c are constants. Then marginal utility is $U'(x) = (a + x^{-\frac{1}{2}}, a)$, and it is readily apparent that $\tilde{X} = \emptyset$ since there is no point in D such that $u_1'(x_1) = u_2'(x_2)$.

Suppose, however, that we have picked a function U such that $\tilde{X}$ is not empty. Assume also that U is strictly concave or strictly convex. Then U has an inverse, and we can express the equal marginal utility condition as: $x_1 = [u_1']^{-1}[u_2'(x_2)] = g(x_2)$. The function $g(x_2)$ is strictly increasing since $g'(x_2) = u_2''(x_2)/u_1''(g(x_2))$ is positive for all x^2. Thus the reference set for state-dependent utility function U can be expressed as $\tilde{X} = \{(x_1, x_2) \in D: x_1 = g(x_2), g' > 0\}$. Note that the vector-values of utility and the coefficient of risk aversion for any point $(x_1, x_2) \in \tilde{X}$ are, respectively, $U(x_2) = [u_1(g(x_2)), u_2(x_2)]$ and $R(x_2) = [r_1(g(x_2)), r_2(x_2)]$.

Next, let $\tilde{X} + Z$ be a gamble with payoff $g(x_2) + z_1$ in state 1 and $x_2 + z_2$ in state 2. For utility function U, the risk premium for this gamble is defined by:

$$(10) \quad p_1 u_1(g(x_2) + z_1) + p_2 u_2(x_2 + z_2) = p_1 u_1(g(x_2) - \pi) + p_2 u_2(x_2 - \pi).$$

Expansion of both sides of (10) with respect to x_2 yields an approximate value for the risk premium of a small gamble:

$$(11) \quad \pi(x_2, Z, p) \approx p_1 z_1 \left[\frac{-(u_1'(g(x_2)) - u_2'(x_2))}{p_1 u_1'(g(x_2))g'(x_2) + p_2 u_2'(x_2)} \right]$$

$$+ \frac{1}{2} \frac{p_1}{p_2} z_1^2 \left[\frac{-(p_2 u_1''(g(x_2)) + p_2 u_2''(x_2))}{p_1 u_1'(g(x_2))g'(x_2) + p_2 u_2'(x_2)} \right],$$

where as before we have used $E(Z) = 0$.

Observe that the first-order term in (11) is equal to zero for all x_2, Z, and p, since the numerator of the expression in the squared brackets is identically zero because of the equal-marginal-utility restriction. Then the (approximate) value of the risk premium for any gamble $X = \tilde{X} + Z$, and for a small Z, depends entirely on the second-order term in (11). It is also clear from an examination of this term why we must ensure that $g(x_2)$ is strictly increasing: if $g'(x_2) \leq 0$ for some x_2, then there exists a vector of probabilities p such that the risk premium is not defined.

Consider once again the comparability of two utilty functions U and V. The following definitions are parallel to those in Section 3:

DEFINITION 3. Two state-dependent utility functions U and V are said to be risk-aversion comparable if the reference sets $\tilde{X}^U$ and $\tilde{X}^V$ are non-empty, and $\tilde{X}^U = \tilde{X}^V$.

DEFINITION 4. Let U and V be two comparable state-dependent utility functions in the sense of Definition 3. Let $\pi^U(x_2, Z, p)$ and $\pi^V(x_2, Z, p)$ be the associated risk premiums. Then U is said to be more risk averse than V if, and only if, $\pi^U(x_2, Z, p) \geq \pi^V(x_2, Z, p)$ for all x_2, Z, and p.

The following theorem is a restatement of Theorem 1 in Karni (1983). Our only departure is to point out that the proposition holds for strictly convex as well as for strictly concave utility functions, since the proof merely requires that the function $g(x_2)$ be strictly increasing.

THEOREM 2. Let U and V be two comparable state-dependent utility functions in the sense of Definition 3. Then the following conditions are equivalent:

(i) $R^U(x_2) \geq R^V(x_2)$ for all x_2.

(ii)   There exists a strictly increasing, concave function ϕ

such that $\phi[p_1 v_1(g(x_2)) + p_2 v_2(x_2)] = p_1 u_1(g(x_2)) +$

$p_2 u_2(x_2)$ for all x_2, Z, and p.

(iii) $\pi^U(x_2, Z, p) \geq \pi^V(x_2, Z, p)$ for all x_2, Z, and p.

We remark in passing that the comparability condition of Theorem 2, like that of Theorem 1, implies that individuals have identical ordinal preferences for wealth. Simply note that this is guaranteed by the requirement of an equal and constant marginal rate of substitution for each and every point in the reference set $\tilde{X}$.

5. Risk Aversion Measures Compared

Here we address the question of the relationship between the measures of risk aversion proposed in Sections 1 and 2. We will refer to the comparability restrictions of Theorems 1 and 2 as RAC1 and RAC2, respectively. Also let C_R^1 and C_R^2 denote the sets of utility functions that are orderable on the basis of Theorems 1 and 2. The next proposition establishes the fact that C_R^1 and C_R^2 are noncomparable, nondisjoint sets.

THEOREM 3. Let C_R^1 and C_R^2 be two sets of state-dependent utility functions ordered by Theorems 1 and 2, respectively. Then:

(a) $C_R^1 \not\subset C_R^2$; (b) $C_R^2 \not\subset C_R^1$; (c) $C_R^1 \cap C_R^2 \neq \emptyset$.

PROOF: (a) Recall the example given in Section 4. There we considered a utility function $U(x)$ defined on $(0, +\infty)$, with marginal utility $U'(x) = (a + x^{-\frac{1}{2}}, a)$. Clearly, RAC2 is not satisfied anywhere on the interval, so U is not in C_R^2. Now let $V(x)$ be a utility function defined on the same interval, with $V'(x) = (x, ax/(a + x^{-\frac{1}{2}}))$. Then $u_1'/u_2' = v_1'/v_2'$ for all x. Therefore RAC1 is satisfied, so U and V are in C_R^1.

(b) Let $U(x)$ and $V(x)$ be defined on an interval I, and suppose that $U'(x) = [\psi'(x) + b, \psi'(x)]$ and $V'(x) = [\psi'(x), \psi'(x) - b]$, where $\psi''(x) < 0$ for all x, and $b > 0$. Since $\psi'(x)$ is strictly decreasing, there exists some sufficiently small, nonzero value for b such that the sets $\tilde{X}^U$ and $\tilde{X}^V$ are not empty. Moreover it is clear that $\tilde{X}^U = \tilde{X}^V$. Thus RAC2 is satisfied, so U and V are in C_R^2. Next, observe that for $x_1 = x_2 = x$ we have $u_1'/u_2' = (\psi'(x) + b)/\psi'(x)$ and $v_1'/v_2' = \psi'(x)/(\psi'(x) - b)$ for all x. But $u_1'/u_2' = v_1'/v_2'$ only if $b = 0$. Thus RAC1 is not satisfied, so U and V are not in C_R^1.

(c) Let $U(x)$ and $V(x)$ be strictly concave functions on an interval I, with $u_1'(x)/u_2'(x) = v_1'(x)/v_2'(x) = 1$ for all x. Thus RAC1 is satified, so U and V are in C_R^1. Now set $x = x_1 = x_2$, and we have $u_1'(x_1) = u_2'(x_2)$ and $v_1'(x_1) = v_2'(x_2)$. But these are just the defining equations for RAC2, and we find $\tilde{X}^U = \tilde{X}^V = \{(x_1, x_2) \varepsilon D : x_1 = x_2\}$, which is not empty. Hence U and V are also in C_R^2. Q.E.D.

6. Conclusions

Equal wealth and equal marginal utility of wealth across states are natural points of reference for determining and comparing individual attitudes towards gambles. If utility is independent of the state, then these reference points coincide, since the equal-marginal-utility condition is satisfied on the set of sure wealths. But the coincidence fails when tastes are state-dependent. Karni's (1983) suggestion that we choose reference points defined by equal marginal utilities does provide a basis for such comparisons. But as we have pointed out, the basis may be very narrow, especially if we want to compare utility functions characterized by sizeable differences in cross-state marginal utilities.

The purpose of this paper has been to show that there are other grounds for comparing state-dependent risk attitudes. Theorem 1 establishes comparability on the set of sure wealths, assuming that the stipulated restriction on the marginal rate of substitution is satisfied. Comparability in this sense requires no prior restrictions on the concavity of these functions. We also examine Karni's comparability theorem and find that it is extendable to the class of strictly convex utility functions. It is demonstrated that neither of these propositions is implied by the other. However, both are properly regarded as generalizations of the Arrow-Pratt theory, since they both contain state-independent preferences as a special case.

This study also points up the affinity of these and other extentions of the classic measures of risk aversion contained in the literature, such as to the case of state-independent utility with many commodities. We find that the common prerequisite for comparability is that decision makers have the same ordinal preferences on the space of goods.

Department of Economics
University of Iowa

NOTES

1. For applications of the theory, see Eisner and Strotz (1961), Hirshleifer (1965; 1966), Parkin and Wu (1972), Arrow (1974), Cook and Graham (1977), and Jones-Lee (1976). For recent axiomatic treatments of state-dependent utility with subjective probabilities, see Jones-Lee (1979), and Karni, Schmeidler and Vind (1983). Excellent general discussions of this theory can be found in Arrow (1974), Drèze (1974), and Hirshleifer and Riley (1979).

2. As has been known for some time, the generalization of Arrow-Pratt to the case where utility is a function of a vector of commodities becomes possible if the individuals being compared have the same preference field. See, for example, Kihlstrom and Mirman (1974), and Levy and Levy (1984). What we have shown here is that this restriction on the preorders has an analogue in the case of state-dependent utility functions.

REFERENCES

Arrow, K. J., Essays in the Theory of Risk Bearing (Chicago, Markham, 1971).

Arrow, K. J., "Optimal Insurance and Generalized Deductibles," Scandinavian Actuarial Journal 1 (1974), 1-42.

Cook, P. J. and D. A. Graham, "The Demand for Insurance and Protection: The Case of Irreplaceable Commodities," Quarterly Journal of Economics, 91 (February, 1977), 143-156.

Drèze, J. H., "Axiomatic Theories of Choice, Cardinal Utility and Subjective Probability: A Review," in Allocation Under Uncertainty: Equilibrim and Optimality, ed. J. H. Drèze (New York - Toronto, John Wiley and Sons, 1974.

Eisner, R. and R. Strotz, "Flight Insurance and the Theory of Choice," Journal of Political Economy, 69 (August, 1961), 355-368.

Hirshleifer, J., "Investment Decisions Under Uncertainty," Quarterly Journal of Economics, 79 (November, 1965), 509-536, and 80 (May, 1966), 252-277.

Hirshleifer, J. and J. G. Riley, "The Analysis of Uncertainty and Information - An Expository Survey," Journal of Economic Literature, 17 (December, 1979), 1375-1421.

Jones-Lee, M. W., "The Expected Conditional Utility Theorem for the Case of Personal Probabilities and State-Conditional Utility Functions: A Proof and Some Notes," Economic Journal, 89 (December, 1979), 834-849.

Jones-Lee, M. W., The Value of Life: A Economic Analysis (Chicago: Univ. Chicago Press, 1976).

Karni, E., "Risk Aversion for State-Dependent Utility Functions: Measurement and Applications," International Economic Review, 24 (October, 1983), 637-647.

Karni, E., D. Schmeidler and K. Vind, "On State-Dependent Preferences and Subjective Probabilities," Econometrica, 51 (July, 1983), 1021-1031.

Kihlstrom, R. E. and L. J. Mirman, "Risk Aversion with Many Commodities," Journal of Economic Theory, 8, (July, 1974), 361-388.

Levy, H. and A. Levy, "Multivariate Decision Making," Journal of Economic Theory, 32 (February, 1984), 36-51.

Parkin, J. M. and S. Y. Wu, "Choice Involving Unwanted Risky Assets and Optimal Insurance," American Economic Review 62 (December, 1972), 982-987.

Pratt, J. W., "Risk Aversion in the Small and in the Large," Econometrica 32 (January-April, 1964), 122-136.

PART V

DECISION MAKING UNDER UNCERTAINTY

Karl Aiginger

THE IMPACT OF UNCERTAINTY ON THE OPTIMAL
DECISION OF RISK NEUTRAL FIRMS

1. The Aim of the Paper

This paper seeks to demonstrate under what conditions risk theory is able to give an unambiguous answer to the question whether firms will produce more, the same or less under uncertainty as compared to certainty.

In part 2 we offer four alternative sufficient conditions under which an unambiguous answer to the question is available. The first of these conditions refers to the <u>risk attitude</u> of the entrepreneurs, it is well known in the literature and is reported only as a sort of reminder. We will not follow this path since it is in my opinion this very preoccupation of economic literature with risk attitude (in the sense of risk aversion, neutrality, or seeking, followed by absolute and relative degress of risk aversion, and finally by differences in the degree of relative risk aversion between two relevant economic agents) that prevented the literature from investigating more objective (technical) reasons for the influence of uncertainty. Our second condition refers to this economic or technological influence of the decision under certainty for risk neutral firms ("<u>technological concavity</u>"). The third condition refers to the case where price stickiness prevents an equilibrium at least in the short run ("<u>disequilibrium models</u>"), the fourth condition refers to a two stage decision process, where fine tuning of the decision variable is possible after the veil of uncertainty is lifted ("<u>ex-post-flexibility</u>").

In part 3 we present an overview of the scattered literature on the firm's behavior under uncertainty, showing how it fits our four conditions. In part 4 we try to find which empirical circumstances are important for a final assessment of the influence of uncertainty on a modern industry. In part 5 we present empirical evidence on these crucial facts, to evaluate the most likely

355

L. Daboni et al. (eds.), Recent Developments in the Foundations of Utility and Risk Theory, 355–373.
© *1986 by D. Reidel Publishing Company.*

influence of uncertainty on a "real economy" in constrast to a normative system of general equilibrium. We want to stress that this paper refers only to partial models (or partial partial models, since we consider only one side of one market), but this is justified because the confrontation of these models with empirical data has - to my knowledge - never be done.

2.   General Conditions

In this part we investigate under which general conditions the optimal value of a decision variable under uncertainty will be lower (larger) than under certainty.

We assume a utility function (1) in which utility U depends on the variable Z (which can be understood as profits): Z itself depends on two variables X and Y, (which usually are quantity produced and price). In the world of certainty, X_o is known and there exists an optimal solution Y* for the decision variable Y, under which profits are maximized (the second order condition is assumed to hold).

$$U[Z(X_o, Y)] => Max\ Y* \quad \text{(certainty maximum)} \qquad (1)$$

Under uncertainty we assume maximization of expected utility (von Neumann-Morgenstern Utility Maximization). Uncertainty exists about the variable X for which a probability density function $f(x)$ is known[1], with expected value assumed to be the same as the fixed value X_o under certainty (mean preserving introduction of risk).

$$E\ U[Z(X,Y)] => Max\ Y' \quad \text{(uncertainty maximum)} \qquad (2)$$

The optimal value of the decision variable under uncertainty, Y', can be shown to be smaller (equal, larger) than the optimal value under certainty, Y*, if U_{YXX}, (suffixes as usual denote partial derivatives), is smaller (equal or larger) than zero[2] (Rothschild, Stiglitz 1971; Diamond, Stiglitz 1974 etc.).

$$Y' \lesseqgtr Y* \quad \text{if } U_{YXX} \lesseqgtr 0 \qquad (3)$$

Unfortunately this condition is not very useful, since U_{YXX} proves for most problems to be neither unambiguously[3] positive nor negative (see Hey 1981 or Kraus 1979).

2.1. RISK AVERSION

An unambiguous result is available (as is well known in the literature) if we assume that Z is linear in X ($Z_{XX}=0$, let us call this "linear technology"). Linear technology (and the side condition that the optimal value of the decision variable reacts positively under certainty to the variable about which uncertainty may occur) leads to proposition 1.

Proposition 1:   Linear technology ($Z_{XX}=0$) plus (dY^*/dX)>0
                  yields the following sufficient condition

$$U_{ZZ} \lesseqgtr 0 \Rightarrow Y' \lesseqgtr Y^* \qquad (4)$$

Proposition 1 implies that risk attitude is the main channel for effects of uncertainty.

In the economic literature the case of biased action[4] in presence of risk aversion (or risk seeking) is well known. But it seems that its impact on economic thinking is smaller, since people's attitutes toward risk are unknown. Furthermore, there are arguments that firms should behave as if they were risk neutral or that entrepreneurs should be at least less risk averse than consumers, if not risk seeking.

2.2. TECHNOLOGICAL CONCAVITY (CONVEXITY)

Other channels of uncertainty like costs or demand conditions are not unknown, but less popular. It is characteristic that Lippman and McCall (1982, p. 212) in their survey on the economics of uncertainty have to recall that "though in many circumstances, risk aversion is a fact..., much economic behavior is a direct consequence of uncertainty and is independent of risk aversion". Neverthless they do not offer any general condition for the influence of costs or market conditions (nor does Hey, 1981 in his excellent book on uncertainty), though such a condition is available as a quite simple application of the Rothschild-Stiglitz condition (equation 3) for risk neutral agents.

Proposition 2: A linear utility function ($U_{ZZ}=0$) and technological concavity, neutrality, convexity ($Z_{YXX}<0$, $Z_{YXX}=0$, $Z_{YXX}>0$) yield the following sufficient condition.

$$Z_{YXX} \lesseqqgtr 0 \quad => \quad Y' \lesseqqgtr Y* \qquad (5)$$

The proof needs only Jensen's inequality and the second condition for optimal choice under certainty ($Z_{YY}<0$)[5].

This channel for an effect of uncertainty ("technological concavity") depends on demand or cost conditions, it is therefore "objective" in the sense that it does not depend on the subjective attitude towards risk. It does not contradict maximization of expected profit under infinite repetitions.

2.3. MARGINAL COSTS OF UNCERTAINTY (DISEQUILIBRIA MODELS)

There is a third channel through which uncertainty influences the optimal decision if we give up the assumption that some ex post control (usually the price) does change fast enough to guarantee equilibrium.

In disequilibria models there are either ex post unsold goods or unsatisfied demand. Ex ante, we have to calculate the costs for both of them (potentially unsold production plus potentially unsatisfied demand). Uncertainty therefore unambiguously increases expected costs and we have to equate expected marginal revenues to the sum of expected marginal costs of production and expected marginal costs of uncertainty. We want to label the extra costs of uncertainty as "marginal costs of uncertainty". These costs reduce the optimal production under uncertainty (given convex costs under certainty).

Assume a certainty model (equations 6-8), where revenue and costs (r and c respectively) depend on production (additively) and we get the well known first and second order conditions. For uncertainty where expected sales depend on the smaller of demand (x) or production (q) we get the conditions 10 and 11.

<u>Certainty model</u>

$$\pi = r(q) - c(q) \tag{6}$$
$$\pi_q = r'(q) - c'(q) \tag{7}$$
$$\pi_{qq} = r''(q) - c''(q) < 0 \tag{8}$$

<u>Uncertainty model</u>

$$E\pi = \min [r(x), r(q)] - c(q) \tag{9}$$

$$\frac{\delta E\pi}{\delta q} = r'(q) - F(q) \cdot r'(q) - c'(q) = 0 \tag{10}$$

$$\frac{\delta^2 E}{\delta q^2} = r''(q)[1-F(q)] - r'(q) F(q) - c''(q) < 0 \tag{11}$$

where r', c' are marginal revenue and costs under certainty and $F(q) \cdot r'(q)$ are the marginal costs of uncertainty (see equation 10).

<u>Proposition 3</u>:   Given a certainty model of type 6 and an uncertainty disequilibrium model of type 9, uncertainty adds on an additional marginal cost component which is positive (since F(q), the distribution function, as well as r'(q) are positive), yielding, for this type of model, the unambiguous result of equation 12 (recall that r''(q) is smaller than c''(q) in the neighbourhood of q* by equation 8).

$$q' < q^* \tag{12}$$

The most prominent special case of this model is where marginal revenue is constant and equal to the price (r'=p). For the purpose of making things comparable, we assume that the exogenous price is the same under certainty and uncertainty which seems natural in the specific partial model, but need not hold in a general equilibrium model. From the empirical point of view it will be a fair assumption for a period of uncertainty which follows a period of considerable certainty, and in which firms will stick to the "old" price at least for some time. The result of unambiguously lower production under uncertainty

was presented in Hymans' model of "competition under demand
uncertainty" (Hyman 1966). It did not become very popular,
since a fixed price is considered contradictory to the
idea of competition. Nevertheless assumptions of short run
price stickiness and price taking firms all selling a
certain proportion of their "normal" production in case of
a negative demand shock, may not be so unrealistic (see
part 5 for empirical support). The model of fixed prices
with demand uncertainty is intensively used in the
inventory literature (it is labelled the newsboy model in
its simplest form) without discussion of the market
environment. In the last years it was rejuvenated by
Mullineaux (1980), Benassy (1982) and Costrell (1983), as a
fixed-price uncertainty model with stochastic rationing,
though none of them stressed the fact that this model
results in unambiguous decreasing production under
uncertainty.

2.4. ASYMMETRIC EX POST FLEXIBILITY

The fourth factor that could change the optimal production
is given if it is possible to make a preliminary decision
about the decision variable; and then, after the veil of
uncertainty is lifted, to revise this decision at some cost.
It is easy to show that if the cost of revising the
decision upwards is larger than that of downward revision
the preliminary optimal production will rise, in the other
case it will fall. Downward irreversibility of gross
investment is one related form of asymmetry.

Proposition 4: Suppose it is possible to make a
preliminary decision Y and revise this upward (downward)
at cost C_1 (C_2) then

$$c_1 \lesseqgtr c_2 \text{ tends to imply } Y' \lesseqgtr Y^* \qquad (13)$$

This asymmetry effect is rather unattractive from a
theoretical point of view[6], from the practical point of
view upward revisions seem often to be much easier (less
costly) than downward revisions. Reselling production,
getting rid of investment goods, laying off personnel in
the short run (especially in business troughs or facing
shocks effecting a whole industry), usually proves very
difficult.

3. Presentation of Some Models

Instead of describing the   host of models presented in
the literature, (see Aiginger, 1985 for an   overview) we
limit ourselves to the case of risk   neutrality, since the
effects of risk aversion are treated so prominently in the
literature.

The competitive model under output price uncertainty
is   a   typical   example   of   "linear technology"   and
uncertainty has therefore no influence on the optimal
decision. The same is true   for a monopoly, if the
monopolist is a quantity setter (Q-ex-ante-model), but
only if uncertainty is additive or of the type $p=f(q) \cdot u$.
If however the demand uncertainty function is of the type
$q=f(p) \cdot u$ then Z_{YXX} is not zero (since the
uncertainty variable enters expected revenue), but under
realistic conditions[7] it is negative. This fact   has
been overlooked in the literature to a surprising extent.

Most authors write - following Leland 1972 - that
uncertainty for a quantity setting monopoly will not
change the decision. He assured this results by a
Principle of Increasing Uncertainty (PIU), which implies a
special setting of the uncertainty (see Aiginger, 1985).
Nickell (1978) has found the contrary result in a quite
different context assuming a second type of multiplicative
uncertainty, without discussing whether or why he assumes
a different type than Leland had for deciding. There are
no a priori reasons as to which type of multiplicative
uncertainty is more realistic.

An unambiguous result (lower production) is given by
the "competitive model under demand uncertainty", which
may be called a fixed price disequilibrium model or which
may be considered characteristic for some situations
of fixed prices under oligopolistic behavior. In this case
it is more important whether the conditions for the model
are realistic - e.g. the identity of the exogenous price
under certainty and uncertainty - than to discuss the
result. Nevertheless we want to stress two issues. First
the extension of the model to goodwill and holding costs,
and to the value of unsold products (they can be sold in
the next period) as well as to the value of backlogged
orders. If these costs are symmetric they do not change
the one period results. Symmetry of these "dynamic costs"
means, inter alia, that the proportion of unsatisfied
demand which can be backlogged is   the same as the

proportion of unsold goods which can be stored.

In contrast to this argument inventory literature favours the result that the incorporation of a future sales value for stock, increases the optimal stocks. This result stems from the implicit or explicit assumption that backlogging of demand is less likely than the storing of goods. In some very influential articles (e.g. Veinott, 1966; Johnson-Montgomery, 1974) the costs of backlogs are included (if consumers wait, the products have to be produced in the next period), but the revenues are forgotten (see Aiginger 1985).

The second aspect to be discussed is that many disequilibrium models assume linear costs (for all cost components) in models with uncertain but stationary demand. The optimal post order stock (or production) in this case cannot be compared to a unique optimal production under certainty, but to expected demand. In this case the result, whether more or less than expected demand is produced, depends on the exact values of some parameters: high profits, goodwill costs, and durability of goods increase optimal production, while lower profits, large holding costs etc. lead to lower optimal values as compared to expected demand.

The infinite horizon model for determining optimal post order (post production) stock is given by the recursive equation (14). The first term in each bracket represents the sales revenue as in the one period model. The h and g terms represent unit holding and goodwill costs. The V terms calculate the future expected revenues from an item stocked or a demand backlogged. In the first case the revenue is positive since an item stocked decreases future production costs (depending on the discount parameter α and the durability parameter a.) In the second case it is a cost since backlogged demand has to be produced in the next period (depending on the degree of backlogging b). The second term in the second line is the term sometimes forgotten in literature, it represents the revenue of backlogged demand.

$$V(I) = \max_{q \geq 0} \int_0^{q+I} \{[px - h(y-x)] + \alpha V[a(-x+y)]\}f(x)dx +$$
$$+ \int_{q+I}^{\infty} \{py + \alpha bp(x-y) - g(x-y) + \alpha V[b(-x+y)]\}f(x)dx - cq \tag{14}$$

Using dynamic programming techniques the solution is (15). This rather complicated formula shows that production in the multiperiod model will be higher than in the one period model if goodwill costs exceed holding costs and if durability exceeds the feasibility of backlogging. If however these are symmetric then the one period model represents a fair approximation of the dynamic problem. If a=b=1 and h=g=0 the formula collapses into the newsboy results (16).

$$F(y) = \frac{(p - c)(1 - \alpha b) + g}{p + g + h - \alpha b (p - c) - \alpha a c} \; ; \quad y = q + I \quad (15)$$

$$F(y) = \frac{p - c}{p} \quad \text{if } a = b = 1 \quad \text{and} \quad h = g = 0 \quad (16)$$

If costs of backlogs are included, but their revenues are forgotten (Veinott, 1966; Johnson-Montgomery, 1974) we get (17), which implies the implausible result that the possibility of backlogging increases optimal post order inventory. If the goods are durable (a=1), but backlogging is not feasible (b=o), holding and goodwill costs are negligible (g=h=o), we get (13), which implies that almost all potential demand should be satisfied however unprobable this is.

$$F(y) = \frac{p - c + \alpha bc + g}{p + h + g + \alpha bc - \alpha ac} \quad \Rightarrow \quad \frac{\delta y'}{\delta b} > 0 \qquad (17)$$

$$F(y) = \frac{p - c}{p - \alpha c} \quad \text{for } \alpha \Rightarrow 1, \quad y' \Rightarrow \infty \qquad (18)$$

4. Crucial Facts for the Evaluation of the Influence of Uncertainty on the Production Decision

The models presented and very briefly discussed in part 3 allow for any influence of uncertainty on the optimal production decision . However, the results show some facts on which the direction of the impact depends.
The first is the well known effect of risk attitude

(question 1). If people are risk averse then a downward pressure on the optimal decision is likely.

The influence of "technological concavity" hinges on a third cross derivate which is difficult to evaluate. The discussion of the monopoly model has shown that in the case of price setting there will be no influence, in the case of quantity setting either no influence or a somewhat larger probability of a downward bias is given in case of multiplicative uncertainty of the type $q=f(p)\cdot u$, a linear or quadratic demand function or a demand elasticity smaller than -1 will suffice. If it can be shown that quantity setting (question 2) is prevalent, then chances exist for a downward bias of production under monopoly.

The existence of disequilibria as an empirical phenomenon would be the strongest channel for uncertainty to reduce optimal production. If a market clearing price (question 3) existed for example in the case of output price uncertainty, then uncertainty would not change the decision. If there were no market clearing price then there exists a heavy downward pressure.

This downward pressure can be lowered if backlogging (question 4) does not exist or if goodwill costs exceed holding costs considerably.

If it is easier to revise upward than downward (question 5), then optimal production under uncertainty will tend to be lower than under certainty.

5.   Empirical Evidence on the Five Crucial Questions

In this part results are reported from a larger study on the impact of uncertainty on Austrian manufacturing industry (Aiginger 1985). Readers interested in more detailed evidence are referred to this book. Some of the results stem from econometric applications, some from a survey conducted among approximately 1000 entrepreneurs.

Question 1: <u>Are entrepreneurs risk averse</u>?

Many experimental studies have investigated this topic. We chose another way and asked entrepreneurs whether they based their decision on the expected return of investment projects alone, or whether they preferred among two investment projects, one with high risks and considerable chances or one where they might forsake some mean expected profits for the certainty of the return.

We defined as small projects those which amount up to approximately one half of an annual investment programme, and as large, those exceeding an annual programme considerably. For small risks, risk-averters (36.82% of the firms) and risk seekers (33.66%) balanced each other out, with less than one third risk neutral. Risk aversion and risk seeking are higher for small firms, risk neutrality is predominant for firms with more than 1000 employees (60.78%).

For large risks, risk averters outnumber risk seekers 53.15 to 12.37. Approximately one third are risk neutral for large decisions. Again risk aversion and risk seeking decreased with the size of the firm. Only 3.92% of the large firms are risk seekers (14% of the firms with less than 100 employees).

Question 2: Price setting or quantity setting?

Using Hay's (1972) technique of testing whether, in case of surprises firms changed their prices, their production, their inventories or their backlogs, a significant quantity reaction (0.65% for a demand shock of 1%), but no price reaction (0.02%) was observed.

Investigating the determinants of price changes econometrically, long-term determinants like labor costs and energy prices outperformed short term demand influences in Austria.

Asked how they react to a short-term surprise, 20% of the firms answered via a price change, 56% via a quantity change, 48% that they would change their inventory level.

Asked if, in case of uncertainty, they set the price or the quantity, 27.64% of the firms said that they set the price (and adjust the quantity ex-post), 15.94% that they have to set price and quantity and 53% that they set quantity.

Question 3: Market clearing price or disequilibria?

It has been said already that only 20% of the firms named price changes as the main response to a surprise, and that econometric results support this survey result.

Confronted with five different modes of behavior under uncertainty (P-ex-ante, Q ex post; Q-ex-ante, market price ex post; Q-ex-ante, monopoly price ex post; P-Q mode; ex post quantity flexibility) only 6.99% of the firms regarded the classical competitive model (Q-ex-ante, market price ex post) as relevant (7.71% of the small firms). The fixed-price competitive model was not listed among the possible answers, in order to force the firms to remain within the framework of normatively appealing models. The disequilibrium monopoly model (P-Q mode: 22.49%) and the ex post flexibility model (preliminary Q, then revision: 31.11%) together got more than 50% of the responses.

Question 4: Is backlogging feasible?

Backlogged orders in modern industrial economies are usually two or three times as large as finished stock inventories. In the US finished stocks amount to 14.2% of annual sales (1954-1982), backlogs to 28.9%, net inventories are therefore negative (-14.7%).

Theoretical considerations imply that net inventories, if they are negative, should decrease (becoming more negative) with increasing uncertainty. Empirical data for the US as well as for Austria comply with these forecasts. Decreasing stock of finished goods in the period of slow and uncertain demand (1980/82) may be plausible. Increased order books, however, have to be interpreted as a conscious shift from production on stock to production on orders as a typical optimal behavior under uncertainty.

Question 5: Are upward revisions less costly than downward revisions?

Entrepreneurs labelled more instruments as feasible in case of pessimistic forecasts. They are especially willing to let inventories run down, but will not allow them to build up, indicating less goodwill costs than inventory holding costs and/or easy backlogging.

Investment plans are more often revised upward than downward. For small firms this tendency is evident up to one third of their annual investment program.

Asked which errors are more costly, 21% of Austrian firms assessed upward and downward errors as equally costly, 63% reported optimistic forecasts as more costly, 16% reported overpessimistic forecasts as more costly. This asymmetry slightly increased with the size of the firms.

6. Summary

The empirical facts seem to indicate that in "real economies" the effect of uncertainty tends to decrease production. The limitations of empirical investigations presented should be stressed: they were performed mainly on an aggregate level, they mainly refer to Austrian manufacturing, they rely heavily on questionnaires. Above all empirical investigation will never be able to decide normative questions or to explain the behavior in the general equilibrium. Neverthless in the short run, given all the rigidities and disequilibria which exist, uncertainty tends to lower optimal production even in absence of risk aversion. Risk aversion becomes important for large, and for once-for-all decisions, but it is not the only channel through which uncertainty changes decisions.

"Technological concavity" created by concave marginal revenues or by convex marginal costs, marginal costs of uncertainty in disequilibrium models or asymmetric costs of revisons of the preliminary decision are able to bias the decision downward in a real world economy without invoking subjective risk attitudes.

Austrian Institute
of Economic Research
Vienna

NOTES

1. All theoretical models will assume maximization of expected utility as the chosen decision technique. Uncertainty is not differentiated from risk (in the sense of Knight, 1933), we assume that the decision-maker has a probability distribution about the uncertainty variable (which Knight would have called risk). The rationale for this assumption is not that I believe that the concept of expected utility maximization is the only feasible one. The Keynesian view that "true" uncertainty changes the very behavior of agents (for example favoring the use of more flexible production techniques, reducing the willingness of people to undergo long term commitments etc., see Rothschild, 1981) is probably the more realistic description for the impact of uncertainty,

albeit less operational. The same may be true for Shackle's theory stressing the importance of "focus values" (1962), for Simon's concept of limited rationality (1955, 1978), or other critics of Expected Utility Maximization like Kahneman & Tversky ("prospect theory", 1979), Radner ("satisficing processes", 1975), or Loomes & Sugden ("regret theory", 1982). Though we use the technique of expected utility maximization our analyses and results may be regarded as "Keynesian" in spirit, since we allow for price stickiness and ex post adjustments in the decision parameters and then get the result that uncertainty changes the behavior and increases the importance of flexibility. This is a genuine Keynesian result proven with von Neumann-Morgenstern Utility Maximization.

2. A suffix as usual denotes a partial derivative. All functions are assumed to be well-behaved in the usual sense (continuously differentiable, integrals exist and are finite).

3. U_{XXY} is ambigous if Z_Y changes its sign. But, in any interesting problem Z_Y must change sign, since in a certain world $Z_Y=0$ and $Z_{YY}<0$ are the conditions for the optimal choice of Y (assuming U'>0), see Hey (1981, p. 344).

4. Bias in the sense of a difference of the optimal action under uncertainty as compared to certainty.

5. The proof makes use of the a ssumption that the second order condition for maximization under certainty holds ($Z_{YY}<0$) and of Jensen's Inequality for convex or concave functions. We prove the case of Y'<Y* defining Z_Y concave in X.

$$Z_Y(X_0,Y') > E\ Z_Y(X,Y) = 0$$

The inequality holds for any concave function (and so for Z_Y), the equality stems from the first order maximization under uncertainty.
It follows that $Z_Y(X_0,Y)$ is positive, and using $Z_{YY}<0$ this implies that Y' is smaller than Y* (where $Z_Y=0$). The result may also be derived from the Rothschild-Stiglitz condition.

6. The expression "tends to" is used since the effect is somewhat complicated. For equilibria models with non linear costs the result depends on the interaction of "normal production costs" and emergency costs (a 3rd

cross derivative, see Turnovsky, 1973).
We   can demonstrate the tendency for a fix-price model
with   linear   normal   production   costs, with upward
(downward) revision costs of
c_1 (c_2) and   feasibility parameters   for   upward
(downward) revisions a (b).
Optimal production is given by

$$F(q) = \frac{p - c - bp + bc_1}{p + bc_1 - bp - ac_2}$$

Optimal   production is very likely to be smaller than
expected demand, especially if upward revisions are more
feasible and less costly than downward revisions.
7. See   Nickell, 1978. The demand function has to be
   linear   or   quadratic or the elasticity has to be less
   than -1.

REFERENCES

Aiginger, K.: 1977, "The Use of Survey Data for the
   Analysis of   Business   Cycles". CIRET-Study, No. 24,
   Munich.
Aiginger, K.: 1979, "Means, Variance and Skewness of
   Reported Expectations and   their Difference to   the
   Respective Moments of Realizations", Empirica   2,
   217-265.
Aiginger, K.: 1981,   "Empirical Surveyed Expectational
   Data and   Decision Theory", CIRET-Conference, Athens.
Aiginger, K.: 1981, "Empirical Evidence on the Rational
   Expectations Hypothesis", Empirica, 25-72.
Aiginger, K.: 1983,   "Die Wirkung von asymmetrischen
   Verlusten auf die Bildung con rationalen öconomischen
   Erwartungen", IFO-Studien, No. 29, Munich.
Aiginger, K.: 1985,   Unsicherheitstheorie   und
   unternehmerische Produktionsentscheidung, Campus Verlag,
   Frankfurt.
Amihud, V. and H. Mendelson: 1983,   "Price Smoothing
   and Inventory", Review of Economic Studies 50,   87-98.
Arrow, K.J.: 1978, "The Future and the Present in
   Economic Life", Economic Inquiry 16, 157-169.
Arrow, K.J.,   T.Harris,   J. Marschak J.: 1951, "Optimal
   Inventory Policy", Econometrica 19, 250-272.

Arrow, K.J. and M.D. Intriligator: 1982, Handbook of Mathematical Economics, North-Holland, Amsterdam.

Arrow, K.J., S. Karlin and H. Scarf: 1958, Studies in the Mathematical Theory of Inventory and Production, Stanford University Press. Stanford.

Arrow, K.J., S. Karlin and H. Scarf: 1962, Studies in Applied Probability and Management Science, Stanford University Press. Stanford.

Baron, D.P.: 1970, "Price Uncertainty, Utility, and Industry Equilibrium in Pure Competition", International Economic Review 11, 463-480.

Benassy, J.P.: 1982, The Economics of Market Disequilibrium", Academic Press, New York.

Blinder, A.S.: 1982, "Inventories and Sticky Prices: More on the Microfoundation of Macroeconomics", American Economic Review 72(3), 334-348.

Buchan, J. and E. Koenigsberg: 1963, Scientific Inventory Management, Prentice Hall.

Carlton, D.W.: 1978, "Market Behavior with Demand Uncertainty and Price Inflexibility", American Economic Review 68, 571-587.

Costrell, R.M.: 1983, "Profitability and Aggregate Investment under Demand Uncertainty", Economic Journal 93(1), 166-181.

Cyert, R. and J. March: 1963, Behavioural Theory of the Firm, Prentice Hall, Englewood Cliffs.

De Groot, M.: 1970, Optimal Statistical Decision, McGraw-Hill, New York.

Diamond, P.A. and J. E. Stiglitz: 1974, "Increases in Risk and in Risk Aversion", Journal of Economic Theory 8(3), 337-360.

Falkinger, J.: 1983, "Modellierung der Unsicherheit - Keynes'sche Position". Vortrag für die Tagung der National - ökonomischen Gesellschaft in Wien. Erscheint in: Quartalshefte der Girozentrale, Wien.

Fishburn P.C. : 1977, "Mean-Risk Analysis with Risks Associated with Below-Target Returns", American Economic Review 67, 116-124.

Gordon, R.J.: 1981, "Output Fluctuations and Gradual Price Adjustment", Journal of Economic Literature 19(2),493-530.

Hartman, R.: 1975, "Competitive Firm and the Theory of Input Demand under Price Uncertainty", Journal of Political Economy 83.

Hay, G.A.: 1971, "Production, Price and Inventory

Theory", American Economic Review 60, 531-545.

Hay, G.A.: 1972, "The Dynamics of Firm Behavior under Alternative Cost Structures", American Economic Review 62(3), 403-414.

Hay, D.A. and D.J. Morris: 1979, Industrial Economics, Oxford Press University, Oxford.

Hey, J.D.: 1974, Statistics in Economics, Martin Robertson, London.

Hey, J.D.: 1979, Uncertainty in Microeconomics, Martin Robertson, Oxford.

Hey, J.D.: 1981, Economics in Disequilibrium, Martin Robertson, Oxford.

Hey, J.D.: 1982, Goodwill-Investment in the Intangiible, University of York. Discussion Paper 46, York.

Hillier, F.D. and G.J. Lieberman: 1980, Introduction into Operations Research, Holden Day, Oakland.

Hirsch, A.A. and M.C. Lovell: 1969, Sales Anticipations and Inventory Behavior, Wiley, New York.

Holt, C.C., F. Modigliani, J. Muth and H. Simon: 1960, Planning Production, Inventories and Work Force, Prentice Hall, Englewood Cliffs.

Hymans, S.H.: 1966, "The Price Taker: Uncertainty, Utility, and the Supply Functions", International Economic Review 7, 346-356.

Johnson, L.A. and D.C. Montgomery: 1974, Operations Research and Production Planning, Scheduling and Inventory Control, Wiley, New York.

Kahneman, D. and A. Tversky: 1979, "Prospect Theory: An Analysis of Decision Under Risk", Econometrica 47(2), 263-291.

Knight, F.H.: 1933, Risk, Uncertainty and Profit, Houghton Mifflin, Boston.

Kraus, M.: 1979, "A Comparative Statics Theorem for Choice Under Risk", Journal of Economic Theory 21(3), 510-517.

Kon, Y.: 1983, "Capital Input Choice under Price Uncertainty: A Putty - Clay Technology Case", International Economic Review 24(1), 183-197.

Leland, H.E.: 1972, "Theory of the Firm Facing Uncertain Demand", American Economic Review 62, 278-291.

Lim, C.: 1980, "The Ranking of Behavioral Modes of the Firm Facing Uncertain Demand", American Economic Review 70, 217-224.

Lippman, S.A. and J.J. McCall: 1981, "The Economics of Uncertainty: Selected Topics and Probabilistic Methods", In K.J. Arrow and M.D. Intriligator, Handbook of Mathematical Economics, North-Holland, Amsterdam, 211-284.

Loomes, G. and R. Sugdan: 1982, "Regret Theory: An Alternative Theory of Rational Choice under Uncertainty", Economic Journal 92(4), 805-824.

Malinvaud, E.: 1980, Profitability & Unemployment, Cambridge University Press, Cambridge.

Mullineaux, D.J.: 1980, "Inflation Expectation and Money Growth in the United States", American Economic Review 70, 149-161.

Muth, J.F.: 1961, "Rational Expectations and the Theory of Price Movements", Econometrica 29, 315-335.

Nermuth, M.: 1983, "Modellierung der Unsicherheit: Moderne Theorie und Keynes", Vortrag für die Tagung der Nationalökonomischen Gesellschaft in Wien 1983. Erscheint in: Quartalshefte der Girozentrale, Wien.

Nevin, A.J.: 1966, "Some Effects of Uncertainty: Simulation of a Model of Price", Quarterly Journal of Economics 80(1), 73-87.

Nickell, S.J.: 1978, The Investment Decision of Firms, Oxford.

Petersen, R. and E.A. Silver: 1979, Decision Systems for Inventory Management and Production Planning, Wiley, New York.

Pindyck, R.S.: 1982, "Adjustment Costs, Uncertainty, and the Behavior of Firm", American Economic Review 72, 415-427.

Radner, R.: 1975, "Satisficing", Journal of Mathematical Economics 2, 253-262.

Rothschild, K.W.: 1981, Einführung in die Ungleichgewichtstheorie, Heidelberger Taschenbücher, Band 212. Springer Verlag, Berlin.

Rothschild, M. and J.E. Stiglitz: 1970, "Increasing Risk: A Definition", 2. Its Economic Consequences, Journal of Economic Theory 2, 225-243, 3, 66-82.

Rothschild, M. and J.E. Stiglitz: 1971, "Increasing Risk - Its Economic Consequences", Journal Economic Theory 3, 66-82.

Shackle, G.L.S.: 1955, Uncertainty in Economics and other Reflections, Cambridge University Press, London.

Simon, H.A.: 1978, "Rationality as Process and as Product of Thought", American Economic Review (Papers and Proceedings) 68, 1-16.

Streissler, E.: 1969, "Hayek on Growth: A Reconsideration of his Early Theoretical Work", in E. Streissler, G. Haberler, F. Lutz, F. Machlup (eds), Roads to Freedom, Essays in Honour of F.A. von Hayek, Hayek, Routledge, London.

Tichy, G.: 1976, "Die Bedeutung der Lager für die Konjunktur", Empirica 1, 3-45 and 2, 153-196.

Turnovsky, S.J.: 1971, "The Theory of Production under Conditions of Stochastic Input Supply", Metroeconomica 23, 51-68.

Turnovsky, S.J.: 1973, "Production Flexibility, Price Uncertainty and the Behavior of the Competitive Firm", International Economic Review 14(2), 395-413.

Veinott, A.F.: 1966, "The Status of Mathematical Inventory Theory", Management Science 12, 745-777.

Winckler, G.: 1977, "Walrasianische und Keynesianische Aspekte der Lagerhaltungstheorie", Österreichische Akademie der Wissenshaften, Wien.

Zabel, E.: 1972, "Multiperiod Monopoly under Uncertainty", Journal of Economic Theory 5, 524-536.

Zarnowitz, V.: 1973, Orders, Production and Investment - A Cyclical and Structural Analysis, NBER, New York.

János Ács

STRATEGIC PLANNING MODELS
AND RISK MANAGEMENT

1.   Introduction

Although   strategic   planning   had   been   developed   to match the   growing risk   and uncertainty in   business, its theory and practice ignored the latest development in risk management   until now.   There are   only a   few cases known, where the instruments of risk analysis and risk management are   explicitly   considered   in the   process   of   strategic planning.   The   reason for   this curious   development lies, among   others,   in   the   fact   that   risk   management   was regarded by   many academic   theorists only   as some   sort of insurance management. In the prevailing discussion about the scope   of   risk   management   there   are   opinions   which understand by risk management only a very limited field of management   activity.   This   is   all   the   more   surprising because   in   the   German business   administration there   was important   research   work   done   under   the   topic   of   risk policy by Nicklisch and Leitner as early as the beginning of   this   century.   Some academics   are   now   rediscovering these works   and they   consider risk   management as   a very important   part of   corporate management.   Some enthusiasts go even   further and   put risk management   on a   level with corporate management. This view   cannot be accepted because there   are   management   functions   which   are   not   closely connected with uncertainty and risk.

The objectives of this paper are: (1) to describe the application   of some   known   and some   new   models of   risk analysis   in   strategic   planning,   together   with   their problems and limits; (2) to describe and discuss a kind of Decision Support   System (DSS)   in strategic   planning; and (3) to   present a concept   of risk management   in strategic planning.

2.   Risk and Uncertainty in
Strategic Planning Models

375

L. Daboni et al. (eds.), Recent Developments in the Foundations of Utility and Risk Theory, 375–391.
© *1986 by D. Reidel Publishing Company.*

Strategic planning models are important analytical tools for evaluating strategic decisions. Annex 1 summarizes the main characteristics of the portfolio models according to Wind. The paper of Naylor, Vernon and Wertz presents a good survey of the most important strategic planning models, but we will not discuss all of them here in detail. Competitive strategy models originally proposed by the Boston Consulting Group (BCG), later adapted by Little and McKinsey, and more recently by Porter, emphasize the interdependence of an enterprise with its competitors. In fact, one of the greatest innovations in management science and practice was the splitting of a firm into strategic business units. The BCG model is based on the growth-share matrix and the experience curve. The basic concept of this model has been discussed exhaustively in literature and applied world wide by many companies.

Unfortunately, the problem of risk and uncertainty is not considered by the BCG-model; the pitfalls in its application are numerous. General Electric, Texas Instrument, Xerox and Mexico's Grupo Industrial Alpha had employed the portfolio approach in strategic planning and recently they encountered a series of problems which were discussed in the literature. The majority of the optimization models described in textbooks is of a deterministic type: in spite of the fact that the essence of development of corporate strategy should be the analysis of risk. We may explain this fact in the following way: a deterministic planning model cannot take any risk into account; the reason is that it cannot scale the risk. The goal of any planning model is certainly to determine risk at the lowest level in the planning cycle. Risk should conform to the level of the Strategic Business Units, which in return determine the capital requirements that influence the alternative business plans and then these alternative projected risk plans flow upwards to corporations. In agreement with Ball we find that it is necessary to work with a consistent definition of risk for a large number of diverse business units. There are problems, namely how to determine the level at which risks are consolidated, to what extent they should be consolidated, and which techniques of computing should be used. The final problem here is to determine the formal, quantitative amount which expresses the attitude of the corporation in question against risks. In the case of the application of deterministic portfolio models, risks and uncertainties could be taken into account by a pessimistic scenario based on the main pessimistic environmental dates. But such a scenario is highly unrealistic because the uncertainties are not always positively correlated. On the other hand, not positively or even negatively correlated uncertainties or·risks (e. g. demands in various business units), also termed statistic uncertainties, are very important from the point of risk sharing.

The relationship between expected returns, systematic risks and the valuation of securities in this context is the essence of the Capital Asset Pricing Model (CAPM) which has been proposed to be applied as a strategic planning tool for corporations managing a portfolio of businesses, divisions, strategic business units, etc. Good descriptions of the CAPM have been published, e. g. by Sharpe and Linter, and its application to strategic planning by Naylor and Tapon.

The objective of management, making strategic decisions within the CAPM framework, is to maximize V, the expected value of the firm's common stock. This value V can be calculated by the following (discounted cash flow) equation, provided that its profit stream and its expected rate of return will continue indefinitely:

$$(1) \quad V = \frac{R - \delta r_m \, \sigma}{i} \, ,$$

where: i is the risk free interest rate, R is the expected rate of return, σ is the standard deviation of the rate of return, r_m is the correlation coefficient between the company's rate of return and the rate of return of the entire portfolio of all n firms (securities) in the market, and δ is the market price of risk determined by the stock market (in a perfectly competitive capital market this is a constant value).

The product $\delta r_m \sigma$ is the risk premium, meaning that for every additional unit of risk $r_m \sigma$ borne by investors, the rate of return demanded must increase by the amount $\delta r_m \sigma$. A company's management wields little or no influence over the risk-free interest rate i and the market price of risk δ. It is obvious that the management has partial control over the company's rate of return R, its standard deviation σ, and the correlation coefficient r_m.

Strategic decisions   should increase R and decrease σ and r_m.

The expected rate of return of the firm is the weighted average of the expected returns from the various businesses in its portfolio,

$$(2) \quad R = \sum_{j=1}^{m} W_j R_j,$$

where W_j is the proportion of a company's asset invested in division j. Thus the management has to increase the rate of return of each of the individual businesses.

The variance, σ_j^2, of the company's rate of return depends not only on the variance σ^2 of the businesses constituting the portfolio but also on the relationship between these businesses, characterized by the covariance σ_{jk}. A portfolio including businesses with low positive or even negative covariance can reduce the dispersion of the probability distribution of possible returns. Finding businesses with such statistical properties is the main task of the strategic management. The correlation coefficient between the company's rate of return and that of the entire market portfolio r_m (not to be confused with the company's own portfolio) is obviously partially controllable by the management. r_m should be as close to zero as possible or maybe even negative. As a result of this effort the value V of the conglomerate firm's share would rise.

There are various cases where such a diversification strategy is pursued. Operating in basic and diverse fields keeps the covariance of returns between businesses much lower than concentrating investments in one field only.

3.   The Necessity of Decision Support Systems in Strategic Decision—Making

The common characteristic of the methods for strategic decisions under uncertainty and risk are among others: (1) the necessity of great deal of quite sophisticated judgmental information to be obtained from the decision maker and/or experts, (2) the iterative nature of the decision-making process and a lot of time and effort wasted by the decision-maker and/or experts, and (3) the necessity of the trained analyst to conduct the decision-making process.

These and other reasons necessitate a co-operation between decision-maker and computer in the decision process. As a result, various software packages have been elaborated for Decision Support Systems. In strategic decision-making such a system has to contain interactive procedures and has to be rather universal, since it has to enable the decision-maker to contruct models and solve decision-making problems with continuous and discrete sets of alternatives, with different kinds of attribute scales (both ordinal and cardinal), and different forms of objective functions. It may be necessary for the decision-maker to be familiar either with programming languages or utility theory, because the application package must be realized as a sequence of dialogue procedures interconnected by common judgemental information. Functions of information gathering, testing, processing, storing, and correction have to be built into nearly all the interactive procedures, so that the decision-maker (expert) has the opportunity to interrupt a decision-making process at any appropriate point, starting again from this or another earlier point. A software package with such possibilities can be regarded as a Decision Support System for Ill Structured Problems (ISPs) in the sense of Carlsson, et al.

4. Strategic Decision Making by an Interactive System

It has been emphasized that a close cooperation of decision-maker and computer is necessary for effective strategic decision-making. Most of the ideas of a Decision Support System described here are realized in the interactive program system developed by Viliums and Sukur, which thus can be considered as a general tool of strategic planning. It enables managers to carry out the major steps of strategic planning in many system models. The co-operation between problem solver and computer is illustrated in Figure 1.

Activity of decision—maker	Activity of computer
1. Problem formulation, pratical decision making	
2. Choice of feasible set of alternative possible values of the decision vector X (e.g. resource allocation among the different projects, or market divisions, or R and D activities etc.) X may have discrete alternatives (to choose a project or not) or may have continuous ones (how much money to allocate for a project).	
3. Determining the set of attributes $R_1,\ldots,R_m$, e.g. profitability, market-share, business strength, competitive position, attractiveness, risk, return.	
4. Construction of the attribute scales and accuracy demanded. Cost of information has to be considered. -> 5.	
	5. Parametrization: making the decision of how to choose the best information for the accuracy demanded in step 4.
	6. Sensitivity analysis consideration of risk. -> 7.
7. Examination of steps 5 and 6 and decision about acceptance of parametrization 8 or to make a new parametrization with finer scales. -> 5.	
	8. Solution of the resource allocation problem -> 9.
9. Decision making about acceptance, STOP or NEW parametrization -> 5.	

Fig.1. Interactive System for Strategic Planning Decisions

5. Limitations of Risk Analysis in Strategic Planning

Even though risk analysis is a popular topic in many theoretical works and papers, a formal risk analysis is not used very often as a practical decision-making tool. Following our analysis, we give here our explanation for this phenomenon (see also Naylor, Vernon and Wertz). Obviously most of the models and approaches described in the literature assume implicitly that the decision-maker has empirical or apriori knowledge of the probability distributions of the random variables in question, at his disposal. But the main problem is that the key random variables of interest are usually unknown or only partly known; they are therefore not a significant representation of reality. What is to be understood by an apriori probability of any executive's evaluation? Don't we idealize the abilities of corporate executives by demanding them to be able to express accurately their apriori probabilities?

There is another serious problem. Risk analyses can be very expensive, expecially when we use simulation models which have to be repeated very often, up to 1000 times. In the case of a large and comprehensive model these iterations require enormous amounts of computer time which average firms cannot afford. Finally, there are too many unsolved methodological problems connected with simulation models, for example: validation of the experimental designs and of all the data generated by the the simulation model itself.

Of course it is difficult to sell the formal analysis of any model to top managers, quite simply because few of them have enough training to be able to understand what probability distributions, random variables and their standard deviations, and the whole theoretical framework really mean for their practical decisions. We therefore agree with most authors that sensitivity analysis, with the help of computer models may be the best and actually the most often used tools for risk analysis. If, for example, we investigate an oligopolistic model of a market, we cannot know in advance what price the competitors will charge. Therefore we have to run the simulation experiments on the basis of several competitors' pricing policies which have been simply assumed. We will take, for example, high, low, and average prices. This is a very intuitive and easily

understandable way of simulating because it is clear to
every manager that the price of his goods will depend on
the impact of the assumed price levels of the competitors.
With this simulation we will be able to evaluate the
sensitivity of his sales relative to the different pricing
policies on the market. Thus computer simulations are
widely used in corporate decision – making and they do not
demand any sophisticated understanding from the corporate
managers who use them (see also Naylor, Vernon, and Wertz
who come to similar conclusions).

6.   From Risk Analysis to Risk Management– The Concept of Risk Management

The difficulties of using risk analysis in practical
decision-making has led to the Concept of Risk Management
which, generally speaking, goes beyond the traditional
scope of insurance management. Risk management is
understood as a systematic analysis, influence and
coordinated control of all risks of a company. Albach
defines risk management from a more operational aspect:
risk management is the attempt to place the firm in a
position where all risks can be identified, valued and,
with the help of the instruments of risk policy, mastered
in a way that the existence of the firm itself can never
be endangered by its environment.

According to these definitions risk analysis is a
part of risk management. Do its limitations influence the
applicability of the concept of risk management? This is
only true if risk analysis is limited to the apriori
knowledge of the probability distributions of the key
random variables of interest in a decision problem. If
risk analysis is regarded as risk identification and risk
evaluation, and quantitative methods are accepted besides
qualitative ones, the concept of risk management is
applicable in theory and practice.

We have presented, in figure 2, a process oriented
classification of the main functions of risk management
following three different points of view. However,
according to Helten, risk management has the following
functions: the identification of risks, risk analysis,
risk evaluation, decision-making. In this context it is
necessary to re-evaluate critiques of the concept of risk
analysis; it is only one tool of risk management. The

shortcomings and pitfalls of risk analysis ought to be
compensated and   amended by other tools of risk management.

Williams—Heins,	Denenberg—Eilers—Melone—Zelten.	Baglini,
Risk Management, 2, 1971 23 f.	Risk, 2, 1974 68 ff.	Risk Management, 1976 28.
Identification of risks	Discovering the sources of possible loss	Discovering the firm's exposures to loss
Measurement of the losses associated with these risks		Analyzing and measuring the loss potential
Considering the alternative tools and decisionmaking	Evaluation of the financial impact of losses on the firm	Developing alternative methods for dealing with these exposures
Effective implementation of the decisions made	Selecting the most efficient method or methods of treating the various risks	Choosing the best method or combination of methods
		Implementing the chosen method(s)
		Monitoring the results

Fig. 2. Process Oriented Functions of Risk Management

7. Applications of Risk Management in Strategic Planning

One of the most important new developments is that of
the differentiation of strategic planning process. Wind
criticizes present (and still valid) theory and practice,
concentrating primarily on financial and organizational
considerations,   and presents a system model for strategic
marketing planning that has been applied in a number of
cases to achieve a more marketing orientation in strategic
planning. A closer investigation of the system models of

Wind and the evaluation of the practice of strategic planning, shows the necessity of the situative approach of strategic planning, which results in a better identification of the main global risks and uncertainties of the firm. Figure 3 shows new system models of the strategic marketing planning process, which has been developed by the author. This framework and its applicability to a computer render it possible to generate a better strategic decision under risk and uncertainty. These models enable the analysts to consider the tools of risk management.

The following two examples will explain the practical applications of the concept of risk management in strategic planning.

7.1. MANAGEMENT OF PRODUCT LIABILITY RISKS

Because of the increasing protection of consumers, the problem of product liability is not only a matter of producing goods and services, but is also increasingly a matter of bearing risk concerning the marketing and financing organizations in business. To explain some difficult aspects of product liability risks, Helten presents the case of a machine factory delivering equipment to produce plastic bottles. Due to a mistake in construction the bottles are leaking. The fault was recognized after a certain part of the order had been finished. The producer of the bottles now faces financial losses as he cannot satisfy his customers. A catalogue of risk management of failures in contruction could be defined as follows: risk avoidance, which means the renunciation of risk products; risk reduction means a change-over to other technologies, connected with less risks or increasing quality control; risk sharing could mean organizing independent sections for research and development, for example, as a limited company. This is the same as with the foundation of corporate laboratories together with business partners; risk transfer means contract-liability or the delegation of risks to suppliers or customers. In an optimal risk-portfolio all these instruments have to be combined with each other.

7.2. MANAGEMENT OF RISKS IN FOREIGN COUNTRIES

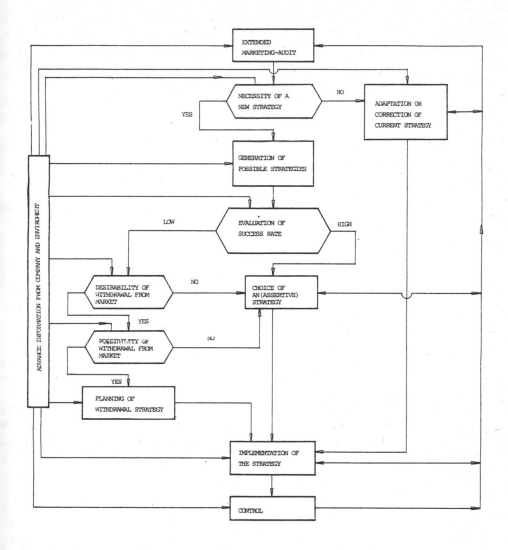

Fig. 3.

Credits in foreign countries are endangered through economic and political factors. Let us explain the possible strategies of risk policy against political factors: risk avoidance means having no business with an unstable country; risk reduction: restricted activities in such countries; risk sharing: regional diversification; risk transfer: securities through international contracts; etc. In an optimal risk portfolio these instruments have to be combined properly with one another. The present state of risk management does not provide proper instruments for every problem of the strategic planning process. For specific problems new instruments of risk management have to be developed and applied in the decision-making process. It is an urgent task of research to find new, adequate instruments of risk management which have to be combined with other well-proven instruments.

The above considerations hold good mainly in case of one decision–maker, with a specific risk behavior. The situation markedly changes in case of group decision-making in a firm. This behavior differs considerably when the interests of the various groups (or members of the same group) clash. It is empirically proved that individual decisions are more risk averse than group decisions (Ács 1980). For this reason the structure of the strategic planning process influences the risk management considerably. Interested parties seize risk assessments that favour their position and try to use them as conclusive arguments. It would be naive to expect that such a misuse of risk analysis could be curtailed by exhorting analysts to reform their practices. Institutional changes, among them new rules of the game, are to be introduced and strengthened, respectively.

8. Summary

Risks, uncertainty within firms and in their environment, are increasingly dealt with by strategic planning, risk analysis and risk management. The present state of strategic planning enables us to consider the greatest part of internal and environmental risks mainly quantitatively - due to the fact that the majority of planning models used are of a deterministic type.

The application of CAPM in strategic planning could take risk explicitly into account and maximize the expected

value of the firms' common stock. Linked to a corporate
simulation model or a DSS it could generate a series of
values for the expected rate of return, its standard
deviation, as well as other output variables important for
the management. The difficulties of the use of CAPM are
numerous but an attempt to optimize the value of the firm
would be a big step in developing new powerful instruments
for evaluating the economic consequences of alternative
strategies.

The implementation of the Decision Support System in
strategic planning could help to find "the best decision"
in an interactive way - as suggested in this paper. DSS
renders the consideration of other factors relevant to
strategic decisions possible; businesses need not be
reduced to portfolio terms.

The limitations of DSS for strategic planning could be
partially avoided through the Concept of Risk Management.
In this concept, strategic planning represents only one
instrument of risk management and is a powerful tool of
risk identification. In this paper the other instruments
have been shortly demonstrated for the cases of product
liability and risks in relation to foreign countries.
The development of new instruments for special cases (e.g.
siting problems, specific strategic decisions, etc.), the
consideration of risk behavior in individual, group and
inter-organizational or even international decision-making
are now the main topics in the urgent task of research in
risk management.

University of Technology
of Vienna

REFERENCES

Acs, J: 1980, "Zu einigen Problemen der kollektiven
   Entscheidungen aus der Sicht der Informationstheorie und
   technologie", in Proc. 4th Int. Wittgenstein Symposium
   1979 - Kirchberg, Wien (Hölder-Pichler-Tempsky).
Albach, H.: 1978, "Strategische Unternehmensplanung bei
   erhöhter Unsicherheit", ZfB 48, 702-715.
Baglini, N.: 1976, Risk Management in International
   Corporations, New York.
Ball, B.C.: 1978, "The Use of Management Science Techniques

in a Corporate Strategic Planning System", European Journal of Operational Research 3, 99-109.

Carlsson, Ch., S. V. Khaynish and A. G. Vlasov: 1984, "Decision Support System for Ill Structured Problems", paper presented at EURO 6, Wien.

Carter, R. L. and N. A. Doherty: 1974, "The Development and Scope of Risk Management", in Handbook of Risk Management Carter-Doherty, London.

Cristy, J. C.: 1965, "Fundamentals of Risk Management", in Property and Liability Insurance Handbook, J.D. Long and D. W. Gregg, Homewood, 1085-1100.

Denenberg, H.S., R.D. Eilers, J.J. Melone and R.A. Zelten: 1974, Risk and Insurance, Englewood Cliffs.

Gallagher, R.B.: 1964, "Position of the Risk Manager in a Business Organization Structure", in Risk Management, H.W. Snider, Homewood, 1-32.

Helten, E.: 1984, "Strategische Unternehmensplanung und Risk Management", in E. Gaugler, O. H. Jacobs and A. Kieser (eds.), Strategische Unternehmensfuhrung und Rechnungslegung, C. E. Poeschel Verlag, Stuttgart, 15-30.

Leitner, F.: 1915, Die Unternehmungsrisiken, Berlin.

Linter, J.: 1975, "The Valuation of Risk Assets and the Selection of Risk Investments in Stock Portfolios and Capital Budgets", Rev. Econom. Statist. 47, 13-37.

Naylor, D., I. Vernon and K. Wertz: 1983, Managerial Economics, New York.

Naylor, T.H. and F. Tapon: 1982, "The Capital Asset Pricing Model: An Evaluation of its Potential as a Strategic Planning Tool", Management Science 28, 1166-1173.

Nicklisch, H.: 1922, "Allgemeine Kaufmännische Betriebslehre als Privatwirtschaftslehre des Handels (und der Industrie)", Leipzig, 1912.

Parkinson, J. R.: 1976, The Role of the Risk Manager in Industry and Commerce, London.

Porter, M.E.: 1980, Competitive Strategy, Free Press, New York.

Risk Management Manuals: 1971, The Merrit Co., Santa Monica.

Sharp, W. F.: 1954, "Capital Asset Prices: A Theory of Market Equilibrium under Conditions of Risk", J. Finance 19, 425-442.

Viliums, E. R. and L.Ya. Sukur: 1984, "Practical Aspects of Alternatives Evaluating and Decision Making under Uncertainty and Multiple Objectives", Cybernetics and Systems Research 2, 165-171.

Williams, C. A. and R. M. Heins: <u>Risk Management and
   Insurance</u>, 2nd ed., New York.
Wind, Y.: 1982, "Marketing Oriented Strategic Planning
   Models", in R.L. Schultz and A. A. Zoltness (eds.),
   <u>Marketing Decision Models</u>, North Holland,   207-250.

An expanded version of this article appears in the journal
<u>Theory and Decision</u>, Volume 19, Number 3, also published by
D. Reidel Publishing Company.

Model	Degree of adaptability	Specific dimensions
1. BCG growth/ share matrix	None. A rigid framework	1. Relative market share (cash generation) 2. Market growth (cash use)
2. McKinley /G.E. business assessment array	Limited through the selection of variables used to determine the two composite dimensions	1. Industry attractiveness 2. Business strengths
3. A.D. Little business profile matrix	Same as McKinsey/G.E.	1. Competitive market position 2. Industry maturity
4. Shell Intern'l directional policy matrix	Same as McKinsey/G.E.	1. Profitability of market segment 2. Competitive position in the segment
5. Product performance matrix	Considerable. The specific dimensions are selected by management	1. Industry sales 2. Product sales 3. Market share 4. Profitability all by market segment
6. Conjoint analysis based approach	Fully adaptable to management needs	No general dimensions. The dimensions determined by management judgement
7. Analytic hierarchy process	Fully adaptable to management needs	As with conjoint analysis, determined by management judgement
8. Risk/return model	None. A theory derived model	1. Expected return (mean) 2. Risk (variance)
9. Stochastic dominance	Same as risk/ return model	The entire distribution of return

ANNEX 1. MODEL COMPARISON

Allocation rules	Comments
1. Allocation of resources among four categories (move "cash" to "problem child", etc.) 2. Consideration for product deletion (e.g. "dogs") 3. No explicit portfolio recommendation except w.r.t. the balance of cash flows.	Widely used but conceptually questionable given the forcing of two dimensions, the unique operational definition, and lack of rules for determining a portfolio of "dogs", "stars", etc. No consideration of risk, no weighting of dimensions.
In its simplistic use, it offers a slightly greater precision than BCG (9 cells vs. 4 and better definition of dimensions). In its more sophisticated uses (as by G.E.), the classification of products on these two dimensions is used only as input to an explicit resource allocation model.	Forcing of two dimensions which might not be the appropriate ones. The empirical determination of the correlates of the two dimensions is superior to the BCG approach, yet, given the tailoring of factors to each industry, comparability across industries is difficult. No consideration of risk.
Same as McKinsey/G.E.	Same as McKinsey/G.E.
Same as McKinsey/G.E.	Same as McKinsey/G.E.
Same as BCG but based on project's results in response to alternative marketing strategies	Limited applications (major user: Intern'l Harvester), yet it offers the conceptual advantage of management determined performance dimension and allocation of resources based on projected rather than historical performance. No weighting of dimensions.
Based on computer simulation which incorporates management utility functions (for the dimensions of the portfolio), and product performance data (supplemented to the extent needed by management perceptions of current and new products and businesses)	Limited applications. Very demanding of management time
Optimal allocation among all items of the portfolio (e.g. products, market segments) determined algorithmically	Limited applications. Conceptually and mathematically very appealing. Allows assumptions and allocates resources across products, market segments, and distribution networks optimally under different scenarios of market and competitive conditions. Weighting of dimensions explicitly considered
Determination of optimal portfolio	Conceptually the most defensible, yet, difficult to operationalize for the product portfolio decision. Limited real-world applications
Same as risk/return	Same as risk/return

ANNEX 1. MODEL COMPARISON CONTINUED

INDEX

THEORY AND DECISION LIBRARY

An International Series in the Philosophy and Methodology of the Social and Behavioral Sciences

Editors

GERALD EBERLEIN, *University of Technology, Munich*

WERNER LEINFELLNER, *University of Nebraska*

1. Günther Menges (ed.), *Information, Inference, and Decision.* 1974, viii + 195 pp.
2. Anatol Rapoport (ed.), *Game Theory as a Theory of Conflict Resolution.* 1974, v + 283 pp.
3. Mario Bunge (ed.), *The Methodological Unity of Science.* 1973, viii + 264 pp.
4. Colin Cherry (ed.), *Pragmatic Aspects of Human Communication.* 1974, ix + 178 pp.
5. Friedrich Rapp (ed.), *Contributions to a Philosophy of Technology. Studies in the Structure of Thinking in the Technological Sciences.* 1974, xv + 228 pp.
6. Werner Leinfellner and Eckehart Köhler (eds.), *Developments in the Methodology of Social Science.* 1974, x + 430 pp.
7. Jacob Marschak, *Economic Information, Decision and Prediction. Selected Essays.* 1974, three volumes, xviii + 389 pp.; xii + 362 pp.; x + 399 pp.
8. Carl-Axel S. Staël von Holstein (ed.), *The Concept of Probability in Psychological Experiments.* 1974, xi + 153 pp.
9. Heinz J. Skala, *Non-Archimedean Utility Theory.* 1975, xii + 138 pp.
10. Karin D. Knorr, Hermann Strasser, and Hans Georg Zillian (eds.), *Determinants and Controls of Scientific Developments.* 1975, ix + 460 pp.
11. Dirk Wendt and Charles Vlek (eds.), *Utility, Probability, and Human Decision Making. Selected Proceedings of an Interdisciplinary Research Conference, Rome, 3–6 September, 1973.* 1975, viii + 418 pp.
12. John C. Harsanyi, *Essays on Ethics, Social Behaviour, and Scientific Explanation.* 1976, xvi + 262 pp.
13. Gerhard Schwödiauer (ed.), *Equilibrium and Disequilibrium in Economic Theory. Proceedings of a Conference Organized by the Institute for Advanced Studies, Vienna, Austria, July 3–5, 1974.* 1978, l + 736 pp.
14. V. V. Kolbin, *Stochastic Programming.* 1977, xii + 195 pp.
15. R. Mattessich, *Instrumental Reasoning and Systems Methodology.* 1978, xxii + 396 pp.
16. H. Jungermann and G. de Zeeuw (eds.), *Decision Making and Change in Human Affairs.* 1977, xv + 526 pp.
17. H. W. Gottinger and W. Leinfellner (eds.), *Decision Theory and Social Ethics.* 1978, xxii + 329 pp.
18. A. Rapoport, W. E. Stein, and G. J. Burkheimer, *Response Models for Detection of Change.* 1978, vii + 200 pp.
19. H. J. Johnson, J. J. Leach, and R. G. Mühlmann (eds.), *Revolutions, Systems, and Theories: Essays in Political Philosophy.* 1978, x + 198 pp.
20. Stephen Gale and Gunnar Olsson (eds.), *Philosophy in Geography.* 1979, xxii + 470 pp.

21. Maurice Allais and Ole Hagen (eds.), *Expected Utility Hypotheses and the Allais Paradox: Contemporary Discussions of Decisions Under Uncertainty with Allais' Rejoinder.* 1979, vii + 714 pp.
22. Teddy Seidenfeld, *Philosophical Problems of Statistical Inference: Learning from R. A. Fisher.* 1979, xiv + 246 pp.
23. L. Lewin and E. Vedung (eds.), *Politics as Rational Action.* 1980, xii + 274 pp.
24. J. Kozielecki, *Psychological Decision Theory.* 1982, xvi + 403 pp.
25. I. I. Mitroff and R. O. Mason, *Creating a Dialectical Social Science: Concepts, Methods, and Models.* 1981, ix + 189 pp.
26. V. A. Lefebvre, *Algebra of Conscience: A Comparative Analysis of Western and Soviet Ethical Systems.* 1982, xxvii + 194 pp.
27. L. Nowak, *Property and Power: Towards a Non-Marxian Historical Materialism.* 1983, xxvii + 384 pp.
28. J. C. Harsanyi, *Papers in Game Theory.* 1982, xii + 258 pp.
29. B. Walentynowicz (ed.), *Polish Contributions to the Science of Science.* 1982, xii + 291 pp.
30. A. Camacho, *Societies and Social Decision Functions. A Model with Focus on the Information Problem.* 1982, xv + 144 pp.
31. P. C. Fishburn, *The Foundations of Expected Utility.* 1982, xii + 176 pp.
32. G. Feichtinger and P. Kall (eds.), *Operations Research in Progress.* 1982, ix + 520 pp.
33. H. W. Gottinger, *Coping with Complexity.* 1983, xv + 224 pp.
34. W. Gasparski and T. Pszczołowski (eds.), *Praxiological Studies.* 1983, xiv + 418 pp.
35. A. M. Yaglom and I. M. Yaglom, *Probability and Information.* 1983, xx + 421 pp.
36. F. M. Wuketits, *Concepts and Approaches in Evolutionary Epistemology.* 1984, xiii + 307 pp.
37. B. F. Stigum and F. Wenstøp (eds.), *Foundations of Utility and Risk Theory with Applications.* 1983, x + 492 pp.
38. V. V. Kolbin, *Macromodels of the National Economy of the USSR.* 1985, xxii + 465 pp.
39. H. J. Skala, S. Termini, and E. Trillas (eds.), *Aspects of Vagueness.* 1984, viii + 304 pp.
40. G. L. Gaile and C. J. Willmott (eds.), *Spatial Statistics and Models.* 1984, x + 482 pp.
41. J. van Daal and A. H. Q. M. Merkies, *Aggregation in Economic Research.* 1984, xiv + 321 pp.
42. O. Hagen and F. Wenstøp (eds.), *Progress in Utility and Risk Theory.* 1984, xii + 279 pp.
43. G. Seebass and R. Tuomela (eds.), *Social Action.* 1985, xx + 302 pp.
44. Karl A. Fox, *Social System Accounts. Linking Social and Economic Indicators through Tangible Behavior Settings.* 1985.
45. N. T. Potter and M. Timmons (eds.), *Morality and Universality. Essays on Ethical Universalizability.* 1986.
46. Yu. B. Germeier, *Non-Antagonistic Games.* 1986.